D1587501

Rescuing the Past

Rescuing the Past

The Cultural Heritage Crusade

Jonathan Tokeley

ia

imprint-academic.com

The moral rights of the author have been asserted
No part of any contribution may be reproduced in any form
without permission, except for the quotation of brief passages
in criticism and discussion.

Published in the UK by Imprint Academic
PO Box 200, Exeter EX5 5YX, UK

Published in the USA by Imprint Academic
Philosophy Documentation Center
PO Box 7147, Charlottesville, VA 22906-7147, USA

ISBN 1845400194
9781845400194

A CIP catalogue record for this book is available from the
British Library and US Library of Congress

imprint-academic.com

Contents

Acknowledgements

This is a single-minded book. I dislike committing thought to paper unless I can lay a claim to it, that of having worked it out for myself, and taking nothing for granted. It is feasible that others have thought along the same lines, entirely unbeknownst to me. It is also possible that lines of thought have been planted, by chance conversations or by forgotten books. That may detract from originality, in the academic's conventional sense. But it is difficult to acknowledge.

There have been, however, certain beauties of intellect that I would be honoured to recognise. Dr. Laura Vazzoler (Rome University) springs to mind, as does Michael Tanner, and through him Nietzsche and Leavis and Trilling. John Keegan's immense knowledge, Bernard Williams' gentle irony, Roger Scruton's sense of the strenuous, and Duff Burrell's (10th/11th Royal Hussars) straight-to-the-bone directness. And, more generally, the British Army.

I'd also like to acknowledge Charles Ede, who did so much to shape the modern antiquities market, and under whose tutelage I became a restorer. He showed me that academics can also be dealers (and vice versa) and both sides benefit.

Any infelicities of thought are entirely my own — that goes without saying. I do not apologise for the light-hearted style, however. I never much cared for prigs. And neither did Charles Ede.

Picture credits: Page 40 was taken by the famous German photographer, Professor Walter Hege (1893-1955), but the author has been unable to trace his legatees. Page 250 is reproduced by kind permission of the British Museum.

Finally, I would thank those who have stood by me, because they believed in me. They know who they are and, more importantly, so do I. Also, I thank my enthusiastic publisher, Keith Sutherland, for being so patient — for not shouting at me, or not very much — and ditto my dalmatian.

Preface

This last decade I have found myself in the eye of the storm. When it began I was successful, and contented, and morally at my ease. I was perhaps the last of my breed — essentially an amateur, what they used to call a 'gentleman smuggler' — in a profession that was fast becoming semi-industrial, dominated by government agencies, and their third-world ruthlessness.

Then the new puritanism took me in its maw. I was to be an example, a scapegoat to be loaded with the sins of the market — of the *ancien regime*, in fact — and cast out, in order to purify the future.

I didn't much appreciate this, nor the means employed. The mere fact, for instance, that since I'd broken no English law (couldn't have, and wouldn't have) the law was changed on the hoof — twisted, made palpably absurd — to make it appear that I had. And the fact that I was sent to prison, and with an 'exemplary sentence'. This was called 'establishing a precedent', and was obviously thought the means to a noble end. My barrister called it a 'show trial', however, and those who were privy called it much worse.

And nor did I appreciate the character assassination that followed, the sheer nastiness and the lies.[1] For the truth, as usual, was rather more complex. I had been working with

---

[1] A London broadsheet, for instance, published an article containing seventeen assertions of putative fact. Thirteen were simply false, and would only have required a telephone call to be proven so (that's all they eventually required from the FBI and the New York Times). Of the four true propositions, three were so qualified by adjectival phrases as to become at best ironic, at worst slanderous. In addition, there were three op-eds, all unfounded and all hostile — the mere stuff of calumny — and three quotes from 'friends', which actually came from hostile prosecution witnesses (later revealed as perjurers). It has to be said, in his defence, that the journalist had no reason to distrust his 'source'. But that hardly excuses his *ad hominem* glee, nor the paper's cynicism in publishing a defamation which they knew I was in no position to contest, and which would have done any tabloid proud.

antiquities for almost thirty years. I had restored them in their thousands, for collectors and dealers — and through them for museums — across the Western world. In my time I had been kindly regarded, as one of the world's leading restorers. I had certainly salvaged many fine pieces. Saved them, I would have liked to think.

I had also become a collector and a dealer, and latterly a smuggler. But I had consistently felt myself in the right place and — as I gradually realized what was going on — that I was doing the right thing. I was part of a grand and impersonal process — what I have called the *diaspora* — which has swept antiquities along, kept them safely in the centre, kept them where they would be cherished. And always I had felt the honour of this. These are glorious things, a legacy from the past, and far too important to be the playthings of dogma, of nationalism and the modern humbug.

The *Cultural Heritage Crusade*, however, had been gathering a head of steam, become part of the fashionable consensus, what everybody agrees at dinner parties. A few allusions to desecrated tombs, and our 'liberal' elite started getting hot under its collective collar, that in our arrogance and colonialist greed we had just sauntered down there and crated up the stuff — and deprived what we have been taught to call the 'countries of origin' of their glorious heritage.

The British Museum's Elgin Marbles are just the tip of this argumentative iceberg. There may be no redress for this stain on our character, except the delicious guilt of it. But the mere idea of such a trade continuing, of anyone in these enlightened days accumulating 'stolen' antiquities as a display of wealth — all this should be anathema to the modern soul. The world antiquities market, in short, was fast becoming the new fur trade.

Lord Renfrew, the Disney Professor of Archaeology at Cambridge, has spelled it all out. Quite simply, he says, it is the fault of the *collectors*. They may appear benign as a breed, harmless even, but their hunger for new pieces creates a kind of suction, which is ultimately responsible for tomb robbing and the desecration of sites. And since the causal connection is so simple, he concludes, so must be the solution. We only need remove the monetary value from antiquities — by making them impossible to sell unless their provenance can be proved beyond reproach — and the horrors will cease. Once there's nothing in it for them, you see, the natives won't be corrupted any more. They won't be tempted to *go a' diggin'*.

This book aims to refute Professor Renfrew's argument — at least as far as regards Egypt and, by inference, the other Middle Eastern countries that share Islam, and Arabism, and the culture that goes with them.

There are many, therefore, who will dislike this book. *Bien pensants* and other members of the liberal elite will dislike it cordially, because it says things they would much rather not hear. It disturbs their comfortable orthodoxy, and puts them to the trouble of thinking. And thinking, real thinking, is always an exhausting business.[2]

The 'politically correct' will hate it even more than they hate their own label. They bear the sacred flame, after all, and are mighty quick to turn the sacred hatred on anybody that disagrees — or any uncomfortable fact that doesn't fit.

The archaeologists will also dislike it, because it challenges their privilege. This is their field, after all, and they expect to pronounce from tablets of stone.

And last but not least, the Egyptians will hate it, because I use them as my example. Indeed, they are the only example I'm qualified to use. I may not be their favourite foreigner, but I should still be taken seriously when I speak about Egypt. After all, I am probably the only Westerner who has seen all sides of their particular game — and the only one, until now, who has nothing to lose by speaking out.

I have seen their official side, the side prepared for Western consumption, and I have felt their official outrage. There are Egyptologists who have also felt this outrage — perhaps you had better call it revenge — when they have dared to pass comment. On the whole, however, Egyptologists are a timid breed,[3] and learn quickly enough to hold their tongues — if they ever want to return, that is, and continue their excavations.

---

[2]   The irony, of course, is the etymology. The Latin *liber* means 'free' — which is what their noble forbears had in mind. But freedom of thought — genuine dissenting thought — is the last thing these modern liberals have in mind. See the footnote on page 297.

[3]   In fact this timidity seems to have infected the whole of academe, given the muted response to the unprecedented assault by the British government on the independence of the university. See Gordon Graham, *The Institution of Intellectual Values.*

I have also seen the *conservation* side of things. I have worked with Egypt's leading conservators and seen every-thing—all the horrors that are hidden from foreign institu-tions and museums and from anybody connected with these august bodies. Worse than this, I saw the widespread indif-ference, bordering on disdain, of the Egyptian field workers. And I have pondered on this.

And, finally, I have seen the black market in Egypt, and come to realize how closely—how intimately—it now works with the very authorities who are tasked with its suppres-sion. I have pondered this also, long and hard, over the decade when I was working in Egypt. And I have come to realize the impossibility of the Egyptians' situation, and how naive we Westerners are if we expect otherwise. Corruption in Egypt is inevitable. It is not a falling away from the norm. It simply and inevitably *is* the norm.

There are others who know this, of course, and know it to their advantage. But they have their own reasons for keeping quiet. They are trying to make a honest living, after all—well, reasonably honest, given the circumstances—and better the devil they know...

I would ask you to bear one thing in mind, when you read this book. That it is written with only one concern— that of the antiquities themselves, and what's best for them. I am asking a single question, and asking it with monotonous reg-ularity: *How can we get as many antiquities as possible through to the future?*

I'm not concerned with their present ownership, or the rights and wrongs of it. Haggling about ownership is a lux-ury I am content to leave to the future. But when that future finally arrives—and sees things, as it usually does, rather dif-ferently from the present—it is essential that the antiquities are still there, still on hand to be admired, and studied and, yes, to be argued about.

This is, therefore, a ruthless book, as any philosopher's book should be. But only in the sense that it's interested in the truth—in how things actually are, and not how we would morally prefer them. It wants to know whether the argu-ments commence with facts—with true propositions—and whether they end with true conclusions. And it's not dis-mayed if the facts and the conclusions seem uncomfortable. Only if they are false.

* * *

Who ought to own antiquity? And who to own its far-flung treasures? These are interesting questions. Of course they are. But they are also damned embarrassing — at least for the West — because antiquity's present distribution is so clearly the result of our past interference. Artefacts may have been scattered to the four winds, but they have ended up — yes, I'm afraid they have — in a mere handful of Western museums. And you can be pretty sure they weren't paid for, or not at the proper prices.

Viewed in this light, the British Museum — that 'magnificent cabinet' — can sometimes appear little more than a *residuum of imperial loot*. Benign enough in its harmless way — like the modern collectors — but somehow stranded, and a trifle embarrassed. Yes, definitely embarrassed.

The *Cultural Heritage Crusade*, however, aims to set this right. It provides an answer — and a suitably unequivocal one at that. These beautiful things, it declares, belong to their *countries-of-origin*. They may have been removed in the past, but that was morally incorrect. In future we should behave better. In future antiquities should always remain where they have been discovered. Anything else would be unthinkable.

So far, so splendid. But why stop there? Once the argument is underway, you see, it's rather difficult to restrain. If we are morally so sure of the future, why not rectify the past? Why not make amends, and just hand the stuff back? Wouldn't anything else be hypocritical?

There are difficulties in such a scheme, and mighty convenient ones, you would have to say, if your own collection was hanging in the balance. Should these things be returned to where they have been *found*, for instance, or to where they were *made*? Where the people *then* lived who made them, or where their descendants live *now*? Where they were last *sold* — legitimately, that's to say — or where the salesmen live now? If these answers were all the same, of course, there would be no problem. But they seldom are.

But prevarication like this won't solve the problem. It will only give our curators a breathing space. In the long term, perhaps, their only strategy is to brazen it out. That is what the Europeans would prefer — those who looted so efficiently through the nineteenth century, and are now sitting on their hoards. They would like to set a date-line — a sort of arbitrary cut-off point, after which the world can be assumed to have grown up, and learned how to behave — and *after which there should be no more movement*. And, ideally, the date-line would be yesterday.

As I say, this is certainly what we would prefer, the post-imperialist great powers; the British and the French, the Russians, the Germans and Austrians. But it is hardly what these newly resurgent countries-of-origin would go for. After all, we're still sitting on their inheritance, which they would like back, all of it, and soon. And returning the occasional 'stolen' piece, in a blaze of self-congratulatory publicity, is just disingenuous. *Beads for Manhattan* is how they'll see it.

And the present antiquities market? The plush dealers in London and Paris, Zurich and New York? They are in a conciliatory mood, these days. They are prepared to admit that, in the past at least, things might have been better. They are prepared to have the market 'disciplined'.

But the Cultural Heritage Crusade has a larger agenda. It's not interested in mere discipline; those who think they can just 'tighten the rules' — and carry on much as before — are sadly mistaken. The Crusade wants to *eradicate* the world market for antiquities, close it down completely, so that 'discovered relics' have no choice but to remain in their countries of origin. More than this, it would rather prefer to have all antiquities repatriated — wherever they happen to be now.

This is not just a scholarly debate, without consequence for the real world. It is not about some minor turpitude of trading, and the means to put it right. It is not *just* about the 'market' at all. It is also about our great nineteenth-century collections — the British Museum, the Louvre, the Hermitage, the Berlin Kunsthauus and Vienna — and even the New York Met. It's about their *integrity*, their moral right to hold what they have acquired. And the consequences of this debate — of getting it wrong, that is to say — would be calamitous, as much for antiquity as for our own *amour propre*.

The Argument

Thesis

Antiquities teach us about ourselves. Our modern selves, that is. They are enchanting clues from the past, reminders of our long journey, from hunting and gathering to the modern city. They are all that remains of that journey.

More than that, or because of it, they are a sacrament. A recompense, if there can be one, for the slaughter and the mayhem.

Because of this, they impose a duty on us. We have to see them safely through to the future. But not because of what they can teach us, or what they can give. Merely because they have come so far. At the moment there is a dispute about who can carry this responsibility. About *who, if anybody, can own the past*.

The liberal elite thinks that *no-one* should own it, which they think is the same thing as governments owning it. But modern governments are rarely liberal. They tend to look out for themselves. Their relation to their subjects is rarely unambiguous. And they are unreliable stewards of any resource, especially one to which their claim is arguable.

Archaeologists side with the *bien pensants*, but archaeologists rely upon governments, so perhaps they have little choice. As for the museums, they are becoming nervous, especially those whose funding comes from government.

Collectors, and traditionalists — they are often one and the same — think that *anyone* can own antiquities, as long as they look after them. And dealers side with the collectors, as you might expect.

As for myself, I don't much mind who owns antiquity, or where, as long as it is cherished through to the future. The artefacts and the sites are more important than their present stewards. But I do think there is too much politics, too much naivety, and far too much humbug.

The politics is the attempt to take antiquity out of the 'market system', in case it's regarded as a *resource*, and somehow sullied. But taking antiquity outside the property realm – in the hope of banishing the wickedness of 'market forces' and 'greed' – is foolish. Worse than that, it is doomed.

Firstly, because whatever is outside the market is to no-one's advantage, and subject to no-one's care. Hence unprotected in a struggling world.

Secondly – and this is the humbug – because state stewardship is effectively the same thing as state ownership, and many governments use antiquity as precisely that, as a resource, whether mythic or monetary.

Indeed, it follows both logically and contingently, that antiquities must continue to be regarded as a resource, if they are to survive as they have so far.

And the naivety? The academic supposition that these two are at odds. That antiquity cannot both carry a monetary value (be bought and sold) – and also maintain its sacrament (the feelings of plangency and haunting imagination that it evokes). As if relics had never been never sold in antiquity.

The solution lies with our concept of *property*, which is ever adapting, ever becoming more sophisticated. If antiquity does carry this benison – the knowledge of our forebears, and our descent – then it should be correctly acknowledged in its market value. For intellectual property also has a value. And if all parties are made to realize this – that illicit or incompetent (or prejudiced) excavation can lose this major increment of value – then they will all be more considerate.

Antiquity, in short, should be accepted as a resource, a very special resource, a form of property that imposes peculiar duties on its present owners, its present stewards.

It behoves, however, that archaeologists also admit the fact. Until now they have gone to far away places, and extracted knowledge by excavation. They have taken something away, an intellectual property, and used it for publication, for academic advancement and prestige. They have consumed sites, and left them bereft – and not only of artefacts. Putting it bluntly, they have been using them, yes, as a resource.

Putting it even more bluntly, they have taken something which has a value, and used it as a commodity – earned their dinners by it – but refused to admit as much, and certainly not to the peasantry. As if they were some latter-day priesthood, whose arcane ceremonies were beyond consideration by the vulgar.

And then they have complained that others, the despised 'looters' — in reality the same benighted peasantry, who have also been trying to earn their dinners — have failed to honour the same value. But how were they supposed to know? How *are* they supposed to know, if nobody bothers to tell them?

Surely, antiquity continues to teach us our *selves*...

A note to the reader

This book has three parts. The *First* proposes an argument, and the *Third* provides its practical proof, which I've derived from a decade spent working in Egypt (and with Egyptians). These two parts can be read in either order.

As for the *Second*, it sketches the background, and aims to see off some counter-arguments. This involves some philosophy, but I've tried to make it accessible. Philosophy is hard enough, anyway, without its practitioners showing off, and making it unreadable. Having said that, this part can safely be skipped by the general reader — although I would recommend the last chapter, the one about Islam. Given recent events, this may prove the key to the whole puzzle.

There is also an *Appendix*, a series of separate articles to which the footnotes will guide you. Treat them as a travel guide — as an anthropology. They explain and describe the strange world of antiquities, the eccentric people who live there, and have their being...

And lastly, at the end of each chapter, I've provided a summary. Taken together, these provide a crib — or, I'd like to think, a continuous argument — for the whole book.

CHAPTER 1

The Curious Case of Nefertari's Head

In the Spring of 2000 the British Museum staged a press conference. The great and the good were all assembled, and the mood was triumphant, for a sculpted head of Queen Nefertari — an Egyptian national treasure, and valued at $10 million — was being returned to the Egyptian government. It was a splendid occasion, and rightly hailed as a token of everlasting friendship, and the fruit of a 'joint campaign against illegal looting'.

There was only one fly in the ointment. Or perhaps two. First, the head wasn't Queen Nefertari. Second, and more pertinent, it was almost certainly a *worthless fake*.

His Excellency Adel al-Gazzar, the Egyptian Ambassador, takes possession of 'Queen Nefertari's Head' for the Egyptian people (or at least for the Egyptian government).

First, the little matter of identity. When I had originally seen the head in Cairo, and promptly bought it—oh yes, I was the one—it had a hieroglyphic inscription on the back. I photographed this immediately (date stamped), as a matter of routine (and recorded the event in my journal):

*Taken on the same day I acquired the head, this photograph shows the original (and **only**) inscription, exactly the same as the White Queen's.*

And then I strolled across to Cairo Museum to follow up the clues. I soon discovered that my head's inscription was exactly the same as the one on a famous statue called the 'White Queen.' Now this had been discovered in 1894 but its inscription had been broken off before it reached a name, so nobody knew who it was. Then another statue was found in the 1980s, this time with a complete inscription *and* a name—Meryet-Amun, one of the daughters of Ramesses the Great. It followed that the famous White Queen was Meryet-Amun. And it also followed, or so it seemed, that morning in 1991, that my head was also Meryet-Amun.

> *JOURNAL: Sunday 24th November 1991, Dokki Flat, Cairo*
> *Ali arrived with the new head. I unwrapped the inevitable newspaper, and saw the perfect necklace and lappets...*
> *I exclaimed that it was either Tiyi, or Meryet-Amun, the Prin-cess-Queen of Ramesses the II–it has a double ureaus, and it's late New Kingdom. I started for the museum, to examine the two candidates, and concluded that it's Meryet-Amun,* **because the inscription on the back plinth exactly matches the 'White Queen's'!**

The famous 'White Queen' in Cairo, found by Sir Flinders Petrie in 1894, and for nearly a century an unsolved mystery.

But its identity hardly mattered, unless the thing was genuine. I was able to smuggle it out disguised as a tourist trinket—Egypt's laws forbid the export of antiquities—but the face was badly damaged, and needed extensive restoration. And as I was struggling with this I gradually realized—to my considerable embarrassment—that it was actually a fake. It was bloody good, as fakes go. But definitely a fake.[1]

Eventually I sold it on, as a fake by the 'Berlin Master'.[2] *And the British Museum should have known this.* I sold the head, incidentally, for £35,000, the going rate for a modern masterpiece, but a tiny fraction of the real price—if it *had* been a genuine antiquity, that is to say.

---

[1] This was eventually confirmed in New York, by the world's leading Egyptologists—Professor Bernard von Bothmer of the New York Institute, now sadly deceased, but the acknowledged authority at the time, and the curators of the Metropolitan and Brooklyn Museums, amongst others.

[2] We don't actually know who the Berlin Master was, only that he was Albanian, worked in Cairo in the 1950s, and was the greatest faker of them all. His title is honorific, derived from the resting place of some of his best efforts. For more of his work, see page 223.

On the advice of the Metropolitan Police Arts Squad, the Egyptian government took its new owner to court — claiming it 'stolen' from Egypt, and rightfully theirs. The owner simply said it was a fake but, interestingly, the case folded without a shot being fired, his legal aid being withdrawn the very day before the case was to be heard. A curious coincidence.

Anyway, since the BM had reluctantly admitted my market reputation — that I was 'one of the world's finest restorers', and could 'only helplessly admire the skill with which [I]...had recreated the face'[3] — it would surely have been sensible to consult me regarding the authenticity of the piece.

So why *didn't* they pick up the phone and ask me? Presumably because at the time I was languishing at Her Majesty's Pleasure, serving a sentence for having 'smuggled' the thing — or things like it — and they didn't have the phone number for Wormwood Scrubs. It was a pity they didn't ask, however, because their own conservator could only devote four hours to its authentication (as opposed to my four months) and his brief, apparently, was to expose my restoration of the face. Consequently he missed everything else.[4]

---

[3] The Guardian, January 22nd 2000.

[4] For those of an inquisitive bent, these are:

• The inscription on its 'back column' was a straight lift from the so-called 'White Queen' statue in Cairo Museum, which ended in exactly the same place, in the same mid-sentence, but with certain modern 'spelling mistakes' (proportion and spacing) which implied a modern 'illiterate's' hand.

• Although the material appeared to be *Gneiss*, a hard crystalline stone much used by ancient Egyptian sculptors, it definitely wasn't. It was a suspiciously soft imitation, most likely an imported marble, and as such, it was completely unknown in Egyptian sculpture. There is no other known example.

• The impressive bronze stump in the head-dress does not 'belong', as the trade says. It seems to comprise a selection of bronze fragments — themselves undoubtedly ancient — but glued together to give a favourable impression.

• The torso was broken at its strongest point, which suggests that the stone was broken *before* it was sculpted and that a composition containing all the most desirable bits was squeezed onto the available space. This unexpected completeness usually suggests a forgery, or that a fragment had recently been cut from an original statue. But in *that* case, the cut-edge would have been raw stone, showing saw-marks, not weathered (patinated) the same as the rest.

• The stone showed microscopic evidence of working by modern (tunsgten-steel) tools, and modern garnet-based abrasives and, last but far from least:

• Its patination was not ancient, but indicative of oxalic acid immersion (or chicken-slurry immersion, in the style of modern Italian forgers).

With all due professional respect to Mr. Ken Uprichard, the BM's head of stone conservation, he is not an Egyptologist. Hence he wasn't the man to 'authenticate' such an object, and certainly not in an afternoon.

The real puzzle, however, was the mistaken identity. Because there is one thing clear in all this. If the British Museum had known that the head's inscription was the same as the White Queen's—ending at exactly the same place, in mid-sentence—they would have been as suspicious as I became. And they would probably have concluded that one was a copy of the other. That's what fakers do, after all. They make copies.

But they were told an extraordinary thing. They were told that I had *'hacked off the original inscription* (presumably naming Nefertari) and *disguised the sculpture with a copy of the White Queen's inscription.'*[5]

No rationale was ever offered for this—for this brutal replacement of an inscription. Why would anyone reduce an object to a tiny fraction of its value—especially if 'greed' was supposedly his motivation? If a racehorse is kidnapped for stud, why geld it for disguise? And how could a restorer who had spent his career bringing such things back to life, and preserving them for the future, be supposed capable of such brutality? Doctors do not habitually mutilate their patients.

But it quickly established itself as a matter of faith—that smugglers *'habitually mutilate antiquities so as to 'disguise' them.'* But changing an inscription as an aid to smuggling? Surely not. The Egyptian customs service would hardly dismiss something because it bore the same inscription as the White Queen's, even if they recognized it as such. Quite the contrary. Any inscription at all would alert them. Hence my smuggler's practise of *concealing* any inscription until it reached a safe haven (as I did with this sculpture—see illustrations overleaf). But a harmless, removable conservator's disguise is a far far cry from 'mutilation.' Considerably farther than face-paint from major plastic surgery.

And the result of all this? That a noble institution—and with a great deal of pious fanfare—has returned a *howling fake* to a foreign government. Which has to count as a splendid joke, unless you happen to be Egyptian, and were expecting—and agitating for—something *genuinely* important, such as the Rosetta Stone...

But how to account for such a farce? The probing reader will already have his suspicions. There are people here—

---

[5] Published in The Times Legal Supplement, admittedly by a lawyer acting for the Egyptian government, which presumably had its own agenda.

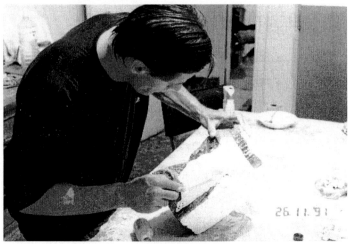

The head being plastered by myself to conceal its inscription from prying eyes...

...and then being gilded by my partner, Ali Farag

parties, factions—with a definite *agenda* in mind. And there are others—decidedly less scrupulous in their methods—who are willing to help it along. Spin, disinformation, propaganda, call it what you like.

For sadly, whatever the high-minded pronouncements of its standard bearers, the *truth* has been the first casualty of the Cultural Heritage Crusade.

CHAPTER 2

The Cultural Heritage Crusade

As I've indicated, the *Cultural Heritage Crusade* has been gathering steam. As a consequence the *countries-of-origin* — the mostly poor countries where ancient cultures were born and produced their art — are fast waking to the fact that this art — their irreplaceable antiquity, a cultural inheritance, something glorious, and a source of pride for them in the modern world — has been filched wholesale by the West. To an alarming extent, it just isn't there anymore.

In the past this was little better than a rape. It may have abated, these enlightened times — grown outwardly respectable — but the pillage continues. It is something shameful, and needs to be rectified. Since the blame lies squarely with the Western antiquities market — the well-known avarice of dealers, and the collectors they serve — it may prove necessary to suppress this market, and prevent collectors from acquiring such things. It may also be necessary to return them. In one sense, *restitution* is the logical end of the argument.

This is more than just an argument. It really is a crusade. It started innocuously enough, with UNESCO's remit against racism. A noble ideal, no doubt, but somehow grown out of proportion, grown into something called *multi-culturalism*, which is hardly an ideal at all, more a reluctance — to consider that any race or any culture could ever be better than another, and in any way — and a reverent determination to ignore any evidence to the contrary.

The prime offenders of course, were the *colonialists*. They remain the force of reaction. If you can invoke colonialism, the weight of the age will be behind you. And the Crusade suggests just this, that colonialism was responsible for a systematic rape of the third-world's heritage. Those who tolerate the market, therefore — a market that continues the desecration — are not just enjoying the spoils of colonialism.

They are continuing that colonialism. Our duty is clear, therefore. We should suppress this market, and make recompense for our theft.

All heady stuff, and as a crusade it may prove irresistible. It catches the spirit of the times. It has something for everybody. It appeals to the liberals, and delights them with a new source of shame. It soothes the academics, who anyway despise the market, which sells art for 'mere profit'. And it gives the poor nations a ready stick to beat us. They can denounce us for past rapacity, blame us for their present plight, and demand the return of their birthright. There is even something for class-warriors: the well-acknowledged fact that coal miners rarely collect antiquities.

The specific argument against the market

All heady stuff, and strangely difficult to engage. Broad sweeps and noble sentiments are too large a prey, too elusive to be pinned down to specifics, and too spongy (a trait they share with political ideologies).

But if crusades discourage analysis, they do attract adherents. The two seem to go together. They demand to be believed, devotedly. And in this they are strangely effective. They get things done because of it, because so little energy is wasted in reflection, and so much available for hatred.

At the heart of every crusade, however, there are small chunks of logic — simple propositions that *such and such is the case*. Every movement and every doctrine has such simplicities, although they usually pass unnoticed until it's too late. The aim of this book is to bring those little chunks of logic to light, to examine them carefully, and ask some simple questions. Are they right? Are they true? Are they justified?

I hardly expect to dissuade the faithful. That is rarely achieved by mere argument — or even by disasters that all the world can see (just look at Marxism). But I do mean to ask whether such a faith is sensible. That is, whether a man of sound common sense would hold it. That is my present task.

Luckily the crusade's propositions have been stated, by Colin Renfrew[1] and his acolytes. Their specific charge against the international antiquities market, it seems, is that

[1] Professor The Lord Renfrew of Kaimsthorn FBA, Disney Professor of Archaeology, Director of the McDonald Institute for Archaeological Research, and former master of Jesus College, University of Cambridge.

it *encourages looting*. Not that it is against the law to take antiquities from countries-of-origin — although it *is* becoming so, by degrees — for such laws are merely *post hoc* attempts to prevent the looting.

No, *the looting itself is the bad thing*. And the reason for this? That only a controlled and scientific excavation — one conducted by professional archaeologists, that is to say — can ever yield *knowledge* to mankind, whereas the market encourages 'illicit excavation', which is clumsy, nefarious and destructive of knowledge. And knowledge is the key.

This is the charge against the market. But there is also a specific charge against *collectors*. It is the collectors, you see, who power the market. They are the cause, the prime movers. The rest is merely effect. We should direct our animus against collectors. Thwart the collectors, and the market itself will wither.

The collector's urge

The *collector's urge* is certainly a curious phenomenon. It turns up in the strangest places. It hoards the unlikeliest things, and arranges them neatly in rows. You might think it silly, or vicious — or just another bit of our biology run amuck, like a bower-bird or an obsessive squirrel with his nuts. There is even the suggestion, rather more than a suggestion in fact, that the *urge to collect* — or, rather, to classify, and take examples along the way — is part of our innate baggage, something that is hard-wired into the brain, another aspect of our evolutionary inheritance.

If so, it may be more a liability than a help to modern city-dwelling man — much like Freud's *id*, Lorenz's 'aggressive instinct', Ardrey's 'territorial instinct', the masculine urge for sexual-dominance, and numerous other unpleasant twentieth-century obsessions. It has certainly become fashionable to question the passion — and with this vague and as yet unformulated agenda in mind, who can say? Also to hint at something not quite right, something out of place, something which needs to be controlled. It has not passed notice amongst the feminists, for instance, that only men collect (or, at least, collect antiquities).

Collectors can certainly be vicious. Every urge has its pathology, and any passion can drift into obsession. Consider the mayhem done by little boys in pursuit of bird's eggs. Or Swiss collectors in the late seventies, commissioning burglaries from provincial Italian museums, just to complete their collections.

But collecting is a universal passion. This much has to be admitted. Every man dreams of discovering treasure, and not just fully-fledged collectors. Every man likes to think that one day his pertinacity will be rewarded — and his knowledge — and he will bring something wonderful into the light.

We all know the stories. The antiquities collector, contentedly browsing the junk shops in the Brighton Lanes, who came across a head and torso, painted a pillar-box red. Underneath this disguise he recognised something characteristic, the features of New Kingdom Egypt. He took a chance, paid his fifty pounds, and consigned the head for cleaning. His hunch was correct. The head was ancient, and a masterpiece. It was worth millions. But somehow the knowledge of it had been lost, and a pharaoh's head doing duty as a garden gnome.

Collectors and dealers all dream this dream of discovery. Whether Sung Dynasty figurines or Egyptian shawabtis or even teddy bears, the dream itself remains the same. Somewhere is the ultimate piece, rare and glorious, just waiting to be rescued. Every collector, in his quiet place, quietly envies Indiana Jones.

Even curators in their tweeds harbour the passion. Or at least they should. These days in England they have no funding, no means to purchase new objects, and hence they rail against the market — its materialism, its corruption and, more recently, its disruption of the gentle pace of archaeology.[2]

All very well, and enjoyable, as long as they have no money to spend, and hence no temptation to sully themselves in the places they would spend it. But if they had the money, as the Americans still do, would they not plunge in just the same? I would certainly hope so.

Collectors, are they really to blame for the carnage?

The collecting of ancient things — their reverence and their protection — is itself an ancient pastime. But these days, as I say, it is under threat, and from a surprising quarter, from

---

[2]   Although, more recently than they care to remember, the market *was* archaeology. See page 24.

the universities. Well, perhaps not so surprising. Academe has invariably been the last bastion of failed ideas.

The debate has been dominated, at least in England, by Colin Renfrew. Professor Renfrew roundly despises the market, and the collectors who drive it.

If there were no collectors, he suggests, *there would be no real problem for antiquity*. They seem innocuous enough as a breed, these collectors — even the 'Peacock Collectors' that cluster the Metropolitan Museum in New York, and attract his special ire. These people may appear benign, Renfrew concedes, but they create a demand — almost a suction — which seeps through the market, until it reaches the original source of antiquities — the *countries-of-origin* — and drags antiquities from their rightful resting place.

If there were no collectors, it seems to follow, and no dealers to serve them, there would be nothing to disrupt the orderly calm of archaeology. Nothing would be disturbed, nothing removed from its resting place until scholarship was ready to record it with due reverence.

And if there is still illicit excavation — clumsy, nefarious and destructive of knowledge — then it is ultimately the fault of these collectors and their cupidity — and not at all the fault of the poor countries themselves, who are just trying to get by, and lack the resource to prevent such an outrage, such a *Rape of Heritage*.

Banish the collectors, and you banish their demand. Cultural heritage would be unharmed, and sleep undisturbed for gentle archaeology to unearth.[3]

The argument has an immediate charm. It is simple and self-assured. And it does all the ancillary things that politically-correct arguments are meant to do. But it does not really bear scrutiny. In reality it simply turns the world on its head. And later I shall disprove it.

The Crusade's solution to smuggling...

The practical version of the argument, however — and what some regard as the remedy — suggests that *any antiquity with-*

---

[3] In fact, Renfrew condemns the Metropolitan Museum *in toto* because it 'has no proper ethical policy — unlike the British Museum — and is indirectly funding the looters... Illicit excavation does terrible damage to our understanding of history. And even if collectors believe they are buying antiquities legitimately, their money is funding illicit excavation. *Collectors are the real looters.*' (Lord Renfrew, New York Times, 23rd February 2004).

out a provenance — that is, without a clear and recorded history, from find-spot through successive owners to the present — is somehow suspect, dubious if not downright dodgy. And that reputable dealers should simply refuse to buy any object — unless it has an exhaustive, meticulous, and preferably *published* testimony.

In other words, in this brave new world every antiquity is to be *presumed guilty unless it can be proved innocent.* A strange argument. How many ornaments in our homes, our homes themselves and even our own families, can we trace back beyond a generation or two? Are they to be indicted because we have forgotten them, or because we never knew? And if this is considered logical for the antiquities market, then why not the general antiques market, or any second-hand goods? And what about the museums, where almost nothing has a provenance — except for those pieces which are now being bought, and bought in an atmosphere of almost cloying sanctity.

Everything has a provenance[4] — of course it has — but most have been forgotten, because just too insignificant, in the bustle of the day, for their history to be recorded, or passed reliably by word of mouth.

And this is part of antiquity's resonance, this lost but plangent history — the wonder of where an object has been, and the events it has seen. It releases the imagination.

...relies upon a false conflation

Renfrew relies on this conflation — that 'un-provenanced' means illicit, means 'stolen'. This is clearly nonsense, because 'attached memories' are easily lost. If I have a collection of a hundred items, say, I will soon forget their individual histories, except for those that had pain or pleasure in the finding — those that had to be tracked down, were expensive or were bargains. And if I sell or exchange them, their next owner will likewise only remember the extraordinary ones. He may remember that they came from me, but bother little about their previous ownership. This is simple psychology.

---

[4] The antiquities trade usually distinguishes between an object's *provenance* — its original find-spot — and its *provenience*, the history of its subsequent adventures, its various owners, or the paper-record of them, if any exists. An object's provenience can be 'disreputable', 'respectable' or even 'noble', depending upon its collectors. For ease and clarity, I shall use *provenance* for the entire history, known or unknown, of an object.

The only antiquities to flaunt their history–or a part of it–are those bearing collection labels. This 'black-top' vase carries a Victorian label, which shows it to have been part of somebody's 'cabinet of curiosities'. The label adds something of charm (if only because it's wrong, by about a thousand years).

Renfrew's conflation also ignores the auction-houses, through which most antiquities are bought and sold nowadays. Auctions impose anonymity, and there is nothing suspicious about that. There are very good reasons for it. An auction-buyer only knows the past owners if they were famous — John Lennon, say, and his New Kingdom Statue of Sekhmet — whose association (might be expected to) improve the selling-price.

But there is more. Every antiquity can be 'read', and reveal a deal of its history. A competent restorer can easily understand — from the materials used, and the techniques — when an object was last restored, and hence when it must have been in the West for that restoration. And if a restorer can tell this, then so can dealers, collectors and even curators. Anybody, in fact, who has access to the restorer or his reports. Consider the following examples, both entirely typical:

previous
infill

join line
of
detached head

chipped
toes

Bought in auction, and thus of 'unknown origin', this statuette clearly reveals (by the type of plaster used, the style of work, and the use of shellac) that it was restored in England in late Victorian times, or no later than the twenties.

My restoration report records everything I have done, as well as the object's starting condition–and hence the fact that it could not possibly be regarded as 'stolen'. But what if that report were lost, or the statuette resold at auction?

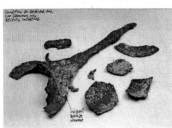

This object has quite clearly just left its resting place in the soil. The bronze has almost completely mineralized, and any (Western) owner would have it restored.

After extensive restoration, the strainer has been saved for the future. But such a work could only be done in the West, which has the technology, the skill and the funds.

The complete 'hoard' after restoration, and the presentation case that will prevent it from being 'scattered'–the other charge against the market.

The complete 'hoard' (in the second example) could have come from anywhere in the Eastern Greek world (any one of a dozen countries). If it had remained there, however, it would never have survived. Of that I am sure. Its relative unimportance, and the extreme difficulty of the restoration, would have consigned it to oblivion. Bear this in mind, those who denounce it as 'stolen'.

It follows, that anyone who insists on Renfrew's conflation is either ignorant — knowing nothing of the market and its subtleties — or is being mischievous. This book should help you decide.

It also overlooks the sheer numbers of antiquities

The *Provenance Argument* is tactical, of course, and usually goes hand in hand with another — that private people have no right, really, these egalitarian days, to possess antiquities, and no right to sell them, for they are 'priceless'. They should all be in museums, where they can be seen by everybody, and available to scholars, and looked after properly by trained people, and not selfishly hidden away.

If this sounds clumsy, gushy even, that is because it is usually delivered so — all in a rush — and laced with plenty of indignation to bolster the shaky logic.

For it overlooks one huge and salient fact. There are just *too many antiquities around* — and most of them too unimportant — for museum display. Or even museum storage. For each Egyptian type the British Museum has a dozen examples, with only the one displayed, and the others just stacked in darkness. The South East Asian Department has entire collections of antiquities, still packed in their tea-chests, bequeathed before the War and yet to be catalogued. In some cases they have not even been unpacked.[5]

What is to be done with all these things, if they cannot be owned and cherished by ordinary people and — yes — passed from hand to hand? Are they to be stacked unseen, wrapped in fading newspaper, and gently decaying? Or should they perhaps be destroyed to further discourage the market — as elephant tusks are even now being burnt to 'discourage' ivory smugglers?

---

[5] Robert Knox, (Assistant Curator, South East Asian Department, British Museum), in personal conversation, 1978.

The European stance

You could say that Europe has already acted on this argument — implicitly perhaps, but acted nevertheless. In the early nineties the EU imposed new regulations on its much-vaunted 'open-market'. Previously antiquities had moved unfettered between member states, as they did elsewhere. Antiquities could be sent from one centre to another — from a London gallery to one in Paris, say — with a minimum of fuss. But such simple twenty-minute transfers were now to require an 'export licence' — with the strongly hinted possibility of a refusal if the antiquity in question was considered important enough. This was just extraordinary. It reversed the 'open-market' principle. It immobilized antiquities, froze them wherever the flow of the ages had brought them, and largely on grounds of national vanity.

Now you could regard this as an expression of the new piety — that it is sinful to trade somebody's '*Heritage*'. Or you could regard it — as I prefer — as an infamous exercise in *realpolitik* — as a political appeasement of Italy and Greece, who have nationalized their antiquities in the strict sense — the only Europeans to do so — but who cannot take care — or can't be bothered to take care — of their claimed inheritance, their hundreds of museums and ancient sites. Or, in the case of Greece, have precious little of it left, having lost all the movables to ancient Rome (what they didn't sell to the Etruscans, that is), and would like it all back, damn you, starting with those bloody Marbles.

Anyway, the real losers were bound to be Northerners; the British and the Germans. And we British had the most to lose, because of our supremacy in the market — our former supremacy, I should now say — and because we alone would bother to enforce the new laws. This is clearly what has happened. Whilst the new regulations were busy-bodily being enforced upon the British dealers, the French just carried on as if nothing had happened (they just 'smuggled' pieces for me to restore, for example). There were some of course — cynical souls indeed — who suspected that the French were quite willing to appease the Greeks and Italians, because they'd always had some such advantageous outcome in mind.[6]

---

[6] A sentiment strengthened by the recent French gains at the expense of the London antiquities market, their vociferous support for the return of the

And the wider consequences of the Crusade

But perhaps the EU position really does represent the future – as they so monotonously claim in other contexts. Professor Renfrew wants to close down the market for antiquities, for only by such means – or so his logic would have it – could there ever be an end to the dreadful looting. And it makes no sense to close the market in just one country. That would only be a moral gesture and Professor Renfrew is not a man who would be content with gestures. No, what he wants is to close down the world market – all of it – and make it impossible to trade in antiquities. He wants to put a stop to their movement across the world.

Renfrew is trying to discredit the antiquities market, therefore. And not just by establishing a causal linkage with looting. No. He also claims a contingent link with drugs and drug money-laundering.[7] (His acolytes go further – they claim a link with terrorism.) And it is only a matter of time before someone cites the link with imperialism and hence – at least according to the fashionable pundits – with dread racialism.

It is certainly true that the European powers used their influence, especially when it came to accumulating other people's art, and especially from their colonies. And it is arguable that the great museums of Europe – the British Museum, the Louvre, the Hermitage, the Berlin and so on – are largely the products of this. Putting it bluntly, that they are *imperial loot* at one remove. Colonialist loot. Racialist loot.

If this idea received full backing from UNESCO, these museums would come under immense moral pressure to make restitution. Precisely how much restitution would depend upon how aggressive the countries of origin became, and how far they pushed the matter.

Elgin Marbles, and their absolute refusal to consider their Napoleonic acquisitions in the same category although, in terms of sheer rapacity, they surely rank as the greatest looting of modern times. They 'make Goering look like a pickpocket', to quote one historian (Paul Johnson, Spectator, March 12th 2005). The argument that Napoleon's agent, Vivant Denon, used in the early years of the nineteenth century – and which the French still explicitly believe – is that Paris is the natural place to acquire a knowledge of European culture, and its roots in Greece and Rome, and the Louvre is its cynosure. Literally, Paris is the tail that wags the cultural dog.

[7]   For the truth of this, see page 333 and *Drug money laundering – is the antiquities market involved?* in the Appendix.

One of the great prizes, the Rosetta Stone

If Egypt, for example, just demanded the return of war booty, it would embarrass the British Museum, whose founding collection was precisely that—booty requisitioned from the French invaders in 1804, and including the Rosetta Stone. If Egypt then demanded what had been stolen from her various governments—in the strictly conventional sense of stolen, that is—the British Museum would have to return the bulk of Curator Budge's collection of the 1890s.

If Egypt went farther, and demanded the return of goods that had been bought, but only from an occupying power which they refused to recognise— the Ottomans say, or ourselves under the Protectorate—that would jeopardize the remainder. Almost the entire Egyptian Collection of the British Museum—which was effectively complete by the end of the nineteenth century—would be at risk of repatriation. And similarly for other European museums.

If the *Cultural Heritage Crusade* proves successful, therefore, and legitimises its moral agenda, it would be a catastrophe, and not just for the world antiquities market. It would allow various countries to demand the return of billions of pounds of treasure and that, dear reader, would be a political nightmare.[8] All the more reason to get the argument right.

Summary

- The *Cultural Heritage Crusade* would have us return all antiquities to their *countries-of-origin*.
- The consequence of this would be little short of catastrophic for the great European museums.
- The Crusade's position is nebulous, more *politically correct* than logically explicit, but it does have a central charge against the market, that it encourages *looting*, and against *collectors*, because they drive the market.
- By muzzling them, it claims, we can prevent further outrage in these poor countries of origin, and further loss of their national inheritance.
- It further claims that all antiquities without a *provenance* should be shunned, because they are probably smuggled.
- The EU tacitly supports this position, whilst turning a blind eye to the reality.

---

[8] A first list would include the following works:

- *The Pergamon Altar* from Anatolia, modern Turkey (now in Berlin)
- *The Winged Victory* from Corinth (now in the Louvre)
- *The Elgin Marbles*, purchased by Lord Elgin from the Ottoman authorities in 1802 (now in the British Museum)
- *The Rosetta Stone*, wrested from the Napoleon's Egyptian expedition of 1798 by ourselves (ditto)
- *The Codex Sinaiaticus*, brought from Egypt in the seventeenth century (ditto)
- Various *Greek Statuary*, looted by Roman emperors and consuls (now in the Capitoline Museum, Rome)
- *The Obelisk* taken by Caligula from Memphis (now in Rome)
- *The Serpent Column* from Delphi, taken by Constantine and placed in the Hippodrome in Constantinople (now Istanbul)
- The famous *Bronze Horses of Venice*, probably originating in Corinth, and taken to Rome after the sack of 146BC, transferred to the Eastern Empire, and taken from Constantinople after the sack of 1204AD
- The *Lion of St. Marks*, from Piraeus, taken as booty by the mercenary Francesco Morosini in 1668 (now outside the Arsenal, Venice)
- *The Head of Nefertari* (now in Berlin)

A comprehensive list would be enormous, stretching from the unanswerable to the absurd. A Jewish group has recently claimed the Coliseum in Rome, for example, because it was built with the proceeds of the sack of Jerusalem in 70AD.

CHAPTER 3

The Nineteenth-Century Legacy

If the past were really to blame, it would make life so much easier. We could simply confess our sins, and start again.

Are the colonial powers really to blame?

The European museums certainly have a lot to answer for, at least by their new-found standards of piety. Their early collecting methods were decidedly frisky, and bear a marked resemblance to what they now regard with such studied stage horror.

For much of the nineteenth century the French and the British fought each other in Egypt—a war by proxy through their agents—for the biggest share of Egypt's antiquity. On the British side was Giovanni Belzoni—the 'greatest plunderer of them all'—and for the French Consul Drovetti and his Coptic agents. These two intrigued and tussled, bribed and counter-bribed with heroic relish.

The French opposition, beaten by a short head

The tussle continued in their respective national presses. Belzoni was abhorred by the French, and frequently denounced, but eulogized by the British as an 'archaeologist of genius'. He certainly was a handful. A circus strong-man — the 'Patagonian Hercules' — turned engineer, turned adventurer, he robed himself like a flamboyant pasha, and boomed his way down the Nile, sweeping enormous antiquities into his waiting boats.

The French tried to restrain him. They plotted and they sabotaged. They even resorted to destroying things, lest Belzoni get his hands on them. When he arrived at Philae, for example, to collect some temple reliefs he had reserved, he found them deliberately smashed, with *'operation manqué'* scrawled on the remains. But Belzoni was indefatigable. He only quit the field when his life was in jeopardy.

The results of this splendid war by proxy can now be viewed — at your respectable modern leisure — in the echoing halls of the British Museum and the Louvre. If I were to hazard a guess, I'd say the British had won, by a short head.

But these were confident men. They had all the certitude of Empire, that they were the natural custodians of such treasures. And they shared a common assumption, that *property rights could be nullified by systematic abuse* — just like the modern RSPCA, when it confiscates a mistreated pet. They believed that many of the sites and objects would be

'Young Memnon', as it is now, safely ensconced in the British Museum, but no acknowledgement of its donor, Giovanni Belzoni, or the drama of its salvage (see illustration on rear end-paper).

destroyed if they remained where they were. The natives would befoul them, and the authorities disregard, or just use them for building material. The only important thing, they believed, was to get as many antiquities as possible through to a less uncertain future. And that meant under their capacious wings.

A classic example of the breed was Sir Wallis Budge, Kt, MA and D.Litt. Cambridge, MA and D.Litt. Oxford, D.Litt. Durham, FSA, Keeper of the Egyptian and Assyrian Antiquities at the British Museum, and warmly commended by the Museum's trustees for his 'remarkable energy'. Budge was evidently a bit of a lad, and had numerous scrapes with the Egyptian Antiquities Service under its French Director Eugène Grébaut.

Sir Wallis Budge, Keeper of Egyptian Antiquities
at the British Museum, erstwhile burglar and smuggler

On his second collecting visit, for example, the Service had him trailed by the police. This hardly cramped Budge's style:

> Before I had been in Cairo many hours I found that everybody was talking about [the] discoveries in Upper Egypt, and the most extraordinary stories were afloat...There were representatives of several Continental Museums in Cairo, each doing his best, *as was right*, to secure the lion's share...The Egyptian officials of the Service of Antiquities behaved according to their well-known manner...M.Grébaut went about the town with entreaties and threats...he threatened me with arrest and legal prosecution, if I attempted to deal with the natives concerned...[1] [my italics]

[1]   Wallis Budge, *By Nile and Tigris*, 1920.

But Budge was made of sterner stuff. He reached Luxor, and was taken under cover of darkness to a newly discovered tomb on the West bank, where he bought an important collection, including the famous *Papyrus of Ani* — now occupying pride of place in the British Museum's collection, and the world's finest example of the *Book of the Dead*. Budge had them crated and secured in the basement of a small house adjoining his Luxor hotel. But several hours later, whilst drinking coffee with the dealer who had taken him to the tomb, he found himself under arrest, pending the arrival of Director Grébaut in person.

Grébaut was but twelve miles upstream, and being thwarted by the natives, whose loyalties lay with the dealers, and against the authorities. Grebaut's steamer was firmly stuck on a sandbank, and the villagers had simply hidden their donkeys, to prevent them from being hired.

Meanwhile the Luxor police chief surrounded the dealers' houses with armed guards, and also the house containing Budge's contraband. The dealers tried to get the guards drunk, but this proved unsuccessful. So they 'commended them for their fidelity', and rewarded them with a sumptuous meal up on the hotel roof. And, as dusk descended, a crew of burly gardeners filed into the garden of Budge's house, and silently dug a tunnel in the soft earth, under the thick hotel wall, and into the basement where the antiquities were being stored. Budge watched all this from the garden, and remarked that:

> As I watched the work with the manager, it seemed to me that the gardeners were particularly skilled house-breakers, and that they must have had much practise.

The British Museum's antiquities, once they had been successfully stolen — or stolen back, perhaps one should say — were spirited down to the river, where the Royal Engineers were on hand to ship them efficiently to Alexandria — as unexceptionable 'military freight' — and thence to England. The British army clearly regarded the natives as reasonable men who were just trying to make a living — and the Government Antiquities Service as venal and corrupt. They had every reason, for Grébaut's staff were even then selling off the antiquities he had collected on the way upstream, and spiriting them off the steamer whilst the luckless Grébaut was enjoying his dinner.

Lady Duff-Gordon

Similarly, the formidable Lady Duff-Gordon admitted that:

> A man has stolen a very nice silver antique ring for me out of the
> last excavations – don't tell Mariette [the French Director of the
> Antiquities Service at the time]. My *fellah* said, 'Better thou have
> it than Mariette sell it to the French and pocket the money; if I
> didn't steal it, he certainly would' – so I received the stolen
> property calmly.

Sir Wallis himself was entirely untrammelled by modern
self-doubt. 'In this way', he proudly proclaimed 'we saved
the papyrus of Ani, and all the rest of my acquisitions from
the officials of the Service of Antiquities, *and all of Luxor
rejoiced*'. [my italics] He also declared, with splendid Victorian assurance, that such things were only safe when they
were in the British Museum:

> Whatever blame may be attached to individual archaeologists
> for removing [mummies] from Egypt, every unprejudiced per-
> son who knows anything of the subject must admit that once
> [the mummy]...is lodged in the British Museum, it has a far
> better chance of being preserved there than it could possibly
> have in any tomb, Royal or otherwise, in Egypt.

By such cavalier methods Budge and his predecessors
were able to assemble – in the British Museum, that is – the
finest repository of Egyptian art in Europe. In Egypt Budge
may have been regarded with suspicion, as a 'well-known
but somewhat unscrupulous collector for his Museum'

(Egyptian Gazette, 1884), but in England he was publicly lauded.

But anyway, please note, here was a senior official of the British Museum resorting to house-breaking and literally stealing antiquities from (the Antiquities Service of) the Egyptian Government. Worse, from the British administration in Egypt, who could hardly be seen to be stripping Egypt of her assets, and had already distanced itself from Budge's activities (although he was eventually knighted for his services.)

How do they feel about their friskier past, these august institutions?

Yes, how *does* the modern British Museum feel about harbouring Belzoni's plunder and Wallis Budge's stolen goods? Their present piety hardly accords with their nineteenth-century antics. They are obviously embarrassed by Budge, and have even suggested that his autobiography — *By Nile and Tigris*, quoted above — was a 'work of semi-fiction'. But having been there myself, and seen much the same antics — almost a hundred years later — I can assure them that it has nothing to do with fiction. It is a careful and explicit record. If anything, a classic of English understatement.

There are some who suggest that the great nineteenth century collections — these hoards of imperial loot now stranded on insignificant shores — should be regarded as museum pieces in their own right. A sort of colonial Emperor's New Clothes, as it were, but on permanent display. All very well, and very post-modern — as I have already mentioned — but hardly useful to the Egyptians themselves. Have these liberal apologists suggested anything practical? Have they considered returning the *Papyrus of Ani*, for example, and to the very body it was stolen from, the Egyptian Antiquities Service?

It appears not. They like to flaunt their 'ethical buying policy' — of not purchasing anything without a verifiable provenance, that is — but as they have no money to spend compared with the other great museums, and as their own collections were effectively complete — courtesy of this same imperial skulduggery — by the end of the nineteenth century, this is hardly a loss.

The Egyptian room at the British Museum:
One of the triumphs of imperial self-confidence

And as for the past, they seem curiously ambivalent. Perhaps they would claim that what happened then was justifi-
able — just because it was then, when archaeology was young
and callow. But that, after 1945 say, and the advent of
UNESCO thinking and a mature and scientific archaeology,
a new era has dawned, and that, well — after all's said and
done and a host of other clichés — sleeping dogs should be
left well alone.

But consider. If denouncing Sir Wallis Budge would oblige
them to return the goods to Egypt, or to make some amends,
then it seems to follow — at least it does for my unrepentant
logic — that hanging on to the goods obliges them to embrace
Budge's contempt for the Egyptian Antiquities Service.
More, in fact. It obliges them to accept that little if anything
has changed. That Egypt is still as corrupt as it was in
Budge's day — and, hence, that Budge's avowed justification
still stands, perhaps even more so.

It is all a question of morale, you see. Most of these august
institutions — with the possible exception of the British
Museum, who can only mouth it with embarrassed hilar-
ity — still more or less believe what Sir Wallis Budge believed
in the 1890s. They believe, that is, that they deserve every-

thing they get — if only because *it is safer for the objects themselves.*[2]

That is, they believe that nothing much has changed, and the same uncomfortable fact applies, that the only safe place for antiquities is wherever they are *cherished*. Which might not be with the Third World regimes who are so busy claiming them, but might still be — dare we admit it — in the democratic West. And I do not necessarily mean the great museums. I mean the despised *collectors*, who also cherish the small and unimportant things — the vast majority of antiquities that don't merit any museum — and preserve them for the future.

They may not believe this as confidently as the American museums, who display the imperial self-confidence in its acutest form, and unashamedly declare that the best and safest place for such things is under their capacious American wing — and the more of them the better. But, nonetheless, they still consider themselves *worthy*, and it follows that any demand for restitution will be met with a very dusty answer.

Or should we simply blame it on the Ottomans?

Of course the British Museum and its competitors paid almost nothing for these treasures, and if the modern Egyptians do have a case it is this, that their heritage — which belatedly they have come to appreciate — was relinquished for next to nothing. But the fault was not ours. It was the Turkish Porte's, who issued the requisite *firmans*, and with them the right to accumulate in bulk, rather than buying the items individually, for a correct and negotiated price, as has since become the practise.

Until the First World War Turkey remained one of the great powers. Greece may have fought for her independence, and eventually gained it through not much merit of her own, but the rest of the eastern Mediterranean — including Egypt — remained inside the lax and chaotic Ottoman Empire.

---

[2] And sadly, as I hope you'll come to agree with me, they were right. The ruin of the Egyptian sites, the Greeks allowing their marbles to disintegrate and bulldozing the site of the Battle of Marathon for a rowing lake (now discarded), the rape of Angkor Wat, the bulldozing of temple sites in Lebanon, and the Afghans using their statuary for target practice. These states *can't or simply won't* look after their 'Heritage'.

Egyptian antiquity was disregarded by the Turkish rulers and Egyptians alike. The Ottoman Satrap, Mohammed Ali, ridiculed the idea that he might gift 'Young Memnon' to the Prince Regent, Albert. What Monarch, he scoffed, would want a mere block of stone? Belzoni knew better.

The Turks, or at least their provincial governors the Beys, did not apparently value antiquity, and freely issued *firmans* — which enabled the other great powers, notably the British and French, to plunder for them — upon the lightest of reasons, and with scarcely a bribe or a gift. Instance the conversation between Giovanni Belzoni — working for the British Museum in the 1820s — and the Turkish ruler of the province of Egypt that contained Luxor and the splendours of Karnak and the West Bank. Calil Bey, a relative of Mohammed Ali Pasha — the *Satrap* for Egypt and its virtual ruler — entertained Belzoni to a convivial dinner of mutton spiced with green peppercorns. The Bey merely expressed his astonishment that Europeans should want more stones, when presumably they had plenty of their own. Belzoni gravely assured him that 'we have plenty of stones, your grace, but we think those of Egypt are a better sort'.

Whereupon Belzoni was issued his *firman*, and with it the indisputable right to collect whatever antiquities he wished, from wherever he wished, and pay nothing more than the workers' wages for digging them up, and boat fees for carrying them away. Truly one of the best deals of all time, and you can see the results in the British Museum.

In one sense the Turks were sowing the whirlwind, because the newly independent countries of origin — those of the former Ottoman Empire — can now claim that their 'heritage' was thoughtlessly squandered, and before they themselves had any say in the matter. The Greeks, for example, can now argue that 'their' marbles may have been 'sold' to Lord Elgin, but that the vendors had no legal title and that, therefore, there really had been no sale.

In one sense the Greeks have a point. I sympathise with them. But they persistently refuse to admit that this was not just hard luck on them, the Greeks, but *good luck* for the marbles themselves — and hence for the Greeks in the long-run — because the 'Parthenon' marbles are still around for them to wrangle about so deliciously. And that I find ungracious.

After all, without the British and their splendid self-confidence, *none* of these marbles would have been rescued. They would have been destroyed, as the other pediment was, the one which Elgin could not or would not afford — and only captured as a plaster-cast — and which has since been completely destroyed by industrial pollution. Even worse, the pediments might have gone to the French, and the Greeks would have no chance of bamboozling them.[3]

And has the world really changed?

This is the real bone of contention between the *Cultural Heritage Crusade* and myself — its underlying assumption that there's been a decisive break with the past. This is never openly stated, of course, never hauled into the cold light of day. But it underlies everything else that *is* said. It's what enables the Crusade to accept my arguments — and then calmly to deny my conclusions.

And this assumption? That at some fairly recent point — presumably the fully-fledged emergence of *UNESCO Man* — human nature underwent a radical conversion, and could now be trusted to husband its heritage, rather than digging it up and flogging it, knocking it down to build something else, or just destroying it for the sheer hell of it. And this splendid assumption — as this book, alas, will serve to show — may be a trifle premature. Consider the rain-forests, just to be getting on with.

If we could assume this, you see — that the world had really changed — then everything would be easy. We could blithely blame the past for everything bad, for everything that has ever gone wrong — and cast it aside like so much soiled and empty baggage. And then we could start afresh. This is indeed what the *Crusade* has in mind — that *history has ended*, and man is created anew. He is closer to God, and

[3] See illustration on page 40. See also Dorothy King, *The Elgin Marbles*.

must be judged by new and very different standards. And because of this the cautions and the caveats can all of them be swept away. Welcome the Brave New Dawn!

This is nothing new, however. It's been a continuing refrain of academics since the 'thirties. There have been numerous brave new dawns, all of them drawing a line between mankind's past moral turpitude, and his blithe and blameless future.

And they all assume that the benign rationality of the academic's armchair extends beyond the Cambridge Court (or the Oxford Quad, if it comes to that) — that all the races of men, and all their cultures, have become as sensible and as candid as they themselves. This is one of the unspoken beliefs that bedevils academics, and makes them human after all. And I have to say that it is just as naive, now — and just as comfortably disingenuous — as it was in the 'thirties, when those same academics knew damn well what was happening in Stalin's brave new world, but managed to turn a blind eye.

As Ferdinand Mount has expressed it:

> The *critical* and the *sceptical* find high praise in academic circles, but are rarely practised in Academe. It is the intelligentsia which provides suckers for each New Dawn, and which buys ideologies wholesale. The rest regard all ideologies as pretentious claptrap which have little to do with real life'[4]

No. I am afraid that reality is still fraught and confused, and men are very much the same. Nothing much has changed, except perhaps the sheer quantity of humbug that's out there — and if we think otherwise we'll only be embarrassed, and the future will laugh at us — just as we laugh at all the other silly idealists of the past. If I have a refrain, therefore — a refrain to counter this premature idealism — it is just this. We should expect the worst, and plan most carefully for it — and then hope for something better. And that way, somehow, anyhow, we'll manage to scramble through.

And those who see farther than the rest — or believe they can? Their duty remains as Keats defined it, so many years ago. They must tolerate the clamour. They must put up with the chaos. They must admit to their own limits, and resist the temptations — and the comforts — of the easy answer. For if they jump too soon, they'll only come up with cliché or,

[4]   Ferdinand Mount, *The Subversive Family*, 1982

worse, they'll just re-iterate the old grudges. As Lionel Trilling put it 'only the self that is sure of itself can do without the armour of systematic certainties.'

When academics pontificate, therefore, that warfare in modern Europe is inconceivable — that it's grotesque even to think of it, after everything we've learned — then the bloody Balkans await them. When they declare that we've entered an age of sweet reason, a second enlightenment, where all nations are mature and responsible — and all of them acting with due reverence for their inheritance — whether rain forest or archaeology — then again they're heading for embarrassment.

And when the same academics maintain that antiquities are being savagely stolen from the countries of origin — that a pillage is afoot — I would enjoin caution. I'd suggest that we take our time, and take nothing on trust. The world is more complicated than it appears from a Cambridge armchair. I should know, if anyone does. I've been there, after all.

Just who, to begin with, is supposed to be pillaging, and from whom? With a responsible democracy the ownership is clear, or clear enough. But what of a junta, a dictatorship or a military regime, whose citizens stubbornly persist in selling 'their' antiquities? Just what does 'their' refer to? Condemn the citizens, quick and thoughtless, and you just bolster the status quo. Should you not, at the very least, give some thought to the matter of ownership?

As I say, it's all rather complicated out there.

Summary
- The European museums certainly have a lot to answer for. Their early methods were little short of rapacious, although they're now curiously ambiguous about them.
- In one sense, it was the fault of the Ottoman Empire, for making it all so easy.
- The important question, however, is whether mankind has really reformed, and whether these protesting *countries-of-origin* can now be trusted with 'their' heritage.

The Beginnings of an Answer – Survival and Value

I would ask you, for a while, to ignore all this – the fashionable clamour, the zealotry, the rough and tumble of crusade – and just consider the antiquities themselves. They should be our sole concern. For they will remain – if all goes well – long after our obsessions are dust.

What is their best hope for the future? Where is their protection best assured? Putting it bluntly, how can we get as many antiquities as possible through to an uncertain future?

For this should be our sole concern. Not who owns antiquities at the moment, or who should own them. Not the vanities, the fashions, the obsessions and hatreds of the age. And not even the knowledge that might come from antiquity – if getting this knowledge endangers the antiquities themselves.

These are my concerns, and Egypt is my example.

Collectors reconsidered

You have heard collectors vilified, as the engine that drives the market. It is my contention, however, that we owe a great deal to collectors, and to the urge that drives them. For it is this urge that has so far saved antiquity. Far from being reprehensible, I see it as an inherited richness of human nature – as God's useful afterthought. The *collector's urge* has always been, and probably always will be, our best means to prevent destruction. Better have it open and honest, therefore, than masquerading as something else.

And the academics' argument against collectors? Something that only academics could foster, after years of training have divorced them from the world and all its ways, and from the fund of wisdom that we call common sense. All the more dangerous, therefore. Arguments like this – and from this source – have been the blight of the last century. We should have learned to distrust them by now.

To survive, antiquities must have a *value*

This is my central contention. That antiquities will only survive if they are valued. Stated thus, it sounds platitudinous. In philosophical terms, indeed, it is little more. But it seems, nevertheless, to have been overlooked.

Just accept, to be going on, that when an object is *well regarded* – when it's considered valuable, or worthy, or sacred, or scientifically and archaeologically important – and in its own right, for itself, rather than as a means to some other end – then it's an object that will be looked after. It will be cherished. And accept, further, that unless it *is* cherished, it will be at risk. I doubt that anybody could disagree with this.

Where antiquities are not valued, however, ownership can be compromised

When a pet animal is endangered, for example, we'd not hesitate to rescue it. We would remove it from its present owner, take it to a place of safety and refuge. And we'd do this upon little more than a *common-sense unease*. Such unease is inarticulate. It finds a voice through action, if at all. But it can be profoundly felt. The English may not be very good at expressing their feelings – even in these method-acting days – but we are still rather good at feeling them. Rather decent, that's to say. And if we were forced to explain ourselves – or at least to make the attempt – we would probably say the animal was at risk because *nobody (seemed to) care about it*. Or, what is much the same, because *nobody (seemed to) value it*.[1]

Whether we could explain why we were acting, however – calling in the RSPCA to have them 'rescue' the animal, confiscate it, that's to say, for its own good – it would be absolutely clear why we were acting. Rather, why we thought we had the right to act. Because *the owner had forfeited his property rights*.

---

[1] The parentheses are another Englishness, a reluctance for the definite and the unequivocal. This is an Englishness upon which English charm depends – or English hypocrisy, as the continentals would have it.

And if somebody was destroying or damaging antiquities because of incompetence, or irresponsibility — or manipulating them as a means to some other end — would we not feel this same unease, this same urge to interfere? And wouldn't it be correct? And laudable? In a sense, you see, these objects are also *living* for us. They represent a past life that has come down to us.

Consider the Taliban in Afghanistan, and their destruction of Buddhist sculptures. All those who saw this on television were shocked that such a thing could happen. All of us wanted to rescue these things, though they were no part of our culture, and nothing to do with 'our' heritage. Merely because we felt how important they were. For whatever reason, we felt this same unease in its strongest form. And we also felt that the Taliban had forfeited any *rights to ownership*. Before they did this terrible thing, we would have granted their rights. Well, some of us would. We'd have regarded these statues as part of their inheritance, their *cultural heritage*. But having seen what they were doing, we felt they'd betrayed their trust, and forfeited their rights.

This could be arrogance on our part, of course. The Taliban clearly scorned us and our paltry concerns. They felt that destruction *was* within their remit. But that wouldn't convince us. We'd feel a dogged moral surety about this — this

One of the Bamiyan Buddhas, before and after its destruction

same *common-sense unease* — inarticulate, but decent and profoundly felt.

And if we realized that more antiquities were at risk to other suspect regimes? Regimes that were showing signs of fragility, that were doomed, in fact — but perfectly capable of dragging wonderful things down with them? Would we not feel it incumbent to act, just to *do* something, as we'd wanted to act — felt we should have been acting — whilst the Taliban were using 'their' Buddhas for target practise?

Even our own very English disputes about planning and heritage — whether of countryside or archaeology — draw upon this same unease, the disconcerting feeling that our political masters are obsessed by present contingencies — by the small and squalid stuff of votes — and are so blinkered that they've lost sight of the more lasting values.

In all these cases the unease is the same — the suspicion that nobody cares, or cares enough, or cares as we do. And that they *don't care because they don't value*. And because of this, that innocent animals or objects are being put at risk.

And the corollary

When you expose your property to danger or destruction, you forfeit your ownership — whether 'you' happen to be a person or a government. That is the nub of it. And the unease that tells us this is not just a residue of bourgeois morality, but something profound.

The corollary also applies. When you save something from destruction — whether it is a pet animal or an antiquity, and whether you be individual or government — you thereafter own it. You have saved it, so now it is yours.[2] This is not just the common fare of folk legend and soap opera. It is equally profound. You save my life, and my life is somehow forfeit to your service (literally so, in 'primitive' cultures and in legend).

It is not often pointed out that Lord Elgin *saved* the marbles that bear his name. But it is often felt, in an inarticulate way, that if he had not shipped them north, they would have been

---

[2] As we shall see, academics also feel this about their precious *knowledge*. They've saved it from the rubble, so it's theirs. No one else can have it, unless they've paid for membership, and that they guard with all the mumbo-jumbo of freemasons.

The Greeks keep very quiet about the fact that Elgin left the Parthenon's west frieze behind, and contented himself with plaster casts. The top photo (of Elgin's replica, taken in 1938) shows the state of that pediment as it was in 1802. The bottom photo, taken in situ in 1938, shows the effects of air pollution before Athens's industrialization had really got under way. By the 1970s, the frieze was almost completely destroyed, so the Greeks cut it off and placed it in storage, safely out of sight. Study these photographs, therefore, pay homage to Lord Elgin, and reflect upon the present humbug.[3]

[3]   'A most striking example of weathering. In what may be called the industrial
      age, the modelling has everywhere lost its sharpness, facial expressions have
      changed, and whole features have gone for ever (for example, the right-most

destroyed.[4] The same is also felt by the Greeks themselves, when they claim the marbles have been 'over-cleaned', or damaged by exposure to the London smog. All parties feel the same thing. The only difference is, the Greeks' claim is a nonsense, and the truth makes a mockery of their pretensions. But ours is well-founded.

If we realized how correct it is to feel this way, we would be more open about it. The British Museum might even put aside its liberal feelings of guilt. Guilt for what? They have no reason, but every reason to feel proud (and defiant).

But what gives this *value* to antiquity? Why, the market, of course

The truth is very simple, I'm afraid, and very uncomfortable, at least for the academics. It is trade, and only trade – what we loosely call 'the market' – that gives any value to antiquity, and thereby ensures its survival in a harsh world. And by 'trade' I mean the mass of ordinary collectors, as well as the dealers and auction houses and experts that serve them.[5]

For one thing at least is clear. Antiquities have safely come down to us because – and, I would suggest, only because – they were considered valuable.

Let me repeat this. *Antiquity has only survived because it was valued.* And if you stop valuing it in the only sense moderns understand – *that of giving it a price* – then you condemn it.

---

figure's face has simply disappeared).... Marbles of all kinds are liable to be seriously damaged by the acids present in an industrial atmosphere. In the presence of moisture these destroy the surface, particularly at angles and corners, and open the joints to the disintegrating action of frost. In the case of exposed buildings, the action can only be arrested by the application of stringent anti-pollution laws, but where statuary is concerned, a practical alternative may be offered by the possibility of covering in the marbles or *bringing them indoors*, so they can be maintained under conditions where conservation is possible.' (*Conservation of Antiquities and Works of Art*, by H.J. Plenderleith, Emeritus Professor at the UNESCO School of Conservation in Rome). 'Bringing them indoors' is what Elgin did two hundred years ago.

[4]   For a technical explanation of this argument, see chapter 10.

[5]   Collectors are necessary, and all of them. The little ones give value to little antiquities, that are of no interest to museums. And the major collectors maintain prices for major antiquities. Prices depend upon competition, as anybody knows who's attended auctions. If the only buyers were national institutions – our great National museums – the prices would be piffling and the countries of origin would suffer. No, prices need competition, and lots of it. And that comes from collectors and the collectors' passion, lots of it.

I can imagine the chorus of outrage at what I have just said. I can hear the academics spluttering. It is the anguish of modernity, after all, that we live in a world of salesmen, where everything has its price, but nothing retains a value. Is that not what they say? And has not modernism attempted to raise art, *High Art*, into a sacrament that could fill the void left by the departing gods.[6] Nonsense, of course, and all that modernism has managed is an unholy alliance between critics and dealers and artists—blurring the distinctions between them—so that art-rubbish is foisted onto a bemused public. The whole modern-art fiasco is based upon a market—a corrupted, subsidised and cash-rich market—that modernism itself has created.

Put that aside for now, and let me reiterate. If you are worried about the ravages of the market, you cannot protect antiquities, or puppies, or elephants—or Golden Geese for that matter—by closing down their market, as academics are suggesting. That is no way to protect any of them, least of all antiquities. It is just an academic silliness. For when you take away their value—their exchange-value that is, their *price*—for most of the world you also remove their sole reason for surviving. You cast them outside the modern way of life—whatever they may be, antiquities or elephants—and you had better give them some other form of value—and pretty quickly at that—or they will surely perish.

You might be surprised by my choice of elephants here. You might even think it repugnant. Are not elephants being killed precisely because of their ivory, because their ivory has a *monetary value*? And is not it the market that's wiping them out? Perhaps so, but only because the market is being mishandled.

Faced with the Goose that lays the Golden Egg, you see, there'll always be some greedy moron who'll try and wring its neck. A stout guard and a big stick has invariably been the answer—funded by the occasional egg.

The moderns, however, have a novel stratagem. They have decided the best way to protect this particular Golden Goose is not to cherish it—and guard it as a resource—but declare that *gold will no longer be acceptable as a currency*. A brave attempt, indeed. But where does it leave the poor goose,

---

[6] The idea of the *sacred* has also been used by the Cultural Heritage Crusade, and just as ineptly, see pages 122 f and 148.

whose only value came from her eggs? Straight into the cooking-pot, I suspect. And what if some might think it useful – just in case – to stash a little bullion under the bed? No, it seems clear that only a properly disciplined market can ever save them, whether they be elephants or antiquities or Golden geese.[7]

It was Bernard Williams, then Knightbridge Professor of Moral Philosophy at Cambridge, who alerted me to the horrors of modernity with his *Elephant Argument*. He asked the forbidden question, the question that nobody else dared ask. Why *should* elephants survive? He dismissed the standard humanist arguments, the ones about elephants bringing pleasure to future generations of children, or the 'knowledge' that somehow accrues to these children, just having elephants around. These were not solutions to the problem. They were the problem itself, the problem that Judaeo-Christianity had left us – that we still tend to regard the world, and everything in it, as having been put there for our personal use. And hadn't started to think in other terms.

It is quite clear, for instance, that an overcrowded world that scrabbles for resource will make everything prey to the utilitarian calculus – *that what is good is what benefits the most people.* It is also clear that elephants will be swept aside, unless they can be seen to benefit the struggling masses, unless they can pay their way, as part of that same economic system. Those who live by votes can perish by them. Anything of value can be voted to the slaughterhouse. That's just how it is.

Williams' argument was meant to expose *utilitarianism* – and wishy-washy humanism – and the poverty of any system that cannot accommodate something as full of wonder as elephants. But, thirty years down the line, and we are actually living in that brutally utilitarian world – or at least Africa is – and elephants must be brought within this horrid utilitarian calculus, or they will surely perish. And the brutal fact is that elephants do have a value – and can pay their way – because of tourism, because of game hunting and, yes, because of ivory. Without these they would rapidly be destroyed by the men who covet their land. The value is

---

[7] Or, even, the African lion, according to a recent Johannesburg conference of the IUCN–World Conservation Union, which concluded that controlled trophy hunting was the best practical method of conservation.

there. It only needs husbanding, and needs to benefit every-body concerned — and be seen to benefit them. And the same applies to antiquity.

There are other means, of course: the sense of sanctity...

Of course there are other ways of finding *value* in antiquity. There is its *sense of sanctity*. You can feel this when you touch an ancient thing — a reaching out in awe, a vibration, and a shadowy sense of the sacred. Archaeologists should feel it all the time — or find some other means to earn a living. And it is part of this sanctity to feel outrage at the thought of money, mere vulgar money, being involved. How can the holy be traded, except for thirty pieces of silver?

Part of the modern problem, however, is that most people have lost this pervasive *sense of the holy*. Whole swathes of our lives were once protected by sanctity, but the Enlighten-ment has seen them all off, and we crouch around the remains like dying embers in a fire. Oh yes, if the world had really changed, and was closer to the ideal — or how it had been before the Enlightenment, when the gods were still alive and worthy of worship — then, yes, the holy things would be holy again, and made taboo, and protected.

And antiquity would be hedged around and protected, if only because it was the work of our ancestors, and carried their resonance. All would be simple again and, yes, I could agree with the Masters of Cambridge Colleges that my argu-ment was a vulgarity. But the world has changed forever, I fear, and the gods are all of them dead. We must find our way through without them, and without their benison. Our task is more immediate, and much more simple. We have to get these antiquities safely through to the future. Somehow, yes, we have to manage this.

Besides, sanctity was never enough in the past — even when backed by the high priest's big stick. There always were tomb-robbers — even in antiquity, when the tombs themselves were supposedly occupied by gods. And sanctity certainly wouldn't be sufficient nowadays. We cannot expect academic scruples from a poor peasant. He has more press-ing problems. His recent history and his harsh religion, all these get in the way. He is poor, his prospects are unpredictable and his government is probably repressive. And he has to feed his family.

No. The *sentiment of sanctity*, I'm afraid, is just not in the running. At least not for the hard-pressed peasant. Try telling him that the antiquity he has just found is sacred, and accordingly belongs to his government, or to his 'cultural inheritance' – or to something equally splendid and vacuous. Tell him that the antiquity cannot be expected – in any practical sense, that is – to benefit him and his family. And then prepare yourself for a very dusty answer.[8]

...and nationalism

Another approach, which the Egyptians have been attempting, these forty years and more, is to foster an entirely different value – a national prestige, almost a vainglory – and back it with all the powers of the modern state. The Egyptian regime, to put it bluntly, has busily been nationalizing its antiquity. They've also been *Egyptianizing* it, as they say, and making Pharaonic antiquity central to their self-image, their image of the *Egyptian Nation*. When you think of Egypt, they have been saying to their people, think of its past and be proud, for the past – *your* past – was glorious. Oh, and by the way, don't get any fancy ideas.

A tried and tested idea, nationalism, and it might just have worked. The Egyptian people might have come to value themselves – and their nation's antiquity – as a glorious reflection of each other. And this would have given another type of value to antiquity, something to replace the despised money value. Unfortunately, however, it hasn't worked. If it had, I would not be complaining now.

---

[8] This is not to say that sanctity – or one of its alleles – is not suitable for the *developed* countries. Indeed, as I shall explain, it may be the only form of value that can 'do the job', that can countermand commercial forces and property-prices. The monetary value of antiquity cannot. Proof of this was Abbey Meads at Swindon, the largest Roman temple complex in England, discovered in the way of a proposed housing estate. Its preservation required a million sterling – a tiny sum, given the developers' cash-flow, but vast in terms of the antiquities involved – and a year's grace for raising it. Nobody was forthcoming, and the day was only saved by a last minute preservation order (as a scheduled ancient monument), and a purchase by English Heritage – effectively as an area of sacred space. But such tactics can create resentment. A specialist contractor – an otherwise equable and civilised man – has admitted to me that he dreads them, and orders his men '*you will find nothing* – bones or artefacts – that'll bring in the archaeologists.'

*How Nasser wanted the Egyptians to see themselves, with a little help
from Cecil. B. de Mille (Museum of Egyptian History, Cairo)*

The problem has always been the little matter of resource.
At a practical level — and the Egyptian populace are a very
practical people, and not much given to flights of fancy —
nationalism has increasingly meant the regime confiscating
antiquity for itself, as if it was a resource that belonged exclu-
sively to its members — and denying it to the people. At least
that is how the people see it.

After three generations, this proud Egyptian experiment
has become just another *Prohibition*, and its main effect, as
Bernard von Bothmer[9] understood — apart from the inevitable corruption, that is — has been *to make the vast majority of
antiquities worthless for the vast majority of the populace.* Hence
they are being cast aside, ploughed over, built over, and forever losing their chance of coming into the light. Nineteenth
century nationalism is not the way, I am bound to conclude.
Oh no, not at all.

---

[9]   In his lifetime the world's greatest Egyptologist, and one who enraged the
      Egyptians — and was thereafter treated appallingly by them — for saying
      much of what I've been saying here. That is, saying it in public fora, and in
      print: *Sauvetage des Antiquitées en Egypte*, The Paris Conference, 1968.

...and the commercial

In these poorer countries – and Egypt is my example, but what I say applies elsewhere in the Middle East – *antiquity will only survive if it can pay its way*. Where something is worth money in Egypt it will be saved from the wreckage. What is 'saleable' becomes 'valuable', and what is 'valuable' becomes 'worthwhile' – the brute equation of the struggling man throughout the ages. Make it impossible to sell, and you put that object in danger because – come the crunch, as the moderns say – there is no reason for anybody to protect it.

Where it is worthless, that is to say – which is merely to say that it cannot be sold, that there is no market for it – then it is vulnerable to the pressing needs of the present. It will be cast aside in the struggle for land and housing and sustenance.

In the end, you see, it is only because of the Western market that a poor Egyptian peasant, when he discovers an antiquity in his fields, will still sometimes attempt to sell it, rather than discard or even destroy it. Because, that's to say, he knows that somebody out there still wants to buy such things. And because of this – because this antiquity can still benefit his family and himself – he will sometimes still save it, and pass it on, until it reaches sanctuary (in the West, it has to be said).

This may seem a brutal vision, and such a care may seem inadvertent. But it is better than nothing, much better, and if you wish to save antiquity – and pass it as a chalice to the next generation – you must allow it to keep this value.

I shall return to this topic. But for now, I would just ask you to note the delicious irony, that it's these despised collectors in the West – they who power the market, as Professor Renfrew contends – who are actually preserving antiquity.

Another irony, of course, is that Egypt is one of the very few countries where antiquity – because of its huge relative value in a poor country – *can* compete with development and modern commerce, and actually see them off.[10]

---

[10] We were able to *prove* this in the field, with our so-called 'Stela Hoard', a collection of six *stelae* found on a building site at Akhmin, South of Beni Suef in Middle Egypt. The site was owned by lawyers, who were prepared to alter the plans of their building, so as to shield the site, and continue an excavation upon orderly principles. In return for this, we agreed to purchase the entire collection for $70,000, which was what they needed to build their six-story apartment building. See *Journal*, 23rd June 1994, page 202.

If the nineteenth-century Egyptians had realized the true monetary value of what they had on hand, they would have prevented the West and its archaeologists from ripping into it. The West was rapacious, in the end, because it was all bargain-basement.

The way of the world

We need to recognise the way the world really is, whether we like it or not. We need to yoke it to our purpose. And ours is a world where collectors have created a market, and this has given value to antiquity. Archaeology has not done this, and neither have the academics — the supposed experts with their quest for 'knowledge' — nor the politicians with their ideas of national resurgence. The collectors have done it, and the value they create is what we call the market. And God bless them for it.

Summary

- Antiquities have only survived because they have been deemed *valuable.*
- This has preserved them in times of conflict, and cherished them between.
- There are various types of value: the *monetary*, the *sacred*, the *sacramental*, the *iconic* and the *nationalistic.*
- *Sanctity* is favoured by the West, for reasons that have something to do with *academe*, and its traditional disdain for commerce.
- *Nationalism* is favoured by emerging countries,
- but *commercial value* is the most effective, at least for these poor countries.
- Commercial value is only given by the *market*,
- by those same despised *collectors*, and their willingness to compete for possession (or for stewardship).
- Collectors are still necessary, therefore, to carry antiquity safely into the future.

CHAPTER 5

The Countries-of-Origin Argument

At the heart of the matter is the *Countries-of-Origin Argument*. Sometimes it refers to *cultural heritage*, sometimes *cultural patrimony* or *cultural property*. But the flavour remains the same — that very modern flavour, with its nuance of bullying — of being rather less an argument, and rather more an article of faith.[1] It declares that:

[1]   Antiquities ('discovered relics') should belong to their 'countries of origin', as an inheritance.

This sounds well enough, as a banner to rouse the troops. But it conflates inheritance and stewardship, and both of these with ownership. And, as we shall see later, it also ignores ancient trade routes and demographic change. And it certainly is *not* — as those who pronounce at dinner-parties seem to think — one of the grand and self-evident truths, which only we moderns have the wisdom to comprehend, and can only be denied by reactionary monsters. Consider the following:

[2]   Antiquities should not be destroyed (or damaged, for that matter).

[3]   Hence, antiquities should not be (in any place) where they are liable to be destroyed (or damaged).

[4]   Hence, antiquities should not be delivered to any such place,

---

[1]   What T. D. Weldon has called a 'Political Principle', the statement of which is meant to foreclose. It's a point beyond which further questions are useless, a door that slams upon argument. Modern debate increasingly involves the slamming of doors, many of them with a deal of force. This is not debate at all, as the Greeks understood it. It is indeed a kind of bullying, what Aristotle feared when he referred to democracy as the rule by orators, by those who would rule at one remove, by manipulating the stupid. Political principles are fast becoming blurts of emotion, aroused on cue, and manipulable.

[5]   or forcibly kept there.

[6]   Hence, antiquities should not be *returned* to their
       'country of origin', if they are liable to be destroyed
       (or damaged) there,

[6a]   or if there's is a demonstrably safer place for them.

[7]   Hence, antiquities should not *remain* in their
       country of origin, if they are likely to be destroyed
       (or damaged) there,

[7a]   or there's a demonstrably safer place for them.

Now this certainly *is* an argument. Call it the *Conservator's Argument*. It begins with a proposition – [2] – which really *is* self-evident, which anybody in his right mind would accept without a murmur. It then proceeds with unexceptionable logic, stage by stage.[2]

Once you have accepted the opening proposition [2] – and as I say, you would have to be seriously delinquent to deny it – then you just have to accept the conclusions [6] and [7]. If the sequence worries you – or you are worried about lumping 'damaged' with 'destroyed' – just substitute 'puppies' for 'antiquities' and you'll catch the argument's full force.[3]

It follows, therefore, that you would overrule anyone who suggested returning antiquities to their country of origin, if you knew – or had good enough reason to believe – that they would be destroyed or damaged once they got there.

You may balk at [7a], the idea that antiquities should be evacuated – pre-emptively, as it were – just because there happens to be a safer place for them. But a line of distin-

---

[2]   If any hack philosopher accuses me of committing the so-called *Naturalistic Fallacy*, deriving statements-of-obligation from mere statements-of-fact – 'ought' statements from 'is', as they say in the trade – I'd point out that we all of us, in our various ways, commit the self-same 'fallacy' every day of our lives. All political, ideological or religious adherents do it regularly, *and a good thing too*. It gives their life a structure, defuses the world by rendering it comprehensible, and therefore less an object of dread. Besides, in this case, I'm merely deriving subsequent 'ought' statements from an initial 'ought' statement. In logical terms, I'm merely drawing out the logical implications of an emotional urge. Accept that opening assertion, therefore – no. [2] in the sequence – and you have to accept the rest.

[3]   In fact, the argument gives logical shape to the *common-sense* unease described in the last chapter. It's a separate question, of course, which came first for our 'rational species' – the emotional imperative, or the logical argument. The New Darwinians would have something to say on the subject, and it's an attractive idea – at least I find it so – that we may tend genetically to conservative behaviour (if only with a small 'c').

guished archaeologists have believed just this — or come to believe it, once they've grasped the hard realities — and acted upon it in good faith. Many still do, I daresay. The difference is, they only dare admit it in private.

But you cannot deny the rest of the argument — and then complain about the Taliban, for instance, and their summary approach to Afghan statuary. And you cannot discount future Talibans — further takeovers by fundamentalist Moslems, who are honour-bound to destroy the works of pagans.[4] What would happen in Egypt, for example, if there was a fundamentalist coup? And what would [7a] have us do, if such a coup seemed imminent?

Retention, restitution and the dinner party principle

The problem seems to be that

[1]   Antiquities should belong to their 'countries of origin', as an inheritance

which seems so morally persuasive — at least to those of a liberal cast — is actually a church of many faiths. Some are reasonable, some absurd, but all rely upon the same idea of inheritance — and the emotional benison that goes with it.

One of the weaker forms, the 'Retention Argument', states that

[1b] Antiquities should be retained by their source country

which seems reasonable enough, unless of course it's countermanded by

[7]   ...unless they're likely to be destroyed (or damaged) there.

And given the modern world — the propensities of nations and *realpolitik* — [1b] is probably inevitable.

Young nations invariably find themselves needy. Governments are expensive things. So they cast around for resources. Usually they find something — and usually they find that the rich nations have already helped themselves. Their first response, naturally enough, is indignation — followed by a summary confiscation. The methods may vary, but the sentiment is the same. The young nation — that is to say, its government — grabs the nest-egg for itself, and pro-

---

[4]   *Taswir*, see page 166.

ceeds to guard it from others. If only to insist upon a decent price.

This usually has an effect upon world markets, and causes a deal of sanctimonious whinging. Sanctimony, because there's nothing so sacred as the way things have been done — for the last fifty years or so. And whinging, because the effects can be catastrophic. Consider the Arabs, when OPEC finally imposed an oil cartel.

It is salutary to consider antiquities in this light, as a straightforward economic resource. Salutary because that's often how they are regarded by emerging nations, in one sense or another — as simple saleable treasure, or as tourist bait for hard currency. And salutary because if *they* think this way, it can only be because they observed the way *we* think, and misconstrued it.[5]

And salutary, finally, because it engenders a delicate irony. An irony which persists when we consider the other things that young nations do. For they also seek an *amour propre* — something that sets them apart, and soothes their natural anxieties, their feelings of vulnerability. And often as not, they seize upon the idea of former greatness; of a greatness that was, and might be again. They look to antiquity, and bask in its vicarious glory.

The classic example was Colonel Nasser, who nationalized Egypt's antiquity, and then exploited it shamelessly for propaganda purposes.

How the West manages the matter

I said that [1b] was reasonable. I didn't mean it was straightforward, or *prima facie*, or even correct. Only that it was predictable, in a rather depressing modern sense. In fact there are difficulties, plenty of them. And they become insurmountable as stronger claims are made.

You may have noticed that I annotated the 'Retention Argument' as [1b].

Apparently I skipped [1a]. Indeed I did, but only to illustrate that these young nations also skip it, and doing so ride

[5]   Or not, as the case may be. There is a deal of ambiguity about our public pronouncements, even now. Many emerging nations could be forgiven for misconstruing them, for assuming antiquity to be a resource, a form of fuel, which various parties — the archaeologists, the television historians and television companies — rely upon for their dinners, not to mention their promotion, see page 294.

roughshod over matters that we in the West hold sacred, that we guard jealously, that we deem essential if the citizen is to stand against the over-weaning state. [1a], in fact, is what pertains in the West

[1a] Antiquities should belong to their finder (where the finder owns the land on which they are found)

We colloquially call this the 'Finders-Keepers Rule', and we accept it as common-sense. It accords with our tradition of common law, of the individual husbanding himself against a powerful centre — whether that centre be the crown, the aristocracy, or some other intrusive body. The individual sees himself as separate from this centre. He stands apart. And he jealously guards what he has.

Finders-Keepers has been sensibly circumscribed, to ensure that special objects — objects of historical importance or outstanding beauty — can be claimed for the centre — for the national collection, as it usually is nowadays. But the original owner is always the finder, and full recompense is expected.

Finders-Keepers underlies the Western idea of property, as it has developed since the seventeenth century. When we acquire something, we also acquire things that are contingent upon it. We own things found on our land, quite simply, because we own the land. The trees and stones, the standing water, the minerals, the discards of past owners. All these go with the land.

There are some who object to this — let us call them the *Glastonbury School* — who say that such things cannot be owned, that the very idea is a brutalism. At most we can be stewards, whose task is merely to preserve them for the future. I couldn't agree more. That's my own underlying assumption. I can even accept their cloying religiosity. At least, in their way, they're trying to articulate something that's deeply felt. But, for now, I would make two points.

Firstly, that our modern concept of property can easily accommodate these people, or at least their concerns (they tend to have problems about property *per se*).[6]

Secondly, that their own arguments are jejune. When pressed, they retreat to sentimental utilitarianism; that the happiness of future children is at stake, and this future hap-

---

[6]   See page 123 ff.

piness—gained by access to what we take for granted, but might well disappear—is what will protect these things (whether they be trees, standing stones, rare species or antiquities). This is not a good defence. In fact, it's lethal. Those who live by the sword run a sporting chance of dying by it, and utilitarianism has been the death of untold millions this last century. Anything that's protected by votes is vulnerable to fashion. Votes can be manipulated. And, as Gladstone gloomily foresaw, they can also be bribed. So any theory that equates *what is most* with *what is best*—most happiness with *morally best*, in this case—can be used to justify the nastiest of things. In this case, and on another occasion, it might well justify wiping them out.[7] It is about time, therefore, that these people did some proper thinking of their own[8]—or accepted the protective shield of property and property law.

Another requirement of property is *saleability*. If you cannot sell something found on your land, you cannot be said to own it, in any meaningful sense.

But being free to sell it is definitely not what the Cultural Heritage Crusade has in mind. The Egyptian people, for example, are not allowed to sell antiquities they find on their land. Nor are they allowed to sell antiquities in their collections. (Nor are they allowed to have collections, for that matter.)

It follows that something else must be the real owner of these antiquities. Some abstraction that doesn't amount to flesh and blood. The Egyptian People with a capital 'P' perhaps, or the Egyptian state.

But these constructs, please note, are radically different from their Western equivalents. The western versions can be

---

[7] The Nazis, for instance, were much happier off without the Jews, without homosexuals and freemasons. And by Nazis, I mean all those many Germans who had been seduced by the creed.

[8] And accepted the importance of the *sacrament*, of things that are sacred in themselves—and have to be accepted as such, without further justification—and *piety* as the appropriate and abiding response to them. Treating piety as an anthropologist would—as a means to some larger and adaptive end—just makes its task impossible. As Roger Scruton has put it: 'Piety is a means to social unity only when it's not treated as a means. The function of piety is fulfilled only when people do what piety requires, but for no other reason than that piety requires it.' Modernism—which was nothing if not the attempt to find new sources of the sacred (and hence new reasons for piety)—has been a failure, largely because it could never shake off the modern fascination with justification, with explaining—to our own satisfaction, as the litany goes—why we are doing what we are doing.

forced to sell, and the people, whose welfare they represent, can pocket the proceeds. This is one advantage of the family silver, after all, as a rain cheque against hard times. But not in Egypt, at least for ordinary Egyptians.[9]

But I am getting ahead of myself. I leave the puzzle for now, and make the point only to show what strange company the Crusade keeps. Fellow travellers and liberals, who would be in arms at the least infringement of their own civil rights, are complacent about such arrogations in third-world countries. This is indeed puzzling. Or not, as we shall see.

Summary

- The *countries-of-origin* argument has two active forms, both of which are now being used. The weaker wishes to retain antiquities in their *source countries*. The stronger wishes to repatriate them.
- The weaker (*retention*) form may be practically incontestable. If emerging nations want to apply it, we cannot stop them,
- although it goes way beyond our Western ideas of property. With our own *finders-keepers* praxis, the finder of an antiquity becomes its owner. He may be required to sell — as a matter of national *amour propre* — but it is still a genuine sale, rather than a requisition.

---

[9]   See page 196 ff.

CHAPTER 6

A Confusion of Claims, and a Working Principle

As we have seen, the 'Retention Argument':

[1b] Antiquities should be retained by their source country

goes way beyond our ordinary sense of inheritance. We tend not to notice this, because the idea of heritage has such a warm glow about it. It has become fashionable and commercial, not to say promiscuous.[1] And this lulls us, and dulls our scepticism. A pity, because scepticism is what we need

For [1b] is actually quite radical. It does not claim ownership for the person who actually finds an antiquity — which is what the Western tradition would expect—but for something much larger, for an abstraction. For something that can overrule both common law and common sense. For something called a 'source country'.

The claim is that modern nation states can inherit antiquities from *defunct states that occupied the same land* (or partly overlapped it). And not the people who make up the modern states, please note, but their governments (which may or may not represent 'the people').

This is an enormous claim, if you consider that *heritage* simply denotes an *inheritance*, which in turn means 'a property, or an estate, which passes by law to the heir on the decease of the possessor'.[2] In effect, therefore, modern states are claiming to be the strict heirs of the ancients. And this is

---

[1] And discrete enough to be pointed at by road-signs, the brown placards that proclaim 'heritage trails', 'heritage theme-parks' and even 'heritage villages'. These are little more than labour-saving devices for harassed parents on holiday. They degrade a noble word, and deliberately confuse the central idea of possession. Used in this way, the word merely suggests that there's something here that's old and interesting, and worth stopping for.

[2] This dates from 1473. The first recorded use was Robert of Gloucester's (and the *Cursor Mundi*) in the thirteenth century, and derives from the

something that has to be justified. It has been variously attempted:

[1]   by the modern state claiming the *same culture* as the ancients.

[2]   by claiming the *same race*

[3]   by simply being in the *same place*, or

[4]   by claiming an *escheat*

We shall consider these in turn. First, however, a minor complication. Did the ancients themselves have title to the goods, which the moderns are so keen to claim? And were they actually made by them, or by a different race or culture?

For if they were made by another people — or stolen from them — then trying to link ancient inhabitants to the modern state — on the facile ground that 'their' objects have been found in this particular place — may be ill-advised. There may be a stronger link, and a better claim. Perhaps it's the *makers* of the objects that should signify, not their last 'owners'.

For ancient ownership is problematic. Many antiquities have been stolen, and not just by us dastardly moderns. The ancient Etruscans were notorious. As pirates, their record was exemplary. And antiquities have been traditionally pillaged by conquering armies — the Mesopotamians, the Greeks under Alexander, the Romans, and the waves of conquest that followed the decline of Rome. They all assiduously looted.

Manufacture is easier. We can at least be sure who made the objects. Well, usually. We can identify a style, and link that with a people and a specific time. And even a group of artisans.

We can link, say, *Corinthian Late Ripe Animal-Style* pottery to a specific Greek City — Corinth — and a specific period, between 540 and 520BC. We can be sure of that much, but little about its subsequent owners. There may be no point in

---

ecclesiastical Latin *hereditare*, from the same root as *heir*; and means 'one who succeeds to an estate, or is entitled to'. Another, dated to 1535, defines it as 'possession, ownership, of something as one's birth-right'. The standard modern definition is Wharton's: 'a perpetual or continuing right to an estate, vested in a person, from his heirs'. All figurative uses derive from this, for example Darwin's of 1859: 'These characters may be attributed to inheritance from a common progenitor.' All these definitions — including such figurative ones — stress the related concepts of 'heir', 'birthright', and 'lineage'.

even asking. The pots were only made as packaging, after all, as the containers for oils and unguents, which the Greeks were exporting across the Mediterranean. And packaging is rarely regarded as property.

For modern Greece to reclaim Corinthian *aryballoi* — exported throughout the Mediterranean as disposable containers — would be as absurd as France reclaiming all the Chanel bottles that are scattered around the world, merely because some of them — the ones manufactured by Lalique — are now considered valuable.

It appears we have a simple choice, therefore, between the country where an antiquity was found (its 'source country') and its country of manufacture (its 'country of origin'). Not so, alas. There are more worms in the can. Many of the manufacturers no longer exist, as distinct peoples whose descendants can be traced — the Etruscans, for instance, or the Phoenicians.

Trade routes, emigrations and magpies

Etruscan tombs in Italy are filled with all manner of objects. There are objects from the eastern Greek islands, and from the mainland. There are things from Syria, from other Italic peoples, and from south Italian Greek colonies. There are Etruscan things, and Etruscan copies of the Greek. There are far flung exotic things from Egypt, or even from India.

Pride of place goes to Greek pottery, however. It is not generally known, but almost every Greek vase in every museum and collection came from these Etruscan tombs. Nor that many were made for the purpose. Greeks rarely mention the fact.

The immediate question, therefore, is whether these famous vases — the red and black figure-painted vases that many consider the finest small art ever made in antiquity — should be regarded as Italian property, because they have been found in Italy? Or Greek property, because they were made in Greece? Or Etruscan, because the ancient Etruscans bought and stored them — probably commissioned them — and certainly saved them from destruction?

The Etruscan race itself has disappeared. They were defeated by the Romans, their land was overrun, their tombs were rifled and their culture obliterated. Their language was suppressed. It has not been deciphered, and none can understand it. So my last option is a non-starter. There are simply no Etruscans left to claim them.

So who should inherit Etruscan property? The modern Italians?[3] But they consider themselves the inheritors of Rome and her greatness. That is the myth which sustains them (despite, or because of, their little excursion into fascism). And to allocate foreign produce found in Etruscan tombs to those who honour the destroyers of Etruscan culture seems rather droll, to say the least. I am not sure the Etruscans would have appreciated the joke. Especially as the Romans—when they looted the Etruscan tombs for their gold and jewellery — deliberately smashed these same Greek vases. Now that particular barbarism— if you have accepted my *RSPCA Argument*[4]—would certainly affect their descendants' property-rights.

It looks like the Greeks must carry the day in this particular squabble.

Peoples who disappear...

And the Etruscans are not the only people who have disappeared. So have the Phoenicians. They were as carefully obliterated. So what about my two Ostrich eggs, which were found in a tomb in Civitavecchia, and brought to London in the late 'seventies? These astonishing artefacts were gathered on the African coast, carved by the Phoenicians, or so it is thought—although to complicate matters, the Etruscans were accomplished craftsmen, and sedulously aped their fashionable imports —and then secreted by the Etruscans in their tombs.

Should these eggs be returned to Tunisia, because the Phoenicians' capital Carthage was sited there (even though it doesn't exist anymore, courtesy of the Second Punic War and the Romans)?

Or to Lebanon, to Jordan or Egypt, where the Phoenicians settled and had workshops, and where these particular examples might have been worked (and where, presumably, there are traces of Phoenician blood)?

---

[3] That is to say, are they *justified* in inheriting these things? Because, of course, they have already filled their museums with them, and nobody has thought to contest the matter, (except the Greeks, in a rather perfunctory way).

[4] See above, page 37.

Or to modern Italy, the land of the Etruscans, who ensured the survival of Phoenician art, because they sedulously stored it in their tombs?

Or to the Aegean sea, because that's where the Etruscans would have pitched them, if they'd had an inkling what the Romans would do?

...or were transplanted

And what about the products of the many other settlements, clustered around the Mediterranean? There were Greek colonies, and Greek settlements in various non-Greek places There were Greeks in southern Italy and Sicily, keeping themselves and their culture aloof from the native Italics and busily making Greek-style things. And these also ended up in Etruscan tombs.[5] The modern Italians claim them because they were found in Italy, and because the descendants of these Greek colonies are now Italian-speaking Italians. But the modern Greeks—who are in a very claiming mood—would claim them because they were made by Greeks.

Of course, these are largely academic squabbles, because the objects are unimportant in the *national vanity stakes*. The Egyptians have never bothered to reclaim mere shawabtis from Etruscan tombs, for instance. They would not be worth the cake.[6] But it would be different, I suspect—and the arguments really begin to bite—if some wonderful late-period Egyptian statuary turned up in an Etruscan tomb. Oh yes, this is feasible. Far stranger things have been found in Etruscan tombs—Buddhas, for instance.

There can be no 'correct' and definitive solution to these problems—that much should be clear by now—if only because we can never really know the facts. We can never

---

[5] If you are wondering why the Etruscans figure so largely, it's because they continued steadfastly interring things in their tombs—the necessities for the after-life—whilst the rest of the Mediterranean was cremating their dead. Very kind of them, at least from the modern Greeks' point of view.

[6] If you find this wilful on my part—the implicit suggestion that Egypt might be tempering her moral outrage to the prizes on hand, then I'd mention the case of *Roger Box's shawabtis*, in the late 'nineties. At first the Egyptian government claimed the return of this matching but uninteresting set of shawabtis, until they realized that their legal fees would hugely outstrip the market value of the objects themselves, whereupon they despatched an 'expert' to London, and this fine fellow suddenly 'discovered' they were fakes, and of no further interest to the Egyptian nation. Nonsense, of course. The shawabtis had already been authenticated by the best Egyptologists in the world.

learn how any given antiquity got where it is now. They have no passports, these things. No record of what they've seen, and where they've seen it. Oh that they had!

Conflicting claims

The 'countries of origin' argument is clearly a broad church. Behind its bland facade and its emotional appeal — not to mention its modern self-righteousness — there is schism and confusion. And, I suspect, a great deal of opportunism.

[1] Antiquities ['discovered relics'] should belong to their 'countries-of-origin', as an inheritance.

could mean any of the following:

[1a] Antiquities should belong to their finder, (where the finder is assumed to own the land on which they're found)

This is Finders-keepers, the common-sense Western solution

[1b] Antiquities should be retained by their source country

that is, the country where the objects have been found

[1c] Antiquities should remain where their origin (-al maker) was,

that is, where the objects were made

[1d] Antiquities should remain where their origin (-al maker) came from

that is where they were born and bred, if they were working abroad.

[1e] Antiquities should remain where their origin (-al makers) are now

that is, where the makers have since moved to, or moved back to.

The Cultural Heritage Crusade is trying to keep the lid on this lot. And in the process it's squeezing ancient realities into a very modern strait-jacket.

It ignores the complexities of six thousand years of history, of everything that has happened since men first lived in cities and found the leisure to make things of beauty, and to sell them. And most of that complexity means movement.

The diaspora

The word 'diaspora' comes from the Greek to *scatte*r or *sow*, and shares the same root as the word *sperm*. Deuteronomy used it of the Jews' dispersal among the Gentiles,[7] and we use it of the Irish and the Scots, for any race that has scattered from their homeland, dispersed afar and wandering, achieving fine things, but bearing always the image of their homeland.

Diaspora, therefore, is the word for a process. And the *diaspora of antiquities* is their movement across the ages, flowing here and there with the flows of wealth and power. The idea I want to catch is just this, that the Jews kept their identity — as did the Irish, and the Scots — because of the diaspora, and probably *only* because of it. Without this flow they would have lost themselves, and been absorbed. Similarly with antiquities. They have reached us because of the diaspora, and probably only because of it.

The basic mechanism is clear enough. For more than 5,000 years a network of trade routes has shuffled art objects around the Mediterranean, as far afield as Asia and Africa. And, more than this, there's been the rise and fall of empire. Nations have clambered into supremacy and, as they have risen, these new powers, so they have gathered to themselves the spoils of conquest.

But this is more than triumphalism. More than the Roman processional, and the delight in booty. It also concerns submission. Enemies can be defeated in the field, but they may rise again. There is one sure way to bring their leaders to heel, and that is to confiscate their regalia, whatever carries the resonance, the mystic force of their tradition. This will emasculate them, be they princes or priests.

Seen in this light, there was nothing new about European colonialism. And nothing uniquely reprehensible. It simply followed an ancient pattern. In 1897, for example, English troops were ambushed by Edo warriors from the ancient kingdom of Benin. In retaliation the British confiscated the so-called Benin bronzes — the adornments that proclaimed the King of Benin's power, and carried his accumulated pres-

---

[7] 'The Lord shall cause thee to be smitten before thine enemies: thou shalt go out the one way against them, and flee seven ways before them: and shalt be removed unto all the kingdoms of the earth.' *Deuteronomy* xxviii, 25.

tige. By doing so they allowed the office to remain, but nullified its power.

But empires do not last. They follow their own logic. They drift into desuetude, and pass out of memory. And then others take their place. Others usurp their treasures, their objects of beauty and display. Witness the British Museum, that 'magnificent cabinet', which is nothing if it's not a *residuum of Imperial loot*.

We can indulge ourselves — as a romantic exercise, at least — with the history of particular objects. We can thrill ourselves with the sense of the past — with the large movements and the chance encounters, the failures and the serendipity. A given antiquity, after all, may have been bought and sold, lost and found, filched or looted many times before its present resting place. These are fingernails screeching down the blackboard of history. But as I say, it is rather difficult at a practical level. Antiquities do not have passports. And in the end we can only daydream.

And we have been rather spoilt, this last century. The *diaspora* has continued, of course, but it has all been rather orderly. As our own power waned, so America's grew, and with it the westward flow of treasures. There was nothing wrong with this, however hurtful it might have been to our own national vanity. It simply followed the age-old dictates of the diaspora, by which new wealth and new power attract the beautiful things to themselves.

For it is the American museums, and their great collectors, who now have the imperial confidence, the certitude that these beautiful things belong with them. But it has been a gentle transfer, with correct prices being paid. There are no bargains any more — no taking advantage of the natives — and the Americans have paid generously.

The transfer has not always been such a pretty sight, however. In the British era, it has to be admitted, there was markedly less scruple. We were dedicated, of course, and set about things with our customary efficiency — systematically gathering the fruits of antiquity, everything in fact we could lay our hands on. The whole world was there for us to harvest; the Indies and the classical lands, the Middle East and Africa. And I daresay we saved an immense amount from destruction.

But our collectors, whether private or institutional, paid almost nothing for their treasures. They simply helped themselves, Gatling guns at the ready. As collectors, you see, they had the rich confidence, the certitude of empire. They had that almost serene sense of *deserving what they were crating up*, as a recompense for what they were offering—justice, order, roads and the like, the grand Roman settlement, in fact.

If there is embarrassment now, therefore, it must be the British Museum's. They have to accommodate their new-found piety—their suspicion that they no longer deserve by right what they find themselves the keepers of—by right of God's dispensation to the English race, that is—with the clear knowledge that they actually behaved outrageously to get it, and often got it for a song.

But in another sense the British behaved rather well. They took great care of what they looted. Compared with their predecessors, that is. The noble Romans, for example, subdued Greece and then scoured her ruthlessly for bronze statuary. They left almost nothing behind. To put it bluntly, the Romans raped Greece. They may have bowed to Greek culture, but they stripped her larder bare of bronzes, and then melted most of them down, to make their own second-rate copies.

And when they crushed the Etruscans, and looted their tombs, they were far more careless. They were only interested in the jewellery and precious metals. They ignored the rest—or smashed it up for fun—and left it for us to find.[8]

In their turn the Romans were pillaged—quite thoroughly, in fact—and many of their treasures trundled north, from where they emerged much later to confuse the issues of ownership. What they had looted, or sequestered or confiscated, or requisitioned—whatever you will—was dispersed around Europe by all the confused migrations of late antiquity—the Goths, the Visigoths, the Franks and Vandals, the Tartars, Slavs and the Celtic residue—until a resurgent classicism returned them to fashion and to notice. That is, until the English milords invented the Grand Tour.

---

[8] And lucky it is that we rate their discards—the incomparable Greek pots of the Archaic and Classical periods—far higher than their thefts. It is because they left the Greek pots—or smashed them and left them lying—that we have been able to stock our museums with these treasures. Very few, if any, as I've already mentioned, and would like to stress, *were actually found in Greece herself.*

In other cases we can only guess at the movement, and how it went. How did all those early Christian relics get into medieval Europe—fragments of the cross, artefacts of the saints—relics enough to sustain a complete system of idolatry and of commerce? Some transfers must have been legitimate—purchase or gift from hand to hand, through the Eastern Empire and into Byzantium—but others must have been more murky. One suspects the Crusades—and the Knights Templar, with their enormous wealth—had more than a hand in the matter. But who can ever know for sure?

It behoves us anyway, we in the modern West, to be honest about what we have, and how we got it—and to see this as part of a larger pattern. For what we actually have is a huge—but not necessarily a permanent—repository of other peoples' art, brought here by the diaspora—the process which scatters art, then inexorably drifts it towards safety, to the newest power and newest wealth.

And so it must continue—in the form we now choose to call the free market—for there is little enough safety away from the centre, even now, as I hope to demonstrate. The Lebanese government, for example, discovering a temple complex in the path of their new coastal dual carriageway— pillars intact and magnificent mosaics—and bulldozing it into the sea overnight, before the journalists could hear of it.[9] And all the nonsense and corruption of Egypt...

But has the diaspora ended?

Nowadays the movement seems to be at rest. The flow seems to have stilled. But this is an illusion. It is only stilled for us, and from our perspective. What we see in the British Museum—or the Louvre, the Hermitage, or Vienna's Kunsthaus—has a massive air of static certainty. But don't let that confuse you. These are just dammed pools in the flow, static pools where the stream was once strong, but has dwindled. They don't convince me, these great imperial repositories, that the flow has ended. There may be power enough to hold

[9] Except in this particular case they weren't quite quick enough. A French journalist saw the site when it was discovered, videoed it briefly, and returned the next day to record it in more detail, only to discover that it had been bulldozed overnight, and no longer existed. He then hired a diver, and confirmed that it was now on the sea-bottom, and utterly smashed, see page 170, footnote. Another example that these countries—whatever their platitudes— cannot be trusted to care for their heritage.

them intact — though the Hermitage has been looking a bit
shaky of late — but is there still the will?

Take a look at the great American museums — The Metropolitan and the Brooklyn, Boston, Denver and The Getty in
California — and you can see the diaspora in self-confident
action. They are swelling with new treasures, even as we
watch. The British Museum, by contrast, buys nothing. They
have no funding to compete with the Americans, but more
importantly they've lost the will. The vital idea has gone —
that stringent sense of deserving, of wanting to freeze the triumph of the present by acquiring treasure.

And when this sentiment departs — as it largely has for the
Europeans, and especially for the British — then the decline
has begun. The curators become troubled men, troubled by
the 'rightness' of their hoard, their moral grounds to deserve
it. They dare not speak of empire, or the past. They become
embarrassed by the idea of loot. They become vulnerable to
moral exhortation. And yes, I daresay the British will return
the Elgin Marbles, whatever the rights and wrongs of the
matter, because in a very real sense — the sense in which they
have lost that sense of rectitude, and of deserving these wonderful things — they no longer *do* deserve them.

The politics of the matter

If nothing else, it will be clear that this is a political problem.
The Cultural Heritage Crusade is not driven — or not primarily driven, or not driven at all in the minds of those who matter — by selfless conservators' zeal. Far from it alas. There are
other virtues at play, and more suspect. Pride figures large,
as we shall see. Pride in country. And also resentment. What
we are witnessing is a political movement, backed by
UNESCO, and largely anti-Western in sentiment — punish-
ing both our colonial past, and the power of our cultural
present.

Not that this would signify, I suppose, if it wasn't for the
confusion behind the Crusade's blameless facade. Given
that, the tendency has been to settle things by diktat. By arbitrary edict, by political fix. It is here that Aristotle's political
virtues — those of hard sense and moral courage — are most
needed, and so far have been most notably absent.

The first political candidate, and still the most popular — if
only because it leaves things roughly as they are, and ratifies

what has been going on—is our old favourite [1b]. This blandly declares that, from now on, 'origin' just means *where an antiquity's been found, where it has lain in the soil through the long ages.*

Would this solve the problem? Not always, alas. As my argument unfolds it will seem increasingly silly. And there's still the little matter of the soil, and who stands for it. Should it be the state which owns the land now, or the state which held sway when the object was found? And whether they're still talking to each other...

This is more than casuistry. Consider the Elgin Marbles, bought by Lord Elgin from the Turkish Porte in 1802—at least with their active permission—long before there was any such thing as a Greek state, and when the Greek people was little more than a nostalgic concept.

At that time the marbles were clearly the property of the Ottoman Empire, which had every right to sell them. And that, presumably, is why the Turks aren't claiming them from the British Museum, rather than the Greeks. Because Turkey recognises the sale as legitimate. But why aren't the Greeks claming them back from the Turks—or at least a suitably massive compensation—rather than from the British? Because they'd obviously get a dusty answer. All very difficult, and this for something really straightforward, a large chunk of somebody's building, what the Egyptians call an 'immovable' antiquity.

What about the last legitimate purchaser?

Perhaps we should we redefine 'origin'—again, by arbitrary diktat—and declare that, from now on:

[1f] Antiquities should remain with their last legitimate purchaser

Another can of worms, I fear. Not for me, of course, but for our great European museums. The diktat would sometimes help them. The British Museum would get to keep the Elgin Marbles, for instance, because they were legitimately bought by Lord Elgin.

But it would pressure them to return most of their Egyptian collection to Egypt, including all the big statuary and the Rosetta Stone, which was quite simply French loot, confiscated by Nelson's squadron from Napoleon's expedition in

1804, as part of the arrangement whereby we evacuated his troops to Cyprus.

Certain it is, however, that the English did not legitimately purchase the Rosetta Stone from the French — or any of the other baubles — and I very much doubt that the French purchased them from anyone. Egypt was still part of the Ottoman Empire, administered for the Turkish Porte by the Mamelukes, which gentlemen had just been obliterated by the French infantry. I rather doubt they were consulted, and gave their free permission. And the long-suffering Egyptians? I doubt they saw a sou.

But returning the Egyptian Collection or the Rosetta Stone to Egypt is just not on the agenda — even less than returning it to the Louvre — so any argument that suggests as much must be faulty. Mustn't it?

What about 'time legitimates possession'?

Or should we impose a 'cut-off point', and accept that however an object was obtained — whether by correct purchase, chance discovery, organized dig or simple pillage — it becomes legitimate after a given time. Thus:

[1g] Antiquities should be where they've been the last x years.

This would be preferred by the western powers, those like ourselves, that have a shady past to account for, but are reluctant to return their loot.

It would also ratify the status quo, and protect the Egyptian collections of the British Museum and her great competitors. And it would sweep a deal of imperial skulduggery under the carpet.

More importantly, however, it would force the liberals to acknowledge the diaspora, the flow of objects from power to power, from empire to empire, the flow which has always taken antiquities where they'd be cherished and protected. That is, it would force them to accept that what our great museums did in the nineteenth century — or, rather, what the imperial collectors were doing, whose collections are now nationalized and housed in these great museums — was exactly the same as dominant powers had always been doing (and probably always will).

But it *would* upset the natives and — more to the point, perhaps — suggest their next move. At a recent UNIDROIT conference, for instance, an attempt was being made along these *time legitimates possession* lines — proposing to fix x at 75 years. But the Greeks promptly responded with 5,000 years, and apparently without irony!

But this is national vanity gone mad. It would reclaim every ancient Greek object for the modern Greek state — every pot, bronze or fragment of statuary anywhere in the world, however acquired, and whether rescued, cherished down the ages, legitimately purchased or inherited, found or just plain stolen. It denies that any transfer of any antiquity could ever have been legitimate.[10] It blatantly ignores the trade routes, the merchants, and the export sales upon which ancient economies often depended. And it deserves a very dusty answer indeed.

The argument so far

The last few chapters have cast doubt on the *countries-of-origin argument.* An interesting question now arises. How much doubt do I need — from you, the bemused reader — to have gained my point? Surprisingly little, I suspect. Accept the following, and you are still on board.

Firstly, that [1b] the 'retention argument' is rather confused and rather difficult to justify.

When it is applied by emerging nations, it really is *realpolitik.* It just happens to be something that these countries do (and short of invading them, there's nothing we can do about *that*). It may be beneficial in some circumstances, but harmful in others. Which it is depends upon the antiquities themselves, whether they are helped or harmed. Either way, we must put the antiquities first. We must consider them first — and their welfare — before we think of ownership, and who has the best claim. And when we do ponder ownership, we can temper it — overrule it even — when there's demonstrable abuse.

If you agree with me so far — with this series of propositions — then you have accepted that my *common sense unease* should be trusted. That my *conservation argument* can disqualify property rights. That what you felt about the Taliban was correct. That our first duty is to the antiquities them-

---

[10] Rather as if, in a hundred years time, an impoverished and debt-stricken Germany were to demand the return of every BMW, wherever it might happen to be. 'But you bloody sold them!' would be the correct response.

selves, and not to fashion. That what's actually happening out there is more important than what's politically correct.

And that is all I need, because you've also accepted — if only in principle — a *working principle for the living day*, which should be in the back of everybody's mind; every archaeologist, every conservator, collector, dealer, reader, or writer on the subject. Everyone who cares, in short.

[2a] Antiquity (as much as possible) should get through to the future.[11]

This is the only important thing, in the end. Nothing matters as much. And when the *countries of origin* argument goes against the well-being of antiquity, it should be disregarded. After all, you can talk solemnly of cultural heritage and grand principles. But grand principles have been the blight of the twentieth century. They have destroyed whole swathes of beauty. We should be more modest, and more workaday.

Retain or return?

I have no doubt — well, not much, and not for much of the time — that in *some places* the original 'retention argument' [1b], would prove benign. But not because it is correct, or true. Merely because of serendipity.

But it may be quite the opposite, and harmful to the antiquities themselves. I have little doubt that in many places it would be little short of disastrous — for the antiquities themselves, that is. Whichever it turns out to be, when the dust has settled and we can see more clearly, rather follows from the probity of the governments concerned. If we have the interests of antiquity at heart — that these things are properly cared for, and passed on safely to the future, a future when we will ourselves be dust — we should watch what happens, watch very carefully, and not just rely upon anybody's fine speeches. Fine speeches are altogether too easy.

We need to get beyond this vague and vaguely commendable liberal sentiment — that every antiquity is part of some twentieth-century nation's patrimony — which already sounds far less convincing, please note, when you put it like

---

[11] Which is quite close to the working principle of archaeologists:

[2b] *Knowledge of antiquity (as much as possible) should get through to the future.*

but not quite the same thing, please note, see page 295.

this—and consider each of these modern nations in their turn. For each is different.

In some cases there is an excellent argument for government intervention, as a sort of safety net, where commercial pressures would otherwise prove too strong, and antiquity—the archaeological sites, that is to say—would go to the wall when faced with land prices and development. This certainly applies to industrialized countries such as Great Britain.

In other countries there is arguably a need to prevent the large-scale loss of antiquities by sale overseas—or at least the loss of important antiquities, the ones that the country cannot afford to buy in the open market, or can no longer afford. This applies to the South American countries—and used to apply to ourselves, until we regained our economy and invented the lottery.

But in many poor countries—and these are the ones that really worry me—it is evident that the governments concerned simply cannot—or will not—look after their antiquities properly. And of these Egypt will be my example.

The demand for restitution

Which brings us, neatly enough, to the hardliners. For the Cultural Heritage Crusade has its militant tendency, just as every sect has its fundamentalists.

Now antiquity was something they may have overlooked in the past, these poor countries. Their 'birthright' may have survived only because the European powers—the despised colonials—had the pieces commandeered, and shipped them overseas. But now that they are independent—'born-again', as it were—these new nations are claiming it back as their rightful property. They are nationalizing what remains of their antiquity, and demand the return of what's been taken.

[1b] Antiquities should be retained by their countries of origin.

now becomes

Antiquities should be returned to their countries of origin.

And so on, for every version. Just substitute 'returned to'. In each case the demand—and it is no longer just a claim, it properly is a demand—is for us to *give the stuff back*. They are no longer content just to keep what they find, and what is still in their soil. Now they want us to hand over our own collections, as if we had no right to them. As if they had been stolen.

This is more subversive. It is also, by now, beginning to look very primitive indeed, if not absurd. It may be surrounded by well-meaning flummery and rhetoric, but such are the stock in trade of mountebanks and knaves. My sentiment remains, that if an argument is sound, and a cause is noble, it has no need of lies, and none of rhetoric.

For what we are witnessing is the higher humbug, and the modern bullying, the attempt to get something handed over *gratis*, if enough moral indignation and guilt can be generated. It is a type of opportunism.

Summary

- The *countries-of-origin argument* is in fact a family of claims, which generates a confusion of counter-claims,
- depending upon whether *manufacture* or *ownership* is favoured; whether past location or the present.
- This confusion results from the continual movement of antiquities; what I term their *diaspora.*
- The Cultural Heritage Crusade, therefore, is clearly a political campaign, which attempts to impose an arbitrary political solution,
- that, for example, *only the find-spot counts*, or *only the last legitimate purchase,*
- or that *time legitimates possession*, and anybody who has held an antiquity for a certain time acquires legal title, however he acquired the piece, and wherever.
- Each of these political arbitrations will have its adherents, because each benefits one claimant as against another,
- but they all miss the point, which should always be the *present welfare of antiquity*, rather than its 'correct' ownership,
- because, quite evidently, the two may well conflict.

The Support

CHAPTER 7

How Can Modern Cultures 'Inherit' the Past?

We can now return to the matter of inheritance.

The importance of memory

I can inherit art that my immediate forbears bought. I can bequeath it in turn. I can even inherit something from generations before—a family estate, say, or a family nose—but only whilst the passage from kin to kin is unbroken, and only whilst it is remembered.[1] All this I can understand. I can also understand a Dutch Jew claiming paintings from a German gallery, because they had been confiscated from his family by the Nazis. Or claiming them from an American gallery, if they'd been 'liberated' in turn by American GIs.

And I can understand inheritance in a looser sense. A townsman who returns after many years will be accepted—when others are rejected as outsiders—because he (can demonstrate that he) shares the town's collective memory. He remembers past townsmen, and the deeds that gave them renown. He remembers connections and their significance. And he is recognized because of this. He is seen as fit to inherit what he has missed by his absence.

But all this depends upon memory, upon shared memories.[2] And memory is something that can be fabricated. The townsman who returns may be a spy, or a fraudster pursuing

---

[1] Or perhaps one should say *recognised*. Many things that we unwittingly inherit—a propensity for certain diseases, say, or a bloody-minded temperament—are genetically based. To base inheritance in the wider sense upon genetics would therefore make eminent sense, but there are problems here of political correctness—of our modern refusal to 'recognise' certain things, though they stare us in the face. This is the product of that same UNESCO mindset, see page 11.

[2] As modern philosophy has demonstrated—and the movies have depicted—self-awareness reduces to little more than a bundle of memories. You are what you can remember, and what others can remember about you. Lose

an inheritance. And memory is a thread that can be broken. It is tenuous. It rarely stretches more than three generations. Do you know the names of your great-great grandparents? And property memories are even more elusive. Do you know who owned your house before the last incumbents, or who occupied your flat? Do you know who added the conservatory, or scratched that message on the coal shed wall? We are all, all of us, floating in shallow water, and beneath us are the deep cold depths of the unremembered.[3]

How, then, can we inherit property from claimed 'ancestors', two hundred generations ago? What could stretch across such a depth, when there are and, indeed, can be no memories? And what could overrule a *finder's-keepers* claim — overrule the person who actually finds it on his land? How can a modern state justify such a *confiscation* — make it look anything other than a case of judicial theft?

The concept of 'culture'

The immediate suggestion is that *they share a common culture*. But culture is a difficult concept. It has a certain slipperiness. Hardly surprising, given the rate of cultural change, both of theories and the actual thing.[4]

---

these memories, and you lose much of what it means to be a 'self', as distinct from other selves.

[3] It is worth stressing that once the direct link of memory is broken, we can take nothing on trust. Absurdities can follow. The Yemenis, for example, are Muslims of uncompromising stamp. They are militant, and particularly virulent against Israel, even by Arabic standards. Given half a chance they'd exterminate Judaism in the Middle-East. That is their present culture, but as a matter of recently discovered fact — discovered by Professor Steve Jones in his DNA survey — they are not Arabs, or not in any classical sense. They are Sephardic Jews. In fact, they are the purest enclave that now exists — genetically more so than Israel herself — and hence the rightful inheritors of the Temple. It seems there are not only *false recovered memories* over time. There are also *true memories forgotten*.

[4] The word itself comes from *cultura*, which refers to cultivating the soil. A person — and that person's mind — are things to be cultivated, as if they were plants to be coaxed into bloom. A person who has achieved this state is said to be 'cultured', or even 'civilized'. Our modern concept inclines to the finished product, rather than the process of getting there, and is neutral between the different claimants to culture, the high, and the low (and the downright common), the scientific and the humane. These have been admirably demarcated by Roger Scruton (*Intelligent Person's Guide to Modern Culture*, 1998). It is clear that I am dealing with his 'common culture' — the form-of-life that any social group must necessarily have, which it inherits, and which distinguishes it from other groups — rather than his 'high culture', which is

But if culture is what groups of people have, and the having of it — in a particular form — is what makes one group different from the next, then a culture is rather like a uniform. We can recognise it before we understand it. (For our present purpose we needn't 'understand' it at all.) Now a uniform can do many things for its wearer. It can give him a role, specify his duty, assuage his fears and strengthen his resolve. But it does something more immediate — it makes him recognisable to those who wear the same uniform. The important thing if you wear a uniform is to identify those who wear another uniform, or none at all, or whose uniform just doesn't 'fit'. Recognition is all (or at least it comes first).

Once we have understood how a culture can recognise its own, we can understand — or so I would hope — how it can be recognised over time (or not, as the case may be). And then we can understand what has to be proven — in the court of calm reason, rather than of emotion — before clamouring 'inheritors' can get their hands on the goods. And if that last sentence sounds crass, it is simply because — as we shall see — the whole campaign is rather less than high-minded.

The face-to-face culture

Consider an extended family. Such a family does everything by conversation. Its members can talk directly — watching each others' faces, to supplement what's being said — or resort to modernity — to the telephone and the internet. But the conversation never ends. This is the important point. It only ends, in fact, when the family itself has ceased to be. The conversation binds and embraces the family, and its ease and efficiency is a measure of the family's health.

A given member may break off the conversation, or be forced out of it. He my be banished in disgrace, or travel abroad. But bulletins will keep him 'inside', with all that implies.[5] Now these bulletins rely on past conversations. They can only be understood in terms of them. Their writer

---

the result of strenuous application in a context such as the university. If high culture is a rarification — an elocution imposed upon the basic language, and a fascination for its lost *timbres* — then Raymond Williams' 'popular culture' — the third contender in the ring — is a debasement, at best a relaxation into slang (like affecting Cockney when you've been to Eton).

[5] My purpose here, of course, is to tease out those implications, particularly for interlopers — for those who are not family, but pretend to be. They can be exposed by their failure to understand such bulletins.

stands for the whole family, because he has all the family's shared past – all their shared conversations, their opinions and attitudes – to rely upon. A complete family history and lexicon.

So what do these family members have in common? What makes them so relaxedly confident – that they can recognise each other, and interpret things that happen in the same way? Putting it simply, because they all share these same memories, going way back, and they all share these same assumptions. These memories and assumptions go to make a hidden world. It is as if a huge but private map has been draped over everything, putting every landmark in the same place – at least for family members – and making every sign-post point the same way.[6] Because the family shares this map, they share the same significances, the same meaning for each and every act. But no two families can ever share exactly the same map. That is virtually impossible.

Such a face-to-face culture can be taken as a paradigm. It certainly was for the ancient Greeks.[7] Most cultures are larger than families, of course, but the metaphor holds. In fact, it is hardly a metaphor at all, just a clarification, what Wittgenstein called a 'machine for understanding'. Cultures share what families share, and members from one culture can recognise other members in the same way as family – by the things they need not say and need not do, and yet be understood. By the immediate feeling of having so much in common, and not having to spell it out. By not having to bother.

The claims of 'cultural' inheritance

So what, precisely, are the moderns claiming, when they lay claim to their 'ancestors' – or, more precisely, to their ancestor's culture (and the cultural booty that goes with it)?

[1]   That they share the same 'total complex' of culture.

---

[6]   In technical terms, they share a *weltanschauung* – a world-view – that gives a shared significance to every event, a significance that already incorporates moral and religious and even aesthetic value. Hence my disparagement of the so-called 'Naturalistic Fallacy', on page 50, footnote.

[7]   Whose *polis* seems to have been the only successful democratic structure ever invented – with the possible exception of the Swiss Confederation, and the local democracy of the early United States – primarily because the groups were small enough to remain face-to-face. See page 109.

E. B. Tylor was the first Englishman to attempt a definition of culture. In 1871 he wrote of 'that *complex whole*, which includes knowledge, belief, art, morals, law, customs and any other capabilities or habits acquired by men as members of [the same] society'.[8]

The strongest claim, therefore, is that the moderns share such a complete 'complex' with their forebears. This is clearly impossible, because – as we've already seen – the 'complex whole' changes over time. It mutates, and adapts to changing circumstance. Its shared assumptions are discarded one by one. Sometimes because they need to be, other times because they fall victim to stronger assumptions. And more often than we care to admit, cultures simply are obliterated. No, such a claim is absurd.

[2]   That the modern culture is directly descended from the ancient,

stage by unbroken stage, as a son descends from his father, and the father from grandfather, down through the generations. Rather as our ancient families can trace their descent from the Norman Conquest. The present culture may be an improvement upon the ancient, but only in the sense that it has developed and realised what was already implicit, as a modern Ford does from Henry's original Model T.

This is a different claim, and appears more sensible.[9] It is, however, a contingent claim – one that is open to proof. And in nearly all cases it is demonstrably false.[10]

The problem is the matter of *technology* – the fact that very few cultures are responsible for their own. Few are gifted enough to have it all there in the first place – the complete set

---

[8]   E. B.Tylor, *Primitive Culture*, 1871. The first ever definition was Herder's in the eighteenth century, whose *kultur* was 'the life-blood of a people, the flow of moral energy that holds a society together', to be distinguished from *zivilisation*, the veneer of technical know-how, of law and manners. Nations can share a civilisation, but their cultures will always differentiate them. Their culture is *the conversation they pursue with themselves*, in my own sense.

[9]   Anthony Smith, *The Ethnic Origins of Nations*, 1986, for instance, claims a 'continuity between modern nations and pre-modern ethnic communities', which he calls 'ethnies'. But, as we shall see later, this is pie-in-the-sky, given the amount of mingling and muddling. Yes, nations may be 'historically embedded', rooted in a common cultural heritage that predates their modern statehood, but as a claim this is either true and trivial, or important but false (because it ignores warfare, invasions, forced emigrations, assimilations etc).

[10] Hellenic culture, for instance, was obliterated in Greece proper, and only survived outside Greece, from where it was tenuously re-introduced.

of Meccano, so to speak. Fewer are lucky enough — isolated enough, and for long enough — to be able to work it out. And even fewer — and this is the really interesting point, at least for anthropology — show any inclination to do so. Most isolated cultures settle contentedly at a certain level, and just ossify, until the outside world comes galloping rudely over the horizon.

This happened to the Persians and the Egyptians, until the Greeks arrived under Alexander;[11] to the American Indians until the Europeans turned up with repeater rifles and cheap whisky; to the Japanese when Commodore Perry dropped anchor off Edo Bay in 1853. In each case the superior culture — that's to say, the one with the better technology — simply overwhelmed the inferior. There was rarely anything subtle about this. And certainly not when ancient empires were on the *receiving* end — those same empires whose antiquities we are squabbling about now.

Oh yes, a culture can close its doors, as the Japanese did for hundreds of years. But that is only possible for a while. Because it is also clear that most new technology is weaponry, and ignoring a new weapon is generally imprudent.[12] We are not, as anthropologists like to suggest, the 'tool-making animal'. We are a weapon-making animal, and we

---

[11] In the critical field of military technology, the Greeks invented the *phalanx*, and deployed it to conquer the known world. The phalanx was the first modern killing machine, which remained supreme until the Romans developed the *centurionate*, the world's first effective tank (not only proof against missiles but reliable, because funded by equitable taxation). This was, arguably, the Greeks' most important contribution of all — their invention of modern warfare. They were the first modern war-makers to pass what Keegan has called the 'threshold of modern war', and overcome the biological inhibitors against hand-to-hand fighting (both the instinct of self-preservation, and the cultural inhibitions about face-to-face killing). Amongst more 'primitive' peoples (including, presumably, the 'barbarians', who could not speak Greek) warfare had largely been a matter of demonstration from a distance — and the discreet use of thrown missiles — to assess relative strengths, after which assessment the weaker party would gracefully retire without loss. The Greek phalanx, however, and its discipline of drill — the sense of being subsumed into, and protected by, something much larger than the individual self — made it possible for men to overcome their fears. It turned ritualistic warfare into close-quarters slaughter. There are many explanations of why the Greeks did this, or needed to do it. But do it they certainly did.

[12] As the gloriously attired Mamelukes of Egypt, the fossilized embodiment of medieval cavalry, found to their surprise and chagrin, when they came up against modern European infantry armed with muskets.

always have been. We may have invented the cooking pot, and tamed the fire to go beneath it. But first we invented weapons to fill the pot — to make a pot necessary — and then to defend it against those who did not have a full pot of their own, but only malign intentions on ours. This is common sense as well as history.

A new weapon gives an advantage, and cultures that succumb to it are forever changed. Very few cultures have developed weapons — technology — from within themselves, as an oak tree develops from its acorn. At best, therefore, modern cultures are hybrids. At worst they are aliens, something that has been introduced or imposed, something that has simply taken over.

Taking on another culture's technology is taking on more than just the machines. The reason why the rest of the planet is now 'Americanising' — much against its will, and with a considerable amount of whinging — is because American software insinuates American *culture*. We need the former, but also get the latter. The two seem inseparable.

[3]   That their culture is part of a living tradition,

in a looser sense. If the ancient culture had not existed, that's to say, the modern couldn't have. The modern Greeks probably imply this, when they claim the Elgin Marbles. Unfortunately for them it is either untrue, or true in the trivial sense, the sense that's been true for all of Europe — and the extended Western world — since the Renaissance. We are all of us indebted to ancient Greece, not just the Greeks.

But we are also, and all of us, indebted to other cultures. To Islam, for example, first because her scholars preserved Aristotle, and then because her warriors captured Constantinople, and forced these scholars out and away to the West. And then there's the Jewish obsession with monotheism, and the Protestant hunger for truth. There are many influences on our culture, many markings on the map that we moderns use to find our way. Many of these markings are ancient, but only some are Greek.

But suppose the map were ancient — just suppose, for the moment — and has been continuously in use. Suppose its margins were full of alterations, scribbled by many a forgotten hand, as the landscape gradually changed over time. And all of them, say, were in Greek. Would not such a map be a living tradition, through which the ancients could guide their distant descendants? I think it would. And would not the test of such a map — of its authenticity — be whether the present users still saw the world, more or less, as the map showed it? Whether they felt themselves constrained by its imperatives? Whether they followed the wisdom of the people who made it? For if they did not — and do not — we should have to conclude the map was a fraud. More, we should have to conclude that they *knew it was all along*.[13]

So, for example, how *can* the modern Greeks claim the Parthenon, as if it was *pan-Hellenic*, something which *all the Greeks combined to build*? It wasn't, and they didn't. It was specifically Athenian, a blatant triumphalism, built with sequestered funds from a resentful empire, and solely for Athenic aggrandizement. In the modern argot it was blatantly 'in yer face'. And anything that claims otherwise is *modern* propaganda.

[4]   That they still use the same language, and the culture that goes with it.

This has been suggested in the case of the Greeks. Quite literally so. It has been argued that modern Greeks speak the language of Pericles and Pheidias, which proves them the rightful inheritors of the Parthenon (and hence the Elgin Marbles). They are Greeks, simply because they speak Greek. It has been objected, conversely, that the modern speakers and the ancients simply could not understand each other[14] — and that this proves quite the opposite.

There seems a confusion here, and a mutual slamming of doors. But given what I have already said, it should be easy enough to settle. It is clear that when we learn a language — when we learn to converse, that is, when we prepare ourselves for conversation — we are learning more than mere words. Much more. We are learning the assumptions and the

[13] A subtle example of this. An eighteenth-century restorer would have repaired the damage to a medieval painting, say, and done it 'invisibly' in the same style as the original, so there was no way of telling where his work began, and the medieval master's had ended. He could do this, without qualm, because he felt himself part of a living tradition, and his correct task was to 'complete' the work that tradition had begun. Modern 'conservators' disdain the practise, regarding it as a form of forgery. In doing so they are being more honest than their political masters. They admit their distance — their complete severance, their lack of any continuity — from the ancient tradition. They are preserving it, but not living it.

[14] The modern inhabitants of Greece speak a language descended from Byzantium, which is incomprehensible to anyone who speaks classical Greek.

rules, the unstated verities and the values. We are learning a
weltanschauung. In other words, a culture.

This is true, and importantly so. Every culture has its own
language. And being born into that language is as unavoidable as being born into a given family. We cannot choose our
language, any more than we can our relations. We wake up
to them, and by then it's already too late.[15]

But there is more to it than this. For cultures do change.
Slowly for the most part, but ineluctably. And their changing
language charts this change. Your grandfather who served
through the war despairs about you, as much for your slang
as for the disregard it seems to show. And your great-great-
great-grandfather, who served under Wellington? How
would he feel in your family? Entirely at ease, and only needing a few conversations before he feels 'at home' with video-
texts and laptops, and all that's taken for granted by yourself
and the moderns? I suspect not.

Every new cult discards something of the past, and affirms
something that is new. That is what slang is for. And dialects
gradually deepen and diverge. There was once a time, after
all, when the English and French actually understood one
other. When they literally spoke the same language.

And language is not just inherited. It can also be adopted.
The interloper may be easy enough to spot, for the moment,
but his children will have mastered the perfect accent. Natural child or foster child, it hardly matters after a generation.[16]

Language can also be imposed. The twentieth century
taught us that, if nothing else. If Hitler had succeeded in 1941
we should all be speaking German (or at least our governing
classes would), and absorbing the German ethos. And
Franco understood as much. He set about destroying the
Catalans by suppressing their language, just as the ancient
Romans had suppressed the Etruscan language.

---

[15] Since the Enlightenment, Europeans have thought of society as a *contract*. This
is misleading, because it implies that social membership is a free choice. It
isn't, any more than family membership. Oh yes, 'contracting out' is possible,
just as flouncing out of a family meeting. But it's much more difficult than
people imagine. There's no *pathos* like an ex-patriot's loneliness, no yearnings
like those who have severed their birthright—just recall Alan Bates'
memorable performance as Guy Burgess in Bennett's *An Englishman Abroad*.

[16] And that has been the active principle of the English aristocracy, who have
always brought the rising best of each generation into their own family. Many
eighteenth-century ennoblements were Jews, for instance.

The present dominance of English derives from its powerful culture. The present-day French are attempting to protect their language from Anglo-Saxon 'corruption'. And it is not just the words they are afraid of. English carries a culture that many crave to adopt. America has gained her preeminence through this craving. And Americans all speak English, whatever their former race. They do this as a token of their willingness to discard (parts of) their own culture, and adopt a more productive one. But nobody would suggest them the inheritors — in any strict sense — of Stonehenge or the Globe theatre.

It is this very dominance that confuses the issue. If English is a disguise that many adopt, it is increasingly worn in ignorance. How many, when they assume the coat of our language, can explain those peculiar buttons on the sleeve, and that tear on the pocket? How many speakers, when they use its adaptable insults, know that 'bloody' is a concealed invocation to the Madonna — 'by our Lady' [Mary] (and her grace) — rather than to gore and the military? And how many know the history that makes sense of such coyness?

For similar reasons, language can be subversive. It can keep a culture afloat, against all the odds. It is an English myth, for example, that the Anglo-Saxons kept alive their culture — the aboriginal 'English' culture — through their language, and that they gradually 'Anglicised' the Normans, as if by osmosis, until they finally regained some sort of ascendancy and English regained control of government.

All of which leads us back to the beginning. But at least the journey has been instructive. It has shown us several important things. For instance, that our language connects us with other and contemporary users, in many deep and subtle ways. But does little to connect us with past users — users over the immediate horizon of memory. Only that there might — or might not — have been such connections. As I have already stressed, few can remember the names of their great-great grandparents, and fewer can be fluent with the dialect they spoke.

[5]   That, if not their language, they inherit the ancients' 'character'.

This is an interesting idea, but if it's true it's also trivial. And it is impossible to prove, except by hindsight and a deal of government propaganda.

It is true that the moderns, like the ancients, lust after power (or its alleles), cheat on their wives, and come to blows. That much remains. But if the claim is that a specific 'national character' is shared by both ancients and moderns — as a character may be inherited by a son from his father — then there are problems, the same as we have already encountered.

Now I actually believe in national characters — however unfashionable that makes me — as Madame de Staël believed in them, as did the German romantics (and the British Idealists). They spoke of a nation's 'defining essence', its 'shared spiritual force', which shows in its actions, its beliefs and practises. It is clear that when we celebrate Waterloo, we are celebrating more than the nemesis of Napoleon. If that were all, we should long ago have forgotten the battle. No, we are celebrating the qualities of the British troops — the durance, the phlegm, the courage of a particular sort — that made it possible. We are celebrating virtues that we would hope to share with them, even at this remove.

But national character changes with the culture. It is clear that no modern British troops would 'go over the top', knowing that they faced almost certain death, as they did in the Great War. Nor would they stand (or even lie) in perfect formation whilst being shelled, as they did at Waterloo. Nor would any British officer expect them to, or be prepared to ask them. And this is clearly because the modern British are more *sensible* of danger than their forebears. The Great War was the last in which whole battalions were recruited from the country, from men who simply lacked the modern awareness of danger.[17] It is debatable whether the modern British would even be *capable* of the self-discipline and restraint — the doggedness and pride, come to that — that earned us the sobriquet 'the bulldog breed' in WW2.

This may be a degradation, or merely an indulgence. Either is arguable.[18] But it is only necessary to observe, here,

---

[17] A fascinating subject, and I would recommend Keegan's various studies, as well as Lord Moran's *Anatomy of Courage*, for the way in which fear has gradually become central to modern city-bred armies. Both are standard texts at Sandhurst, and are used in training officers, whose major task will be the management of that fear.

[18] One of the first conclusions of being in prison, and observing the self-indulgence and weakness of the majority of young offenders — their complete inability, amounting to fecklessness — to take control of themselves and their

that unless we change, and change rapidly — we should certainly lose another such war. In a hundred years we have changed almost out of recognition. We have changed from a nation that ran the world — and not only expected to run it, but expected to be acknowledged as the best people to be running it — into a diffident nation that is constantly astonished by the efficiency and courage of its tiny army. So what hope has 'national character' after thousands of years?

[6] Because they all happen to believe it,

all the moderns who are making the claim, that is, and whichever claim it happens to be. This is probably the driving force for the modern Greeks. But, as D.H. Lawrence appositely remarked, the million voices that shout the same thing are no more likely to be right than the lone voice in the wilderness that shouts the opposite. They're just considerably louder. The reason for this is writ large in the twentieth century. It is the main problem facing democracy, the fact that behind the million voices there is invariably a single voice, but tactically acute, who is quietly telling them what to shout. Dr. Goebbels understood this well, and his techniques have been studied by modern governments — and television pundits the world over — and used to good effect (or at least to effect). Make something simple, and say it often enough, and people will absorb it, and often without realizing.

Consider the Greeks' claim[19]

Turning to modern Greece — the modern inhabitants of the archipelago — we can ask what remains of the ancient culture. What is *particular* to modern Greece, that is to say, that cannot be found anywhere else? That cannot be found throughout the whole of the western and English-speaking world? The answer has to be, precious little.

The ancient Greeks were pagan. They followed the old Gods. Their worldview accommodated the bloody-minded Gods that Homer described, and then adapted itself to Plato's and Aristotle's intellectual optimism. Above all it

---

appetites, are such thoughts as these. I was not alone in feeling them. The majority of prison warders, especially those who have also undergone military service, realize with uncomfortable clarity what is wrong. And they generally agree that 'there's little wrong that couldn't be sorted out by three years in a good infantry battalion'. But they usually add, after a thoughtful pause, 'but I don't know how long I'll be able to say that. It's almost gone too far.'

[19] I am indebted to Dr. Sean Gabb for his kind help with this section.

made space for *tragedy*, as a means to cope with the world's nastiness.

None of this has been inherited. None has been passed down, generation by generation, without interruption. What the Greeks have now, they have imported from the outside, as a deliberate homage to the modern world, rather than a direct inheritance from the ancient.

Take tragedy. There is no place for tragedy in the modern Greek worldview. There cannot be. There is no place for tragedy in Christianity, and modern Greece is Orthodox. Christians have always been *tempted* by tragedy, to bring it into the Christian worldview, because they can see it's important, and can sense its profundity. But strictly speaking, there can be no Christian tragedy.[20] There can be no senseless waste. There can be no punishment out of proportion. There can be nothing, for the Christian, which is not justified by a benevolent God.[21] And Christian attempts to justify tragedy in terms of *things that are learned* are hopeless, doomed from the start. In the century of Auschwitz and Belsen, the Gulag and ethnic cleansing, this argument is simply vulgar.

Take the Renaissance. The medieval world was intensely religious, and interpreted all phenomena within a Christian framework, which regarded Greek and Roman writers as pagan.[22] The challenge facing the medievals — from the twelfth to fifteenth centuries — was reconciling this framework to a re-discovered classical civilization. There were two approaches, the Italian and the Greek.

In the former, men 'broke through the darkness to return to the pure pristine radiance of antiquity'.[23] Scholars and artists in the fifteenth and sixteenth centuries lived through a 'rebirth' of classical civilization after a long period of degeneration. Vasari (1550) spoke of a 'second birth of the arts',

---

[20] With the possible exception of Judas, whose betrayal — and punishment — must have been pre-determined.

[21] There is not even, as there was in the Western church, the Dionysiac residuum of *Lords of Misrule*; of giving chaos its limited release. This was a healthy component of our tradition until James I had to ban it by edict — there had been too many complaints about it getting out of hand, of Christmas rituals being disrupted by people in masque storming the churches, overturning the candles, mocking the priests etc. The tradition only survives in the great universities, and their *rags*.

[22] Dante, as late as 1320, in the *Divine Comedy* consigned all classical writers to hell because they were un-baptized and 'lived before Christianity'.

[23] Petrarch (1304-1374).

and saw them moving towards a new perfection. There were enormous cultural changes afoot. But this was only in Italy.

The other approach was the Greek. A twelfth-century classical scholar once compared his position to that of a dwarf on the shoulders of a giant. He had been raised high by the achievements of the past – of classical antiquity, amongst others – but could see no further than his predecessors. The Greek Orthodox Church held to that position. It neither inherited – nor transmitted – any of the *optimisme* of Plato and Aristotle, their deep and abiding belief that the human mind can be the master of all things, and can work its way to the truth. In this sense, the church was profoundly anti-intellectual, and profoundly anti-Hellenic. The classical ideal was dead in Greece. Greek Orthodoxy suppressed it, and meant to keep it that way.

Now the Byzantine church did much to be admired. It kept alive the idea of a separate nation during the long centuries of Ottoman rule (and it has not shared in the moral collapse of the Western churches). But the 'national idea' it kept alive was also specifically Byzantine – the revival of an Eastern empire – and nothing to do with Greece *per se*, or the Greek-speaking people.

Again, there was much to be said for the Byzantine empire. It kept alive everything we now have of Greek civilization, when that had been extirpated in Greece proper. It re-introduced some sort of Hellenism into Greece, after the two centuries of disorder and Slavic invasion that followed the Great Plague of 542.[24] But the Hellenism it re-introduced was Byzantine. And after the sack of Constantinople in 1204, and the final Turkish conquest of 1453, the Greek spirit departed to Italy – where it found more fertile soil – and all that remained was the anti-Hellenism of the religious establishment. And the Greek church, as I have made clear, shares nothing with ancient Greece, either Apollonian or Dionysiac. It took nothing from the Greek revival which has so changed the modern world. It has had no reformation, no Counter-Reformation, no ferment of thought, and no surge into the future.

---

[24] To this extent, the linguistic evidence is important because, with the exception of the Tsakonians of the Peloponnese, the modern inhabitants of Greece speak a language that is clearly descended from Byzantium, and not from Greece proper. This suggests that the Greek language had effectively died out under the Slavs, and had had to be re-introduced by invasion.

The foreign Philhellenes of the Greek War of Independence may have seen themselves a fighting another Persian War, to be followed by another classical age. What they actually got was a long period of intellectual and cultural torpor, frequently disturbed but never improved by a cycle of revolution, civil wars (including the attempted Communist putsch of 1946, which we British crushed, thus saving Greece from Stalinist dictatorship), assassinations, military dictatorship, jingoism and jejune economics. There's nothing commendably 'Greek' about any of this, unless the modern inhabitants want to draw a comparison with the internecine squabbling of the ancient Greek city states.

In short, everything that was really Greek has been re-adopted, brought in from the outside, from Byzantine and from the Hellenised North — and from the civilized classes of the West, who could just as legitimately claim themselves the true heirs of Greek culture.

What the Greeks have in mind, I suspect, is something different. They have noticed that modern art — perspective, realism and anatomical exactitude — was invented by the fifth-century Greeks. But, again, the modern Greeks lost all this, and took no part in the Renaissance. And the main modern use of Greek art, at least in the twentieth century, has not been the classical, but the 'severe style' — its triumphalist precursor — which has ranged from the jingoistic to the out and out fascist. Nothing there to be proud of.

So, I conclude, the modern inhabitants of Greece cannot claim to 'inherit' their culture from a group of people who lived thousands of years before, who shared no cultural commonality, who would have disagreed with them and everything about them if they could ever meet — even as a thought experiment — and who didn't even share a common language to disagree in.

They cannot make the claim, unless they refuse to consider the wishes of these same ancients. And that in itself is a denial of continuity — or an admission that there is no real continuity, just an empty claim. A family that refuses to consider the wishes of its 'ancestors' is effectively admitting that they never were its ancestors. A family can only loot someone else's mausoleum. (They would get really upset if they discovered they had looted their own relatives, stolen their own family's silver. Similarly, they'd feel remiss if they blatantly disregarded their own family's traditions.)[25]

Summary

- Inheritance depends upon proven continuity. And continuities, according to the philosophers, depend upon memory. So how can the moderns claim anything beyond the reach of memory, which is limited to a few hundred years?
- For a modern nation to 'inherit' something after thousands of years — rather than the person who finds it on his land, *faute de mieux* — is another matter. It needs justification. Otherwise it's just a confiscation.
- The first suggestion is that the moderns share the same *culture* as the ancients.
- The paradigm of a culture is the face-to-face society. By analysing this, we can understand how members of a given culture can recognise each other.
- It becomes clear that sharing the exact same culture as the ancients is impossible, because cultures change over time; they lessen, they adapt, they are corrupted. They are never static.
- Similarly for any culture that claims its *descent* from antiquity. There may be an unbroken line of inheritance, of course. But there could also have been obliteration by a stronger culture. And that wouldn't justify a claim on the stronger culture's property.
- Claiming that the modern culture could only exist because of the ancient — that the ancient was a pre-condition — is too vague. It applies to all of Western culture.
- *Language* has also been suggested, but speaking the same language (or its descendant) could imply many things — conquest, assimilation, absorption, infiltration — which give no grounds for inheritance.
- The modern Greeks, for instance, are no greater inheritors of ancient Greek culture than any post-Renaissance Western culture. And possibly less.

---

[25] Tomb robbing in ancient Egypt, for example, which was systematic and highly organized — and economically necessary as a means of recycling gold in an inflated economy — was always a robbing of 'them' by an 'us' — of Pharaohs and nobles by the ordinary people, or by a hereditary cult of 'outsiders' (those of Seth, the god of chaos).

...and How Can Modern Nations?

It is clear that few modern cultures can muster what is required. Few can claim a continuity with ancient culture, in anything more, that's to say, than the sense in which we are *all* of us heirs to the same past — the minimal sense in which we are all of us Greeks, we in the democratic West. Which sense doesn't enable our governments to claim Greek relics, please note — or describe them as 'stolen' if they are not promptly handed over.

It is also clear that a cultural link, even if it could be proven, would not suffice. It may be a necessary condition, but it's certainly not sufficient.

What must a *people* show, therefore, to claim an ancient people as their ancestors, and hence to claim their property?[1] Apart from the fact that they — the supposed 'ancestors' — made the things in the first place, or had proper title to them.

[1] That they have continuously occupied the same territory as the ancients...

This would seem to be common sense, and beyond question.[2] But it would already disqualify most Middle-Eastern states — whose boundaries only date to the 1920s[3] — and the majority of African states, whose borders were fixed by colo-

---

[1] I am using *people* as an appropriately neutral term. It connects with 'family', as I have been developing it — with any group, that is, the members of which feel an immediate affinity, an easy recognition of each other (even when they're unrelated by blood), and an easy detection of strangers.

[2] Although it apparently scuttles Israel's claim to Hebraic antiquities found on their land. I can only suggest that, like others dispersed in diaspora, the Jews have 'burned the bright flame of their homeland, forever in their hearts', and that Israel's present borders are no more artificial than any others in the Middle East, rather less than most, in fact, since they've been tempered by war, rather than the stroke of a bureaucrat's pencil.

[3] See page 153 ff.

nial land grabs, owing more to serendipity than to tribal groupings and traditional hostilities.[4] Of all African states, the only one with virtually incontestable frontiers is Egypt.

And how are we to decide when two or three modern nations claim the same 'cultural heritage', because they infringe the same ancient territory? And when they're at each others' throats?[5]

[2]   ...and that they share the same blood.

That is, they share a high proportion of the ancients' genotype, as measured by DNA testing. This may be impossible to prove, however, because of the ancients' inconsiderate habit of cremating their dead, or exposing them as carrion. The only available samples may be battlefield bones, and battlefields are muddled places, by definition. The bones may be of the invading enemies, or mercenaries, or foreign looters caught and killed as they went about their grisly business. Without memories — in this case memories about battlefield customs, and whether the enemy dead were honoured with ritual burial or cremation, or only the native troops, for example — the task is almost impossible.

There is another problem, however. There is a stout resistance to DNA testing. Not on grounds of sacrilege, that the supposed 'ancestors' are somehow being violated; rather because of what it might reveal, especially if that goes against the pieties of the age. The Middle East, it should be remembered, is a place of entrenched orthodoxies. Bloodshed is predicated upon them — and past sacrifice aplenty — and anyone who questions these pieties — or worse, who sets about scientifically undermining them — will be most unwelcome. Professor Steve Jones discovered this, and abandoned his DNA survey because of the opposition he encountered.

---

[4] Thus Gambia, with a population of only 300,000 — effectively a single town and its hinterland — became a full state, with all the state's unwieldy apparatus, which eventually bankrupted it in 1981. Nigeria, conversely, was a huge potpourri of two hundred separate races which, with the arrival of nationalism in its Afro-Asian form — and the emphasis that each 'ethnic community' should have its own 'rights' — made the country virtually ungovernable except by dictatorship. These have proved far from benign, however. In the forty years since independence, they managed to squander or embezzle some $200 billion of aid and oil revenue (figures from the present government's own commission), leaving the country an impoverished wreck, despite its oil.

[5] This is, incidentally, why civil wars in Africa invariably become foreign wars, because none of the contesting parties are neatly contained by national borders (the borders themselves being artificial).

An opposition, it should be noted, that included Western liberals, UNESCO and the forces of political correctness. The Yemenis are a merely one example of this nonsense.[6]

All of which is a pity, because the occupants of any region secure within its borders—whose borders have been enforced by Prince or by mountains or the deep blue sea— will tend to become inter-related. Modern biologists have proven this statistically. Prohibitions between classes prove no match for lust. *Bars sinister* abound, and after sufficient time all the inhabitants become distantly related to each other.[7]

Failing such a definitive proof, however, we shall just have to make do with:

[3a] That their occupancy of the territory has been continuous and justified.

that is, they haven't displaced the 'rightful' occupants—the makers or owners of the antiquities in question, and

[3b] That they haven't been so diluted by immigration, that they have effectively ceased to be the same people.

A *people* is not like a river, which remains the same river, and bears the same name, though there is not one drop, not even in the most sluggish of backwaters, that was there a year ago, let alone a millennium. A people is more like a *wood*, where the trees are all the same type, the same type as they were, say, two thousand years before, and this because they grew from the seed of those former trees. Of course a wood can tolerate the presence of other trees. An oak wood remains an oak wood, despite the occasional beech or ash, or even an exotic cedar lost in diaspora. But there comes a point when it ceases to be an oak wood—to be recognisable as such—and becomes something else. A beech-stand, or an Aspen scrub.

It is necessary, therefore, that the wood has been unmolested. That it hasn't been burned, or wiped out by disease. That the bare site has not been re-seeded, or deliberately re-planted. (Recent history has seen a deal of displacement. Whole peoples have been forcibly removed—not only in Russia—and migrations usually follow the plague.)

If all these conditions are met, however, the wood can be considered the same wood as in antiquity. The problem,

---

[6] See footnote, page 75.

[7] It has been calculated that, in fourteenth-century England, almost the entire population was related—at least to the extent of fourth cousins.

however, is that we can hardly ever know. Once memory has languished, peoples are as dumb as trees, and memories can be falsely planted, just as woodland maps can be forged (when, say, ancient mineral rights are being contested).

So it is not only culture that depends upon memory. Ultimately race depends upon it — at least one's awareness of one's race, and its traditions over time. How else have the dispersed peoples survived; the people who have been pushed here and there, the Jews and Romanies, the nomads and outcasts? They have kept their 'race memories', their myths of themselves, and they have kept them precisely because they were migrating and not moored to the land. Woodland people, settled people, do not have such strong myths of themselves. They have no need.

[4] That the modern people are a democracy.

This may seem a strange stipulation. Almost arbitrary, given the word's inexactitude, the haziness of the thinking behind it, and its peculiar benison — its 'feel-good factor' — that has politicians of every hue attaching it like health certificates to some very dodgy regimes.[8]

But it is important. For unless *the people themselves* can benefit from a claim — in the sense that the claimed relics can be shared amongst them, or held in trust for them — then it is clear that a fraud is being perpetrated. That some other party is making use of them. The crucial test, as I hope to make clear, is whether 'the people' can force their governing body to sell the antiquities — that is, to exchange them for some preferable currency — and distribute the proceeds. Of course they may have no such intention. But if they cannot do this, *de facto* or *ope legis*[9] — in reality or in imagination — then they cannot be said to have 'inherited' them in any meaningful sense.[10]

---

[8] And getting away with it for a surprisingly long time, aided by Marx's 'useful idiots' in the West, most of whom should have known better, and probably did, if truth be told.

[9] By virtue of the strength of the law.

[10] In the sense of having *sovereignty*. Political sovereignty rests with the group or body in a nation that 'can make its will prevail, whether with or against the law' (Bryce), or 'the will of which is ultimately obeyed by the people' (Dicey). In a democracy this would normally be the people themselves, in the form of the electorate. And the problem is just this, whether 'the people' retain any real leverage in a modern democracy, or whether sovereignty — in a 'coercive'

The necessary and sufficient conditions of inheritance...

We should be clear about this. For a modern territory to claim the previous incumbents' property as its 'heritage', it has to prove these things. Unless they can be proven, and reasonably so, the moderns have no case. They cannot claim the antiquities as an 'inheritance'. Their claim is wishful thinking, and their motives suspect.[11]

They can seize the antiquities, of course. Nobody can stop them. Modern nations — their political class, that is to say — have extraordinary powers. But what they are doing is only that, a seizure. It gives them resource, much as an oil field is a resource, but establishes no vital connection with the past. It gives them no moral increase, no cause for pride or celebration. And that, as we shall see, is the real purpose of the exercise. Antiquity is claimed by the modern nations because it somehow increases them. Antiquity cuts a dash on the stage of life. And oil fields are useful for cashflow.

...and of escheat

This rather stark fact — that modern nations are acting in bad faith, claiming what is not theirs to claim, and puffing themselves because of it — is often overlooked. I suspect the sentiment of *escheat* is to blame. Escheat was originally an incident of feudal law, whereby a fief reverted to the lord when the tenant died without heir.[12] Land would lapse to the lord of the manor, or to the crown, or to the state — or be confiscated

---

sense — resides in the internal politics of the supreme group (the party), which group can safely ignore the rest. And bloody knows it.

[11] Benedict Anderson (*Imagined Communities: Reflections on the Origin and Spread of Nationalism*, 1991) suggests that nations are just 'imagined communities', existing more as mental constructs — created by mass media and education — than by virtue of 'family' as I've described it, that is, of any genuine face-to-face interaction. Eric Hobsbawm goes further (*Nations and Nationalism since 1780*, 1992), and suggests that nations are 'invented traditions', that historical continuity and cultural purity are just myths, and 'national consciousness' is a nineteenth-century development fostered deliberately by propaganda and national totems, (for the purpose, he opines, of sustaining working-class loyalties, and thereby preventing social revolution). And this analysis is not just limited to Marxist historians: Linda Colley has also famously argued that 'Britishness' is a myth — a fabrication of recent provenance.

[12] The etymology is interesting. The Old French *eschete* derives from the Latin, *excidere*, 'to escape the memory', and the variants all stress this idea, of losing legitimacy by *passing out of memory*.

as forfeit, as in Scottish law — when its owner died intestate without heirs.

This is an idea that modern citizens have reluctantly accepted — that a citizen's unclaimed property will revert to the state. But there's a problem in our case. Modern states are claiming antiquities found on their soil as an escheat, as something unclaimed which naturally reverts to the state. But for this to be the case, they'd have to prove that the antiquities originally belonged to their citizens — that is, to subjects of the state, to 'family'. Otherwise they're simply begging the question. Worse, they're giving an aura of calm legality and moral suasion to what is an unwarranted seizure.[13]

Nations that do satisfy the requirements...

There are several modern-day stone-age cultures where these conditions do apply, and where *inheritance* is beyond dispute. The Inuit of Alaska, the Red Indians of North America, and the Aborigines of Australia occupy the same isolated territories as their ancestors. They are largely unaffected by inter-breeding or immigration. They are immediately recognisable. They speak the same languages as their ancestors, and honour the mythic traditions that go with them. And their culture, although under attack, has been preserved, if only temporarily, and if only in aspic. Nobody could possibly doubt their claim, if only because so little time has passed. Their claim is based on living memory, on memory kept alive from father to son. The 'ancients' and the moderns are still very close. The only problem is that such cultures, being pre-metallic, have produced very little by way of art.

Perhaps the paradigm, from our own milieu, are the Icelanders, whose comprehensive genealogies stretch back to the original Viking settlers of the tenth century, and whose blood is 95% Viking, with just a dash of Celtic. The same applies, with reservations, to others on the northern fringe of Europe, who escaped the repeated invasions that swept the mainland. The Picts, the Gaels, the northern Celts, the Scandinavian peoples, even the Jewish Catalans — all these have

---

[13] It is worth noting that *escheat* only exists in modern English law in the form of 'treasure trove', where discovered relics are judged to have been *nest-eggs* — valuables or currency put aside for future use, and then forgotten. The notion only applies to the period when England was already a nation, under a central monarchy. The required proof for treasure trove, for example, are coins from more than three realms. This is sensible, and justified.

good claim to a heritage — largely because they were pushed to the periphery, and could only resist further encroachments.

...and those that fail

But few other claimants can satisfy these requirements. There may have been a time in antiquity, before the first empires started shuffling the pack — invading each other, and shifting populations, corrupting ethnicity, and changing culture — when every nation, every people, was pure and separate from each other. But diaspora and empire have made that an impossible dream for the moderns. Since the homogeneity of pre-agricultural antiquity, there has been — between the River Tiber and the River Oxus — a continual succession of empires. Empire seems to have been the commonest form from classical antiquity to the dark ages. Peoples and their cultures have been jumbled together, muddled and diluted by technology and by warfare.

Most important perhaps, for central and northern Europe, have been the successive waves of horse peoples — the Huns, the Avars and Bulgars, the Scythians, the Tartars and Buminid Turks and the fearsome Mongols. Having domesticated the war horse — and solved the age-old problems of subsistence on the move[14] — these warrior peoples swept out of the Asian steppes, and pushed the European races from their homelands. Very few remain where they had been during the bronze age. For Europe and the Mediterranean fringe, therefore, the requirement becomes impossible. Modern nations rarely have anything in common with the makers of 'discovered relics' on their territory.

The only legitimate European claimants, in fact, are the aboriginal nations, those who united early under strong monarchies, and because of this could resist the flow. England, for example, has been a nation, with a clear sense of its own progression, for over a thousand years. But the present English could only claim the works of that period as their

---

[14] 'An army of hunters can seldom exceed two or three hundred. Their precarious existence seldom allows a greater number to keep together. An army of shepherds, on the contrary, as long as they can go from one district, in which they've consumed the forage, to another which is yet entire, can scarce be limited as to the number who can march together. The judgement of Thucydides, that neither Europe nor Asia could resist the Scythians united, has been verified by the experience of all ages... Nothing can be more dreadful than a Tartar invasion.' Adam Smith, *The Wealth of Nations*, Book Five.

'heritage'. They could mount a case for their medieval cathedrals, for instance — although 'multicultural' Leicester could hardly claim theirs, at least not with a straight face — but not Stonehenge, nor the stone circles of Avebury, nor even the Viking relics. But even that is considerable, compared with the claims of a modern Syria, say, or Iraq, who have only existed, in their present form, since the 1920s.

And again the Greeks[15]

We considered the cultural pretensions of the modern Greeks. Now we can ask whether the modern inhabitants of that glorious archipelago are the descendants of the ancient inhabitants — in the necessary sense, the sense that would give them claim to the Elgin Marbles?

There is no reliable demographic evidence from antiquity, but it is clear that after Alexander the mainland population of Greece dwindled. It was a commonplace of Imperial Rome that the Greek city-states states were a mere shadow of their former strength. A letter to Cicero remarks upon it, and Nero's inscription on the Parthenon implies it. Plutarch concluded that the Greek oracles had fallen silent because nobody now required their services. It is further clear that, after the fall of the western Empire in the late 4th century, there was a dramatic decline in the fortunes of the Greek City-states. They effectively ceased to exist.

The Great Plague of 542AD further reduced the population. By that time, however, we can assume that the majority of inhabitants were the descendants of barbarian invaders and slaves, rather than the stock of the classical period, of Pericles and Demosthenes, Pheidias and Praxiteles.

In the two centuries of disorder and chaos that followed the great Plague, the land was almost entirely lost by the Byzantine Empire. When it was finally re-conquered from the Slavs, it had to be culturally re-Hellenised from Constantinople. That's to say, at some time the Greek *language* itself had to be re-introduced into the archipelago. And the fifteenth-century Turkish conquest further shuffled the pack.[16]

---

[15] I am again indebted to Dr. Sean Gabb for this section.

[16] For an accurate portrayal of the 'family' cultures that survived under the Ottomans, and the way they kept alive their amalgams of folk-belief, fumbled theology and credulous superstition — all of which have since been swept away by imposed nationalism — and the extent to which these cultures were

When Elgin arrived in 1802, the population of Athens — by now a remote and unimportant village in an unimportant corner of a vast empire — was little more than a thousand, of which half were Muslim, and only some of these were 'Greek' converts. They were literally camping amongst the ruins, of which they knew nothing and cared even less, and which they regarded as the work of past Gods or of demons.

Finally, Athens was re-colonized in the 1920s by Asiatics, whose claim to a Greek connection is less well founded than that of West Indian blacks to the English. And the result of all this? Modern Greece is occupied by a rich ethnic mix that embraces every shade from Nordic blonde to Moorish brown.

The inevitable conclusion? That the present inhabitants of the Greek nation state have almost nothing to do with the ancient inhabitants of the land — racially or culturally or linguistically. They just happen to live on the same land. And that's just not enough. It's especially not enough when the claim can only be made — for very clear reasons — by the descendants of the ancient city-states, and not by anything as vague as the 'Hellenic peoples' or the 'Greek races'.[17]

Summary

- If *cultural continuity* cannot — or cannot alone — justify a claim to heritage, what more would be needed?
- *Territorial continuity* would be necessary,
- and also *genetic continuity* (although this may be difficult to establish, for very modern reasons).
- Failing that, a *continuous occupancy* by the same people would perhaps suffice,
- and the assurance that *the 'people' themselves* are the beneficiaries of the claim.
- Very few modern nations can satisfy these conditions, and almost none in Europe and the Middle-East.

---

based on tribe, and race, but no hint of being connected with territory in other ways than the peasant's brute-sense of tilling the soil, his particular patch of soil, in despite of the rulers that came and went (were uniformly 'non-family', that is to say foreign) — for all this, and the way it belies moderns the opportunism of 'cultural heritage', I'd recommend Louis de Bernières excellent *Birds without Wings* (especially Chapter 31), Iganzio Silone's *Fontamara*, and of course *Hamat, an Egyptian* (Egyptian Ministry of Culture).

[17] As is the case with the Elgin Marbles, which could only correctly be claimed — if the moderns are to pay any attention to the wishes of the peoples from whom they are claiming descent — by the descendants of Athens itself.

CHAPTER 9

Only by Manipulation
and Bad Faith

Why, then, are modern states so keen to claim what they have no title to—or none they can justify—and why have academics and archaeologists been so very keen to help, when a moment's reflection should give them pause? It certainly is a puzzle.

The late twentieth century, the arena of the Cultural Heritage Crusade, is profoundly different from antiquity. Almost anybody can see that. Our world is partitioned in a way—and according to principles—that would have been anathema to the ancients, even if they'd managed to understand them.[1] The mere idea of any modern nation claiming as its 'birthright' the remains of their culture—including their cadavers—would have struck them as sacrilegious. And yet that is what has been happening. So why can't we see it?

Before I suggest anything, however, a caveat is necessary. So far my argument has been uncontroversial. But now I have to touch on larger matters. It's not just psychology I have to consider. Why certain failed ideas linger on, and create such havoc. And not just Nietzsche's observation that ideas only become powerful when they begin to smell, as cadavers smell. Nor the commonplace that academe has become a last refuge for such ideas.

It is, more importantly, that philosophy still runs the world. The ideas of past philosophy—or the past ideas of philosophy, to be correct—permeate everything we do. People often think that science runs the modern world, and politicians—for reasons of which I'm unsure, but suspicious—are content to let them. But it isn't true, I'm afraid. It's just technology that gives the impression.

---

[1] No mean feat in itself, since we most evidently haven't, and are still arguing the toss, and killing each other in droves about it.

Firstly, because the science that underpins the technology — and proves itself when the technology works — was
only made possible by a particular culture. And this culture — call it Western individualism — is so dominant and
pervasive, at the end of the century, that it tends to pass
unnoticed. But any other culture, and modern science would
never have made it.[2]

---

[2] This may strike the reader as a bold claim. But for the empirical method to
     have become established — or even been given a chance — a very special frame
     of mind was needed, both curious and fearless. Or, perhaps, with a
     fearfulness so profound that the truth, however horrible, became preferable
     to the usual comforts of indecision and ignorance. Only a few times in history
     have men actually preferred the truth. In this case, at least according to Max
     Weber's narrative, it was Protestantism that provided the spur — or, more
     precisely, the strenuous loneliness of the Calvinist worldview.
         Whereas the medieval church had taught that man was lost without its
     guidance, could only stumble in the dark, as if blind, unless Mother
     Church — its priesthood, that is to say — led him by the hand, the Renaissance
     began to suspect that man indeed had the means. Man could manage it by
     himself, given time enough and — at least for the early thinkers, for Erasmus
     and Descartes, for Locke if not for Hume — the reassurance of a God who
     would underwrite his efforts, and catch him when he stumbled. We call this
     the Enlightenment.
         But it was Protestantism that took the really bold step, and declared that
     man not only had the *capacity*, in the form of reason — the light that could
     shine into darkness, and whatever it illumined, could never be mistaken — but
     he also had the *motive*. For there had to be a motive. Protestantism supplied
     this, as a sense of fearful urgency.
         Well, at least Calvin did. Luther merely denied any power or freedom on
     man's part. He famously compared man's will to that of a beast of burden. He
     is ridden either by God or by Satan. They vie for the saddle. If ridden by God,
     he goes where God wills. If ridden by Satan, he goes where Satan wills. In
     neither case, however, can he influence the rider. It followed that man's fate
     was already decided — and nothing he attempted could alter the outcome. It
     seemed to follow that it hardly mattered *what* he attempted.
         This was obviously unsatisfactory. It created a problem of resignation and
     even despair — at least for the unsophisticated — which Calvin sought to
     alleviate by suggesting that men could, in fact, discover what was in store for
     them. Calvin's masterful idea was that *man's time on earth mirrors his pre-
     destined fate*. If a man was destined for paradise, God would not allow him to
     fail on earth. And vice versa. It followed that if a man was successful
     — whatever his 'calling', and however humble — this revealed him to be one
     of the Chosen. In brute terms, a man could discover his fate through work. If
     he applied himself, and became rich and successful, that would demonstrate
     much more. It would show him his destiny. This created a tremendous new
     energy, an energy born of desperation. Men worked not to become rich. They
     became rich to save themselves. Hence the success of Protestant commerce, of
     homo economicus. (Hence, also, the short-time span of puritan sects, which
     rapidly became rich and forgetful).
         But this compunction to discover the truth went farther. It was willing to
     try things out. It took nothing on trust. It morphed into the empirical method

And secondly, because anybody can use the technology, even cultures which are hostile to it — militant Islam, for example, which hates and fears the Western world, and seeks to turn the clock back. Jihadists are quite content, it seems, to use mobile phones and GPS to destroy the culture which made them possible. And no reason why not. It doesn't require a Western faith in ballistics to fire a Kalashnikov.

I say that philosophy runs the world. But I don't necessarily mean good philosophy. Only that cultures are based on ideas, those implicit ideas that families never need speak aloud, even if they could, because everybody takes them for granted. These ideas started life in some philosopher's mind — and not necessarily a first-class mind — before they burrowed deep and disappeared from view, only to emerge as a banner to rouse the troops.

The horrors of the twentieth century can be seen as a testing to death — literally, and of a large number of people — of some very simple ideas, as well as a stumbling across others which are still at the burrowing stage.[3]

All this is of consequence for my argument. If I am to consider why governments claim things they cannot justify, I have to engage these larger forces. I have to talk about governments, what they do with their subject peoples, and what consent they claim. I have to talk about politicians, manipulation and the higher humbug.

---

and, hence, into modern science. Of course there was opposition, and a yearning for discarded sureties — or rather for the old dubieties, the old limitations, and the succours and salves they made necessary (and, in large measure, delightful). The Reformation and the Counter-Reformation are the names we give to this raging battle, which was to decide the modern world.

[3] And definitely *not* the produce of first-class minds. Michael Tanner called this the *problem of third-rate critics*, who should, by rights, be devoting themselves to third-rate authors, and producing suitably slender books about them. Better this, he suggests, than misconstruing the great authors. But they do neither. They have their own 'third way', which is to produce large and important-seeming books about the third-rate, attempting to persuade the rest of us that they are actually up there with the great (and, by implication, the critics themselves, for having 'recognised' them). They may even believe this, which is even more depressing.

Similarly with third-rate philosophers, who secrete themselves where no self-respecting mind would care to be seen, and where they are safe from exposure. But this doesn't prevent them from mischief. Far from it. Witness the philosophers of education — and sociologists generally — with their heads full of social engineering and the same sad and silly ideas that have already caused so much heartache.

Modern nations are a strictly modern invention…

This is the first point. For our purposes, modern history began with the Reformation, when the ancient states — notably England — struggled scratched and bleeding from the medieval thicket, and gained the undivided attention of her subjects (which, for good or ill, she has held ever since). It was then the modern idea of loyalty took root, *loyalty to an abstract ideal*.

Until then people had thought only of realms, of principalities and fiefdoms. Feudal man had floated in a network of quasi-contractual relations. His political duties and rights had been clear, and clearly had linked him to the land. He'd been *his lord's man*, and then *his king's man*. Or he was *the church's man*; part of an over-arching Latin-speaking culture that hardly recognised national boundaries, and often begrudged them. His loyalties were never directed towards anything as hazy as a 'nation'. His was a world of flesh and blood. It divided into small groups of men, who owed allegiance to other men. Both the knights and the archers of Agincourt — the two classes of men, the two strata of that world — cried 'for Harry and Saint George'. And neither for an abstraction such as 'England'.[4]

Gradually, however, a new idea was starting to emerge — that of the *state* as the maker of laws, and bedrock of the culture.[5] A state that recognised no higher authority than itself, neither international law[6] nor the church.

---

[4] Shakespeare may have been a Tudor apologist, but he was pertinent enough with *Henry the Fifth*. As Keegan has made clear, Hal's men were fighting for various reasons — for loot, perhaps for glory, perhaps as bondsmen — but none of them for what we'd call patriotism; for the state, for the concept of state, for the state *über alles*. (John Keegan, *The Face of Battle*, 1976).

    And, according to Hazlitt, things had not changed much three hundred years later: 'Defoe says that there were a hundred thousand country fellows in his time ready to fight to the death against popery, without knowing whether popery was a man or a horse.'

[5] Sometime about the Reformation, or even as early as Machiavelli, the idea arose that the *body politic* — the people and their political instruments — might itself be an object of government action, worked on and moulded by an enlightened ruler. And who more enlightened, for their own affairs, than the people themselves.

[6] As fatuous a concept then as now.

The real watershed, of course, was the French Revolution. This shifted power in a tantalizing way — that has never since been abandoned, and never adequately realized — from the monarch to the people, who ceased to be mere *subjects* and became *citizens*, and who were now to exercise supreme power — rather surprisingly, it must have seemed — over themselves. The modern *republic* had been born.[7]

Since 1789, the world has been remade according to this principle. Every state or country was now to correspond with a *nation*, which was to be a homogeneity, a group of people who felt they belonged together — implicitly understood each other — because they shared the same race, the same language and outlook. Because they shared the same culture, that is to say, in a slightly weaker sense than my own.

Ideally, each nation was to be its own master, an equal amongst other equals.[8] Such nations have multiplied, as the European empires gradually crumbled, and hegemonies lost their control. There are now one hundred and ninety-one such nations,[9] of which only fifteen existed in 1810.[10]

They have been aided, ironically, by the very idea of *nationalism* — by its conviction that since all peoples were different, some would be better at certain things than others. In particular, some would be better at running countries, both their own and others. That is, to run empires. This idea had become quite serious by the 1870s. It had decked itself out with all the paraphernalia of modern patriotism; the anthems, the regalia, the public ceremonies and the lamentable poetry.

I say ironically, because this same creed was planted in the colonies, and by the colonists themselves. They taught their subject peoples the doctrine — or at least they taught the chosen elites — and they in turn took it seriously. They wanted to try it for themselves.

---

[7] Defined by Bacon as a 'common-weal; a state in which supreme power resides in the people'. The word republic derives from the Latin *res*, 'affair', plus the feminine form of *publicus*, 'public'.

[8] Although some would be more equal than others. Some would be dominant, and the weaker would still need to protect themselves by forming alliances.

[9] Recognised by the United Nations, itself a misnomer. The UN is an assembly of states, only some of which are homogeneous nations. Witness Yugoslavia, which has recently disintegrated into five separate nations.

[10] Including Great Britain, France, Spain and Portugal, The Lowlands, Turkey, Russia, Japan, China, and the United States.

The resulting eruption need not have happened, or happened so precipitously. But after the German Wars it was probably inevitable. The losing empires were simply dismembered. The first world war dismembered three empires – the German, the Austro-Hungarian and the Ottoman – and created eight new states in Europe alone.

More ominously perhaps, the strongest of the remaining powers, the United States, committed herself to 'self-determination', to the idea that since empires had caused the War, free nations would surely prevent another one. Nations were thus a 'good thing', something to be encouraged, whereas empires were most definitely not.

The pause for breath between the wars saw the beginnings of unrest in the remaining empires. Nationalist uprisings took place in Egypt in 1919, and quickly spread throughout the Middle East. The powers held their nerve, however. At least they appeared to.[11] But the second world war finally destroyed their confidence. When it commenced there were six great powers, all but one of them empires. When it ended there were only two, and a massive decolonisation, as the Dutch, the Portuguese, the French and above all the British – some of whom had nominally been winners – quite simply lost the will to govern.[12] And then, in the eighties, the last of the empires followed suit. The USSR collapsed.

---

[11] Although Amritsar was a watershed. After Amritsar, the British were no longer prepared to 'enforce the rule of law at any cost'. The work of Lytton Strachey had been done, and done well. In their hearts they no longer believed.

[12] Much has also been made of Gandhi, and the demi-urge to freedom that he supposedly unleashed in the sub-continent. Gandhi certainly revealed something, but it was only the exhaustion of the British race for government, the loss of their sense of rectitude for the task, a loss of will that saw Macmillan precipitously opting to cut and run from Africa. 'Much of the world today, including the US, is living in the social, cultural and political aftermath of Britain's achievements, its industrial revolution, its governments of checks and balances, and its conquests around the world' (Thomas Sowell, *Conquests and Cultures*). But the British no longer believed in this.
     As for Gandhi, his legacy was a deal of muddled thinking, a confetti of unsuitable constitutions and Anglo-Saxon style political institutions (all attempting to pre-empt tribal warfare and internecine strife, which British governance had efficiently controlled), and some ruthless underhand work by the new self-appointed elites which neatly discarded these good intentions. In India, for example, there was a partition by massacre, economic stagnation and corruption, and a self-perpetuating dynasty that has wasted fifty years in attempted state socialism.

The enormity of all this is difficult to grasp. The world has been literally created anew. Since 1959 a hundred shiny nations have been created — 'set free' in the argot. And of the sixty-five present states in the Middle East and Africa, only three existed before 1910.

...which are entirely different from anything in antiquity

These modern nations are a modern invention. As such, they are completely different from anything in antiquity. But they have deluded themselves — shackled themselves, more like — with the idea that they somehow revive an ancient custom, and an ancient glory, that of fifth century Athens.

The simplest difference, however, and the most important, is that ancient groupings were indeed homogeneous. They were Etruscans, Phoenicians, Nabateans, Spartans, Corinthians, and so on. They were 'families', in my sense of culture.

Modern nations may have been conceived on this heady ideal, but it was always a flight of fancy. It could only have been, for it ignored everything in between — the 3,000 years of invasion and strife, the forced migrations and interbreeding, the death of cultures and the impositions of faith. With very few exceptions — and those mainly on the periphery, such as Iceland — modern nations are a hotchpotch, a confusion, and can only ever be so unless they split into unworkable fractions.

The idea that nations could be homogeneous was one of the last century's sweetest delusions. And that they'd usher in peace and prosperity was perhaps its most disastrous. Modern nations have proven just as quarrelsome as empires.[13] And far nastier to their citizens.

Largely this has been a matter of intellectual baggage...

...what these nations set out with, and what they acquired along the way. Because they were Western inventions — liter-

---

[13] On the other hand, empires have been justified — if only in retrospect, and only to clear common sense — as an efficient means of persuading the unlikeliest of companions to get along. The Austro-Hungarian empire was probably the only means — the only successful means so far devised by the wit of man — to keep a lid on the Balkans. If anyone doubts this, just observe the chaos that succeeded Tito's Yugoslavia. The same argument probably applies to post-Saddam Iraq.

ally so, in Africa and the Middle East, and whole swathes of south-east Asia — they inherited Western styles of representative government and market-based economy.

But the inheritance was illusory. The Western ethos may have been written into their constitutions, but their own sentiment negated it. And de-colonization created its own sentiment. Few of these nations were actually bred in adversity — whatever their own propaganda — but they were bred in resentment.

And in particular, the resentment of *Bandung*.[14] This held that colonization had only ever been a conspiracy of capitalist states to exploit colonial resources (including their antiquity, though they didn't realize this until recently — didn't realize it until the Cultural Heritage Crusade kindly pointed it out). Former colonies were not impoverished because they lacked resources, but only because they had been 'stolen'. At a certain stage, so the theory went, it had been easier for capitalists to keep the natives under the thumb by switching to something called 'neo-colonialism', that is, to economic domination at a distance. 'Freeing' these colonies, it seemed, had just been a sham.

It hardly matters whether this was true, false, or arrant nonsense.[15] It only matters that the people believed it, or could be made to believe it by government propaganda. And become resentful because of it. Resentment has been the key.

---

[14]   The notorious Conference of 1955, at which Sukarno launched himself and his rhetorical idea of 'unaligned nations'.

[15]   Although the case for *nonsense* is very strong. Consider Nkrumah: 'The colonial powers were all rapacious: they all subserved the needs of the subject lands to their own demands: they all circumscribed human-rights and liberties; they all repressed and despoiled, degraded and repressed. They took our lands, our lives, our resources and our dignity. Without exception, they left us nothing but resentment' (*Africa must Unite*, 1958). And this from the man who took Africa's first and most prosperous state, which by any standard of civilized human life — absence of tribal savagery and slavery, the rule of impartial law, relative prosperity, medicine, secure and free communications — had improved dramatically under benign colonial rule, and reduced it to effective bankruptcy under a 'bastardised Stalinist dictatorship'. By which time Nkrumah, the model *thaumatocrat*, had arrogated quasi-divine powers for himself, demanded to be called 'The Redeemer', and had probably gone mad. 'All Africans know' he declared in 1961 'that I represent Africa and speak in her name. Therefore no African can have an opinion that differs from mine'. And so it was for the others...

...in particular, the shadow of Hegel

The question that has dogged us since we took that fateful step — and assumed political power over ourselves — was how far we could use it. How far could we allow our leaders to coerce us, even for our own good. The English-speaking tradition has generally erred on the side of caution. It has set clear limits on what the state can do. The state can hinder the hindrances to the good life, but it cannot force us to live that good life. Anything that is spontaneous and free is outside its scope, and for rather good reasons.

But there is another tradition, that of Rousseau and Hegel. And the twentieth century has seen the two traditions come to blows. The greatest difference between modern nations and antiquity is just this, that the moderns were born and bred within this conflict. And I'm inclined to say, in the shadow of its victors, of Hegel and his *totalitarianism.*

For Hegel regarded the state as no ancient could ever have done. He saw it as a living organism, something that was far more than its constituent parts. You can dissect an organism. You can pin out its organs and list them. You can describe them minutely. And yet you'll always overlook something. You cannot explain, for instance, why a cat stalks, or a wolf howls. You've somehow missed its life, that intangible extra. So it is with the state, according to Hegel. The state has a *geister*, a 'national soul', which cannot be deduced from any listing of parts, of mere citizens and their institutions.

Of course, a state's *temperament* will be influenced by its citizens. England may be obdurate because Englishmen relish a fight, and staunch because of their fairness. But England's *geister* is somehow larger than these humdrum virtues. And England plays its part in Hegel's *historical process* — the ineffable chess game between states and their fate, where the moves are largely inevitable, because the result has already been decided.

This idea has proved irresistible. If the organism that is the state has a part to play on the grand stage of history, then the heads of state become correspondingly important. Mussolini, Hitler, Nasser, Pandit Nehru, Nkrumah, Sukarno and countless others were not just political leaders. They were *thaumatocrats.*[16] They could lead, because they had 'incarnated' the nation in themselves, just as the 'nation' was supposed to incarnate the spiritual yearnings of its people. They were the head to the nation's body. Unfortunately they were also largely humbug.

It has been a terrible dream, this dream. The real winners of the twentieth century, as Paul Johnson has noted, have been professional politicians, mostly self-appointed and mostly lawyers, who have never done anything but politics—never even considered it—but have devoted their entire lives to the gaining of power, and mostly doing it through this flexible concept of 'democracy'. And they've proven eminently successful. They have inherited the earth.

We tend to disregard this difference, because we inherit so much from the ancient Greeks

The late twentieth century, as I have explained, is profoundly different from antiquity. But why can't we see this, as the ancients would have seen it, if they were here and watching us squabbling over their remains? Why can't we understand this? Mostly, it appears, because of our inheritance from the Greeks. In particular, the political ideas we have taken from Plato and Aristotle, which have been something of a mixed blessing.

Since the rediscovery of Aristotle, we have been entranced by the idea of the Greek *polis*, which he considered the ideal association of peoples, the perfect polity. He undoubtedly had a point. His *polis*[17] could not only embrace small groups such as family and village, but was also large enough to provide everything for the good life. Its citizens didn't just claim the 'rights' that we moderns so petulantly demand. They actively participated. The city state was a face-to-face culture as I have described it, with all this implies about common knowledge, and implicit assumptions, and knowing intuitively how to react in crises.

---

[16] From the Greek *thaûmat* meaning wonder and *krátos*, (cracy) meaning rule or power. Hence, 'rule by the wonder-workers' or, more ironically, 'rule by wonder'.

[17] I say 'his', because Aristotle's conception was rationalized, even nostalgic. He was witnessing the demise of the independent *polisea*, as his employer Philip of Macedonia gathered them in like errant sheep, and his pupil Alexander mobilized them—and their murderous phalanxes—to conquer the world.

But these city states also squabbled incessantly.[18] They united with great reluctance — and only the once — when faced with imminent extinction. We obligingly overlook this — the simple fact that there never was a 'Greece' in antiquity[19] — because we are awed, simply awed, by the art — the amazing floruit of the *severe style*[20] and the *classical* — which followed this fleeting consensus, and its defeat of the Persians.

But modern nations are huge by comparison with Greek city-states...

Aristotle surveyed numerous city-states across the Greek mainland and colonies. They were certainly a diverse bunch. Most were ruled by autocrats — what the Greeks called tyrants — others by aristocrats or oligarchs. Some few were democracies. But one thing was absolutely clear. They were small. By modern standards very small indeed. They averaged between one and ten thousand citizens. For Plato, the ideal figure was 4050, for Aristotle the number that a single herald, shouting without strain, could immediately summon to arms.[21] Even with an extended train of females and slaves, they never exceeded 20,000.

---

[18] Little wonder that Renaissance Italy was so attracted to Greek antiquity. The Italian cities may have declined in late antiquity, but they'd never entirely disappeared, and never lost their memories of (Roman) empire. By the time of Dante, they were independent urban communities, holding diplomatic relations with each other and with the territorial monarchies, each possessed of hinterlands and colonies, and feuding interminably. They were, that's to say, the closest modern thing to the quarrelsome Greek *polis*.

[19] Except under the fragile and short-lived Athenian empire, that is. We ignore this because we rely on Herodotus as historian, and Herodotus 'was in the pay of the Athenian state, which is why Athens comes out so gloriously in the reckoning.' Bertrand Russell, *Government by Propaganda*, 1924.

[20] The *severe style* was the first style of national celebration — celebrating the success of something larger than a city state, and celebrating the warrior ethos and the virtues — selflessness, self-discipline — that had made it possible. Some would regard it as the first 'fascist' style, of warriors and workers gazing off-stage, lantern-jawed and steely-eyed and suitably vacant of mind. National Socialism or State Socialism, Russian or German or Chinese, the styles are remarkably similar. And interchangeable. (Ridgeway, *The Severe Style in Greek Sculpture*).

[21] By comparison, the lifeboat crew in my Devon village, which numbers under 500 — the village, not the crew — have to be summoned by exploding rocket. No normal shout could attract their attention.

Greek politics, and especially the supposed miracle of democracy,[22] was therefore the creation of tiny face-to-face cultures. And no one has managed to show, however ingeniously, how a praxis that worked for a few thousand citizens could possibly work for millions.

Many have tried Greek theory with modern numbers. The twentieth century has tried very hard. But everywhere, and under every circumstance, democracy has degenerated into the tyranny of a particular majority, of rule by rotating and increasingly indistinguishable cadres of professional politicians, if not military regimes and dictatorships.

The simple fact remains that the largest city in antiquity, Rome under the Antonines — which was an autocratic dictatorship, please note — numbered a mere million souls, and Rome's entire empire less than twenty million. There are modern cities approaching this, and modern nations, even those claiming homogeneity, are gigantic by comparison.

What worked for the Greeks, for a fraction of their city states, and for a fraction of their history — about thirty years — could hardly work for us. And yet we cling to the dream, and convince ourselves that things done by ruthless dictators — steeped in the ruthless myths of Hegel — are being done 'for their people'. This can only be moral cowardice, at best wishful thinking.

...and easy prey to tyrants, and their propaganda

None of this would matter, of course, in a perfect world, in classical Athens or Switzerland. But it does matter, and that is why I use the Greek word *tyrant*. Because, if there has been one net gainer from the twentieth century, as I have already suggested, it has been big government. Politicians have inherited the earth. There is now a class of salaried and full-time politicians in every country on the globe — a class that sees itself as a permanent fixture, with permanent bureaucracies to enforce its will.

Whatever their fanfare of 'liberation', their lip-service to western models — and however watertight their constitu-

---

[22] Which Aristotle regarded askance, as being 'rule by orators', that is, rule by individuals who bore no formal responsibility, but could manipulate the rest by their invidious eloquence.

tions[23] — these newly-hatched nations have fallen like nine-pins. In Africa and the Middle East, for pertinent example, there remains but one genuine democracy, where the people can not only dismiss their rulers, but occasionally bend them to their will. The rest are run by party cadres, dictators and military regimes. And few of these are benign.

The conclusion has to be that modern politicians have hit upon something, something they can manipulate. And manipulate so that entire states can be regimented. But, however brilliant the thaumatocrats, it could never have worked — and continued to work with monotonous regular-ity — unless it played upon some depths of the human psy-che. The interesting question therefore, is which?

The biology that's involved

I am assuming it's our biology that's being manipulated. Bear with me awhile. The early Darwinists worked with *structures*. They proved that animal bodies, including our own, had *adapted* over time. Extremely long periods of time, that is to say. Rather as a locksmith files a blank key to open a particular door, and then files it again as the lock gets worn or distorted, so evolution files away at life. The key never gets 'better' or 'higher' than it was. There is no 'progress' towards the perfect key, as the Victorians were inclined to believe. The Red Queen never catches up. The key merely changes as the door changes. Sometimes it works quite splendidly, and sometimes not at all, at which point the ani-mal becomes extinct.

Modern Darwinians assume that *behaviour* has been sub-ject to similar pressures — that broad swathes of our behav-iour have adapted over the three million years of successive *homo* species. They also became keys of a sort. They gave a tactical advantage to those who had them (at least over those who hadn't). As such, they proved useful.[24]

---

[23] Of which vast numbers were produced during de-colonization, over five hundred for Africa alone. None survived — and preserved the Western idea of the people having a serious choice in their own government — for more than ten years. In fact, the only democratic constitutions to have worked are those the US drew up for Japan and Germany. And, of course, Israel.

[24] Where 'useful' means 'conducive to reproduction', that is, 'conducive to a particular gene (that is responsible for a particular behaviour) thereby getting itself (more efficiently) into the next generation'.

Darwinians therefore assume such behaviours have been *hard-wired* into the brain (to use the cant expression). That they are now an *inheritance*, a legacy from the past, and can be recognized as such, in part because they are triggered by certain hormones.[25] But it doesn't assume that they're still efficient. Or useful. Quite the opposite, perhaps.[26] The last ten thousand years have seen enormous changes in our circumstance, and these behaviours may now be inappropriate.[27] Worse, they may be available for deliberate manipulation. Our political masters may have discovered how to trigger what, in another world, would have served another purpose entirely. But which trigger?

---

[25] Technically, that a deeply-felt propensity to act, which occurs in response to certain events, and which occurs throughout mankind, *ceteris paribus*, is an adaption that has developed over evolutionary history, what is called an *Evolutionary Stable Strategy* (ESS). It comprises a *propensity for certain types of situation* (to be identified in such a way as) to trigger (certain hormones, which then elicit) certain behaviours. Whatever their present utility these ESSs were once useful enough to have become embedded. As such they have to be recognised as a given. And as such they have given endless trouble to philosophers, who tended to assume them part of God's heritage, and called them 'moral sentiments'.

[26] From which it follows that the Abrahamic religions were probably right after all, when they declared that man is a flawed creature, carrying the burden of himself, his infelicities. The expression varies between the Religions of the Book. Christianity taints man with original sin, whereas Islam taints him with weakness. But the concept is the same, that the *natural* state of man is fraught with unhelpful possibilities which must needs be curbed. For man to live in civilization he must suppress some parts of himself.

This is quite at odds with social thought since Rousseau, which assumes that man is unflawed — potentially perfect — and only turns to the bad because of his *culture*. Cultures ruin the man, and therefore the culture is at fault and the man must be forgiven. Many still cling to this hopeless idea, even though it now requires them not only to reject Christianity — one of its original spurs to action, one suspects — but also the new biology, which will prove more difficult. But doomed ideas live on, as I've said, and do their damage in a thousand innocuous places.

[27] For example, we are a species that needs to do a lot for its young. They require a *High Parental Investment* (HPI). And the nature of that investment has been changing of late. A dominant male in a hunter-gatherer group would have given his 'bolt-on' family — his females' children by previous males — a deliberately hard time. He would even go so far as to kill them off, before himself inseminating their mothers. That made a deal of sense, in terms of *getting himself into the future* (getting his own genes into future generations). But it doesn't go down very well with city-bred moderns. And it is not much use pointing out that 'altruistic' genes — those of a step-father who brings up another man's children (and hence that man's genes) at the expense of his own — will not be passed on to the future by such generous behaviour, but quite the opposite. Magistrates take a dim view of such arguments.

The religious urge...

The popular candidate has always been *religion*. It is almost a commonplace that politicians, in the twentieth century, have managed to harness the 'psychological aspects of religion'.[28] It is certainly commonplace that the great ideological movements have been quasi-religious. The idea has a long history, since Bertrand Russell first noted the structural similarity between Marxism and Christianity (and the temperamental similarity between Bolshevism and Mohammedanism), and observers first experienced the *religious shock* of the Nuremberg rallies.[29] Modern politics has created its own priesthood, with party doctrine as its *revelation*, and elections — where they still occur — treated almost as a *sacrament*. But I would balk at simply *identifying* religion with politics. There is more to it than this. Something far subtler.

The *sacred* is at the heart of religion. It is clearly the profoundest of human needs, and produces the profoundest response. The Enlightenment may have killed off the gods,

---

[28] Peter Laslett for example: 'it is to religious activity...that the social psychologist should look, when he investigates the relationship between the *directive group* and the whole... These men [the politicians], who have succeeded in establishing power over the whole society... and can be said to have conquered it...will tend to maintain and increase the power they possess...by the manipulation of psychology.

Politicians know how to do these things; they know how to gather the leadership which arises from the 'religious' life...They can do all this, without being able to give an analytical account of what they are doing, and how they are doing it, and without the political analyst being able to do so, so far at least...

If this is what they are doing, it's not obvious how it can be said, of any society, that political power can depend upon consent. This psychological picture makes an impossibility of the *classic picture of a community of rational individuals rationally deciding which of their number shall exercise political power for what rational ends and within what limits'* [my italics, in reference to Greek doctrine], *Philosophy, Politics and Society* 1, 1956.

[29] It has an even longer history, if you consider Aristotle's famous perplexity about stepping from the tiny arena of the Greek *polis* — in which everybody and everything was known — into a larger arena where nothing and nobody could be properly known. It seemed a mystery to him, how to do this, and still keep some control, some sense of 'family'. He could only suggest religion. 'To give order to an excessively large number' he suggested 'must surely be a task for divine power'. (Although he carefully refrained from specifying which of the bloody-minded Greek gods he had in mind).

His suggestion of religion, and religious control, was certainly penetrating, and not just because [modern] tyrants have tended to regard themselves as gods, and their antics as divinely ordained.

but the prolonged withdrawal of the sea of faith[30] has not left much silence in the void. There are millions of whispering voices, chanting the modern loneliness, and seeking something to replace the gods,[31] something to satisfy their need for the sacred, something to elicit their reverence, anchor them in something larger than the merely present, and make them feel they're continuing what past generations have begun.

This is not just a nostalgia. It is not just something that dotes on ancient churches, their hushed interiors, and their memorials to the glorious dead. It *is* this, of course, but it is much much more. It's a straining for contact with something that can sanctify the present, and make it more noble. Or at least more bearable.

This is something profound, and I suspect as necessary as any hunger. It is a hunger that must be fed. And it really is part of our biology. It weakens people who cannot satisfy it, or find themselves severed from it. Such feelings are central to all the cultures that we have ever studied. They are as central to our own strong traditions — those symbolic systems by which we honour our past family and their wisdom — as they are to ancestor worship, which is, strictly speaking, a simple refusal to admit that they really are ancestors (that is, that they really are dead). And it is this, I suspect, that professional politicians have been manipulating.

...and the political manipulation of 'antiquity'

At one level the techniques are obvious enough. In the countries of origin it's become textbook stuff. First, the reaction against the colonizing power, and against the West generally. Then the rejection of any parting legacy the West may have left — even if it had been working at the time — and the use of this rejection to bind the nation (quite a useful exercise, actually, given that most of these new nations were potentially lethal ethnic and tribal cocktails).

Then there's the *völksgeist* — the distinctive national spirit — with its ersatz traditions, its symbols and regalia. And it is here that antiquity has proven so useful. Having 'discarded relics' on hand allows politicians to create a glori-

---

[30] *Dover Beach* by Matthew Arnold.

[31] 'When men stop believing in God, they don't believe in nothing. They believe in anything', G.K. Chesterton, 1936.

ous past, or at least the myth of one, and the propaganda to go with it. A glorious past that predates the West, and defies it.

Antiquity can also distract from the present, if that's faring badly. Antiquity is a better distraction than the traditional one, that of inventing a threat and going to war. Wars can always be lost — as General Galtieri learned to his cost — whereas antiquity is more pliable. Antiquity is a proof of past glory, and there's no-one on hand to snigger.

LA VITA DEI POPOLI SI MISURA A SECOLI QUELLA DELL'ITALIA A MILLENNI

'The life of a people is measured in centuries, that of Italy in millennia.'

Mussolini and Caesar depicted in a fascist poster of the early 1930s.

Mussolini was a master of the process. He brandished the Roman Empire as proof of the latent genius of the modern Italians, which he personally took upon himself to re-create. He relished all things Roman. He even modeled the fascist salute on (what he took to be) the original Roman *'ave'*. Himmler used a similar nostalgia — in his case, for Teutonic vigour and a bowdlerized mythology — in creating the SS. Many recent nations have employed the same techniques. Colonel Nasser promoted himself as a modern Pharaoh, the direct successor to Egypt's glorious past.[32]

---

[32] Which didn't go down terribly well with ordinary Egyptians, after their first excitement had worn off. Only Western liberals still maintain the pretence. Christine Hobson, *World of the Pharaohs*, for example, claimed that after

Nasser the Great Leader (Museum of Egyptian History, Cairo)

Such myths have proven invaluable. They have served to
unite people who actually have almost nothing in common
(the modern Greeks, for example). The problem is that the
governments doing this are often fascist. And that politicizing antiquity — apart from besmirching it — exposes it to
retaliation. We can expect this in the near future. Indeed, it
has already begun.[33]

The question of bad faith

If there *is* anything valuable in UNESCO and the Cultural
Heritage Crusade, I would suggest it is this, that they have
correctly sensed the connection between antiquity and the
sacred. They have understood that 'antiquities testify to the
consecration of the land in which they're discovered'.[34]

For the rest, however, it has been a cynical manipulation.
Quite simply, they have been riding the crest of cultural
nationalism — the gravy train, I'd be inclined to say — the
myth of themselves these new nations create (or at least their
leaders). Antiquity has become a weapon to be used against
the West. It is a humbug, of course, and one into which pro-

Nasser's death he was 'mourned as the last pharaoh'. An astonishing but
revealing naivety.

[33] In Afghanistan (p. 323), Egypt (p. 184) and recently in Iraq (p. 329).
[34] Roger Scruton, in correspondence, 2005.

fessional archaeology is being insidiously drawn. This may not matter much to antiquity. Who knows? It may even serve its best interest. But it does matter to archaeology, which risks bad faith.

An interesting thing this. The only people, nowadays, who aren't busily claiming their 'cultural heritage' are those who are still living it, who are still within a living tradition. And they wouldn't dream of 'claiming' it. They don't need to and, besides, they are hardly aware of it as something apart from themselves. They are unconsciously inside it.

As Roger Scruton has put it 'Modern people long for membership. But membership exists only among people who do not long for it, who have no real conception of it, who are so utterly immersed in it that they find it inscribed on the face of nature itself'.[35]

Let us be clear about this. Only those who are standing outside a living tradition — and looking in from the outside — are liable to claim it as their 'cultural heritage'. If they were still inside — and still connected — they would be paying more attention to what it was telling them to do. To what their ancestors really wanted, that's to say. Which almost certainly wouldn't involve them being dug up and put on public display.

So if they *are* claiming cultural heritage, they are doing so for a reason. Either they are suffering the modern loneliness, which has afflicted us all since the Enlightenment killed off our gods, and failed to provide any replacements which could assuage our need — our quasi-biological need — for the sacred, for sacrament (and for sacrilege that puts us in our place).

Or they are in need of a past, a mythical past which will justify their present, make it more bearable, and give it some shape. Fledgling nations need something like this. It binds them together. It gives them pride, an end for which they can strive (as well as a protection against more powerful and more predatory cultures and nations).

Or maybe it's their self-appointed rulers who need it. All those Garibaldis, Mussolinis, Sukarnos, Nkrumahs and Nassers who strut the modern stage. For such as these, cul-

---

[35] And he goes on to add 'such people have access, through their common culture, to the ethical vision of man', *An Intelligent Person's Guide to Modern Culture*, page 10.

tural heritage is a gift. It validates them and their pretensions, and provides a ready-made propaganda.

Or, more justifiably, a culture is losing its living tradition, and becoming aware of it — almost certainly for the first time — as a sort of innocence that is being lost. The Laplanders and the Australian Aborigines[36] were until recently — until the arrival of the mechanized races — steeped in a culture that had been unchanged for millennia. Unchanged because there had been no need of change. As hunter-gatherers and pastoralists, they had been perfectly adapted to their niche.

But now their customs and beliefs — and the rituals and festivals which express them — have acquired a half-hearted and fluid quality. They have a new self-consciousness, which shows that they are being staged for strangers. The family conversation has faltered and become nostalgic, a grasping for the past, a sort of fancy dress that's only half-serious. It has become a suspension of disbelief, in hopes of regaining something that's lost. But when this starts to happen it is already too late.

But, yes, such aboriginals have right on their side. Their artifacts still constitute what I have called a 'family silver', their family's accumulated wealth and wisdom. They should be regained, if they were taken without permission.[37] They are still sacred, though the benison is fading. They correctly belong in the family's sideboard, even though they will never again be in unthinking daily use, only be taken out in nostalgic remembrance.

In fact, they belong in a folk museum, but a museum that is only for family members. Their ultimate indignity would be to earn revenue, to be squandered on the goods of the culture that has made them obsolescent — be it transistor radios, booze, or mobile phones. In that case the family silver has become a commodity, and a sacrilege has been committed. Better they should be hidden from view, and only available to the family. Better by far.

---

[36] And, arguably, the South American Indians, who were invaded and exploited by the Spaniards and Portuguese.

[37] In this case, the recent legal sleight-of-hand in which aboriginal artefacts loaned by the Victoria and Albert Museum were effectively confiscated by the aborigines would be morally justified — however illegal — but only if they were thereafter treated as sacred. To display them as a source of revenue would be dishonest. In fact, it would be little less sacrilegious than the British Museum's display of 'Ginger' — see page 259.

A family can display its portraits on the chimney piece, to honour the family's notables — the one, for instance, who went exploring, the one who became a bishop or a minor poet. But they can only do this for the ones they can remember, and they can only do it for a reason, because it connects the family to its achievements. It provides what the moderns would call a 'role-model', and what anybody sensible would call a sacrament, something that binds and inspires, that creates feelings of awe and pride and piety — what a regiment expects to achieve when it parades its battle honours, and tells the tales of their glory.

But no family — and this is the point — would allow anyone who is non-family to display their portraits, let alone dig up their grandparents and display them. It is only because the corpses in question and their goods aren't anybody's family anymore that they can be treated like this. Think about this. It is true and important, and it's on the borderline — the fruitful borderline — where metaphor and reality meet. Imagine going into an abandoned graveyard and digging up somebody's mausoleum. You can only do this because there is none of their family left. And not because you belong to that family. If you made the same attempt in a graveyard that was still in use, there'd be hell to pay.

So perhaps we have been asking the wrong questions. Not whether this or that claim is legitimate — since very few of them can ever get to first base — but why is anybody bothering to claim them, and whether — to achieve that end — they actually need to regain the stuff? Perhaps it would suffice just to go through the business of making a claim?

Because it begins to seem that all such claims are a sort of bad faith — and the claimants less than honest. It is a matter of disquiet whether, in our naivety and desire to please, we are making antiquity a hostage to fortune, in what is becoming a conflict of civilizations.

Summary

- Since they have no grounds, why *do* modern nations persist in claiming antiquity as 'their' cultural heritage,
- when the idea would have been hateful to the ancients themselves?
- Modern nations are a modern invention, and completely different from anything in antiquity.

- Ancient groupings were homogeneous, but modern nations can only aspire to be, and only by ignoring the evidence.
- Modern nations carry modern intellectual baggage, notably Hegel's totalitarian philosophy, which we overlook,
- because of our reliance on Greek political philosophy, especially the concept of *demos*, although this only ever worked — could only ever have worked — for tiny groupings, for Greek city states (*polisea*), besides which modern states are gigantic.
- There are now many new nations, all of whom are in need. They need *resources*, and they need *credibility* against their former overlords, a sentiment that is actively fostered by UNESCO.
- Antiquity is usefully on hand for these purposes,
- and so are modern politicians, who have proven adept at manipulating the masses,
- particularly their need — their biological need — for *reverence*, for the *sacred*,
- which we in the West have lost since the Enlightenment.
- So, when modern nations claim antiquity as 'their property', they probably cannot do so,
- and it is probably not 'the nation' that is doing the claiming at all, but the tyrants and ruling cadres, the juntas, the parties and regimes,
- who will be using it for *cultural nationalism*, to give themselves a spurious legitimacy (or an undeserved wealth).
- We should, therefore, question such claims. Who is the claimant? Is it really 'the people' or another party that's manipulating them, and for other reasons?
- And if it's merely a case of *realpolitik*, is it in Antiquity's best interest?
- And is archaeology — archaeologists, human all-too-human — also being manipulated, and also acting in *bad faith*?

CHAPTER 10

Has Private Property Failed Antiquity?

One can understand emerging nations claiming antiquity as a heritage, however threadbare their case, however spurious. They have an agenda after all—they need to bolster themselves, and their ruling elites need to justify their power—their presumption to power—especially if it is dictatorial. And antiquity is a gift. All this is clear enough.

But what still isn't clear is why our own liberal Establishment so assiduously supports them, and seems so keen to bring antiquity under state control. What, in the modern parlance, is *their* agenda?

We do not have, as I've already regretted, a sociology of archaeology, or of the Crusade's fellow travellers.[1] Pending that, I can suggest three alternatives:

First, that they are being duped

That they are academics, worthy souls devoted to the pursuit of knowledge, who care nothing about worldly matters, and know even less. This is plausible, given a cosseted existence, a secure salary and a pension. But it hardly explains their presumption, or their bullying. And one recalls George Watson's famous question: 'Were the intellectuals duped?' —whether the academics who visited Stalin's USSR in the thirties and came back as blissful converts, actually knew what was going on.[2] Watson's eminently sensible conclu-

---

[1] You may think the very idea is unworthy. But they have a sociology primed for their enemies. They accuse them of greed, mutilation and vainglory. So why should they be exempt?

[2] [*Encounter*, 1970] that even as they were being soft-soaped, justice was being debased by brute expediency, state torture and murder were commonplace, and systematic purges were driven by nothing more noble than Stalin's increasing paranoia. Academics were willing to disregard this in their cold

sion — with the possible exception of 'useful idiots' like the Webbs — was that they *were* aware. They had worked it out. Further, they'd have been a disgrace to the Socratic inquiring intellect not to have done.[3] They were, however, swayed — seduced, corrupted, it comes to the same thing — by the proximity to power that they had felt — been allowed to feel — the caress of power that is so heady for academics, and seems to stimulate their abstract cruelty.

Second, that it is political

The last century has witnessed a titanic struggle between rival economic theories, between the Anglo-American tradition and the Hegelian. On one hand there's been a reliance upon the market, upon individual effort and private ownership — and on the other a craving for state planning, for collective ownership and control. And property has been at the heart of the squabble.

The contest came to a head in the 1980s, with the collapse of the socialist command economies and then the Berlin Wall. Brute Marxism may have gone out of fashion, but its influence lingers. Academics have simply morphed their arguments. They are still as bitter about private ownership. They still deride its insensitivity to 'higher' needs, such as cultural heritage.

Is this to be antiquity's fate — the last battleground of a failing cause — a cause which has seen its every dream turn sour, seen the forces of rage and resentment, of inhuman cruelty and squalor, where the promised land should have been? Is the academic's contempt for collectors the last gasp of a dying idea?

Third, that it is a genuine moral disquiet

almost a disgust, at the thought of art — high art, art made sacred by our forebears — being sold for money. But, as I have already suggested, reverence can be combined with material

fervour, and to re-interpret it for the benefit of a 'higher' truth (what Orwell termed 'newspeak', and modern academics have almost made respectable as political correctness).

[3] Proof of this is that Bertrand Russell wasn't fooled for a minute, and made his views abundantly clear in print, for those who followed. The most honest of these, André Gide, certainly wasn't fooled. He called for more of the same, and more brutal...

value. Indeed it must be, if transfer is to be orderly. There was a thriving medieval market in relics, after all. This may have encouraged forgeries, but it did no harm to the originals. Nor did it besmirch them. On the contrary it protected them, kept them safe and cherished. Sacrament is only felt by the few, after all. It is something for a sensitive minority. The rest need other reasons for respect.

Given this, the academic's scorn for material value becomes a self indulgence, and a dangerous one. It is also liable, as we shall see, to a charge of disingenuity.

There are many questions here, and I am not sure that anybody has ever laid them out. Some are matters of doctrine, some of contingent fact, and others of sociology — that is, as Durkheim and Weber saw it, of trying to work out why certain people are likely to believe certain things, and especially things to their own advantage. The present and following chapters attempt these questions. They examine the specific arguments against private ownership, and those against the market. They also consider the rejoinder. Nations may be playing fast and loose with antiquity, but *who else is there?* Who or what has any better claim? And a claim that's not already discredited?

Property

Property is an institution, and it needs a culture. It presumes one. I cannot own this antiquity — this anything, for that matter — unless everybody understands what it means to own something. For example, that taking it away without my consent constitutes a theft. Robinson Crusoe on his desert island had no need of property, precisely because he was separated from his culture, and hence from those who made property understandable. It was only the dreaded re-appearance of that culture — in the form of hostile raiders — that continued to make it necessary.[4]

---

[4] On the island, Man Friday and Crusoe were equals before God. Crusoe may have been the acknowledged leader, a chieftain by virtue of his expertise, but otherwise the two were comrades. Only when Crusoe was rescued, and re-entered his culture, did Man Friday become a resource, and the boy Xury got sold into slavery. One wonders what Friday's fate might have been, had he not conveniently got himself drowned. It was the genius of Defoe to introduce the modern mind into literature — the self that seeks always to be efficient, to use efficiently what God has provided for his use. It was also his

This is more than a matter of law. Law only gives voice to the culture. It is a matter, rather, of what has already been accepted by all, by all the members of that culture.

And this is the problem. For as our culture has changed and adapted to commerce and industry, so has its concept of property. There are new forms of property — 'futures', for example, and joint stock companies — that would have puzzled Robinson Crusoe, just as his ideas of property puzzle us (and more than that, disquiet us).

In fact, as I have said, the last hundred years has seen a right royal squabble, at a doctrinal level, between the rival economic theories of socialism and capitalism. And politics has been dominated by the idea of property. Whether things should be owned by private individuals — and be used solely for their benefit — or owned collectively by the community or the state — what has misleadingly been called 'social property' — and harnessed to the 'common good'.

The doctrinal battle has now been lost, and the Left, which favoured 'socialist ownership', has clearly been routed. Market-based systems are being adopted everywhere, even by erstwhile socialists.[5] But Marx's notorious idea — that 'private property appeared long after the emergence of humanity', that it's something recent, something that needs justifying — has a certain romantic appeal even now. It was, after all, the emergence of commercial economics that caused men to regard themselves, more and more, as separate individuals — as *homo economicus* — with a duty before God to efficiently use what God had made available. And caused material objects to be seen as a *resource on hand*, making ownership vital, and hence the idea of property and title.

So it is worth pondering whether private property really is such a modern invention.

---

genius to show the peculiar priggishness of such a mind. Robinson Crusoe, in our terms, was the first prig in literature. Strictly speaking, of course, he was also wrong. If Crusoe had been (old enough to have been) a serious student of Locke — had accepted that all men are born equal and equally free, and owning themselves — then it would have followed that no man could be enslaved unless he'd agreed to it, either because he'd been captured in a just war and accepted slavery as the only alternative to just execution, or because he'd agreed to sell himself and his labour in settlement of debt. And I don't recall young Xury making any such compact.

[5]   Although they still assume the right to intervene and to regulate, as if the market was a mindless obdurate, whose *raw energy* was the only recompense for its *turpitude*.

The laziness of thinkers

The answer, I suspect, lies with the traditional reluctance of philosophers — or their temerity — to do the difficult work of thinking. And their predilection for whatever theories are conveniently on the shelf, discarded there by previous thinkers. But you'd hardly appreciate a mechanic trying to fix the electronic injection system on your shiny new BMW using a hammer and a wrench — however conveniently to hand, and however effective they'd proved for Model T Fords. So why accept the equivalent in social thinking?

The seventeenth century, at the dawn of modern commerce, was genuinely troubled by a problem. It had to justify how common property — the bounty of nature which God had made available to all men — could have been taken into private hands, and denied to the rest.

To solve this problem philosophers envisaged a 'state of nature', a golden age, a pre-lapsarian Eden (or post-lapsarian hell for Hobbes) before the fall, or outside of time altogether, where things could be examined in simplicity, shorn of the contingent complexities of life. In this mythical space, Locke envisaged, a man could 'mix his labour' with un-owned objects — things in *res nullius* — and by taking such trouble could make them his own.[6]

The argument is ingenious, and sensible, if you believe, literally, that the world was made in seven days for man's exclusive use. But if not, it is a dangerous device. We have not, for many thousands of years, laboured on things and thereby made them our own. We have inherited, earned them, found them occasionally, and above all we've *traded*. This is a contingent fact.[7]

And the effect of this philosophical obsession with old tools and tools-to-hand — with seventeenth-century capitalism and the enclosures? That private property is still regarded as something *recent*, something modern. Oh yes, houses and cars and washing machines have only recently become private property. But private ownership itself is ancient. It is communal ownership in its politicised

[6] John Locke, *Two Treatises of Government* (1680-90)

[7] Which explains why in the battle between the American Founders, Alexander Hamilton's free-market capitalist model won out over Thomas Jefferson's (Lockean) agrarian democracy.

form — state ownership, 'social ownership' — which is the modern invention, the artificiality that needs to be justified.

The biological argument for property

In fact, private property is as old as the species, if not older. It's also biologically important. When the first weapon was invented by the first *homo* species — probably *homo habilis*, or maybe *erectus* — at least three million years ago, it gave him an advantage over his fellows. It made him more efficient in the provision of food, and this gave him a selective advantage in passing on his genes.[8]

Of course he would have been copied sooner or later, and at some point weapons may have been shared — or loaned — and likewise the proceeds of the hunt. But the evidence from biology is clear,[9] that any sharing outside the immediate circle of kin was part of a process of mutual exchange — a benign process of tit-for-tat, in which tallies were carefully kept of favours owed and owing. And this presupposed that the objects were already in one party's possession.

This is no scientific fancy to replace a seventeenth-century fancy, but a growing body of evidence, and powerful theory at the heart of the new biology.[10] The evidence had already been noticed (long before there was a theory on hand to make sense of it). Durkheim certainly felt it, the sense that our

---

[8]   It is a charming conceit of social scientists to call us 'tool-making' animals. We are not, or only secondarily. Cooking pots came after weapons, and the sequence remains. Modern technology from Teflon to the computer to the internet has either been invented as weaponry, or developed as weaponry, and only subsequently for more placid use.

[9]   Robert Trivers' theory of 'reciprocal altruism'.

[10] The argument would run as follows:
   • That we as a species require a *High Parental Investment* (HPI). Rearing offspring is difficult, and needs both parents to contribute resources.
   • Hence males with better resources will make better parents and be sought after by females.
   • Possessions have, from the beginning, been an indicator of resource (of 'fitness'), in the early period literally so (when *weapons* = *food* = *resource*).
   • Latterly, when patterns of behaviour had been selectively embedded as ESSs, possessions (property) were taken as an indicator of power, of prestige, of resourcefulness.
   • Hence Property has become enmeshed in reproductive behaviour,
   • and been hard-wired into the brain, especially the female brain. (cf. Sarah Blaffer Hrdy's *Mother Nature*)
   • And so, presumably, has 'collecting' (where *collecting* requires *wealth* hence *resource*).

immediate property has a 'sacred' feel, as if the self-that-owns extends beyond the mere body, and finds expression — literally, self-expression — in its property. As if we see ourselves — and expect to be seen — as an amalgam of our bodies, our clothes and our immediate property. If our houses are burgled, that immediate circle is disrupted, and we feel much more than we should — if we'd only lost mere 'possessions', that is to say. We feel some profound hurt. We feel it as a violation.

Goffman also noticed this, from the sociological perspective.[11] He described a 'personal space', a projection of the self onto the area that surrounds the body, a space whose infringement is felt as a trespass, and whose size reflects the (felt) importance of the self. It could be queried whether the property within that space is there to delineate it — as boundary markers, say — or whether it does something more important, and give that space a peculiar character, identifying it as that person's. I suspect the latter — thinking of men and their sports cars, women and their inner rooms — but it hardly matters. What matters is that for such a reaction to have developed, and become embedded in our biology, a long stretch of evolutionary time was required, hundreds of thousands of years if not millions. And as such, it points to something ancient.

All of which leads me to agree, for once, with Hegel, who regarded property not as an economic resource, or as a consumable wealth — as something that arrived quite recently, as the by-product of agriculture and its surplus — but as a *fulfilment*. People represent themselves through their property. They stake their claim, as it were. It follows that they are diminished if their property is denied them (if it is removed, or 'made to stand in the same relation to more than one self').[12]

It follows, that any confiscation of private property has to be justified. The onus is on the confiscating body. And this also applies to collections — of antiquities, for example.

Property evolves, adapts, and configures

The critics of property, of private property, that is, and of the market where it is freely exchanged, and which goes hand-

[11] Erving Goffman, *The Presentation of Self in Everyday Life*, 1984.
[12] Roger Scruton, *Modern Philosophy*, 1994.

in-hand with it—rather than hand in glove as critics maintain—invariably make the same mistake. They assume they
are dealing with something static, immutable, set forever in
the same obdurate concrete. Hence their relish in blowing it
up.

In fact they are dealing with something that behaves as a
life-form. It evolves to overcome challenges. It adapts to
changing circumstances. It becomes ever more efficient—at
satisfying the changing requirements of men. As I say, *property evolves alongside the species.*[13]

This explains the famous *bad aim* of the critics. They complain that 'property' does this and that harm, but fail to
notice that it is already adapting, like any creature that is
challenged by its own deficiency. Marx bemoaned Manchester in the 1840s, quite correctly, but set it in theoretical concrete as an inevitability of private property. He failed to
realize that Manchester of the 1840s was in its way as vulnerable and as inefficient—as imbalanced—as those moths
whose silvery wings no longer camouflaged them against
trees that were blackened by Manchester soot. And the naturalist who bemoaned that man was 'standing outside
nature', and that the moths were doomed (to be eaten by
predators) quite failed to realize that the moths he was looking at were doomed, yes—because they no longer 'fitted
in'—whereas their fellows had already adapted by blacken-
ing their wings. But of course the naturalist hadn't noticed
those ones, precisely *because* they had adapted so well.[14]

The Cultural Heritage Crusade is similarly short-sighted.
It claims that *private property* has failed antiquity—that it has
been dazzled by its cash value, to the detriment of the knowl-

---

[13] An overlooked aspect of evolutionary theory. Since Julian Huxley *cultural
evolution* has been a commonplace idea. It has been broad-brushed, however.
In fact, man's biological advantage is that he adapts more rapidly to changing
circumstances, because he now *adapts through his property*—that is, through
his *extended self*—and not through long-winded bodily change. Hegel was
right after all, and it is only the emphasis upon culture and consciousness—as
agents in evolution—that conceals the fact that *it is through a man's owned tools
that he evolves.* Modern man can radically adapt in one generation, whereas
other mammals need two hundred for any significant adaption.

[14] And the naturalist hadn't noticed, either, as modern critics invariably haven't,
that by complaining and forcing change they are acting within the system—as
a 'market force'—rather than standing outside the system altogether, as if
little gods, and judging it (as having failed). The idea of standing outside—the
'god's-eye view'—is a conceit and a delusion.

edge it also carries.[15] It concludes that private ownership should be abolished, and replaced with something more 'responsible'. Antiquities should become another type of property altogether, something called 'state property', which is held in trust and safety by a benign government — without advantage and without greed — like a governess who puts aside her charges' toys, lest they be broken.

The Crusade's mistake is therefore fundamental. It overlooks the simple fact that property as a cultural institution can only be 'responsible' for *what it knows*. And it overlooks how easily property — and its owners — can adapt and learn; in this case by simply adding another increment — that of *intellectual property* — whose additional value has to be protected.

The modern concept of ownership (and its presuppositions)

Ownership is no longer restricted to things. That much is clear. Intellectual rights, film rights, broadcast rights, New York overlook and shadow rights are only things in an abstract or a dispositional sense.[16] But they can still be bought and sold.

Now, to own such a thing is to have, in respect of it, certain rights and liabilities as against other persons (or the culture as a whole). It seems preferable therefore, to define ownership not in terms of physical things, but in terms of this *'bundle' of rights and duties* that we have towards other people in respect of the thing that is owned. In terms, for example, of your glass's fragility, or my dog's bite.[17]

---

[15] By virtue of its position in the ground relative to other antiquities — and other 'traces' — in the three-dimensional puzzle that it is archaeology's task to decipher. See page 143.

[16] In the sense in which glass is fragile, and will break when dropped. The 'thing' involved is usually of this nature, a *right to drop* or an *undertaking not to drop*. Such dispositions have to be taken into account, even though they have not yet happened, and probably never will.

[17] A.M.Honoré, working along these lines, defines ownership as 'those legal rights, duties and other incidents which apply, *in the ordinary case*, to the person who has the greatest interest in a 'thing' that's admitted by *a mature legal system*'(my italics). He goes on to list these 'incidents', each of which has its corresponding duty:
- the right to *possess* the thing (and be secure in its possession)
- the right to *use* it

Now to say that *A* owns *P* — that I own this antiquity, say — is not to say that I am subject to all these rights and duties. There are certain rights I clearly do not have — I cannot destroy, damage or consume for example. And I need not have been subject to them all in the past.

The reader may now recall my *common-sense unease* of an earlier chapter. There are some types of property, I suggested, where ownership just drifts into stewardship. Where the mere fact of owning *x* doesn't allow you (any right) to harm *x*, but rather requires — demands — that you (have a duty of) care for *x*, and where any failure (in this duty) seems to cancel your (rights of) ownership, and even allows *x* to be confiscated (whether or not that is supported by current law). We have now seen the biological basis for this *unease*, quite simply, that it is something ancient.

Another thing should now be clear: parts of the present bundle are improvements, solutions to past problems (now backed by case-law and precedent). And there will be further improvements, as and when they are needed. Of that we can be confident.

Private ownership is normal, anything else is exceptional

In fact, the history of property can be viewed as a series of attempts, getting ever closer to the mark, of making (private) property completely efficient, including its duties of care and protection. There is even a theory for this. It is called Pareto's Criterion.[18]

- the right to *manage* it
- the right to (enjoy) *income* arising from it
- the right to *alienate* it (that is, to sell or transfer or exchange it)
- the right to *consume, waste* or *destroy* it
- the right of *inheritance* by one's successors indefinitely
- the *absence of term* (of a fixed date when the owner's interests end)
- the *liability to execution* (of the property being distrained for debt or insolvency)
- the *reversion to the owner* on termination of other interests which encumber the property (usufructs, leases, mortgages etc) and, lastly,
- the *prohibition of harmful use* (although this one is arguable, since I'm forbidden to stab you with anybody's knife, and not only my own).

[18] Wilfredo Pareto's (1848-1923) 'Criterion of Economic Efficiency', whereby resources are allocated in such a way that no possible further change could make someone better off and no-one worse off. He argued that only the free market is capable of achieving this.

It is my contention that private property is not only *ancient* and embedded in our biology — whereas public ownership is a recent development, and still on probation — but that it is also the *best* way to ensure the duties of ownership. In many contexts it is the *only* way. The reason for this is simple. There has to be one *legal* person who is liable for damage. That much is clear. But I would go further. I would say it has to be a *real* person — flesh and blood and conscience — who knows that he will be held to account if anything goes wrong, that 'the buck stops with him'. If *nobody* is liable in this brute sense then nobody will bother. And unless that person also enjoys the *benefits of ownership* — at least some of them — he will not put up with the liabilities. No man will sow where another will reap.

And the real problem with 'social ownership', 'public ownership' and 'communal ownership — all of which actually come down to *state ownership*[19] — is that *nobody* is accountable in this way. Oh yes, as the third part of this book will demonstrate, they do have some of the benefits — the rights to sell, to enjoy income, and to use — but they have none of the liabilities.

Roger Scruton argues as much, when he says that 'private property... is the necessary price for exacting a private duty of property. And we need to extract such duties to ensure that property is not misused, squandered or destroyed by neglect'.[20]

---

[19] These are often confused, and deliberately so. 'Public ownership' (for example nationalization) seems to refer to property owned collectively by all the citizens. But their ownership is only nominal. Control rests entirely with the government, which has both the rights and the duties of ownership. Ordinary citizens have no more rights of access to state property, such as police cars and council computers, than they have to any other private property. And so on for all Honoré's 'incidents'. I would suggest the crux is *alienation*: whoever can *sell* the goods is their real owner. Everything else is window-dressing.

[20] *Modern Philosophy*, 1994, and he continues: 'all who witnessed the environmental catastrophe of communism know the price that must be paid when there is no person (whether individual or corporate)...with liability for damage.'

The Tragedy of the Woods[21]

This is part fable, part contemporary history. It is usually taken to show that vital resources, when left to private individuals, will always be misused and over-used, because of the avarice—and the short-sightedness—that is part of our nature. Hence that private property cannot be trusted with anything that's in any way significant. Actually it shows no such thing, but what it does show is very interesting.

Imagine a woodland, an ancient wood, common property to the villages that shelter within it. As common property, *res nullius*, it provides firewood for their needs. As long as the villages remain small, and villagers only cut what they need for themselves—for heating their cottages and cooking—a natural balance is maintained. New trees can grow to replace those that are felled.

But now imagine a change. Perhaps the villagers become too numerous. Perhaps they begin to take more than they need, and sell the surplus. For whatever reason they cut down trees faster than the woods can replenish them. The trees thin out, and everybody discovers what nobody had realized before—that the trees had been protecting them from the wind. They discover this the hard way, because the soil is blown from their fields, and their crops begin to fail.

There are several solutions to the problem:

[1] Self discipline
The traditional means is for the villagers to discipline themselves. They can either defer to the judgment of the village patriarch—who allocates trees according to status—or abide by the edicts of the village priest—who makes the trees sacred, hence inviolable. The problem here is that traditional authority can wane in an age of chainsaws, and sacred trees inhabited by gods can become a laughable superstition. We call this secularization, the invariable result when any peasantry encounters the modern world.[22]

What if a scientist were dispatched from the city, to teach these recalcitrant villagers why the trees are necessary—that

---

[21] Usually known as the *Tragedy of the Commons* although, in my form it has a greater resonance for modern problems—such as rain forests, and the impossibility of expecting governments to be 'responsible' about them.

[22] And of modern agriculture, once the idea of husbandry, of 'give and take', of sharing with nature, has been banished by city-bred accountants.

they protect the soil from erosion? Would that give them pause? Probably not, for what the villagers will conclude is that the *majority* of trees must be standing for them to do their job (and prevent soil erosion), which only requires the majority of the villagers to desist (from cutting them down).

But that, notoriously, is no reason for any *individual* villager, personally, to desist from cutting some down for himself, since the ones he cuts down will not affect the majority. This is the 'amoralist's argument'.[23] And if you asked the amoralist how he would cope if everyone did the same — if he found himself on the other end of the stick — he would be entirely unruffled.[24]

Whatever the arguments, however, the trees will be cut down, all of them, and everyone will suffer. The argument may not be irresistible, but it is for the trees, and it demonstrates that in the modern world — the world of commerce — 'communal property' will invariably suffer.

---

[23] As an argument, it is as old as the hills or, rather, as old as the Greeks, who first formulated it as *The Paradox of the Heap*. As paradoxes go, it is quite deadly, certainly for trees. It starts from the intuitive thought that if a heap of sand comprises an enormous number of grains, removing one grain will still leave it indubitably a heap, and proceeds by repeating the same operation — taking away one more grain but still having a heap on hand — until there's only one grain left, which is quite evidently *not* a heap.

Logically, (n)(where n is a heap) implies that (n minus 1 is still a heap), and so on, until (n equals 1), so that (n both is and is not a heap) — but nobody's to blame...

[24] He would merely observe that:
• as a matter of fact they wouldn't (do exactly the same), because he would persuade them not to,
• which wouldn't even be hypocritical of him, because
• he sincerely believed that the majority of the trees needed to be standing, which only required that
• the majority of the villagers also sincerely believed it,
• which he would be doing his sincere best to achieve, and that,
• if he failed in this, and the other villagers looked as if they were going for their axes
• he would still have the advantage, because he'd get there first, and he'd end up with the most wood.

This is not just an intellectual game, however. It is precisely the argument proffered by Egyptologists for not desisting from excavating in Kings Valley. 'If the mountain is moving' it has been said 'we had best get what we can before it's too late', carefully omitting to mention *why* the mountain is moving. See *The sad plight of Kings Valley* in the Appendix.

[2] Imposed authority

The second approach is for some authority — the king, say — to take control of the woods on the villagers' behalf. He could then impose rationing. This would certainly save the trees, at least for now, and prevent soil erosion. In modern terms, the wood would become a 'sustainable resource'.

The problem is, however, that once a communal property is entrusted to a king it effectively becomes his property, his resource (because he holds the entire bundle of rights and duties, and cannot be forced to sell). And just as kings have a habit of going to war without bothering to consult their citizens, so they have a habit of cutting down forests to make ships.

Nor does a modern republic — where 'the people are the government' — improve matters. They will probably be worse, in fact, since the wood is now effectively owned by an 'office', rather than a person. The temporary occupant of this office may be corrupt, and sell the wood's rights for a bribe, or to benefit his favourites. He may be subject to political pressures. Or he may be incompetent. But whatever his failings, he is only liable while he remains in office. Whatever the damage, he is unaccountable as soon as he leaves.[25]

[3] The wood in private hands

There is another option, however. The wood could be parcelled out as private property. At first sight this seems crazy. If it was the villagers' greed that caused the trouble in the first place, then giving them unrestricted access would only make it worse. Well, wouldn't it? And showing them the errors of their way would only make them furtive. The Tragedy of the Woods will surely follow. The only difference is, it will come quicker.

But I am not so sure. The villagers may be peasants, and traditionally treated with disdain, but they are perfectly capable of self-interested thought. And now they are aware of the problem. The next villager who fells his trees for lumber will feel the brunt of this awareness. His neighbours will take him to task. They will arraign him for damaging their fields. The court — or tribunal, or council of village elders, it hardly matters — will decide against him. It will order that, since he has reduced the value of everybody's property —

---

[25] Which is, as we shall see, almost exactly the situation in Egypt.

reduced their income or their expectations, or increased their insurance premiums, again it hardly matters — he has to compensate them from his lumber earnings. A precedent has been established. Every villager now knows that felling trees on his land will depreciate the other villagers' land. And that he must pay for this. If he decides, having done his sums, that the necessary recompense (to the other properties) exceeds his profit (from his own) — that paying the other landowners uses up his earnings, and more — he'll simply desist, and spare his trees. And if not, then not, but only to a graduated extent.

Either way, the outcome is the same. Owners will think twice before damaging their property, because of the damage they will do to others.[26] The 'bundle' of property rights and duties has been amended. The rights have been circumscribed, and the duties refined. Property has learned something, and adapted itself. And 'government' has played no part in it. The woods have been treated as a private resource, and this has protected them.[27] And the villagers' 'greed' and intractability have actually aided the process.

'Invisible Hand' mechanisms

This is an example of an *invisible hand mechanism*, whereby a group of individuals, who keep their eyes firmly to the ground and ignore anything larger than their own immediate needs (and their families') — and don't behave particularly well in the getting of 'em, either — can come to benefit everybody — to achieve 'social goals' in the modern argot — in spite of themselves, and probably to their astonishment (if they ever bothered to look, that is).

The immediate conclusion is that people's *intentions* are not actually very important to the outcome. Suspect inten-

---

[26] This principle is in fact widely applied — in the form of 'licenses to pollute' — and operates effectively through insurance premiums.

[27] Compare this with the rain forests of South America, which are still *res nullius* — inhabited by hunter-gatherer Indians, but lacking any formal title, and hence brushed aside — and effectively being treated as state property, (the rights to which, those of consumption and destruction, are being) sold to lumber companies on the pretext of providing fields for agriculture, even though it has been proven that the resulting fields are useless. In the terms of the fable they are blown away by the winds that the trees would have prevented. It follows that the simple solution is for private people — Western or otherwise — to buy those rain forests.

tions can achieve a 'good thing' (as Plato would have put it), and good intentions can create chaos.[28] There is more to it than this, however. Mandeville argued, in his 'scandalous' *Fable of the Bees*, that it did not matter why people acted as they did — whether from self-aggrandizement, greed, revenge or other 'vicious propensities'. But that, if the whole thing — his imaginary 'hive' — was to work it seemed that they *had* to act like this.[29]

As I say, the puzzle which 'invisible hand' mechanisms attempt to explain is why unpromising complicated things often turn out so well. Why they return to equilibrium, like a boat that is tossed by the waves, but always rights itself.

The original suspicion was that God had a hand in the matter. That the 'invisible hand' was actually his.[30] But invisible hand mechanisms have survived the much-publicized death of God.

---

[28] It puzzles me, therefore, that 'liberals' should so hate the market — which buys their dinners and the limousines to reach them — when they are to a man *consequentialists*, that is they judge a man by the *results* of his actions, and not by his *intentions* in performing them. They judge a successful murderer more harshly than an incompetent one (the man who ties his intended victim to the railroad tracks is judged more benignly if he misread the timetable) whereas the television producer making a programme about the dangers of railways is judged harshly simply because he overlooked the timetable. ('Culpable manslaughter' will seem much the same thing as murder to the man in a small cell.) So why do liberals refuse to judge the *market* by its consequences?

[29] That their vicious propensities were necessary, because of the *raw energy* they provided. They were the motor that drove the vehicle, in modern terms. Take them away, as Mandeville did in the last part of his fable, and you'd only get complacency and decline. This also appears to be true.

Modern biology comes down firmly on the side of Mandeville. Not in his chosen example of the hive, of social bees, but in the matter of cultures. And not in any crude *Social Darwinist* sense of the 'survival of the fittest', as Herbert Spencer had it, but in a subtler way, by showing that 'vices' are essential, or at least inevitable, and definitely not to be dismissed or disparaged.

Biology has shown for example, that the basis of altruism is indeed self-interest. What is hailed as an epitome of self-sacrifice, generosity, mutual co-operation and comradeship is actually something else. It is evolved behaviour. And it has evolved because it (eventually) serves the interests of the individual's own genes, by transmitting them through to the future.

[30] The originators of the genre — Mandeville's 'grumbling hive' and Adam Smith's 'market' — believed precisely this. Smith spoke of 'Natural Order' — which echoed Locke's 'Natural Law' — and assumed that only God could possibly see everything that was going on, and intercede at just the right time and place.

Such matters may indeed be too complicated to write down on a single blackboard, however large.[31] And too large for anyone to comprehend in one sweep. But the modern mind is untroubled by this. It accepts that *grasping* things — as the modern mind does 'grasp' them — is not the same as being able to *explain* them. And certainly insufficient for making another for ourselves (if only on paper), or even repairing this one when it breaks down. But it *is* enough for us to operate them — to 'make them work', as we say. And also to reassure us that there are people on hand who can repair them (if only because they made them in the first place).

'Grasping' also reassures us — when things have evolved over time, and now seem huge, erratic and complicated — that we have a means on hand, a reassuring theory net — which can be thrown over these things, and somehow constrain them, by predicting where and when they are liable to lurch.[32] Game theory is this theory, and statistics its tool. And these are enough to satisfy us. This is a confidence that is based on Humean induction. It's similar, and similarly based, as the belief that the bread I am eating as I write this will nourish — rather than poison me — simply because it always has in the past. And there is nothing wrong with that.

In the modern world, therefore, invisible hands are staple fare. They all employ the same idea. Many forces seem to be in opposition, and yet the result is an equilibrium. The best way to 'grasp' invisible hands is by analogy — by a picture that is held in the mind. If you insert a straw into a spider's web, for instance, and gently push it sideways, the strands behind your straw will tend to drag it back to where it started, like a network of bungees. The farther the straw distorts the web, the harder the web pulls back. And this hap-

---

[31] As Adam Smith supposed, back in the eighteenth century.

[32] We may not ourselves know how a thermostat works, for instance, but we know that it *does* work and that other people know *how* it works, and we are familiar with self-regulators — switch-on-switch-off devices that succeed in running complicated things — and we believe, moreover, that we can muster the computing power — if we had nothing better to do — to actually track every movement that it makes, and explain it in a classical sense.

pens however you move your straw. The spider's web absorbs any distortion, and returns to a stable state.[33]

An ecosystem, as biology regards it, is just like a spider's web, except that an ecosystem has three dimensions, and also time. Time, which stretches backwards to explain evolution, and forwards to predict future hazards, and the adaptions they will provoke.

An ecosystem, moreover, is a paradigm of *modulated conflict*. It is driven by the unfortunate ungodly fact that the lion never does lie down with the lamb but insists on eating him, the fact that most animal life insists upon eating other animal life (or getting free rides, as with parasites). And yet the result is an equilibrium. The relative numbers — of predators and free riders and prey — always form an equilibrium. If one increases at the expense of another, then it will be drawn back by a third, or a multiplicity of others.

Summary

- Why *are* liberals — UNESCO, the academics, the Cultural Heritage Crusade — so intent on bringing antiquity under state control?
- Is it naivety about the *state*, and its real intentions, revanchist politics, or academic disdain for profit?
- Private property is not a modern invention, although post-Enlightenment philosophy gives that impression.
- Private property is actually pre-historic, and serves a biological function.
- But property is also a *cultural institution*, which evolves and adapts as culture changes.
- It may have blundered in the past, but that can easily be corrected.
- The *Tragedy of the Woods* demonstrates the dangers of communal ownership, and of state ownership, and the resourcefulness, the adaptability, of private ownership.

---

[33] Although as the strands are progressively cut it becomes less adept. A stage comes, after many strands have been cut, when your straw will lurch sideways with the least impulse. Thus we have dust bowls and modern agricultural disasters because, in our greed, we have refused to allow any competitors, little realizing that these competitors, like strands in the huge web of the ecosystem, are also a buffer.

...and Has the Market?

These, in the day when heaven was falling,
  The hour when earth's foundations fled,
Followed their mercenary calling,
  And took their wages and are dead.
Their shoulders held the sky suspended,
  They stood, and earth's foundations stay;
What God abandoned, these defended,
  And saved the sum of things for pay.[1]

Another 'invisible hand'...

The free market is another invisible hand mechanism. It is similar to an ecosystem — a place of conflict and compliance, of vice and virtue, of predator and prey — and can be 'grasped' in the same way. It seems to have evolved without a designer on hand, but with many a hand in its development, its gradual trial and error. And it still evolves.

On one level the 'market' is quite simple. It is the place where property is exchanged, where buyers seeking a good or a service — including intellectual property — are brought into contact with sellers offering them for purchase or hire. Where antiquities dealers, say, meet their collectors, and archaeologists meet their publishers. The exchange can be by barter, but usually a currency is employed as a convenience — money, what Marx called the 'universal equivalent'.

The mysterious and maligned 'market forces' which 'compete' together are merely these buyers and sellers, these suppliers and demanders, these consumers and producers — these dupes and mountebanks and con-men, it may sometimes be. Together they create a 'price equilibrium', which can be likened to an enormous three-dimensional web. As with other such invisible hands, a complete 'explanation'

---

[1]   A.E. Houseman, *Epitaph on an Army of Mercenaries.*

would be exhausting, but it is logically possible. And economists assume as much.[2]

Such a *market* does for western economies what the *plan*
was supposed to do for socialist economies, but does it
incomparably better, because it accepts the actual complexity of things.[3] The western market has shown itself, in fact, as
by far the best mechanism for generating wealth and technology. It has given us two hundred years of unremitting
advance, from eighteenth-century steam to the twenty-first
century super-processor. Everybody now admits this, however churlishly. Even the former communist states are sedulously aping the Western models.

They may have other things in mind for the wealth once it
has been created, just as a jockey and his a horse have differ-
ing ideas about direction. Social democrats — socialists in disguise — may see the market as a mongrel energy, and one that
needs taming and refining. They may tolerate it only as a
means to fund their cherished 'social projects'. And argue
whether government should step in and apply the bridle, or
whether this would only be doing, in a blundering way,
what the market does with more delicacy. But they do admit
its superiority. They really have no choice.

...which might just save antiquity

This is the crux. Whether antiquity has come down to us
because of the market, which has always shifted valuable
things to where they've been valued. Or whether bad things
have happened to antiquity *because* of the market — because

---

[2] They have developed a model of 'perfect competition' comprising an infinite
number of producers and consumers, each possessed of perfect knowledge
about what is going on in every part of the economy. In such a 'pure market'
the economy will be perfectly regulated by the price mechanism, which
perfectly responds to market forces, the forces of supply and demand (where
demand is the willingness and ability to buy a particular good or service at a
particular price, and supply is the quantity of goods or services that will be
available for purchase at a particular price). This enables economists to
explain why, in certain cases, the market doesn't get it right — because, in
those cases, the market is 'impure'. Something is not known by somebody, or
nobody is available to supply something or to demand it — to make it, or sell
it, or make too much of it, or sell too little.

[3] It was estimated for example, that the Soviet command economy had
20,000,000 products. No wonder the planners proved so inept. A just
recompense for their hubris.

of private ownership, that's to say – and whether they'd happen again. Whether there is something inevitable about it.

The general accusation seems to be:

- that the market cannot preserve the past, because
- the market only works with *money* value
- and overlooks other values, whereas,
- the past has a *social* value, or serves a 'social need' (like an unpolluted environment, or lighthouses),
- which is to nobody's monetary advantage,
- and, hence, gets ignored.
- Moreover, when the past *does* have a monetary value, it is actually damaged because of it – disrupted, dislodged, or otherwise dissipated.

This seems straightforward as an argument, but it's actually rather elusive. It has many variants. Show one to be groundless, and it promptly morphs into another, and then another, until only a sentiment remains. And sentiments give little ground to reason. Nevertheless, the truth does matter.

We have seen that private property is the ancient norm, and state property the newcomer. Until recently, antiquity has invariably been in private hands, and under private stewardship. There has been no suggestion that the state had any rights of ownership, any first or overriding claim. And hardly any interest. The idea that it has – any or all of these, and with them a duty of care – is a child of nationalism, with UNESCO as its midwife (not to mention the new caste of professional politicians, who have their own agenda).

This is a radical change, and should be seen as such. If antiquity – the tangible remains of the past – are now to be regarded as state property (whatever that means) then arguments have to be made. And they have to be convincing. A gloss riding the crest of sentiment, of easy outrage, is just not good enough.

This chapter considers the arguments for such a *confiscation*, for that is what it amounts to. They mostly turn out to be accusations of past misconduct – of a 'failure of duty' – although that duty had not then been specified, and was barely understood.[4] There is also, as I have intimated, a

---

[4] Which is, ironically again, the excuse offered by the great museums for not giving anything back: 'objects acquired in earlier times must be viewed in the light of different sensitivities and values, reflective of that earlier era. The objects and monumental works that were installed decades and even

latent hostility—even a resentment—of the sort which lingers from discredited ideology, lingers in quaint corners, amongst those who have gotten their dinners from that ideology.

Archaeological sites are a property, which needs protecting

Archaeologists have cited the mayhem—the apparent free-for-all in Egypt, for example, over the last two hundred years—as grounds for bringing antiquity under state control. Antiquity nowadays seems too fragile to be exposed as a resource, where resource means 'consumable'—as firewood can be consumed, or machines can be worn out.

This is clearly an argument for *something*. But I don't think it is an argument against private ownership, because most if not all of the sites concerned were commonly owned. They were isolated from agriculture—the brilliant green of Egypt, hemmed by the sterile desert—either because they were too full of ancient stone to be farmed, or because they were sited above the Nile's annual flooding, and hence without water.

Such land was *res nullius*, subject no man's control, or at least to no man's care. Until the Westerners arrived these areas were largely ignored, except for sporadic quarrying. The Western interest changed everything, however. It gave value to what had been worthless—the sites, or at least their contents—and made of them a resource.[5] In all cases however—'legitimate' quarrying or 'dastardly' plundering—these sites were held in common, something to which the Tragedy of the Woods applied.

The Tragedy of the Archaeological Site *can* be avoided, however:

[1]   **Sites should be placed under one legal person's ownership,[6] clear and simple, and**

[2]   **subject to up-to-date duties of ownership,**

---

centuries ago in museums throughout Europe and America were acquired under conditions that are not comparable with current ones'. Universal Museums Declaration, 2002.

[5]   See page 200.

[6]   Control may be in another's hands than the owner's, of course, but this is not a good idea. Unless one legal person has both ownership and control [3] will prove difficult to ensure.

[3] which includes a 'duty of care' — a duty not to harm,
     degrade, derogate or to destroy,

[4] and also a duty to prevent and rectify lapses by other
     owners.

It does not follow, however, that the owner should be the
state. The argument says nothing about that. Only that there
should be an *unequivocal* owner, who clearly recognizes his
duties of ownership.

It does assume, however, that sites and their artifacts
should be regarded as resources, which can be benignly used
to earn income.[7]

And this includes their *intellectual* property

Part of this resource is their intellectual property. The intellectual property of an archaeological site rests in a juxtaposition — a sort of three-dimensional pattern — of objects to
buildings, and artifacts to the layers in which they are
embedded. This is a code that archaeology can decipher,
when it digs down, level by level, backwards through time,
dating each level by, say, the pottery shards it finds,[8] and
interpreting the other finds — the technology, the utensils,
the remains of feeding — so as to create a picture of the life
that was led there and the way that it was changing. It is a
type of translation, comparable to what a radar operator
does. And like modern radar, it is capable of some sophistica-
tion.

----

[7] One of A.M. Honoré's incidents, *the right to (enjoy) any income arising from
     ownership*. Now the theory which states this — the economic theory of
     property rights — also states that such things always end up where their value
     is greatest. Always have, and always will. And that this is a *good thing*,
     because that's where they will be safest. Sound familiar?

[8] Modern archaeology tends to date all the strata by the pottery shards found
     there, not only because pottery can be easily dated (plus or minus fifty years
     from their last firing) by the famous *thermo-luminescence test*, but because the
     Grand Old Man of archaeology, Flinders Petrie, completed the monumental
     task of placing all Mediterranean styles in order, and tying the sequence to
     datable events. Modern technology has simply made his sequence more
     accurate. Egyptologists have a different time-scale, that of the 'King-Lists', the
     lists of Pharaohs, each of which numbered their reigns by year (Year one, Year
     two etc.,) and which therefore can date any sizeable structure by its
     inscriptions. Apart from a few contentious periods, when rival dynasties
     were fighting it out — which caused us, for example, to be a couple of hundred
     years askew in the Third Intermediate Period — the system has proven
     remarkably accurate.

This intellectual property — this extractable knowledge — only exists as long as the juxtaposition exists. Excavate the site in due process, and you transfer it to living memory.[9] Disturb the site by an undignified scramble, however, and you destroy it. The one suggestion that has everybody aghast is the idea of such sites — once they have been discovered — not being confiscated to save them from being dismembered, hacked to pieces and dispersed God knows where, but actually being allowed to remain in private ownership. But why ever not? The market can easily safeguard them. It only requires an intellectual *property value* which the law recognizes, and the site's owner understands — which especially he understands — and which he squanders if he abandons 'due process'. It follows, therefore, that:

[5]   **'intellectual property' should be recognized as a separate value that attaches to the site.**

[6]   **and should be subject to the same duties-of-care,**

[7]   **and not jeopardized by excavation without 'due process'.**

And if an owner chooses to dismember the site 'on the sly', and sell off the artifacts cheaply — simply ignoring the intellectual property that goes with them? Or even to blackmail the authorities that he might be forced to this, by pressing circumstances? Again, this is unproblematic. As a market device it is well-established. Agricultural policies rely on it. It is just not called blackmail anymore. It is called *subsidizing good praxis*.

More generally, if we accept the history of property (rights and duties) as a history of increasing efficiency, then we must also believe that efficiency — in the morally respectable sense — would also be subject to the law courts, who will eliminate abuses. 'The filter that lets in virtuous users will soon stamp out the vicious ones'.[10]

---

[9]   Although this is also a form of destruction, see pages 147 and 294.

[10]   Alan Ryan, *Property*, 1987.

The problem of peasants

Hassan Fahti, the great Egyptian architect (and Prince Charles's favourite) was commendably clear about this.[11] He had none of our Western squeamishness. In 1949 he was tasked to 'solve' the problem of Qurna, the village that squats — and feeds — upon the ancient necropolis of Luxor's West Bank. His solution was to build them a new village.[12]

Fahti spoke of seeing gold bars in peasants' houses, gold bars which had formerly been antiquities, but melted down for bullion. He commented, in his forgiving way, that the peasants had simply not understood how much more valuable this gold would have been, if it were still in the form of artifacts.[13]

The real problem for antiquity, he gently intimated, was the *problem of peasantry*. Academics and liberals are an urban elite, and they have always despised and feared the country — seen it as subversive — and tried to control it from a distance. Hassan Fahti himself had the unwitting condescension of the city-bred. His family had country estates, but detested them as a breeding ground for vermin and flies. Fahti himself was not allowed — or never inclined — to visit the country until he was twenty-seven!

And the half of the world who were peasants? They continued their age-old struggle against their city-bred rulers, whom they failed to understand (or understood only too well). Rights and duties had no meaning for the peasants — as Fahti soon grasped, once he finally met them — unless they could be 'cashed in' for something more useful, like food or animals, or the money to buy such things. His project failed, of course, because the villagers foresaw their loss of income. Academics, he almost suggested, should accept the peasants' predicament (or abandon their salaries and try it out for themselves). They should certainly abandon their suspicion, their condescension, and stop treating peasants like backward children — amusing enough, as Dr Johnson regarded

---

[11] *A Tale of Two Villages*, 1969, essential reading for all who would honestly understand the peasantry — the necessity of their 'enlistment' for archaeology — as well as the 'oriental' corruption of administration.

[12] He failed, of course, as all twentieth-century attempts against the peasantry have failed unless conducted with Stalin's ruthlessness.

[13] As soon as they did realize it (he might have added), they promptly turned it back into antiquities (which they sold to gullible collectors.)

dogs who could walk on two legs — but hardly worth taking seriously.

The moral is simple. The fate of much of the world's antiquity is in the hands of the peasantry. They must be educated — not re-educated, which is merely state bullying, and will have the opposite effect — and made to understand intellectual property and the value of archaeological sites. The peasant must become the *ally* of the city-bred archaeologist, and not his bugbear.

It is of little use, it follows, to blame collectors for 'misleading' or 'corrupting' the poor and childlike peasantry, as if they were colonial subjects, who know not what they do, poor things. The peasants understand condescension very well, and they resent it. Almost as much as they resent government. And it is no use archaeologists being charmed by the sight of cheerful native workers, hauling baskets of earth all day for a pittance, and then wonder at them pocketing the odd artifact at sunset — and doubling their income — or doing much much worse.

JOURNAL: 14th October 1993, Cairo

Cairo is buzzing with the latest story. The workers at the Polish Expedition's site have discovered a statue—six foot long and made of Aswan granite—which they managed to conceal from the Polish archaeologists and overseers. Then, after dark, they all came back, dug it up and rolled it out of the designated area, and reburied it for themselves.

The peasant asks why should 'they' — these foreign unbelievers and city-bred bullies — take away our Gifts from God? And that is a question that needs to be squared, the whole world over.

Archaeology must also pay

Archaeologists will not like this, however. Until now they have been going to distant places, seeking something — Champollion's 'un-hoped for knowledge'[14] — which they have regarded as free, or free-for-them. Archaeologists have taken this *knowledge* into their possession. They have made it their property in the classic Lockean sense (by mixing their labour with something that is *res nullius*). And thereafter, it

---

[14] Perhaps the most famous phrase of modern archaeology, spoken by the (part) decipherer of hieroglyphics.

has to be said, they have used it as a commodity. And destroyed the sites in the process.[15]

I say again: the archaeologist's excavation will have destroyed the site — more effectively than the pathologist destroys the corpse (and without the benefit of the mortician's cosmetic skills). Directly, because digging down through the layers destroys each layer in turn, and leaves it somewhere as a heap of 'spoil' (interesting choice of word) — and indirectly, because a site shorn of its protective soil and exposed to the elements will rapidly deteriorate.

The proof that they have taken something away is that, after a site has been properly excavated, it has no further value. No more value, say, than an unclaimed corpse after its first autopsy, where a second opinion may be called for. The dissected organs can be bottled, and displayed for public edification (or for private reference). And the dismembered corpse? That will be wrapped in plastic, and shoved back into the freezer. This preserves a semblance of dignity — at least while somebody pays for the electricity. But who pays for a dismembered site?[16]

And the proof that this something is being treated as a commodity — in the classic Marxist sense — is that it is then exchanged, or converted, into other currencies — into publications, academic salaries and tenure, into prestige and advancement and honours. In short, it's been merchandized.

But, and this is the rub — at least it will be, for the countries of origin, once they realize what has been going on — *archaeologists have paid nothing for it.* This knowledge is not God's Gift, theirs simply because only they can make use of it. I might have minerals on my land, for example, which are useful — as commodities, that is to say — only after they have been processed. But that's no reason for me to give them

---

[15] In formal terms, the argument is as follows:
  • Knowledge is (being treated as) a commodity
  • Archaeological sites contain knowledge, (intellectual property)
  • without which they are diminished.
  • Archaeologists unearth this knowledge, this intellectual property
  • which they take into their possession, in the strict Lockean sense
  • and then merchandize it, in the strict Marxian/Liberal sense

[16] The conventional piety has archaeologists 'covering up the site after their work... Normal archaeological practice would mean that we would preserve the site by covering it over again for future archaeologists to excavate and examine'. Chris Thomas, *Spitalfields Development Excavation.* But this is a polite fiction, and as much an admission of a very careless past.

away free, just because I cannot process them myself. I can sell them in various ways; by selling licenses to extract, for example, or by taking commission.

The Hobbit Man precedent

This argument will bite. Make no doubt about that. The recent case of 'Hobbit Man' — the skeleton of an apparently diminutive *homo* species — is just the first of many. If the Australian anthropologists who discovered this skeleton had been able to exploit their discovery — and if it had turned out to be an 'new' species — they would have been made for life. Conferences, appointments, honour, fame and wealth. All would have been theirs.

But there was a fly in the ointment. The 'competent authority' — the Indonesian with responsibility for such things — promptly confiscated their find. More than that, he had their license revoked. The anthropologists were outraged. They cited the loss of knowledge to mankind. They waxed indignant. They called the Indonesian a thief.

Strictly speaking, however, *they* would have been the thieves. By the UNESCO Convention, to which Australia is a signatory, those bones were the 'cultural property' of Indonesia, and their removal would have been 'illicit'.[17] Similarly, any use of those bones — any publication, any self-serving publicity, that is to say — would be an exploitation of Indonesian intellectual property.

That is what the Indonesian official understood. So will his *confrères*, the whole world over. And so will Zahi Hawass in Egypt.[18]

And finally, the revulsion about 'resource'

I suspect this is at the heart of the matter. Its heart, if not its head. Readers may simply balk at regarding antiquity — or high art generally — as a resource. Academic archaeologists certainly do. And I used to myself. As a young academic I remember being impressed by Jonathan-the-Restorer talking to Dennis Hopper's Ripley in *The American Friend*, and delivering the crushing line 'I just don't like people who sell art for

---

[17] Assuming that Indonesia has the relevant laws in place. But, given the confusion of international law, the Australians should have assumed as much.

[18] Who shows a sophisticate's grasp of intellectual property — and of its theatre.

money'. I was so impressed, in fact, that I became a restorer on the strength of it. I have to thank that impulse for getting me close to antiquities but, looking back, after nearly thirty years — of restoring, of collecting, of dealing with other dealers and collectors and museum curators and Egyptians, of beauty and humbug and skullduggery — I blush at my naiveté. And I blush for my former colleagues.

For I am sure that the real impulse behind the Cultural Heritage Crusade is just such a feeling, a vague and jejune revulsion that antiquities should ever be defiled by filthy lucre. And a consequent outrage when it is suggested that this is exactly what the countries of origin had in mind.

Readers may also remember my unease at 'vulgar' utilitarianism, the idea that, as a matter of brute fact, when times are hard and people are struggling, only those things that can be exchanged, that have exchange value, that can be used as a commodity — in short, as Mr. Micawber would say, *can be sold* — will be attended to. The rest will be ignored and go to the wall.

Now I don't like utilitarianism, any more than I like hammers on shiny BMWs — or abolishing entire systems because of the occasional glitch. I find utilitarianism fickle, crude and calmly capable of horrors — of sacrificing (relatively) blameless individuals for the 'greater good'. I should know, for I was sacrificed myself.

And utilitarianism has very little to say about ownership, except that in the interests of efficiency and the 'greater good' every object ought to be owned, clearly owned, and in each case by a legal person. That is, that every object is a commodity, where commodity is used in the correct Marxian sense (the correct anybody's common-sense, as a matter of fact) as something which can be exchanged for money, for Marx's 'universal equivalent'.

At one level, however, *vulgar utilitarianism* says it all. For this is the world we live in, and we cannot afford to be prim about it — at least not yet. We have to get antiquity through to the future, and any means will suffice. It's at another level, however, that the idea shows us something else that's wrong about our world. For this fashionable distaste is actually very interesting. It tries to be morally superb — but its logic is decidedly shaky. In fact, it's damn hard to make any sense of it.

Is it being suggested that antiquities should be sold for *less* than was paid for them, because they 'depreciate' as cars do? But antiquities do not wear out. That is the whole point. If anything, they resemble classic cars, which 'appreciate' in value.

Is this *appreciation* the problem — the being aware of it, and deliberately making use of it? If so, then the objection is really to dealers. But dealers are merely brokers, providing a high-risk service. And like any broker — whether insurance salesmen, realtors or car-dealers — they are only human, with human virtues and human vice. As such they reflect their culture.[19] We get the dealers we deserve, just as we get the policemen. To improve the standard of dealers — as I have been at pains to explain — we must improve our concept of property.

Is it a resentment that art should be judged by money? That the market — the collective of buyers — should be judging what is better and what is best, merely by their willingness to pay more or less for it? But who is to do the job better? The consensus of curators, and of 'art experts'? But they are notoriously fickle.[20]

Or is the objection to *profit*? But it is difficult to see how that can be avoided. Antiquities cannot be sold for the same as their purchase price, because their owner has incurred costs — for storage, conservation, insurance and so on — and because the currency is always depreciating. All these have to recompensed. And then there's the increase he would have made if he had invested his money elsewhere.[21] Is he to

---

[19] See *The wickedness of dealers* in the Appendix.

[20] And their tailoring has always been decidedly imperial. The Tate, for example, bought no impressionists at all until they changed curators in 1939 — because they despised the paintings as ephemeral — and none afterwards, because they lacked the funding, and the paintings were no longer to be had as bargains. As a result our 'national collection' is bereft compared, say, to the Americans. What impressionists we do have are all in private hands, and reflect the genius of the despised *market*. And now that the Tate has money, it is squandering it on true ephemera, that the market ignores.

[21] Adam Smith's famous argument for including profit as a 'legitimate portion' of the price — that not including it would be effectively to force a loss on the owner who, had he known of this loss, would have foregone the purchase in the first place — and chosen to do something else with his money, something that *would* have given him increase. The argument replaces the idea of

lose by his stewardship of antiquities? By the care he has lavished on them? Be punished for it, rather than recompensed?

Or, lastly, is the objection to 'greed', which is assumed to go hand-in-hand with profit?. But this is facile. And the correct response is 'so what?' Greed does not matter. Invisible hand mechanisms pay no attention to greed. Antiquity is not 'defiled' by contact with greed. And if it is, then it is likewise contaminated by priggishness and ambition, by spite and the 'ringing' of knowledge—none of which are unknown to academics.

Put like this, the argument—and the revulsion against resource that lies beneath it—becomes a Western indulgence, because it assumes a regime of Western-style care, of Western museums and Western conservators, and the Western sentiments they rely on. And that will only ever apply if the West dominates the poor world, and imposes its own values. But colonialism is quite out of fashion, and the non-Western world is increasingly, well, anti-Western.

The important question remains. Who will ensure this duty of care, and who can enforce it, when things get difficult? And will anybody bother, unless they have the advantages that the rights confer—specifically, the owner's right to derive an income?

Summary

- The market is an *invisible hand mechanism*, which until recently has been 'responsible' for antiquity,
- but is now being blamed for damage to archaeological sites.
- To rectify this—and prevent future damage—is quite simple. The *intellectual property* that attaches to a site must be clearly understood, especially by the peasantry.
- It follows that private ownership is at least as efficient — if not more so—than any other.
- The revulsion against the market is, therefore, a simple matter of sociology.

profit-as-greed with *profit-as-commonsense* (and saves pious liberals from the guilt of selling their houses at a vast profit.)

CHAPTER 12

The Problem of Islam

Modern Islam, assertive and self-confident Islam, presents a particular problem, both for antiquity itself — the visible or yet-to-be-discovered relics of the past — and for archaeology, the profession that studies them. This is an industry that needs to *publish*, and therefore needs access to new sites. Many of these sites are on Islamic territory. The problems about this are easy to state, but that's just the easy part.

Islam imposed a cultural caesura...

'Islam destroys all that preceded it.' *Hadith*[1]

When Mohammed and his splendid generals invaded the Middle East, snaffling up the punch-drunk empires of Byzantium and Sassania — the remnants of Greek culture and the Persian — and pushing east to India and west to the Atlantic, they imposed a brutal caesura on every culture they overran. Whether these cultures converted freely, or were compelled at sword-point, hardly matters. Islam cut their link with the past, with paganism and polytheism. It follows that *they cannot now claim any continuity with that past*. They cannot claim it as a cultural heritage. Not as Moslems, anyway.

Secular governments can make the claim, of course, but only as infidels or apostates. And that puts them on a collision course with modern Islam. This seems fraught, but it is actually very simple. From the beginning Mohammed understood the Muslim faith as 'socio-political' in the modern sense. His 'national mission' was to purify and restore the monotheistic faith that had existed since antiquity. And

---

[1] The *Hadith* — also known as the *Sunna* (literally, the 'beaten path', in our context 'custom' or 'usual way of action') — are the orally recorded sayings of the Prophet and his companions, and a record of their customs. A vast number survived from the early period, and were codified by ninth-century scholars into six orthodox collections, the *Sahih* ('authentic'). They form the second sacred text of Islam, and the *second pillar of Islamic law*.

the *True Faith* does not distinguish between politics and religion. To adapt Clausewitz, the new Islamo-puritans regard politics (and quite evidently warfare) as a continuation of religion by other means. But then Islam has always been a fighting faith.

The pre-Islamic period in the Middle East is now referred to as the *jahiliyyah*, the 'time of ignorance'. It is seen as a spiritual corruption, specifically because it was polytheistic. Mohammed's teaching was simple, that '*God is one God, and has taken no child*' (*Sura* 21, 25-26).[2] It is notable that although pre-Islamic Arabs produced several great and original cultures—the Nabateans,[3] for instance, based at Petra and Bosra—they have been almost completely ignored. Their art has been overlooked, and they are 'barely present, if not willfully obliterated, in the collective memory of traditional Islam'.[4] The point is important. These powerful cultures have been dismissed from Islamic memory, simply because they were polytheistic.

It seems that Mohammed, and hence Islam, had especially clear ideas about pre-Islamic art, and its possible malign effects upon the believer. The early art of Islam may have continued that of Byzantine and Persia—it could hardly have done otherwise—but gradually it was reined in. Within a short time the major arts of sculpture and painting simply disappeared, and the concept of the artist as a creator of images was replaced by that of the artisan, the creator of patterns and decorative surfaces. There was a clear reason for this, as we shall see (and for the occasional exceptions, and the tensions they created).

...and a Middle East redesigned...

The second problem is one of simple geography, that the modern Middle East was invented by ourselves. The nine-

---

[2] And Mohammed's immediate adversary was therefore Arabian polytheism, in particular the *Shirk*, the idea that the one God might tolerate subsidiary gods, as if they were his children—the pre-Islamic divinities of Mecca—Uzza, Lat and Manat (sun, moon and evening star)—sometimes described as the 'daughters of Allah'.

[3] The Nabateans of Petra (fourth century BC to first century AD) of Jordan were probably the strongest Arab culture, and much influenced by Greece. They derived great prosperity from the silk route to China, especially after their annexation by Rome in 106BC.

[4] Oleg Grabar, *Islam, Art and Architecture*, 2004.

teenth-century powers were famously worried about the Ottoman Empire, and especially the Levant. What concerned them was its impending demise, and the power vacuum it would leave. We British had especial cause for concern, as the Suez canal formed our strategic link to India.

The Divine Porte was clearly moribund. It was fast losing its periphery. Bulgaria declared independence in 1797, Serbia gained it in 1815, Greece in 1830 (largely through our agency), Egypt in 1804 (ditto), and Romania in 1829. As for the heartlands—Syria, Lebanon, Iraq, Palestine and Persia—they were still nominally Ottoman, but increasingly subject to a power struggle for influence between Britain and France.

Our influence was indeed extensive. Regarding Islam as an antiquated religion—an obsolete and obstructive social system which stood in the way of progress—we urged modernization based on the nation state, its discipline and its modern efficiency. We encouraged cabinet government. We imposed free-trade, and attempted to limit Islamic law (Sharia) by centralizing and secularizing justice.

This worked, but only to an extent. The *Salafiya* movement—those very same elites chosen by ourselves as vanguards of the new order, and trained in our own countries— were keen enough about European administration and the European military,[5] but less convinced about secularism. They still saw Islam as the keystone of their future, their 'cultural identity' against the West.

In short, we gave these former Ottoman colonies the idea of a future, part of which was independence, of being nations in their own right. This had to count as an achievement. But we also showed them how to create a national identity through Islam. And that was less fortuitous. The *Salafiya* (the 'forefathers') were not just spiritual fathers to modern Islam, therefore, but also—in their desire to reintroduce Sharia law—they were godfathers to 'fundamentalism'.[6]

---

[5]   The embarrassment of coming up against disciplined European infantry— when Napoleon invaded Egypt in 1798, and contemptuously dealt with the Mamelukes—had bitten deep.

[6]   As early as 1885, the 'Mahdi's' rebellion in Sudan gave augur for the future. Even more successful was the strictly puritanical movement of the *Wahhabis* in the Arabian peninsular, in whose name the al-Saud family became the dominant power.

The Great War was the death knell for the Ottoman empire. Quite simply, Turkey and her newly 'Europeanized' army chose the wrong side, and paid the price. Her remaining territories were stripped, and mandated to Britain and France.[7] The French were allocated Syria and Lebanon, whilst Britain had Palestine and Mesopotamia (including the prospective Israel). This was not perhaps the wisest solution, given the strained relations between France and Britain.[8]

The post-war Arab National Congress — one of the post-dated cheques of the war effort — chose Prince Faisal, son of Sharif Hussein of Mecca, to become king of a united Syria, Lebanon and Transjordan. He was promptly expelled by the French, who cited their mandate. The British as promptly made him king of Iraq, and thereby founded the Hashemite dynasty. The British also made Abdullah, his brother, king of Transjordan,[9] establishing the Hashemite dynasty in Jordan, which still persists.

The Kingdom of Saudi Arabia was founded in 1932 — with explicit British support — after ibn Saud had expelled Sharif Hussein, the father of these Hashemite princes. In Persia, the Pahlavi dynasty was founded in 1925 when Reza Khan overthrew the Kajars and declared himself Shah. But again, only on British sufferance. And as for Egypt, Britain responded to the rioting of 1919 by granting nominal independence under British protection in 1922, and full independence in 1936. But

[7] Nominally by the League of Nations, but actually by the Sykes-Picot Agreement of 1916, by which the two powers had secretly agreed to a post-war division of spoils.

[8] France had suffered worst by the Great War, which had fatally exposed her as a non-industrial and shrinking state. In order to rectify this, she toyed with the idea of a Greater France, Poincare's country of 100 million — *la mère patrie* bolstered by *France d'outre-mère*. Such a grandiose scheme needed money, and they looked to the Mosul oilfields of Syria. But after the scramble, France was left with the Lebanon and western Syria — no oil, but a host of voracious Arab nationalists, the *Salafiya*, and a full-scale rebellion on her hands, which she put down at enormous military expense in 1925. And this brought her into conflict with the supremely confident naval power of Britain.

[9] Palestine and Jordan combined. At a certain point Israel was to be hived off, leaving the present Kingdom of Jordan. Abdullah accepted a future Jewish state as his part of the bargain, and also agreed to house its displaced Palestinians. He eventually abrogated the agreement — expelling the Palestinians for bad behaviour — but only after the zionists had also transgressed, by wildly exceeding their allocation of Jewish immigrants. Abdullah was eventually assassinated by a Muslim fanatic for his pains. But this, the manufactured turmoil of the Middle East, is only marginal to this book.

still retained a powerful economic and military presence to safeguard the Suez canal. Effectively, Britain still ran the country.

In summary, the entire Middle East, its structure of states, its boundaries and many of its present problems, are a British invention, or at least a British exercise in pursuit of greater security for her own empire, the lion's share of trade with countries concerned — and, increasingly, their oil — and security for the Suez canal. Of the present Middle Eastern nations, only Turkey existed (in anything like its present form) before 1914.[10]

...according to an imposed and alien concept...

This might not have mattered, so very much, if these modern states had borne any resemblance to ancient formations — which they didn't, except for Egypt, and possibly Persia/ Iran — or to any division the Arabs themselves would have chosen. Again, they didn't: witness the Arabs' desire to create a single entity from Syria, Lebanon, Jordan and Palestine — the equivalent of ancient Phoenicia or the medieval Sham.[11]

But there is a third problem. It is arguable, to put it mildly, whether Islam understands the western concept of *nation*, that of a territory and people somehow combined, to which the people owe their loyalty — their first loyalty — as well as their obedience. It is arguable that, for believers, the very idea of the *nation state* is an imposition;[12] whether Arab Moslems even now consider themselves citizens of this or that state, rather than subjects of this or that school of Islamic law;

[10] Most gained their present independence after WW2: Syria and Lebanon (from France) in 1945; TransJordan and Syria (from Britain) in 1946; Libya (from Italy) in 1947; Israel (effectively from Britain) in 1948; Egypt (from de facto British control) in 1952; Morocco and Tunisia (from France) in 1956-57; Iraq by coup in 1958; Algeria (from France) in 1962; Yemen by coup in 1962 (after independence from Britain).

[11] A territory that covered present-day Palestine, Israel, Lebanon and south-east Turkey.

[12] Thus Dr. Siddiqui, Director of the London Muslim Institute: 'we aim to eliminate all authority other than Allah and his Prophet; to eliminate nationalism in all its shapes and forms, in particular the nation-state; to unite all Islamic movements into a single global Islamic movement to establish an Islamic State; to re-establish a dominant and global Islamic civilization'. Nationalism and the nation-state (and democracy) represent *kufr*, literally *infidelity* but equivalent in the modern context to atheism. Quite clear and unambiguous, it seems to me.

whether state comes before faith, and can be held separate from it; whether, in short, any such entity exists which has any business claiming any such thing as a *cultural heritage*. The Egyptian peasantry, it is well known, resent their regime as 'Pharaonic', and their resentment has many levels.

Of course, Moslems since the Prophet have resented a series of 'oriental despotisms', of which the Ottoman Turks were merely the last. But they've also been — and far more importantly — subject to Sharia law, that is, to the *Madhab* embedded in the state. Islam regards itself, after all, as 'God's Law on Earth', a law both detailed and extremely practicable,[13] and administered on God's behalf by religious judges, the *Qadi*, who have traditionally tried to suppress 'reprehensible un-Islamic innovation' — anything that is unauthorized by the Prophet.[14]

...which is both secular and vulnerable

Since the nineteenth century, however, 'modernization' has been trying to break this authority — to sever the link between religion and the state — by limiting Sharia law to local or family matters. The conservative countries, such as Jordan and the Gulf states, have been hesitant about the process, and the traditionalists — Saudi Arabia, Libya and the Sudan — have left Sharia entrenched. But the mainly secular states, such as Turkey, Egypt, Tunisia, Algeria, and the Lebanon, have overhauled their education and military training, and introduced European-style state courts, administering a European-style codified law.

Since the War, Egypt has generally set the pace. Her charismatic leader, Gamal abd El Nasser, was regarded in the Arab

---

[13] The *Koran* (*al-Qur'an* from *Umm al-kitab*, 'the Mother of the Book') creates a 'community code', which extends to such mundane areas as the payment of dues and the giving of alms (Suras 6 and 58), the marriage contract (Suras 60:10-13 and 33:50-52) and divorce (Sura 65), the guardianship of orphaned children (Sura 4), inheritance and family law, ritual acts and physical punishments, the *hadd*, such as lashing, stoning and the amputation of hands (Sura 5:33-40), and so on.

[14] *Bida*, defined by the 17th Turkish scholar, Katib Celebi, as: 'any new development in matters sacred or mundane appearing during or after the 2nd age; that is, anything which did not exist in the time of the Prophet (on him be the peace and the blessing of God) and his noble companions, and of which there is no trace in any of the three categories of the *Sunna* [the *Koran* and the *Hadith*] and concerning which there is no tradition'. Such scholars regularly produced treatises — *Hisba* — which made great play with this notion of *Bida*.

world — especially by himself — as a hero of the new Arab
self-confidence.[15] In 1956 he suppressed the Moslem Brotherhood,[16] and imposed a form of secular state socialism, based
upon his military regime. After the infamous 'Bandung conference' of 1959, he assiduously played off the USA against
the USSR under the aegis off 'non-alignment', and made
himself leader of the Arab pack against Israel.[17]

These new Pan-Arabist states dallied with state plans and
collectivism, the whole socialist bag of tricks. But their series
of defeats against Israel discredited Arab socialism, and
made the Arabs feel their impotence. During the seventies,
therefore, Egypt, Syria and Iraq quietly renounced their
socialist principles, whilst carefully retaining the Leninist
controls that went with them (Nasser had always admitted
'the usefulness of a little terror').

What has been replacing socialism is a resurgent Islamism,
uniformly hostile to the West — and anything that the West is
interested in. Until now the Islamic movements — the Muslim Brotherhood in Egypt and Syria, say — had been kept
away from political power. They demanded a radicalization
of political Islam in its struggle against the modern world —
against secularism, liberalism and religious freedom — and
they generated a deal of energy from the discontent and
demographic problems of many Islamic countries. But they
had been kept firmly under the thumb.

---

[15] His own people were not quite so convinced, despite his perfection of
European-style nationalistic propaganda. The damning opinion of Nasser in
the Egyptian countryside has always been 'half-and-half', with a
characteristic gesture of the hand. His pharaonic pretensions have
particularly irked the pious, and done much to alienate the country, see page
16.

[16] Founded in 1928 by Hassan al Banna. Its aim was to revitalize a corrupt faith,
and provide the faithful with a political voice. A party of Islam, it sought an
Islamic government that would be an alternative to both socialism and
capitalism, that would finally liberate Egypt from foreign control, and
eventually liberate and unify all Islamic peoples. It spread into Jordan, Sudan
and Syria, where it gave military training for *jihad*. The Brotherhood was
essentially a movement to free themselves from the west, from colonial
control and influence. It remained on the fringes, however.

[17] It's revealing, and unfortunate, that President Nasser — who so relentlessly
espoused Egypt's *Pharaonic heritage* — should have rejected the Pharaohs'
closest and most reliable allies and dependants throughout antiquity — the
Jews of Palestine. Such a blatant disregard for the wishes of his vaunted
'ancestors' reveals his true modernity — and the *meretrice* of his agenda.

But in 1979 the peacock throne fell, and the Persian Shias established the first Islamic republic of modern times, the first Islamic theocracy. Until now, Islamic 'fundamentalism' had been regarded with condescension by western theorists. It may have been our fault for interfering – or so the Liberals claim – but it was airily dismissed.[18] But after Iran, no Arab state was immune. The Lebanon, the Sudan and Afghanistan have been in turmoil, and Egypt is divided into two mutually-suspicious factions, the secular westernized cities of Alexandria and Cairo, and the puritanical rural areas (the majority of southern Egypt is now under curfew).

Nationalism may have a limited life expectancy in the Middle East, where a panoply of dictatorial regimes now exist ambiguously amongst Sharia law, increasingly nervous about the new puritanism.[19] Most are forced to tread a careful path between Islam – keeping the way of life, and their identity as against the West – and retaining access to the West's technology. More hazardous a task than is commonly realized, as Saddam recently discovered to his cost,[20] and Mubarak and his secular regime might also discover.[21]

---

[18] 'Religious fundamentalism is not a viable project...merely a symptom of the difficult adjustment that modernization requires'. It is not a 'viable project', because it is 'implicitly totalitarian, laying down principles for political organization that are by definition absolute and unquestionable.' Heywood, *Political Ideologies*, 1998.

[19] Islamo-fascism, as it is increasingly called, has become 'a kind of stripped down religion that travels light and fast.'(Garvey, *Fundamentalism and the State*, 1993), and it shares a significant advantage with Bolshevism. Both employ the whole of the human psyche, the parts that hate as well as the rest, whereas Christianity restricts itself – officially, at least – to the benign aspects. And there are a lot of very active haters in *Wahhabi*, as we have been discovering to our cost.

[20] Saddam was slow to grasp the political potential of Islamic fundamentalism. At first Ba'athism was based on Nasser's pan-Arabic nationalism and socialism. When he attacked Iran in 1980 he declared war on fundamentalism, but then on the eve of the Gulf war he embraced Islamic principles, and declared *jihad* between unbelievers and the faithful, putting 'God is great' on the Islamic flag. It didn't seem to work, however, apart from annoying the Arab members of the coalition.

[21] According to Sayyid Qut'b, Egypt's secular-nationalist government is presiding over *jahiliyyah*, and is therefore guilty of apostasy from Islam, punishable by death. This justified the assassination of Nasser's successor, Anwar Sadat, in 1981, and would justify the present government's overthrow. President Mubarak's problem is, therefore, increasingly that of the deposed Shah of Iran, of having to rely upon an army conscripted from the peasantry, who are increasingly hostile to Mubarak's own stance. There

The sacred texts have primacy...

It is worth stressing that neither the Koran nor the Hadith are *negotiable* in the sense that modern Christian scholarship regards the Bible as negotiable, as a potpourri of historical record, parable, allegory and metaphor (and apocrypha) written by many hands, from which parts may be chosen or excluded as fashions demand. For the Muslim believer the Koran is quite simply the Word of God. It was recorded in heaven at the beginning of time, and eventually dictated to Mohammed by the Angel Gabriel, word by faultless word. Only its original un-altered and un-translated version is authoritative. There are no King James' or Good News or Happy-clappy versions of the Koran. There cannot be.

There can be debates, with different slants being put on a particular quotation—and the Hadith certainly allows for manoeuverability—but apologists cannot disregard inconvenient parts, if they fall foul of political correctness. And nor can they argue that such parts—the diatribes against Judaism and Christianity, say, or the orders to destroy 'idols'— were influenced by events, such as Muhammad's exasperation with the Jews of Medina (because they wouldn't convert), or his aesthetic distaste for Arab polytheism and pagan images cluttering up the Kaaba.

For the Moslem this is to put cart before horse. As the Koran dates from the beginning of time, so the relevant passages predated such events. It follows that these events must have been engineered by God—or foreseen by God, which amounts to much the same—as opportune illustrations for the texts. And not the other way round.

And for the Moslem, the first of the five pillars of the faith is his public profession of faith—the *Shahada* ('confirmation')—his saying aloud before witnesses, with serious intent, 'there is no God but God, and Muhammad is his messenger' . There can be no going back on the Shahada.[22] As the Koran is the word of God dictated infallibly to his messenger Muhammad, it follows that to doubt the Koran—to suggest

---

may come a time when he cannot rely on them to fire on their own.

    Modern Islamists are heavily influenced by Qut'b, a member of Egypt's Muslim Brotherhood, and mentor to Al-Queda's present leader Ayman al-Zawahiri. Qut'b was arrested by Colonel Nasser in 1954, tortured, and eventually executed in 1966.

[22] As Salman Rushdie might have noted, and saved the British taxpayer a considerable expense.

that it is Muhammad's word and not God's, or that it was in any way affected by contemporaneous events — is *apostasy*, and punishable by death. All very straightforward.

...but can be manipulated

The functional weakness of Islam, however — as Dostoevsky's Grand Inquisitor would have realized — is that it has no clergy, and hence no imposed orthodoxy, no central control, neither Pope nor conclave of bishops. It is vulnerable to fire-brands, to charismatic preachers, and those intent upon mischief, especially when the textual references are unclear, and allow them the scope.

The opportunity arises because of Sharia law — because of its peculiar structure, that is to say. Because there is not just one Islamic law, one Sharia, but five separate schools, four of which are Sunni.[23] Each school interprets the canonical texts differently, and has very different ideas about the proper conduct of human life. They form a spectrum.[24] Each Muslim country tends to abide by a particular school — but they are

[23] The *Madhabib* were formalized in the Abbasid period (after 750AD), during Islam's period of internal 'stabilization', which corresponded to the Christian third century, and its numerous councils. The schools are the *Hanafi*, the *Maliki*, the *Shafii*, the *Hanbali*, and the Shiite *Jafari*.

[24] At one end is the Hanafi school — which has many adherents — flexible and comparatively liberal, and encouraging of *Ra'i* (personal evaluation), and reason. At the other end is Hanbali, the most conservative school, rigorous and uncompromising in its traditionalism and piety, and the most opposed to rationalism, for which read 'thinking things through' or 'compromise' in the Western sense. Because of its rigidity Hanbali has never been widespread, but has always backed puritanical reform — for instance the Wahhabi movement in Saudi Arabia — as have the extremist movements of Shia, the *ghaliya*, ('those who exaggerate').

The Shiite school of legal interpretation — the Jafari — is different again, because it 'keeps open the gate of Ijtihad' ('utmost effort'), which the Sunni schools slammed shut in the twelfth century, and have kept firmly bolted ever since. This means, in our terms, that Shiite legal scholars feel a duty of independent reasoning, rather as Protestantism placed the onus on individual men to discover the truth for themselves, and then to stand by it. Because of this Shiite scholars are known as the *mujtahid* (those who 'struggle with themselves'). The effect of this is important. In simple terms, 'keeping open the Gate of Ijtihad' enables Islam to adapt itself to the modern world. Closing the gate is closing out the modern world.

All the more ironic then that the first Islamic theocracy was established by the the only Islamic faction with an effective clergy — the 'Twelvers' of Shia, the established school in Iran since 1501. Legal scholars in Iran (mullahs — from 'maula', meaning lord or master) occupy a special position because they can exercise Ijtihad. There are several ranks, of which ayatollahs (from *ayatu'Allah* — 'sign of God') are the highest, and considered 'authorities for

not congruent with modern national borders. And dissatisfied Muslims can always appeal to another school, or combine their decisions.

In the West we regard the law as a *boundary*. It delineates an area within which we are free to move, more or less as we wish. Our movements may be slowed or diverted by morality or custom. But of Moses' ten commandments, only three are still enforced by law.[25] The others are either decriminalized,[26] or matters of moral suasion.

In Sharia, however, the provisions of the law are still presented as God's commandments. Transgression, therefore, is not just a matter of breaching decorum or byelaw, but an offence against the divine order of creation. And the penalties can be severe, both in this life and the hereafter.

On one hand, therefore, Sharia is both more powerful and more pervasive than anything we can conceive, unless we put ourselves in the mind-frame of our own fourteenth century. On the other hand it has no centralized control. Herein is its weakness. It has proven as easy to manipulate—by those that have evil in mind—as our own working-class movements were to Bolshevik agitators.

Since Islam has no clergy, Muslims must turn to jurist-scholars (*faqih* or imams) for their guidance. For most problems the two written 'roots of the law' (the *usul*) are sufficient. Either the Koran or the Hadith will provide an answer, without equivocation.

But when there is a real problem the third 'root' is called into play; the *ra'i* (understanding) of these individual scholars.[27] And here lies the hazard. The process gives enormous power to individual imams or preachers (*khateeb*), who are unrestrained by any higher authority, and can easily become tyrannical (as did Khomeini). They attract adherents by their

---

imitation'. A grand ayatollah has the power and the infallibility of a medieval pope. Oh dear.

[25] Numbers 6, 8 and 9—murder, theft and perjury.

[26] For example numbers 3 and 4—blasphemy and Sabbath inaction.

[27] The believer with the problem, the community—or even a government—will now appoint a *faqih* to deliver an expert legal opinion, a *fatwa*. The faqih's task is to draw analogies (*oiyas*) between earlier cases and the present, and to conform the laws into a sort of harmony with reason, and with the divine order of nature. Whoever commissions this opinion—or is on its receiving end—must then exercise 'imitation' (*taqlid*). In simple terms, they must comply with the judgment, and if they do so in good faith, they will not be held responsible for the consequences, however horrendous.

charisma and radicalism, by what Islam calls their 'dynamic interpretations' of the texts — and the West would call their 'personal agendas'. And these modern imams are not restricted to their Friday sermons, and to those who can attend their mosques. They have Western technology at their disposal. Through websites and mass media, any given imam or khateeb can sway a vast audience.

But the really lethal tenet is the fourth 'root' of Sharia. This is the *ijha*, the 'consensus' of scholars, which is deemed infallible on the assumption that God may allow one mind to go astray, but not an entire community:

> 'My community will never agree upon an error.' *Hadith*

Basically, therefore, if the imams all plump for the same opinion, however outrageous, then it is by definition infallible, because vouchsafed by God. If the imams claim in synchrony that the *umma*, (the collective population of Islam) has been attacked by Israel, by the US and its allies, and that this justifies war, then that's what goes. And if Middle-Eastern dictators and their secular regimes are denounced as jahiliyyah, they become apostates from Islam, and their own nationals can put them to death.

Islam's dubiety about the living image...

All this being the case, it behoves us to inquire just how Islam and its imans — especially its imams — feel about antiquity. It is generally assumed that Islam has no figurative art, and will tolerate none. This is actually a simplification. There has been no major painting or sculpture, that much is clear. But there has been a healthy tradition of miniatures, comparable to the Western tradition. And it seems that early 'desert palaces' made free with human images. There is much scholarly debate about all this, based on very scant evidence.[28]

---

[28] Whether these *qusur* of the early caliphs (Umayyad Dynasty 661AD until 750 AD) were a means to enjoy *nazh* — fresh air and remoteness — and whether the images were pleasures best hidden from the puritan gaze; and whether the miniatures are to be seen as Sufist allegory, as aids to mystical contemplation. A pertinent question is why is there 'scant evidence'? Why almost all excavations have been in Egypt, with the rest of the Levant and the Arabian peninsular largely ignored. Largely, I suspect, it is a matter of merchandizing. To be brutal, there has been no money in it — no academic prestige, no glamour, no publishing contracts.

There has also been debate about whether 'Islamic art' is itself a Western construct.[29] What is certain, however, is that its early ambiguity gradually hardened into iconophobia — a clear ideological position — and that scholars found enough in the Koran and the Hadith to justify it. In Sura 3:47-49, for instance, Jesus gives life to an effigy of a bird, as a miracle, to demonstrate that only God has the power to bestow life.

The scholarly consensus, and remember that this becomes law, by *ijha* — and its refusal becomes apostasy — was that God was the great *musawwir* (fashioner or shaper) and anyone who made images of living things was arrogating God-like powers to himself:

> Those who make these pictures will be punished on the day of judgment. They will be instructed: make alive what you have created or be tossed into hellfire. *Hadith*

One exasperated artisan, so the story goes, asked a Hadith specialist 'once and for all, am I not (to practise my trade, and) to represent animate beings?' 'Yes' came the scholarly reply, 'but you can chop the animals' heads off, so they won't look alive, and do your best to make them look like flowers'.[30]

The general tradition, therefore, and the feeling that went with it — went beneath it rather — was one of profound unease, not only at the images themselves, but the greed and luxury that inspired them. Large and gorgeously decorated buildings aroused great hostility amongst the pious:

> Verily, the most unprofitable thing that eats up the wealth of a believer is building. *Hadith*

> An angel may not enter a building in which there is a painting. *Hadith*

Occasionally this erupted into iconoclastic vandalism, reminiscent of our own Puritans hacking their way through church statuary. This extended to book miniatures, where

[29] The Arabic word *fann* (plural *funun*) does not really correspond to the Western word 'art', in its sense of 'the application of skill to objects of taste'. In medieval times *fann* meant a type, a mode, a manner. By extension it meant a skill or a craft. But only recently has it acquired an aesthetic sense, as in *al-funun al-mustazrafa*, the 'fine arts'.

[30] But this gave piety a problem. How could the faith express itself visually? For there was also a strong tradition of beauty in Islam, of making functional things beautiful. It seems that geometric decoration — the complex patterning of every surface, but without figures — solved the problem..

necks were slashed with a black line—as if cutting their throats —to 'kill' the image, and make it impossible for it to breathe (much as pharaonic statues had been 'killed' to make them uninhabitable by spirits or the gods).

The recent break with Islamic tradition—the re-appearance of figurative sculpture after almost fifteen hundred years—has been purely nationalistic, and Europeanized. These sculptures carried a political message, like all 'fascist' art. Steely-eyed and lantern-jawed, these figures gaze off-stage into some nebulous future. It is doubtful whether these will survive resurgent Islam any better than Saddam's statue in the main square of Baghdad. It's also doubtful whether they deserve to.

Cultural nationalism at its stylish best

...and its certainty about idols

It is now clear that the texts used against figurative art—the representation of living things—were originally aimed at *pagan* idols; the objects and images used to worship other gods, and the sites sacred to those gods:

> Oh believers... Idols (*taswir*) and divining-arrows are an abomination, some of Satan's work; then avoid them. (Sura 5:92)

Taswir refers to any form of image, and in later centuries the word and its related forms (all derived from *sawwara*, referring to paint) were generally used for painting, but in the seventh century they clearly referred to sculpture, and particularly to idols. When the prophet announced that 'Islam destroys all that preceded it' (Hadith), he was referring to polytheism. And one thing is absolutely clear, which is Islam's hatred for polytheism, for the *jahiliyyah*, 'the time of ignorance', and for anything that smacks of idolatry. This absolute opposition to idols has always been because they challenged God's omnipotence, if they were thought to create things (Sura 6:74).[31] It was widely believed, for example, that the ancient sites, especially the Egyptian ones, possessed wondrous and demonic powers, and that the ancient Egyptians had used their symbolic frescoes to preserve and transmit illicit knowledge.[32]

The only exceptions were images sacred to the other religions of the Book. When he returned in triumph to Mecca and 'cleansed' the Kaaba, Mohammed destroyed the pagan shrines and their idols—all the images of other gods—but famously exempted a painting of Mary and the infant Jesus, because *Isu* was recognized as a prophet, albeit an unsuccessful one.[33]

---

[31] Islam's early fear of statues as the foci for pagan worship melded with its fear of statues as devices for sorcery. Mohammed was clearly very nervous about the persistence of these ancient practices. He made careful attempts to distinguish the world of spirits, of angels and *jinn*—all of which derived from the resident Arabian polytheism—from that of the prophets, the *hanifi*, the 'seekers after God', those who tried for monotheism in a polytheistic culture. And he denounced soothsayers and magicians, those who attempted to manipulate the spirit world for their own ends. This folk tradition seems, however, to continue healthily enough even today, for example in rural southern Egypt, where shamanism co-exists with puritan orthodoxy.

[32] The 10th century alchemist Ibn Umail gave a detailed description of pharaonic Ashmunein—then still intact—specifically because he believed it built to withstand some predicted catastrophe, the deluge perhaps, and to transmit this illicit knowledge.

[33] And the Kaaba itself was held to have been constructed by Abraham and his son, Ismail, who is revered by Islam as the first *Hanifi*.

Why, then, Islam's overriding indifference?

If Islam's attitude to pagan images — to antiquities, that's to say — is so clear, why have they been allowed to remain? Why haven't the sites been destroyed, as the Taliban recently dispatched their Buddhas?[34] Or can we take it that the Taliban's studied insolence — allowing the press to film an artillery operation that lasted for several days, and primarily to enrage UNESCO and the Western mindset — was an augur of things to come?

As I have said, there *have* been puritan forays, and they have tended to coincide with periods of uncertainty — famine, plague, military defeat and the rest. Finding a culprit for God's wrath has been a common pastime for all religions of the Book — and despots are anyway more likely to pay attention when times are hard.

> So, when the sacred months have passed away, then slay the idolaters whenever you find them, and take them captive and besiege them and lie in wait for them in every ambush, then if they repent and keep up prayer and pay the *jizya*, leave the way free for them, surely Allah is forgiving, merciful.' (Sura 9:5)

But how can statues repent? And how can antiquities pay the *jizya*? Thus the austere Caliph Muhtadi (who reigned 869–870AD) ordered that 'the painted figures that desecrated the rooms be obliterated...and the gold and silver vessels be brought out of the Treasury and broken up'. The records omit to mention what he did to pagan antiquity.

And thus Yazid II in 722AD ordered that all relics of pre-Islamic paganism in Egypt should be destroyed. This 'proved impracticable' — mainly because so much of it was still buried in the sand — but we have no idea how much was destroyed. When Napoleon's academicians arrived in 1798 they reported no defaced monuments. The conclusion, I suspect, is that when sites have been assaulted it has been done so thoroughly as to leave nothing behind to remind us — as we are reminded by the empty niches in our churches.[35]

---

[34] Buddhism and Hinduism went un-mentioned in the Koran — and un-condemned — because Mohammed knew nothing about them. He only knew Mesopotamian polytheism, and of course the pre-Islamic Arabic versions. So the Taliban's *fatwa* was modern — a *dynamic interpretation*.

[35] It is worth noting that Ashmunein was completely intact in the tenth century. Now it has all but disappeared. Also, that the Palace at Ctesiphon has lost half its bulk in the last century, most probably to builders.

Such assaults continued throughout the medieval era. In
1378, for example, the Sphinx (*Abul-hawl*, the 'the father of
fear') lost her nose to a fanatical Sufi. And the gleaming surface of the Great Pyramid was stripped to build mosques. We
shall never know the true extent of damage. But the question
remains. Why are there still so many visible remains of antiquity? Why haven't they also been destroyed? And why have-
n't recent events in Afghanistan been the order of the day?

The Sphinx minus her nose

The answer is interesting. It seems they were tolerated
because of another central tenet of Islamic thought — the *transience of the day* — the fleetingness and unimportance of tem-
poral things, when compared to the afterlife.

> Be in the world as though you were a stranger or a wayfarer.
> *Hadith*[36]

> In the evening, do not expect to live until the morning, and in
> the morning do not expect to live until the evening. Therefore,
> make peace with your God before you sleep.' *Hadith*

Medieval Muslims were well aware of living amongst the
ruins.

> Many ways of life passed away before your time. Then go about
> the earth and observe what happened. (Sura 3:137)

---

[36] The Prophet, as reported by 'Abd Allah Ibn 'Umar, the second caliph and
Mohammed's son-in-law.

They moved amongst shadows of former glory, the exploded presumptions of the past. Ibn Khaldun, the fourteenth-century historian, noted that:

> The Yemen where the Arabs lived is in ruins... Persian civilization in Arab Iraq is likewise in ruins... the same applies to Syria... The whole region (the Levant) was formerly settled... This fact is attested to by the relics of civilization.

These almost mythical monuments represented both magnificence and impermanence, wonder and menace. They were marvelled at, but suspected. The good Moslem took warning from such ruins, and the fates of their creators:

> Hast thou not seen what thy Lord did with Pharaoh, he of the tent pegs[37] who was insolent in the land, and worked corruption therein? Thy Lord loosed upon them a scourge of chastisement; surely thy Lord is ever on the watch.' (Sura 89: 5-15 'the Dawn')

Until the Europeans arrived, and the 'Gifts from God'

Until Napoleon landed in 1798, that is, with his academics in tow, and began our Western fascination — our almost obsession — with all things pharaonic. Until then there had been absolutely no reason, as we have seen, for any Muslim — or any Muslim polity — to be at all interested in antiquity. No reason to feel anything but loathing for its polytheism. The best antiquity could expect was a melancholy contempt, an indifference tinged with poetic sadness at the transience of mere pomp.

But then the Westerners arrived, and brought their wallets with them. Antiquities came to have a monetary value. What had been worthless could now be sold. And this triggered another native tradition, also grounded in the Koran, that *the earth belongs to the believer*. This has clear legal implications under Islamic law. For what is found in the earth also belongs to the believer. And if it benefits him and his kin, it correctly becomes a *'Gift from God'*.

The West may have disturbed antiquity from its long sleep in the sand — and its occasional sacrifices to Islamic piety — but the West also gave it a security it had lacked since the Roman era. The security of a *cash nexus*. This is very impor-

---

[37] *Pharaoh of the tent pegs* was part of mythology of pre-Islamic Arabia, one of many Arabian myths commemorating lost peoples who were damned because they had rejected the messages of God's prophets.

tant to grasp, because the West seems determined upon making antiquities un-saleable again. And this may not be such a good idea. Removing cash value will remove the security that cash value gives. It may only consign antiquity — these polytheistic and pagan relics — to the flames. For what we are now seeing is a renewed fervour in Islam, a return to Sharia law, and a rekindled hatred for the decadent infidel West, and for anything that interests the West.

It would be doubly ironic if antiquity were now to be 'branded' with the West, and excite the latent puritanical hatred of the imams, but without the West's cash nexus — the Gift from God tradition — that alone can protect it.[38] For *it is only the West that has any interest in antiquity*. This must be clearly understood. It cannot be overstressed. Middle-Eastern regimes have no interest in archaeological remains, and none in their preservation.[39] They have more pressing problems.

And the conclusion?

That no Muslim *polity* has any reason for any interest in antiquity. Quite the opposite. Antiquity is *anathema* to Islam. It is everything that's hateful. The idea that Islamic authority might claim polytheistic images as their 'cultural heritage' is grotesque. The very idea, if spoken aloud, would have been apostasy, and punishable by death. At best antiquity has been ignored, at worst destroyed.

Hence any Middle-Eastern regime that claims antiquities — pagan, polytheistic relics and idols — 'for the nation', and imposes a prohibition against possessing what is found in the soil, can only do so as a secular regime, and must tread a delicate path. It may have its own reasons for claiming the antiquity — using it as a mythic resource, or as an economic one — but it flies in the face of the believers, and risks the

[38] And here it is of some interest — it clearly confirms my argument — that the Taliban in Afghanistan were not only destroying their monumental statues of Buddha, but also selling their minor antiquities — yes, to Western dealers. The minor antiquities were being saved for posterity because they had a cash value — if only because that cash was needed for artillery shells.

[39] When I mentioned to an eminent Arabic scholar that I had video evidence of a temple site in the Lebanon, complete with outstanding mosaics, that had been bulldozed overnight into the sea by the government because it lay in the path of a dual carriageway, he merely shrugged, and replied that they would do as much to a village. Such things were of no importance except to the West.

sleeping antagonism of Islam, that is, of the resurgent imams.

It is therefore putting antiquity at grave risk. It negates the traditional protections, *the transience of the day*, and — what the West itself has elicited — *that the earth and its gifts belongs to the believer*. A delicate path indeed. And archaeology, which is a western science, risks getting caught in the middle, risks compromise, risks backing the wrong horse, in short. Western archaeology should ponder the fate of the Peacock Throne.

Summary

- Modern Islam presents a particular problem for antiquity, and for its welfare.
- The seventh-century Arab invasions destroyed all cultural links with antiquity, so modern Muslims cannot claim 'discovered relics' as a 'cultural heritage',
- and nor would they, given their hostility to polytheism — to idols and pagan sites.
- The present Islamic nations were invented recently — largely for our own convenience — and bear no resemblance to any ancient polity, indeed, the very concept of the modern 'nation' is problematic for Islam.
- Consequently, there is no reason for any modern Muslim 'nation' to have the least concern for 'discovered relics' on its land. *Cultural heritage* is a western idea, moreover, and hateful to Islam on various grounds.
- The only reason Islam has not — or not more efficiently — destroyed polytheistic antiquity is because of a native tradition, the '*transience of the day*'.
- This has recently been overridden by another native tradition, that of found objects being a '*Gift from God*' to the believer, and bearing a monetary value (which of course depends upon Western *collectors* and their ready finance).
- The growing danger, therefore, is the low-grade war that militant Islam — Islamo-fascism — is waging against the West, a war which is very difficult to curtail, because of Islam's lack of any centralized religious control,
- and which threatens the present saving-grace of antiquity — its financial value as a 'Gift from God'.

The Proof

CHAPTER 13

And Then There's Egypt...

Interestingly, there is only one Islamic nation that shows the least interest in pre-Islamic antiquity, and that is Egypt. Hers was the first ancient civilization to be discovered by Europeans, and Egypt herself has been aware of it since Napoleon's arrival. Aware of it, roughly speaking, as a resource, as something other than a 'given' in the landscape.

Egypt is also a genuine 'country of origin', where the other geographical and historical problems — those I've been at pains to explain — are less than acute. Egypt has invariably been isolated, protected against invasion, and sufficient unto herself. Very few Egyptian things were ever made for export, very few strayed abroad during the Dynastic period, and 'Egyptian' art was never made outside Egypt, and certainly not by Egyptians.[1] In fact, Egyptian antiquities only began their diaspora in the eighteenth century.

Hence the huge majority of Egyptian antiquities were made in Egypt, by Egyptians and for Egyptians. For much the same reasons, modern Egyptians share much of their blood with the ancient Egyptians. They have only been invaded a few times — in the sense of being over-run by people who seriously interbred with the natives, rather than just pushing them around for a while and then leaving.[2]

Admittedly the *cultural* side is more difficult. Since the Romans obliterated Dynastic Egypt, there have been five centuries of Christianity, then twelve of Islam. Both of these regarded Egyptian antiquity as the work of the devil, and did their competent best to suppress it. The modern Egyptians, as a result, have absolutely nothing in common — culturally speaking — with their forbears. And they have been subject,

[1] The only possible exception being faience technology, which was adopted by Greek trading communities in the Egyptian delta, and spread to the eastern Greek islands.

[2] As we ourselves could be said to have done, mainly because of (the strategic importance of) the Suez canal.

these last fifty years, to a virulent cultural nationalism, which has used antiquity as a tool for propaganda (as well as a consumable resource for tourism). Apart from that, theirs is a fairly simple case.

All this is fortuitous. It prevents us being sidetracked, and allows us to concentrate on the more important matter — that of antiquity being *valued*, and valued correctly. And of the sad things that happen when it isn't.

The emotional response to art and antiquity

If we are to care about an object — feel better merely for having seen it, for having been able to hold it and know it safe — we first have to think it worthwhile, literally, *worth-our-while*. For a poor man, as I have said — with mouths to feed and little to feed them — this equates to being *valuable* and that, I'm afraid, means *capable of being sold*. You might call this the vulgar beginning.

But it is only the beginning. We need more than this. I have heard Egyptians praise a piece so as to justify a higher price. I have heard it almost every day. But this is different from actually feeling the object to be rather splendid, being moved by it — feeling closer to creation just because you have been able to touch it. You may say that this is a rare response, anywhere. But I think not. It is just a part of *being cultured*, and I don't mean this in any snobbish sense; merely one of feeling yourself at ease in your own culture — being roused by your own past, and by what it sends down to you.

And this *emotional response* — for that is what it is — is not something that just happens spontaneously, whatever the moderns may think. You do not just recognise this thing called 'art' — and begin to feel emotional about to it — whenever you happen to see it lying around. There is no peculiar quality, no *essence*, that makes one thing an 'art object', and another a kitchen utensil. Sure, some kitchen utensils are regarded as art objects — the Scandinavian 'fifties ware, and art-nouveau — but it takes *training* to realize that they are, and why they are. In the end, you see, they all started as kitchen utensils, but the quality of their workmanship, the skill and beauty of their design, raised them to another category.

Learning to recognise something as an *art object*, and responding to it emotionally, this is all part of the collector's wardrobe. It is something that develops gradually. It is not something that you are born with, fully-fledged. You can be born with the propensity to feel it — the peculiar sensitivity — and that may put you beyond the common run of men — but it still needs practise and training, before you can use your skill, before you can recognise and then respond, with the surety and confidence that typifies the cognoscenti.

The origins of this response[3]

As I say, this emotional response — this feeling of awe and pleasure at just holding such a thing, this urge to cherish, and to see it safely through — this does not exist in everyman. It is simply not part of his makeup. At least it's not there to begin with. But it can develop. It can develop in any man who finds himself with such things on hand. And it can turn that ordinary man into a *cognoscente*, a man who feels and cares about art — this branch of art — as much as any museum curator. But how does it get there, this apparently *physiological* response?

Oh, of course, it can be installed by academe. Study art history or archaeology at university, and like as not you will develop this response to the things you study, day by day. But it is not inevitable. You cannot assume that because a man has a degree in art or archaeology, he actually *cares* very much about art objects themselves. He may have other fish to fry, as I shall explain later. Indeed, if his degree is Egyptology, you would be wise to assume as much.

But we are not talking about academics here, who are anyway salaried to care about such things. We are talking about *everyman* — your ordinary fellow, strolling the urban streets, or the ordinary *fellah* working the Egyptian fields. He has little enough access to academe, and little enough interest in art objects, or antiquities, at least to begin with. And yet he can develop the full-blown emotional response — the true care of the *cognoscente* — what the antiquities trade calls 'object-mindedness'. How is this achieved?

There is a sequence of events here and it is, I am suggesting, a strictly *causal* sequence. I may have got the order

[3] In this, and all that follows, there is an *aesthetic theory* in play — or more than that, an encompassing theory of the moral sensibilities. This was originally the stuff of my (un-submitted) PhD, and since seems to have been confirmed, obliquely, by advances in evolutionary psychology. Until I publish this, however, you will just have to oblige me, and assume it correct. I'm confident it is.

slightly wrong, but these are anyway the parts of that sequence. Of this much I am sure.

Imagine yourself with an object on hand, an antiquity say. You know nothing about it, save that it is valuable. But this makes you *curious*. You want to know *why* it is valuable — if only because you don't want to appear stupid if you come to sell it, and you don't want to be cheated. So you examine your antiquity. You consult experts. You read books, and compare your antiquity with others of a similar type. You gain knowledge of it, in other words. Perhaps you even try and acquire those others — just to see them side by side, and know that they are also yours. And whilst all this is going on, you begin to feel a genuine *affection* for it. You have begun to respond.

It may be difficult to pin down the precise moment — when you begin to feel the full-blown emotional response. But some things are clear. You cannot begin to respond in affection until you *know* about your object. And you would have no interest in knowing about it, unless you were first convinced that it was worth the trouble and the effort to find out — unless you were convinced it was worth your while...

This emotional response can be a useful indicator. It tells us a great deal about a person and about his culture.[4] Whether he is being honest, for example, with others, and also with himself. I can forgive a great deal, for example, when I see a dealer's emotional response to an object — when I can see his heart *going like a Honda*, as they say, and the waves of elation and joy sweeping through him. If nothing else, this tells me that the object is *safe* in his hands — that whatever his ambitions, he will only ever protect and cherish the object. It shows me what he holds sacred. And it also tells me that he has taken the trouble to learn. Because — and this is my central point — *without careful study and application, there can be no such emotion.*

Oh yes, there is an immediate response to holding antiquities, at least the first few times — a sort of vibration at things so old, and a hair-prickling plangency for the sacred.[5] But it

---

[4] Both his background culture (his 'family' in my sense), and his 'personal culture' (the degree of his personal development and refinement).

[5] This response may seem stronger, and more immediate, for what you take to be your *own* family silver. And you may think this feeling — the mere fact of you having it — proves the vital connection — that you can only feel for your

soon wears off. What *I* am referring to is the *emotional response of the aficionado*, and the deep knowledge that alone makes it possible.

When this emotional response is missing, conversely, I know that something is wrong, and the object is at risk. Either this person has not yet learned his chosen field, and hasn't started responding with emotion. Or, as I have said, he has other fish to fry. This is what reconciles me to the antics of collectors — and dealers — but worries me about academic archaeologists.[6]

There is another pertinent point. Given Islam's nervousness about the sculpted figure, and its abhorrence of polytheism, it is debatable whether Muslims can readily develop this emotional response to pre-Islamic sculpture — as they easily can, say, to calligraphy or plant-based designs. Their taboos may simply inhibit it. I have come to believe, after observing Egyptian 'antiquarians' for many years, that this *is* indeed the case. They are psychologically corralled by their faith.

---

ancestors' art their because they *really were* your ancestors. Not so simple, however. I would agree that we are more sensitive to our own past culture's artifacts — but only because we have already taken the trouble to learn about them. Or because we've been manipulated. Because if these *actually weren't* your ancestors, then what you are feeling is mistaken, or serves some other end. And whatever that end may be, it is almost certainly a bad faith.

Trying to understand our birthright — the behaviours and the feelings that we owe our distant ancestors — is anyway an important part of coming to terms with ourselves and our biology. And it's all the more necessary, these troubled days, when we're ceasing to feel these things — or feeling them in the wrong places. Either because something has passed out of our lives, which leaves us the poorer, or because something has intruded into our lives, that has no business there. Learning to feel, and learning when to trust our feelings — and when to discount them as bad faith — this is a problem of modernity, of being adrift in strange waters, waters we were never meant to swim.

[6]   The risk to an antiquity varies with the *unfeeling person's* profession, and the way he earns his dinners. If he is a dealer, then he may alter the object to enhance its value. This is prevalent amongst Islamic dealers, and it may or may not be a vandalism. If he is a Western archaeologist, he may discard or dismiss the object, or the site that contains it — after it has been recorded, because it has now served its purpose — as if it were an empty container, a mere wrapping, see page 290. If he is a pious Muslim, he may throw it away, or worse. There is also a risk of the feelings becoming *too* intense. The collector's passion can become an obsession, even a pathology, and the collector may sequestrate the object just so as to 'have' it, that is, to live with it. If this sequestration amounts to straight theft — rather than 'competition to acquire' in the marketplace — there is a risk of the object getting itself lost or overlooked after his death.

The biological mechanism that is involved

Let me flesh this out, just a little. This whole response rests upon a biological trick that, in other circumstances, can be immensely useful — in the moral sphere, for example. We do not respond to an old lady being knocked down in the street, and her handbag snatched — with horror, outrage, or shame at our own reluctance to intercede — because there is anything *intrinsically* horrible there. After all, she might be a terrorist, her handbag a bomb, and her assailants secret service men — in which case the virtue lies with them, or at least they think it does, which is much the same thing. And neither do we sit ourselves down and ruminate, weigh the pros and cons, and eventually decide that, *ceteris paribus*, we ought to be feeling anger or outrage. There is no time for that. It's much simpler and quicker. As children we were trained to think such things *wrong* and thereafter — after the lesson has been absorbed, and the program primed — we respond immediately. As if the felt emotion were actually *leading the way*, and not just following a trail that has already been laid.

Underlying the emotion, of course, there is a great deal of mental activity — of analysing what we see, pigeon-holing it, and hence judging it — but all this goes on out of sight. The first thing that we actually notice — on the surface, that's to say — is the immediate, the 'given', the surge of emotion.

It follows — and this is proof of the matter, incidentally — that children can be trained to respond in outrage or delight to practically anything. We have found this to our cost, this last century — the century of the Hitler Youth and the Cultural Revolution, of children denouncing their own parents, exposing them to outrage and sometimes to death. And we are probably about to find it out again. Children are born with the *propensity to respond* — in outrage at the 'bad' things, in beaming pleasure at the 'good' — and their culture just fills in the blanks.[7]

Once this has been done — and it has to be done by a certain age, as the Jesuits have always known — they respond thereafter with emotion, and without the least suspicion of the

---

[7] I am assuming that this is another part of our biological inheritance, another Evolutionary Stable Strategy (ESS), see page 112. We are born with it as a labour-saving device — this ability to respond in emotion, and apparently without thought — but our cultural 'family', must specify the (classes of) events or objects that (serve to) trigger it. The philosophy involved is also beyond the scope of this book, but I hope to develop it elsewhere.

trick that has been played on them. The present generation, for instance, will grow up to feel more strongly about race jokes than about buggery. Fashions come and fashions go.

Similarly in the art world. The *cognoscente* looks at an object — of a class he knows well, and understands — and he responds with joy perhaps, or repugnance. These are emotions, sure, but in such cases they have become a shorthand — you might say a results slip — for the huge unseen calculation of his experience and knowledge, as it is brought to bear on the object. And how could it be otherwise? There is so much going on here — recognition, analysis, judgement — and most of it too fast for spoken language. The *cognoscente* looks at an object, he lets his mind go blank, and a hair's-breadth moment later he feels a joy that tells him — quicker than he can articulate — that the thing is authentic, and splendid. Only then, once he knows the answer, does he cast around to justify the decision that he has already felt.

Aesthetics, unfortunately, is as easy to manipulate as morality. In the modern art world it is easy enough to create a market, which is quite a different thing from discovering one. The impresarios know this well. They know that we respond because we are familiar with the objects, because we took the trouble to learn about them, and did so because we assumed — or had some smart-arse tell us with monotonous regularity — that they really *were* important and valuable. This, I conclude, is the real sequence: first there has to be an *idea of value*, then the *research* to understand the whys and the wherefores of that value, then the *knowledge*, and finally the immediacy of *emotional response.*[8]

---

[8] It follows that we would eventually respond to an unmade bed — or any other gimcrack devoid of talent or technique or vestige of beauty — if it was introduced with the appropriate reverence. Well, maybe not. The crowds at the Tate Modern regard it as an Emperor's New Clothes theme park (which the director, Nicholas Serota, should perhaps consider, rather than judging the *quality* of his museum by the turnstile figures).

But there has been some really nasty art of late, which *has* also elicited the full emotional response. Now *art of national celebration* has a long history. The first ten years of Greek classical, for instance — what we call the 'Severe Style', because of the severe and calm self-possession of the figures — was a celebration of the Greeks defeating the Persians. But twentieth century fascist art, whether of the Right or Left — whether Stalins' workers standing shoulder-to-shoulder and gazing into the glorious future, or Nazi soldiers doing much the same — was often turpitudinous, even though it inspired genuinely powerful feelings.

How do the modern Egyptians feel about 'their' antiquity?

But all this, alas, is denied the Egyptians. They are forbidden contact with their claimed 'cultural heritage', and hence have no means to learn about it (in the necessarily intimate way). Oh yes, they can visit the museum, if they are middle-class and living in Cairo — and provided they show no *comparative* interest in the objects, which would attract the attention of the guards, and have them suspected of being dealers. But for the huge mass of Egyptians there is no intimate contact, and no hope of developing an emotional response.

> **JOURNAL: 2nd July 1993, Cairo**
>
> *To the museum with a nervous Ali.[9] He explained that no Egyptian ever looks at antiquities as we do, with our intensity. And if they did—especially if they were photographing— they'd be arrested on suspicion. I watched carefully, and it was true. Egyptians simply don't look at antiquities. They only glance in passing, as proprietors sometimes do. They're never absorbed, because what they're seeing is beautiful or important. They never look as a lover looks. In fact, they really aren't interested. You hardly ever see an Egyptian in Cairo museum, other than children on school-trips, who take it at a giggling run. [Antiquity] is strictly for tourists. And as for tour guides, they could be comparing football teams. 'Our ruins are bigger than your ruins' is about the sum of it.*

And how do the ordinary Egyptians regard 'their' antiquity — the *fellaheen* working the fields, for example? They're uncertain and distrustful, a I have explained, and riven by contradictions. There is an official attitude — slightly bombastic, and tirelessly repeated for the tourists — which celebrates their past, and the genius of their forebears. I call this the *Egypt Air syndrome*.

This is taught — indoctrinated, perhaps one should say — to those who study Egyptology at university. This equips them as tour guides (and for little else, I have to say, since there is

---

The point is different from Bernard Williams', who mentioned that what *really* worried him about Catholicism was not its depth of pious awe, but that such awe could be *elicited by such kitsch*. The poster art of the Third Reich was certainly not that. It was graphically superb. It's partly that it was used by the losing side.

[9]   Ali Farag, my one-time partner, scion to one of the great trading dynasties.

no postgraduate study in Egypt, and if an Egyptian wants to do research in Egyptology, he has to go to Khartoum, or one of the Western universities). The syndrome might even be shared — without irony, that is — by those who work the bazaars, and hang around the grand and showy sites. It gives them a pride of sorts, after all, and makes their present plight the easier to bear.

But the ordinary people, the swarming city dwellers and the peasantry? If these people really are synonymous with the Arab Republic of Egypt — a moot point, this — then they are *the official owners of antiquity*. For Colonel Nasser claimed to have nationalised in their name. But these same people are forbidden to own antiquities — or even to touch them — where antiquities are defined as anything over 100 years old (or even more recent, if the 'competent standing committee' or the 'competent cultural minister' so decides).[10]

A pious Muslim, therefore, commits a criminal act — courtesy of Law 117 of 1983 — if he holds in his hand, or inherits, a single page of a nineteenth-century Koran. Can you imagine — and would you relish it — being criminalized for inheriting your grandfather's Bible?

Who actually *owns* Egypt's much brandished antiquity?

The Egyptian people may be the 'owners' of their antiquity, but they are not to be trusted with it, apparently. And they certainly don't respond to it — except as a form of display, or something that supports their ambition.

There really is a *prohibition* in place, and it is clear that if anyone owns Egyptian antiquity it is the *regime*, the military regime which pulls all the strings in Egypt. It certainly isn't 'the Egyptian people'. A simple thought experiment will prove the point. Just ask yourself who can sell Egypt's antiquity? Suspend your moral qualms, and just ask the question. Who can sell her hoards of treasure? And who can benefit from the sale? Because only an owner can *sell* a property. And if he cannot sell, he cannot really own it. His 'ownership' is make-believe.

The British people can correctly be said to own the British Museum, if only because we could envisage the sequence of

---

[10] See page 196 ff.

events whereby they — the said people — could force the sale of its contents. A private member's bill perhaps, the lobbying of MPs, and so on, or maybe a referendum. We can also envisage them benefitting from the sale. From which it follows that *they* actually own the museum, rather than the crown, for instance, or parliament.

But there is nothing similar for the Egyptian people. There is no conceivable sequence of events by which they could force their government to sell Cairo Museum — or the stored surplus of antiquities, in its guarded depots — and give them the money. It is simply inconceivable. It follows that they don't own 'their' antiquities. The regime does.

The attempt to *Egyptianize* antiquity

Nasser's triumphalist regime came to power, and promptly confiscated Egypt's antiquity. They did so, one has to suppose, simply because it was there, and because it was deemed important. They'd have needed no grander idea than this. They'd have done the same for a bed of coal, and with scarce less reverence. But having confiscated antiquity, if only to prevent anyone else from getting their hands on it,[11] they had to look after it. They had to assume the mantle and the responsibility. In practise, this meant kicking out the British and the French, who had been running the Antiquities Service and the museums.

The regime decided, effectively, to *Egyptianize* their 'heritage' But this has been a disaster. Three generations have passed, and the Egyptians have yet to become object-minded. That is, they have yet to care as a genuine collector cares — for the objects in themselves, rather than for their symbolic glory, or their significance in the scheme of things.

Hence the peasants' ambiguity. As we have seen, Muslims have traditionally shunned pharaonic antiquities. Over the last two hundred years their attitude has changed, and

---

[11] Especially the Egyptian people, please note, who were not to be trusted with it, *lest they enrich themselves*. The only plausible justification for the Prohibition was just this, that given half a chance, Egyptians would sell antiquities to foreigners, and thereby enrich themselves. And become much more difficult to control. I think this last is the important part. In fact, I've never met an Egyptian who was not happy to sell me his particular antiquity, and who was not perfectly at ease with the idea that this antiquity was really his — his by rights, his to do with as he thought fit, and to benefit his family — and nothing to do with the government, who were only trying to filch it from him.

changed again. They came to regard them as Gifts from God. But now they are forbidden any contact, and told that antiquities are government property.

So how can they now regard them but as the devil's spawn, as idols, as *taswir* from the *jahiliyyah*? The fundamentalists take their scripture very seriously — any Muslim must needs be fundamentalist about the Koran — and hence polytheistic antiquities are *anathema*. They would destroy them, as soon as look at them. Indeed they have already begun. Not with the thoroughness of the Taliban, perhaps, but that is something we must anticipate. But unguarded outlying sites are already being attacked and destroyed.

> **JOURNAL: 11th December 1992,**
> **Government Hostel, Minea**
>
> *Dr. Hussein's just back from the escarpment edge, south of Assyut, where he's been inspecting a small Middle Kingdom temple for the [Antiquities] Commission. He'd heard of some damage, but it's proved much worse than he thought. Decorated surfaces have been literally hacked to pieces. In fact, there's hardly anything left. Nothing in the press, of course, either about this or the other instances. The regime seems coy about this sort of thing.*

Summary

- There is an emotional response to beautiful things, which is an inherited propensity,
- but has to be trained (that is, have its objects specified).
- Where it's present, the objects will be cared for, and safe from destruction and damage.
- Where it's absent however — as in Egypt, and for the vast majority of working Egyptians — the objects are at risk.

CHAPTER 14

Why Aren't the Egyptians 'Object-Minded'?

The problem

It was the great Egyptologist Bernard von Bothmer who put his finger on the problem. As early as 1968 — at the Paris Conference, *Sauvetage des Antiquitées en Egypte* — he announced, with characteristic bluntness, that the Egyptians were simply not '*object-minded*'. He meant, of course, that they didn't respond as we did to ancient things, with awe and reverence, and the desire to cradle and to cherish, and to nurse them through to safety.

We have an Egyptian shawabti on our desk, for instance, and somehow it radiates antiquity for us. We cherish it for that, and because we feel its beauty. And because we respond to it in the way I have been describing, we are incapable of acting against its best-interests — an interesting notion this — any more than we could act against our own childrens'.

All this leaves the Egyptian cold, however. He feels none of it, and it puzzles him that we should feel it, and feel it so strongly. But until Egyptians do become object-minded, Bothmer concluded, we should expect nothing from them, and certainly not trust them as the guardians of their antiquity.

It is not a matter, for example, of the Egyptians not being very good with their hands, although strangely enough they aren't — considering that their forbears were probably the greatest craftsmen the world has seen.

Nor is it a matter of funding, that they are not prepared to spend any money on conservation (although, again, they aren't). Nor, finally, is it a problem of ignorance. The Egyptians are ignorant about conservation, and rather shockingly so, but they are also convinced — their own version of the *cargo cult*, indeed — that the problem is simply one of materials. If they only had the correct materials — the latest magical consolidant from the West — then all their problems would be solved.

No, the real problem is that Egyptians simply don't care about their antiquity, or care in the right way. And it is important to understand why.

> ### JOURNAL: 10th March 1993, Cairo Museum
> *Dr. Hussein[1] distracted the guard outside the Nineteenth Dynasty room., whilst I photographed the shawabti cabinet. The shelves were dramatic enough, with shawabtis just toppled over, like soldiers fainted on parade. But it was down below— out of sight unless you leant on the glass and stretched—where the real drama lay. Down there were about a dozen, all tumbled off their shelves by the earthquakes, and lying smashed to pieces. About $30,000 worth. But the earthquakes were last October, six months ago, and the missing spaces on the shelves are obvious enough— you can count the clean rings in the dust—but nobody's even noticed! The curators are too busy drinking tea in their offices, according to Hussein, and the soldiers are conscripts, who all hate the place. We'll send the photos to al Ahramb [the Cairo daily], and that should rouse them.*

Is it because they are really 'monument-minded'?

You might say, of course, that Egyptians do not care about mere objects — what they call 'movables', and we would call 'free-standing' — all those shawabtis that sit so proudly on our desks in the West, or lie smashed in Cairo Museum's cabinets — because they are really *'monument-minded'*. They only respond, that is, to the grand things and the grandeur — to the temples and the massive ruins, to the pyramids and Abu Simbel and the Sphinx.

And these certainly do have a value for the them — apart from the tourist revenue that keeps their sodden economy afloat.[2] They appeal to Egyptian nationalism, to Pan-

---

[1] Dr. Hussein is probably the best Egyptian conservator. He is certainly the best qualified — the only one with a foreign doctorate (from Heidelberg), and one of only two chosen to work in Nefertari's Tomb, under the aegis of the Getty Institute. He now runs the conservation department at Minea university, where his students are middle-class aspirants to professional status. He is also the most honest Egyptian I have ever met, and one of the gentlest.

[2] The figures are stark enough. The Egyptian economy has lashed itself to a massive food subsidy, which it cannot relinquish without inciting riots. In my

Arabism. They brandish Egypt as a former power, when she 'bestrode the known world like a colossus'. And they make the febrile present bearable even if, just out of sight, there is another idea that lurks — and not half so satisfying — that the moderns are just camping in the ruins of the past (and this past, however glorious, was *jahiliyyah*, and had got it completely wrong.)

All well and good, and feasible, but there also happen to be millions of objects in Egypt that are not monumental. What about them? If the Egyptians are not object-minded about these, there must be a reason. Monuments have a value — giving them a sort of vicarious pride, over and against the dominant West — but why not the smaller things?

As I have already explained, there is confusion of cause and effect here, and it's easy enough to get muddled. Do you need an *expertise* for antiquity, before you can begin to *care* for it? Before, that is, you can feel any real passion for its objects? Or must you feel some stirrings of affection for these same objects — before you have any desire to learn about them? You could go round and round in circles here. But which may be chicken, and which is the egg in this vicious circle — of low pay and low self-esteem, of disdain for the work and disinterest in its objects — the Egyptians have yet to break out of it.

In the end, it all comes down to value

In the end, as I have already said, it comes down to *value*. For the majority of Egyptians — except those lucky few who are still in a position to sell — antiquities are slighted because they have no practical value. Oh yes, the Egyptians may say that they are 'priceless' — that wretched journalistic word. They might consider, in a loose sort of way, that such and such an object is worth a vast figure, but not to them — not to benefit them and their families, that is, and make their life any easier. Such 'pricelessness' signifies nothing — any more than counting the stars. It only fosters a gentle contempt. For

---

day some 55% of GNP went on this subsidy — for example the Nissen-hut bakeries in the cities, that churn out subsidized bread, and feed the poor. Despite cotton and oil, their two staple products, there is always a deficit — in my day about $8 billion — which has to be made up by tourism. Despite attempts to open up the Red Sea as a diving resort, it is clear that nobody would dream of visiting Egypt were it not for the pervading glamour and ambience of Egypt's past, which means the famous archaeological sites.

what use is pie-in- the-sky, when Egyptians are paid almost nothing for an object's restoration, and even less for its care and display? It is this figure — *what the government thinks fit for its upkeep* — that shows the real value of an object. Or not, as the case may be.

Yes, I am convinced, in the end it is just a matter of value. An object has to be considered valuable — in the sense that it is saleable, and could actually be sold — before it becomes interesting. And if it isn't interesting, in this fundamental sense, there will be no real desire to learn about it, and no chance of that emotional response developing, upon which its safety ultimately depends. It is of little use recruiting young people, offering them security through government employ, and explaining how glamorous etc., to be working on such treasures — and then paying them less than the lowliest hotel porter. Because the pay is so poor, no self-esteem attaches to archaeology, which is seen as just another poorly-paid government make-work. The employees pretend to work, but actually idle their time away, doing nothing that might bring down responsibility upon them — and that might jeopardize their pensions. And the government pretends to value their work despite paying pitifully for it.

Sooner or later these young people will make the connection — the penny will drop — that their *government thinks nothing of antiquities because it pays nothing to protect them.* And the government's contempt is catching. The brightest and the best will depart soon enough — to be tourist guides, and hotel staff — and leave behind them the tea-drinkers and the time-servers. Oh, and the rare man with a conscience, such as my good friend Dr. Hussein.

JOURNAL: 10th October 1988, Cairo

With Hussein to Marwa Palace in Cairo, to see some of his conservators.[3] We found a group of contented girls drinking tea. There was no electricity that day, so they were gossiping, until it was time to claim their day's wage and depart. These four had just spent three years with their needles and thread restoring an eighteenth-century settee. The work was good, but I was struck by the timings. Twelve woman-years?! And for one chair? And with three larger ones still

---

[3]   At this time Hussein was still head of conservation for Cairo and the Delta. Soon after he resigned from the Antiquities Commission, and embarked on his doctorate. His title until then had been honorific.

waiting? Here was a work-for-life, a Forth Bridge work. As long as they turned up and performed their little daily task, they'd be paid their daily pittance. It was something that could be eked out for ever. But what disturbed me most— other than the costings, that is—was the restored chair itself, the product of those twelve woman-years.[4] It was sitting in the bright sun, without any covering, covered in dust, and already fading. Where was the care in this?

Compare this with the Egyptian peasant, who has no more idea — of the real value of antiquities, that is — than the government conservator. If the government's man judges antiquities as worthless because he is only paid a pittance for their restoration and protection — and after all, this is the only means he has to judge their value — so the peasant can only judge them by the effort this same government expends in keeping him away from them. To judge by the penalties, and the troops on the ground, the peasant must assume that the antiquity he has just found on his land is worth a king's ransom. There has to be a moral here.

But, as I say, you must start at the right end of the equation. You cannot expect people to take their work seriously if they are paid a pittance for it (especially when they can see how much revenue is being earned from the monuments, and can read the tourist notices promising that it will all be lavished on their upkeep). They will just refuse to be judged by their 'work'. They will distance themselves, reduce it to a joke, a charitable joke, or treat it with contempt. The government pretends to pay? Then they'll pretend to work.

And you cannot expect a peasant to overcome his prejudices — his Islamic taboos against *taswir*, and his resentment against an overbearing secular government, and its claims — unless, quite simply, there was *something in it for him*.

Conservation and bureaucracy

And the time-servers, the ones who just hang in there, and make a career in the Antiquities Commission? What of them?

---

[4] In our own cash-driven context, of course, such a restoration would be inconceivable. It is common-sense that you cannot spend more to conserve an object than it is worth (because it would be easier to buy a better example with the money). Unless, of course, the object is the only remaining one, or the best remaining one But even so, the high wages of the conservator will inhibit you. A good argument, I suppose, for 'outsourcing' restoration.

They were just bureaucrats, Hussein said, with the bureaucrat's agenda. They were incompetent and lazy, but that hardly mattered, because they needed other things.

A Western conservator can rest content on his laurels with a line of well-restored antiquities behind him. This is what makes him successful. It is his testimony, if you like. But when an Egyptian conservator looks back, and comes to judge himself, antiquities restored or otherwise just don't come into it. He will consider himself successful if he is well placed in the hierarchy of the Antiquities Commission, and safe from denunciation, if he has managed to get through unscathed. As I say, antiquities just don't come into it. His purpose may *appear* the same as a Western conservator's, but his real end is quite different.[5]

These fine fellows may hanker for prestige and importance. But more importantly, they want to be safe. And for this, their best course lies in immobility. To undertake something is to undertake responsibility. And that is to put themselves at risk. Much better, therefore, to do nothing at all. Or to do it very slowly, without attracting any attention. The ideal task, therefore, is one that commences with fanfare, gradually fades from sight, and is conveniently unfinished when its instigator retires. The credit of starting will be his, but not the costs of failure. And if antiquities have been damaged, the fault will be his successor's. You think me harsh?

JOURNAL: 4th March 1986, Cairo

To Heliopolis, where Hussein was greeted by a crowd of conservators, taking their tea in a long wooden hut. I thought it was their rest room, but it turned out to be a sort of poor relation to the Boat House [built beside the Great Pyramid, to house the famous Solar Barque]. It seems they'd found a third boat–after the two solar barques at Giza–but this time a working river vessel. It was fine when found, except its

[5]   An important distinction, this, for philosophy and anthropology both. If the army makes its soldiers clean the floor with their toothbrushes, for instance, the *purpose* is just that — to clean the floor — but the *real end* is something else; perhaps to punish, perhaps to teach extremes of hygiene, or that what a soldier does affects his comrades, because his mess has to be cleaned up by them. And when the army teaches drill to its soldiers, the purpose is to have them march in step — quite a useful thing in itself, you might think, except when crossing Sir Norman Foster's bridge — but the real end is to develop their prompt and absolute obedience, and hence their *esprit de corps*. These are the real ends of those in authority, and toothbrushes and foot-stamping are merely the means.

planks were wet with the flooding. But what an amazing find! A working boat from antiquity. They just don't exist.

Now there are accepted techniques for conserving water-logged-objects, and they're little more than applied common sense. A sensible man could work them out on the back of a cigarette packet. If the wood is fragile, for instance, it must be supported before it's moved, and it must be strengthened. Modern synthetics are on hand for that. And you mustn't lose track of how the pieces were lying when you first found them, because that's your evidence of the original structure—of how the boat looked before it fell apart. Again, that's common-sense. And since things can go wrong, you'd best stage a dry-run, if only to understand where it's likely to go wrong when you do it for real. And if something does go wrong, you'd best stop before it's too late. And so it goes, all common-sense.

But what did these people do? They chose an Indian technique, as a means to strengthen the planks, the so-called sugar treatment. They simply shovelled the whole lot into a large tank, full of sugar solution. The planks disintegrated into a mass of fragments, pencil-sized or smaller, and these were painstakingly rinsed, dried, and laid out on the shelves of this hut. About a hundred thousand of them.

They wanted me to admire the fragments. Yes, I agreed: they were very strong fragments. But that was hardly the point. Several score of planks—which could have been reconstructed into something wonderful—had been reduced to little more than a pile of shavings. They'd as much chance of re-building their boat as they had the Wooden Horse of Troy.

What did I think should be done now? asked the ever gentle Hussein. What could one say? What could anybody say? One of the world's treasures had been utterly destroyed. It was outrageous. It was obscene. At that moment I could have wept or broken bones. In fact I was very English about it, and suggested they set up in the barbecue fuel business…

I suppose I date my cynicism from this point. It was then I began to watch Egyptian conservation from the outside, as it were—as an anthropologist watches a native tribe. I was puzzled by the sense of difference, you see. What these Egyptians were doing seemed familiar enough. It resembled what we did in the West — the saving of antiquities, their health and protection, that sort of thing. But it wasn't just a difference of quality — that we were rather good, and they were incompetent. They were, of course, but it was more than that. What these Egyptians were doing was done for a different reason. As I say, its real end was quite different from its purpose. They were just going through the motions.

And there was something missing — something vital, which we took for granted, but made all the difference. Putting it bluntly, they just didn't seem to care — or care about the right things. They cared about something all right, but it certainly wasn't these endless shelves of wooden fragments — or what they had once been, an archaeological rarity worth millions. Perhaps it was just a matter of accountability?

JOURNAL (continued)

I asked Hussein why hadn't we heard about this, this—this monumental fuck-up? What about the man responsible, the one who'd decided on the sugar-sauna? Hadn't he been sacked? Hadn't he been thrown in prison?

—'No, no, of course not. He is over there, and we are drinking his tea.'

But hadn't he been reprimanded? Hadn't anything at all been done?

—'No, because he has not reported his results. How do you say? His restoration is still in progress.

But when were the pieces taken out of the sugar mixture and put on the shelves?

—'It was a year ago, I think.'

Now I began to understand. These contented restorers, six tea-drinking women and their overseer, were still 'working on the project'. And it was expedient for them to carry on 'working' as long as possible. But how long, I asked Hussein, could they just hang around, drawing their wages and doing nothing but drink tea, before somebody noticed? Hussein looked hurt.

—'But they have other things to do as well. They guard the obelisk, and they are paid very little, just enough to live. And they are very kind people'.

As I've said, this is a matter for sociologists. And what they would find is a self-serving bureaucracy, who judge themselves by anything at all — ambition, survival, safety — rather than their service to the cause. And they'd also find the usual bureaucratic turf-wars — in this case enlivened by oriental denunciations:

> **JOURNAL: 24th April 1995**
> *The politics of restoration are really becoming vicious. Dr. Shawky Nakhlar [Head of Conservation for the whole of Egypt] is angling for a more prestigious position, and three or four others have the same idea. All of them are busy denouncing each other's heresy–their materials, not their techniques, please note. Nakhlar's sin–according to his rivals, at least–is his use, in the Sphinx and other sites, of silicates in the mortar. His real sin, of course, is riding the B72 bandwagon so carelessly.*[6]

Summary

- The Egyptians just don't have this vital response to antiquity — this *'object mindedness'*. Could it be because they are 'monument minded', and not interested in the little things?
- No, it all comes down to *value*. For the majority of Egyptians, and increasingly so, antiquities have no value.
- This is clear from their efforts at conservation, which are inept, uncaring and bureaucratised.

---

[6]   See page 270.

CHAPTER 15

The Effects of Prohibition

What happens when antiquities are found in Egypt?

Consider. A farmer discovers an object in his fields, what the Egyptians call a 'movable' antiquity, and we'd call 'free-standing' — something that belongs to no place, or to any place — a household object, an item of jewellery, a utensil or a toy. Then the farmer discovers another, and yet another. He seems to have come across a hoard, or an *undiscovered site*. He alerts the authorities, who immediately investigate, and pronounce his find important enough to merit a *controlled excavation*. The site is closed, to keep it undisturbed, and the farmer's extended family mount guard — alongside the antiquities police — so as to protect it from thieves.

The farmer is obviously delighted by all this, because the *find* was on his land, and this gives him first claim to the objects. He can sell some of them in the free market — subject, of course, to government restrictions — and his family will be richer for it. He can send his sons to school.

The government is also happy, because it gets first refusal of the important pieces — a percentage tax, if you like, or a fee for the excavation — and can ensure they remain in the Egyptian *national collection*. The nation needs important antiquities, after all, but has little use for the rest. They would only duplicate what it already has — many times over, indeed — and could only be put aside in storage. Better for the minor things to be sold abroad, at international rates, and earn much-needed hard currency.

And after the recent liberalization, and the arrival of the auction houses, there is immediate pricing on hand. Christies has offices to cover the Delta, Bonham's has an agency in Luxor, and Sotheby's covers the South. New finds — and old 'treasures' — can be authenticated by Western experts, and given a proper market valuation.

Unless they are considered important enough for the national collection — or the archaeologists want them to remain on site — they will be stamped with invisible ink and despatched to Europe or New York for the regular auctions. This stamping provides an easy means to identify 'rogue' pieces in the market — those that haven't followed the prescribed course, but have been smuggled out — although they are few enough these days. Quite simply, there is no point in smuggling any more. There is nothing to gain by it.

If the farmer's site proves important enough, with buildings of note — a temple complex, for instance — it can be properly conserved. The objects found can be displayed on site, tourism encouraged, and extra revenue earned for all concerned. In such cases the farmer takes a fixed percentage of the earnings. In many cases a full-blown site is more beneficial than the occasional find, because the farmer can quit the back-breaking labour of the soil, and become the effective janitor of his own museum. He can become middle-class.

And lastly, the archaeologists are happy, because the sites are now well guarded — by those who have an interest in their preservation — until they are ready to excavate. And the excavation will be orderly and scientific, with no knowledge lost. There will be publications in the international journals, Egyptology will be advanced — not to mention the careers of the Egyptologists concerned. The antiquities police, who had always been tempted by the wealth on hand — and always corrupted by it — have become more or less redundant. Ordinary Egyptians no longer have to be kept away from their 'heritage', after all — there is no longer a *Prohibition* to enforce — and the remaining police can do something useful, and guard the important sites and tombs. And tomb-robbing is now rare, since there's now a ready flow of legitimate new discoveries. If a man has enough bread of his own, after all, he won't think to steal another's. Besides, 'stolen' antiquities from 'protected sites' — are immediately recognizable, in Egypt, by the auction-house scholars. They no longer have to wait until they reach those same scholars in Europe. I dare say the death penalty — for smugglers and thieves from protected sites — has also helped concentrate their minds.[1]

---

[1] This may seem extreme by Western standards, but the Egyptians learned the lesson in the 'nineties, when they completely stopped the heroin problem in Egypt — not by heaping opprobrium on the dealers, as we tend to do — but simply by allocating eighteen death penalties a year for drug dealers. They literally cut the supply route, right or wrong.

All this is possible, of course, because Egypt is a poor country where antiquities, relatively speaking, are hugely more valuable than they could ever be in the West. Their relative worth — their purchasing power, that is, in the native economy — is perhaps a hundred times what it would be for us. A single shawabti worth $100, for example, would make little difference to us, who expect $3,000 a month — but a huge difference to an Egyptian, who earns only $30, and whose cost of living is less than a fifth of ours. If you assume that correct international prices are being paid for the objects — as they certainly are, now the auction houses are on hand — then the antiquities recovered from a new site will make *them* the commercial option, at least for many years to come. The antiquities will pay for any eventual buildings, in fact. This was occasionally the case before liberalization, though it was highly illegal.

This would anyway be unthinkable in the West. No archaeological site can compete with commerce, let alone pay for a development. If a site is discovered in England, however important — and happens to be in the way of a property development — it will simply be swept aside, unless the government steps in and applies artificial criteria, against the will of the people.[2] But in Egypt the reverse applies. Archaeology can compete.

Forgive me, dear reader, I have misled you

This is not the reality. I have just described the *ideal*, what I have come to regard as the best hope — perhaps the *only* hope — for Egyptian antiquity. Now I would have you consider what actually happens. You will find it far less reassuring.

The farmer discovers his 'movable' antiquity, as before. But Egyptian law demands that he now relinquish it, within forty-eight hours:

---

[2]   For example, the recently discovered late period Roman villa outside Bath, with one of the finest mosaics ever discovered in England. This was unearthed in a playing field, and after the archaeologists concerned had expressed their exhilaration at the 'greatest moment of their careers', was promptly buried again. Why? Because the monetary value of the site and mosaic were less than the profit on a single bungalow, and apparently there is not even enough interest — or possibility of revenue — to create a museum around it. And the value of sacrament? Not in the running, it seems.

> Whoever finds a moveable antiquity or part or parts of an immoveable antiquity must notify such to the nearest administrative power within 48 hours... The antiquity becomes the ownership of the State... (Article 24, Law 117 of the Year 1983)

If he does this, however, it will not benefit him. Oh yes, if the antiquity is important enough the 'competent standing committee' may recompense him, but the process is open to vagaries and corruption. And I have never known it to happen.

And there is another risk. If there are more objects on hand — if the site is obviously important — the competent standing committee will declare it 'archaeological land' and requisition it — but only for its agricultural value. No account is taken of the value of antiquities already found, or as yet undiscovered:

> Lands owned by individuals may be expropriated for their archaeological importance. The possibility of the presence of antiquity in the expropriated land is not observed in the compensation. (Article 18)

In short, the farmer risks being thrown off his own land.

If the antiquity is 'immovable' — what we would call 'architectural' — the risks are even greater. The committee will declare his land 'archaeological' as a matter of course, and expropriate it but, again, only for its agricultural value.

And the law offers a clear enticement for betrayal. If the farmer fails to disclose — fails to jeopardize his patrimony that's to say, and see it requisitioned for nothing more than its agricultural value — he can be denounced by his enemies, who will be rewarded:

> In estimating the value of the expropriated land, the value of antiquities found on said land is not observed. But the authority may grant whoever guided to the antiquity a recompense... (Article 23)

A clear enough enticement.

And if the farmer fails to disclose within those forty-eight hours? This is the worst case of all. His land can be seized without any compensation, and himself thrown into prison:

> Whoever steals an antiquity...or fails to declare said antiquity... that is owned by the state or hides the same or participates in any such crimes...In this case the sets, instruments, machinery property and cars used in the crime are to be confiscated...and

shall be punished by imprisonment for not less than 5 years and not less than E£3,000 and not more than E£50,000. (Article 41)

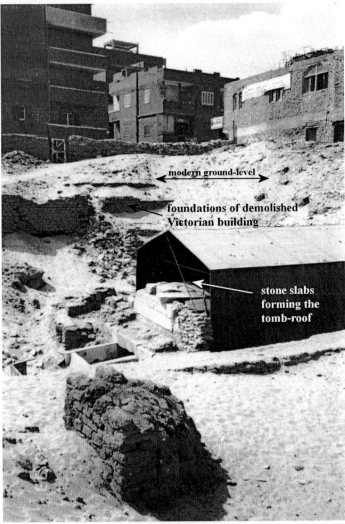

A classic example of how it works. In 1985 some builders demolished a Victorian three-story in a fashionable Cairo suburb, only to discover it had been built on top of a Saite tomb. The site was requisitioned, grandiose plans were mooted to excavate the other two tombs on site, and transpose the first to a safer place. By 1993 (this photograph is dated October of that year) an iron roof had been erected–for no obvious reason–a succession of armed soldiers had guarded the corrugated fence at the front, and two 'restorers' had spent a considerable amount of time drinking tea. But nothing else had been done, and certainly nothing to the tomb. I rather doubt that anything will be done. I also doubt whether the builders have been compensated, except for the 'agricultural value' of the site.

The author inside the tiny tomb, in 1985. By 1993 it already begun to suffer from the damp atmosphere.

The second option, the 'Gift from God'

That is the first option. It is hardly ever used, and why should it be? It does the farmer no good at all, and will probably embroil him with hateful authority — and that, as he knows all too well, will only make him the loser. The Egyptian peasantry fear authority, if they fear nothing else. If the farmer is bold or desperate, however, there is another option. He can contact the local dealers, or make his way to Cairo.

JOURNAL: 27th April 1993, Cairo

Ali has just spent several days with some fellaheen, *looking for the top of a statue. They'd found the lower parts while digging a* shadat, *and came to Cairo looking to sell. But why your shop? I asked Ali. And how do they find you?*

— 'These very simple people, my friend. They never see tourists in their village, and they think pharoni *[tourist copies] and* antikas *[genuine antiquities] are the same. They come into Cairo past our shop–always they go past our shop–and they see my* pharoni *in the window. They think are real antiques, and they think we buy their pieces. Is very easy for us.*

In this way he can sell his objects, but he risks denunciation from his enemies. And that means disaster. In historical
terms this is quite a turnabout. When Napoleon's expedition
first stepped ashore some two hundred years ago, remember, they found the Egyptians living amongst the ruins.
Quite literally so, for Bedouin were living in the tombs at
Luxor, and the tombs at Sakkara were being quarried for
building stone. As for the rest, the attitude was one of puritan
vandalism, or at best disdain for the transience of pomp.

But Napoleon's expedition—and especially his redoubt-
able academicians—created an enthusiasm for Egyptian art,
a passion that has only burgeoned with the years. Collectors
appeared, and with them the idea of a market. Antiquity
became saleable. An antiquity unearthed became a *gift from
God* to its finder, to his family and their descendants. It meant
unexpected wealth, an escape from unending labour.

But this gift from God has now been denied the Egyptians.
Antiquity has been claimed by the regime, and no longer
benefits the ordinary people, unless they are prepared to
accept the risks. A classic case of 'us and them' has developed, as Bernard von Bothmer had grasped as early as the
'sixties. The ordinary Egyptian regards the government's
Prohibition as a simple matter of ownership—and so do I, as
a matter of fact—that the ruling cast of generals, who alone
can get things done in Egypt, are making off with what is
rightfully his.

The fact that the market exists at all, given the apparatus of
the state that is ranged against the poor *fellah*—a dedicated
antiquities police force, with troops to back them up, and a
repressive law—merely shows his desperation, his hunger.
Oh, and the fact that he still knows that such things are saleable, that someone 'out there' is still prepared to pay good
money. The despised Western collectors, in fact.

And the third option?

As I am suggesting, the world is more complicated than you
might think. What seems morally persuasive from a Cambridge armchair is less so on the ground. For there is always
the third option—apart from declaration to the authorities,
that is, and the covert market—that the farmer simply
returns his antiquity to the soil. That he hides it, or destroys
it. In many ways this is the easiest option. It is certainly the

safest. And increasingly, in my intimate experience, it is the one that is chosen. The *fellah*'s world is a harsh one, after all, and the gradual result of the Prohibition is that antiquities are becoming just too much trouble.

More importantly, if a *builder* finds antiquities where he intends to build — and the majority of new archaeological sites are being found in just this way, when foundation holes are being dug, for the very first time, on the outskirts of ancient towns and villages, which would have been flooded every year until the Aswan High Dam, but are now open for development to accommodate the population explosion — if a builder finds such a site, as I say, he will simply destroy the evidence.

The black market in Egypt is well aware of this. There are many stories of discarded discoveries, and many of them convincing — heart-breakingly so. But very few cases of taking the third option — and only because of countervailing fears. After the earthquakes of the late 'eighties, for instance, when many were destitute, or approaching the first Gulf war, when many were frightened. Only then would they risk it.

JOURNAL: February 10th 1991, [During the Gulf War] Cairo

Ali and I managed to reach the suburbs, despite the road blocks. The builder was waiting with Ali's cousin, and he'd brought the head from Assyut. It was certainly impressive, a greenish stone rather like slate. And as for authenticating it, that only took a glance. It was covered with mud and crusted with calcium, but I could make out a mouth and a striated wig. Down one side, and cutting through the crust, were some new scratch marks;

– 'Ali, these marks here, they seem to be new.'

– 'The builder say his machine do it when they digging for the house.'

All this made sense. If the head had been in anybody's care–dealer, collector or curator–the dirt and crust would have been removed, and something done about these scratch marks. It followed that the builder was telling the truth. His men had only just found the thing. In fact, the builder was very straight about it all. Under ordinary circumstances, he told Ali, he'd have poured in the concrete. But he needed hard currency–everybody did in the south, they were all afraid that Sudan would blow the High Dam and

This more than life-size head of Amenhotep IIIrd is now generally accepted as one of the finest of its kind. It is, quite simply, a world masterpiece that's been snatched from the concrete mixer. And I am very proud to have been there, and to have saved it. Nobody can argue that away.

flood the valley. Give him $6,000, he said—that's what he needed to get his family to Tunisia for the duration—and he'd hand it over. And that's what we've done (well, we will have, when Ali's uncle, the State Governor, lends us the money). So, if it hadn't been for the war, this wonderful thing would have been destroyed. That's what's beginning to sink in. And that's what's horrifying.

And my journals, copious though they were, record only one example of common-sense—of people calmly deciding to flout this ridiculous law. Ironically, they were lawyers:

JOURNAL: 23rd June 1994
Ali's returned from Akhmin, having visited the 'Stelae[3] Hoard' site. The contractors wrapped his head in a towel, and took him a roundabout route (so he could never find the site himself, and denounce them, if it all turned sour). But

---

[3] Inscribed slabs of stone, resembling Western gravestones, and variously used in dynastic Egypt, in this case as boundary markers and commemoratives. This particular site was obviously important, and mentioned officials and titles previously unknown. The location of the site remains unknown, but at least the entire contents were saved, rather than concreted into an office block. And, yes, it would have been nice to (have been able to) save the knowledge as well.

once he was inside the hoardings, they showed him every-
thing. The architect was there, and provided a scale drawing
of the site, with the proposed building, and the find spots of
each stela.

It even showed how they'd been lying when they were
found. The owners seem to be a consortium of lawyers, and
they want us to instruct them. The idea is quite simple. We
pay them, and they excavate in an orderly fashion, and even
alter the building, so as to screen the site from view. They've
asked a price of $70,000 for the four stelae so far, and for
anything else they find. Ali says that's how much they'll actu-
ally need for the building. Otherwise, he explained, they'd
simply pour in the concrete and have done with it.

But how could it be otherwise? Ask yourself that. How
could anybody *expect* it otherwise — anybody who had bothered to think the matter through? What is of no benefit to the
struggling man will fall by the wayside. It is as simple as that.
Antiquity may benefit the ruling regime — for increasingly it
is a resource under their direct control, theirs to dispose as
they see fit — but it is little or no benefit to ordinary Egyptians.

After the revolution

This is a tragic situation, and I use the word 'tragic' properly
here, in the ancient sense, the sense that suggests inevitability — and useless purposeless waste — where 'cut is the
branch that might have grown straight and true'.

But this situation did not arrive overnight. It has developed by stages, and there are stages yet to come. Until Colonel Nasser's revolution there was open but restricted trading
in Egypt. Antiquities dealers were licensed, and subject to
inspection and control — largely, one suspects, for the protection of their customers. But it was possible for any Egyptian,
or any foreigner, to go to an established gallery — they were
habitually called 'museums' — and purchase an antiquity of
his choice, much as we still can anywhere else in the world.

The antiquities trade must have been an important source
of foreign currency, for although Egypt was a poor country,
the prices were already high. It is part and parcel of the Cultural Heritage Crusade that the West has been cheating these
poor countries, and paying almost nothing for their treasures. That may have been the case in the nineteenth century,
when our great museums were gathering their hoards. But as

early as the 'twenties — as Lord Caernarvon and Howard Carter found to their cost, when they thought to subsidize their Kings' Valley dig by playing the market — it was easy to pay more for an object in the Luxor bazaar than it was worth in the swish galleries of London or New York.

After the revolution, however, legislation was passed which required all loose antiquities to be registered with the government, and export was officially forbidden. More restrictions were gradually introduced. The nationalization had begun.

But the early effects were perverse, as they invariably are with prohibitions. The dealers were hardly affected, and just carried on regardless — but with a new aura about them, almost a glamour. The same thing as happened in Italy, in fact, where the new and heady atmosphere of forbidden fruit only inclined the erstwhile collectors — the lawyers and doctors, the professionals and technocrats — to lose their heads and lavish their money on fakes. The prohibition only stimulated demand, as it invariably has with all intoxicants.

The market in Egypt remained healthy, in short, but it went underground. It became a black market, and mainly dealt with pieces that had never been registered with the government. Those, and with fakes. Without academics on hand — or at least their expertise — the bad coinage could pass unrestrainedly for the good.

The new restrictions did not *suppress* the market. They just *distorted* it. And corruption blossomed, as it does with any prohibition.

Summary

- Antiquities are still being found in Egypt, but laws have progressively 'nationalized' them. The final stage was Law 117 of 1983, which claimed all antiquities — found or as yet unfound — as the property of the Egyptian state.
- Those who find antiquities, nowadays, have three posibilities:
- They can hand them over to the authorities, effectively without recompense, and risk losing their land by compulsory purchase.
- They can take a risk, and sell them on the black market,
- or they can discard or destroy them. This latter is the most likely, especially if the objects have been found on a building site.

CHAPTER 16

The Black Market in Egypt

With Law 117 of 1983, the legislation was complete. The market was officially closed. Dealers were forbidden to transact. Officially, there were no dealers, any more. Collectors who had antiquities were allowed to keep them, if they had been 'registered' – if they had been recorded with the authorities – but transfer was forbidden. They could neither be sold, nor dispensed as gifts. There were annual inspections to ensure that the same antiquities were still in the same places. And the penalties were severe if they were not.

And the effect of all this? It certainly changed things, but not in the way you would expect. Perhaps I should stress, for everything that follows, that I am speaking from direct experience (and plenty of it). I am not a journalist on assignment – grasping for facile understanding, and with a hidden agenda to coerce the facts. And I am not being fed party-line propaganda by Egyptian officials, or indignation from armchair archaeologists.

In the personal sense, therefore, I *have* no agenda. I have no axe to grind. I am just describing things, as one who lived them day-by-day for a decade, and was guided by those who had gone before, and had accumulated their own wisdom.

In other words, I'm describing things as they happen to be. I would ask you to bear this in mind when I contradict the received UNESCO orthodoxy – or when they indignantly dismiss me. I doubt there's a better informed Westerner on this score (and certainly none who is prepared to talk). This is the way it really is. Sorry.

The market still exists

The antiquities market still exists in Egypt, whatever anybody may claim. There are many objects 'in the flow', as they say. It may no longer be possible to buy from the museum:

> ### JOURNAL: 18th December 1986
> *Delivered [restoration] to the Dutchman,[1] who waxed lyrical about the good old days. In those days, he said, it'd been possible to buy directly from Cairo Museum. You'd negotiate with the guards, and agree a price. And the next day you'd return, and the only way you could tell the display had been re- arranged was by looking sideways. Then you could see the clear spaces in the dust. But what about important pieces? I'd asked.*
> *— 'Ah, for those', he said in his light guttural, 'for those, you had to speak with the Director'.*

But there are many other sources. There are *new finds*, fresh from the soil — things that have floated to the surface, and caught the eye.[2] A flash of colour in the rich brown soil, a child's curiosity, and another faience amulet has been found. These litter the soil in their thousands around the old sites:[3]

> ### JOURNAL: 13th December 1992, Luxor
> *...then to the West bank, to spend the afternoon with Old Ibrahim Ali. He may have retired–he founded the family dynasty, having started life as a farmer–but the village children still bring him what they've found; mostly amulets of course, but the occasional fragment of Roman glass or shawabti. And he pays a fair price, something to double their income. That's why they still come, from as far afield as Qena. An oriental gentleman, and someone from a gentler time.*

Once these antiquities have been unearthed, they pass to a 'catchment dealer' like Old Ibrahim Ali, and eventually to the northern cities. On the way they will pass through many

---

[1] See *Journal*, 15th March 1991, page 219.

[2] And probably not for the first time. It pleases me to think of such things performing a leisurely circle, as the aeons pass. And it's not only Egypt where this happens. One of the finest Saxon arm-torques — half a pound of solid gold — was discovered on Weymouth beach in the 'eighties, just sticking out of the sand. I imagine this piece had been buried and revealed by the shifting sands, many a time, until some newly-weds chose that spot to spread their towels — on the lucky first morning of their honeymoon.

[3] The Malkata Palace, for typical example, is nondescript grassland on the West Bank, with nothing to show but a few monuments. There is an occasional goat and its urchin keeper, and the hot drowsy days pass slowly. But just beneath its surface are tens of thousands of broken blue faience rings. In the fifteenth century BC it was a thriving palace — one of Amenhotep the Third's — and these exquisite but fragile rings were everyday wear. They are of no interest to professional archaeology because they bear no new knowledge. But they *are* cherished by collectors the world over.

Old Ibrahim Ali, the founder of the Farag dynasty, the most powerful and well-connected traders of the 1990s.

A Roman period terracotta being offered for sale in Alexandria (note the single long fingernail, of significance in Egyptian culture). Most antiquities are just like this–quite ordinary small things, of little interest to archaeologists or museums. They do not figure in the grand scheme of things. At least in small (private) collections they can be guaranteed of proper care.

hands, and each time their asking price will increase. From Cairo they'll go to a native collection, or travel abroad and slip into the 'world pool' of Egyptian art.

Then there are thousands of *old finds*. Objects from old collections, and family nest-eggs, that are placed on commission with a local dealer. The majority of stone items are in this class; fragments of wall reliefs and statuary, terracottas and cartonnage.[4] Because of their size, the objects remain in safe-houses, and when potential buyers appear, they are taken to the objects, rather than the other way round. The buyers come from all classes, but are mostly professionals; doctors, lawyers, businessmen and government apparatchiks:

> ### JOURNAL: December 17th 1990, Cairo
> *The Frenchwoman in the L'Orientaliste Bookshop, in Kasr el Nil, after chatting about antiquities, asked me to authenticate some pieces she'll bring in tomorrow. Apparently they belong to a government minister, who wants to sell, but hasn't any idea of prices. I get the feeling we're supposed to buy them, or at least place them on commission. Not the first such request, these last few weeks. Everybody's getting jittery about the war. They all want dollars.*

Then there are the *registered collections*, those declared to the regime, and allowed to remain with their 'owners', subject to the conditions I have already described. But the government records are scrappy, to say the least. There are numbers painted on the objects, and brief descriptions in the files. But very rarely any photographs. It is an easy task, therefore — given the abilities of the modern Egyptians as forgers — to substitute copies, and then to sell the originals:

> ### JOURNAL: November 27th 1992, Cairo
> *Our friend the Colonel and his adjutant–in their official capacity, that is–arrived at the Anglo-American Shop to ensure that Ahmed was still 'in possession of the Government registered antiquities' that had come with the shop. Of course Ahmed's been assiduously selling them, and substituting copies with the same numbers, as provided by Ali's factory. But I dare say the Colonel knows that already. His colleagues have been providing the paperwork for their export, after all, and charging heavily for it.*

Then there are the *foreign expeditions*. The original praxis, of site-workers selling what they had found to the highest bidder — whether black marketeers or the official excavator — has not entirely ended,[5] especially amongst the poorer expeditions:

---

[4] Cartonnage is linen dipped in plaster, then painted. Reliefs are the most contentious class, see *The problem of reliefs* in the Appendix.

[5] A praxis which had its humorous side. In Mariette's unsupervised digs for example, the first 'official' excavations on behalf of the Egyptian government,

JOURNAL: 22nd March 1988, West Bank, Luxor

In Mentuemhat's Tomb with Dr. Hussein, testing cleaning mixtures and consolidants for his doctoral research. The tomb is like a big square box below ground level. When they discovered it, in the thirties I think, it was literally full of small fragments of the most exquisite sculpted and painted reliefs, which had been blown apart by the salt. Nothing left on the walls, everything lying loose and jumbled. Now the fragments are all around the world, and there's a jolly village crew that works all day trying to piece together what's left. And all through the day, they're visited by friends from the village, who drink tea with them, then slope up the wooden ramp, with a fragment in their robe pockets. Quite a trade, I imagine, but then the whole thing's unsupervised–the Inspectors can't be bothered to leave their office–so what can they expect? One fragment represents six month's income for a villager.

Mentuemhat's tomb on the west Bank at Luxor, showing thousands of wall fragments still lying on the ground. The last figure (the one with the dark robe and white scarf) is an intruder from the village, who left soon after, no doubt with a fragment in his galabiel pocket.

when he was scouring the country to stock his new Museum in Cairo, so many things were sold off that several site-foremen — terrified of losing their lucrative position — resorted to buying in pieces from Cairo to supplement their meagre official finds. Also, see *Journal*, 14 October 1993, on page 146.

A typical fragment from Mentuemhat, such as are scattered around the world in their thousands. Barely four inches long, this would sell for $300 in Luxor, the annual average salary. The world market price, incidentally, would be about $1200 (which effectively quashes the idea that foreign 'dealers' are taking advantage of the 'ignorant' natives.)

Then there are the offerings from *government officials*. The antiquities police are tasked to guard the 'nation's' surplus of antiquities, stored in depots throughout Egypt. These include the finds of foreign expeditions, as well as confiscated collections, and confiscated stock from dealers. All these are apparently for sale:

JOURNAL: 6th September 1993, Cairo

Some delicate canvassing in the Ibis Cafe at the Hilton. A most important person has antiquities for sale—only to foreigners, of course–none other than I..., Head of Antiquities for Siwa province and Marsah Matruh, sacked for misdemeanours, but still using his office it seems—and with all his old authority. His collection, it appears, came from the Siwa lock-up store, which was mysteriously burgled the day before the state governor arrived to inspect it.

Even the top brass are in on the act:

JOURNAL: Friday 2nd July 1993, Alexandria Road

We reached the orange grove, and 'Pyramids Man' produced his famous statue. It was Old Kingdom [probably Fourth Dynasty], wooden, and nearly five foot, but quite crude and horrible. Little more than an objet trouvée, if truth be told. It was also, quite clearly, from the government workshop at Giza. We'd been there recently [Dr. Hussein and

*myself], advising the restorers on getting a better colour-
match for their infill. This one had the same garish orange
around the arm-sockets that we'd been complaining about.
It probably belonged to the same batch. I confronted Pyramids Man about the restoration. He stoutly maintained he'd
done the restoration himself– 'sure'–, and bought the statue
from a farmer–but then grinned like a naughty schoolboy
and admitted that, yes, he'd bought it from Giza, from the
Inspector,[6] and paid a high price. It was clear I'd only been
brought here to advise him on restoration (as he's asking an
astonishing $1½ million for it!). I seem to be a consultant to
everybody, these days.*

Lastly, of course, there is a flourishing cottage industry for
fakes, as much for domestic consumption as for 'tourist-
dealers' in search of thrills:

JOURNAL: Monday 11th October 1993, Cairo

*Ali and Tutu are back from Aswan, their tails between their
legs. Splendid. They'd tried to persuade me to go with them–
the farmer's tale was so convincing, my dear, and Ali was
bubbling–but for some reason I'd refused. So they decided
to prove me wrong, and shame me with something glorious.
But when they reached Aswan, 500 long miles through the
night with George-the-demon-driver–and how much sleep
did that give them!–all they found were some pharoni, fresh
from Ali's own factory in Cairo! I almost wish I'd gone along,
just to see their faces. And then of course the long drive
back.*

This is the *first point*, that a vast number of antiquities are
available, and most — unlike the Polish statue — are too insignificant for national display. Besides, there's simply no
space. If the government has them, they are wrapped in yel-

---

[6] The Chief Inspector at the time was Dr. Zahi Hawass, who had just been
sacked by Dr. Bakr, then President of the Supreme Council for Antiquities,
because of 'the theft of a valuable IVth Dynasty statue' from Giza. Shortly
afterwards, Dr. Bakr himself was sacked, amidst accusations of fraud and
malpractice, and loudly complaining of the 'mafia' which had been operating
in the Sakkara district for twenty years. He was replaced by Dr. Nuur el Deen,
who was himself disgraced in 1996, and replaced by none other than Zahi
Hawass. As for the statue, its vendor remained unknown, because 'Pyramids
Man' died soon afterwards. His kidneys had been failing, hence the
outrageous price he'd been asking for the statue. He was trying to raise
$50,000 for a transplant in Paris. He was widely mourned by dealers and
officials throughout Cairo, many of whom attended his funeral. 'They all very
sad for him,' Ali told me.

lowing newspaper and shoved anyhow into boxes, with hardly any adequate records. I have seen them.[7] It is almost impossible for any given piece to be re-located for research purposes — or any class of objects, come to that. And as for amulets, they are 'stored' in buckets. Foreign expeditions may lovingly catalogue their finds — and publish them — but after they have been handed over to the Egyptians, with all due solemnity, they disappear, and are not infrequently sold.

'Stolen' antiquities...

The *second point* is that these antiquities are not 'stolen'. Or not in any sense that we should recognise. The word 'stolen', that's to say, is being misused. Firstly, because nobody in Egypt feels they are stealing antiquities, or selling stolen antiquities. I have never known an Egyptian who wasn't keen to sell me 'his' antiquities,[8] and I have never known them feel themselves in the wrong, feel they were offering things that were not theirs to sell. Against the law, perhaps, against the regime's imposed law. But morally wrong, no.[9]

How could they feel so confident if these antiquities were really 'stolen'? And how can such things be 'stolen', bought as they have been from those who found them (or from those who bought from those who bought...) Doesn't stealing imply coercion — taking by force or fraud what is rightfully another's ? Doesn't it imply a positive act? So where was the act of theft? And where the coercion or fraud?

As far as the Egyptian people are concerned — the supposed owners of Egyptian antiquity — the real theft has been perpetrated against them by the regime. Not the other way round. 'They' (the regime) have been stealing 'our' Gifts from God. This is the people's attitude, and it's only just below the surface.

These Egyptians, therefore, are guilty of something else. They are refusing to render unto Caesar. Partly this is Islam, and partly a dogged refusal to be pushed around. And yours is a similar refusal when you exceed your duty-free

---

[7] See illustration on page 229.

[8] Or lead me to people who would be able to sell (on a commission basis, of course).

[9] The average Egyptian's attitude to the law is anyway radically different from our own, especially in the South. I dare say it is an effect of religion, that the edicts of Caesar carry a secular burden, but little moral conviction. And the ruling military caste is nothing if not secular.

allowance. You are denying the government its excessive demands.[10] It is a failure to conform, not a theft.

...and the law...

Mohammed Ali Ali Salim, director of the legal department of the Supreme Council for Antiquities, has claimed that 'the possession of an any antiquity without a licence from the Authority is considered THEFT against the State of Egypt who is the rightful owners of antiquities.'

But the relevant law, Law 117 of 1983, distinguishes various offences:

- Section 42c deals with unauthorized excavation;
- Section 41 with smuggling antiquities out of Egypt.
- Section 43e with the unauthorized possession of antiquities; and
- Section 45c with accidental possession, whereas
- Section 43a deals with transferring registered antiquities.
- Section 42b deals with demolishing or damaging immovable antiquities (buildings or sites), or movable antiquities (objects).
- Section 43b concerns the removal of stone from archaeological sites, and building or farming thereon;
- Section 43c considers the removal of soil, rubble or fertilizers from a site, or their addition.
- Section 43d examines the misuse of excavation licences (the catchall section invariably used against foreign excavators who criticize the status quo).
- Section 43f considers faking antiquities for deception or gain, and
- Section 45b deals with graffiti on antiquities,

and so on, in painstaking detail. *Only*

- Section 42a actually deals with stealing them [from government custody]

The law, that's to say, recognises the complexities of life in Egypt, and the various 'offences' that can be perpetrated against the state's *de facto nationalization* of antiquity. Only one of them is referred to by the law as 'stealing'. But Mr. Salim deliberately conflates possession, failure to declare, damage of any sort and smuggling under the one dramatic

---

[10] The parallel is not exact, but it does capture the sentiment. And that is very important. When you avoid paying tax you are not guilty of *stealing*, and your guilt — if guilt you feel — is not on that account.

title — THEFT. This may not be accurate, but it surely is deliberate. It attempts to criminalize the possession of any 'found' antiquity. It also calumnizes its owner. What had previously been a *civil* affair — a case of proper title, to be settled through the civil courts — has now been made a *criminal* act.[11]

...and a distorted market...

This is the *third point*. That the market is seriously distorted.

Until recently the majority of finds were still being made by the *fellaheen*, peasant farmers working the land. They would turn up objects with the plough, or their children simply find them in the dust as they played. In some areas — Luxor for instance, the ancient Thebes, capital of Egypt for over a thousand years — the soil was rich and prolific. The Gifts of God were everywhere under their feet.

Over the river from Luxor, in the ancient 'City of the Dead' — the West Bank necropolis — a tribe of peripatetic

The villagers of Qurna not only live between the tombs, but also on top of them. Until they were shifted, they actually lived inside many of them. Many a family has excavated through their living-room floor.

---

[11]   I am grateful to Dr. Saleh Abdul Hameed, from the Egyptian High Court of Appeal, for this timely clarification.

Bedouin had moved in from the desert centuries ago, living in the tombs themselves at first, but more recently in mud-brick houses that straddled the tombs. These Bedouin have lived off the tombs for centuries, selling what they could find or unearth—and copies of them as well. And they are still there, and still plying their trade, stubbornly resisting every attempt to shift them, and cheerfully suborning the authorities, as they have done these last two hundred years.

This still continues, of course, except that, these days, there is a deal more pressure on the *fellaheen*, whose share of the market seems to be shrinking, as the antiquities police bear down on them. Not, I suspect, that they've stopped finding things; only that they think twice before trying to sell. Either they are stockpiling what they have found, and waiting for better times, or discarding them as just too hot to handle—returning objects to the soil, or just destroying them.

The *fellaheen* are certainly becoming more difficult to work with. I noticed this myself, during the late 'eighties and 'nineties. This is partly a matter of inflation—that they need more and more money—and partly of ignorance. For how is a poor farmer, scratching a subsistence living—and earning on the average $350 a year—how is such a man to research the objects that he finds, and find out how much they're really worth?[12] He has no access to expertise. The only people who have some idea are the dealers, and they are only trying to cheat him, or so he's convinced.

His only source of information is lateral—the amount of effort the regime puts into confiscating his pieces, and stopping him from getting his hands on them in the first place. Given the panoply of the state ranged against him, our *fellah* would conclude that he is holding a pharaoh's ransom in his hands. I discovered this myself, trying to deal with them over many years. They are stubborn, and guileful, but also credulous. Impossible, in other words. However pitiful their antiquities, in world market terms, they acquire a huge importance in their imagination.[13]

---

[12] Some of the more enlightened aid agencies have concluded that providing African farmers with mobile phones—to enable them to monitor current market prices—is a far more effective way of 'making poverty history' than the proposals of superannuated rock stars.

[13] If you think this is far-fetched, consider the *scavatori* in Italy—the bands of tomb robbers, or tomb diggers, who operate in the ancient Etruscan

> ### JOURNAL: 24th April 1994 2am, Luxor
> *Just back from Qurna village, under cover of dark, where a villager offered us a group of stone pebbles—for $100,000! Now, there certainly are some valuable pebbles. Pre-Dynastic palettes, for example, usually have a depression in their surface, and very rarely one finds the hard stone pebble that fits in this depression. But not these. These were just pebbles. And the villager wasn't stupid. He knew about pre-dynastic palettes. And he knew we weren't credulous tourists, but experts from Cairo. And yet he really believed his damn pebbles were worth twenty thousand—rather than a couple of hundred, and only if the matching palette were on hand—which is why he asked the stars for them.[14] Just breathtaking.*

Most new finds, however, are being made by builders, as they throw up apartment blocks around the ancient townships, on land which the Aswan High Dam has freed from its annual inundation. And the problem is that most such finds are destroyed.

...which is becoming centralized

The general trend—and what I've observed over my time in Egypt—is that the market is becoming more and more centralized. The antiquities police are not suppressing the market—far from it—but they *are* gradually dominating it, much as supermarkets are dominating in our own countries.

In recent years, for example, it has become very difficult to avoid the antiquities police. But not in the sense you would assume, of them being the police, and attempting to suppress the market. No, not that at all. Just that more and more

---

townships—who still do have access to museums and to libraries—not to mention Sotheby's catalogues—as aids to correct pricing. In spite of all this they still habitually price their Greek vases, which they find in the Etruscan tombs, by simply counting the number of figures on the vase, and multiplying them.

[14] A matter of *souk* psychology, and of 'maintaining face'. The Middle Easterner asks a high-price, expecting progressively to drop to the price he'd always had in mind. And you must abide by the ritual. If he asks, say, 100 units (whilst expecting 20), you cannot pay the 100, and retain his respect. Nor can you offer him 2 (expecting to pay 10) without grave insult. He cannot drop so far—except over several months—and maintain his own dignity, his face. So, if the object concerned is actually only worth 10, the *bridge is just too far*, and there can never be a sale. You can only walk away, after suitably excusing yourself.

objects in the market actually 'belong' to them, and are being offered for sale through intermediaries.[15]

> ### JOURNAL: Thursday 4th March 1993
>
> *When Ali returned from Switzerland, the police were waiting for him in his flat. Apparently the fellow who sold the bronze Hamish falcon to us shouldn't have. The piece had come from a government depot–not from that village in the delta, which is what he'd told us–and apparently it had been earmarked for the new 'Museum of Treasures' at Giza (if they ever get round to building it). The police urged Ali to retrieve it–very politely, as Ali had immediately summoned his uncle the General–and even offered to get him another visa for England (although they stopped short of offering him an air-fare). It seems they're quite windy about it–about having sold the wrong thing, the one thing that'd be noticeable by its absence.[16]*

The bronze falcon known as 'Hamish'. Sixteen and a half inches from beak to tail, it is one of the finest in the world.

---

[15] Which, if nothing else, throws one's own moral position into doubt — whether the corruption of the Egyptian authorities is somehow contagious? See *Corruption – does it matter?* in the Appendix.

[16] It seems they weren't being entirely truthful, even then — or that some other antiquities police made precisely the same mistake soon afterwards — for after the bronze was returned (actually a perfect copy with 'Made in England' written on it, because we didn't believe them at the time, and they hadn't refunded us) — it re-appeared in Switzerland, some fifteen months later.

Given that the antiquities police are sitting on a stockpile of saleable antiquities, stored in numerous depots throughout the country, I would say this was a commercial tactic. If you have a precious commodity, after all, what would you do to ensure primacy in the market? Why, of course, you'd suppress the other sources. You find this an outrageous suggestion? Then read on.

The 'Merchant Princes', and their masonry with the antiquities police

The real change, you see, has been in Cairo and Alexandria. These are the entrepots, through which all antiquities are exported. For it is the little matter of *transport* that now determines the market, and gives it shape. You cannot send shipping containers to Switzerland, or to the other arab states — large containers full of antiquities, scores of them every year — without the Egyptian government being aware of it. You cannot do this without their active assistance. For this is smuggling on an industrial scale.

The cost of such a container — to the dealer, that is, who has bought the antiquities in Egypt, and now wants to ship them to the *freilagers* — the free-ports of Zurich and Geneva — from where they can be trans-shipped anywhere in the world without paying customs duty, or can be sold directly to antiquities dealers, direct from the freilager *cabines* — the cost of such a container is about $40,000. And of this, only $4,000 is the actual shipping cost. The rest is payment to the antiquities police, who provide the paperwork — the documents plastered with official rubber stamps, with everywhere the Egyptian eagle — the paperwork that certifies the contents of the containers as *pharoni*, copies made for the tourist market, and not genuine antiquities at all. That is how the modern market works.

> **JOURNAL: 2030hrs (yes, on time!)**
> **Friday January 15th 1993**
> *Ali took me to Mohammed's office. His eldest brother is charming. He explained that one paid for the container, not the contents, and the price was $40K, most of which went to the 'secret police' for the documentation.. Two weeks ago we could have shared a container with Ahmed [Ali's other half-brother] and G.., and paid quarter price, but now, if we wanted to transport quickly, we'd have to pay for the whole*

container, even if it only contained the one item. If we went for this, the piece could be processed tomorrow, and be in Switzerland in 25 days.

I remarked that Ali's brother was very matter of fact about it all.

– 'Is business, my friend. He do this for many years, maybe five times a year, maybe more. He make a company with the police.'

JOURNAL: 15th March 1991, Cairo

Ali reported back from the antiquities police. He'd been asking whether they could help with transport. They could do various things, the Colonel says. They could meet me at the airport, and walk me through customs. Or they could drive me to the airport, as if I were a VIP. But that was more expensive. In the Dutchman's day this had only cost him £E100. Now it was a healthy $1,000. But then he had been an MP–head of his party, in fact–and he'd been working for the United Nations. Finally, the colonel said, he could send some of his 'Captains'–that's what Ali calls them–round the back, to put my suitcase directly on the aircraft. But we'd have to take the chance they'd manage to find the right aircraft.

All through the 'nineties it was possible and commonplace to 'go down to Switzerland', and visit the frielager *cabines* to inspect the thousands of pieces that had just been shipped out of Egypt. All the world's dealers were making this pilgrimage, and the auction houses as well, no doubt. And all of them making the same assumption, that what they were seeing had been 'legitimated' by the Egyptian government – that unless the authorities had actively assisted in such a transport, the transport itself would have been impossible. The antiquities were there, in Switzerland, and therefore, by that very fact, they'd been 'legitimised'. That was the dealers' assumption, and I'd have to say it was correct. Wouldn't you?

And it's those dealers who work with the antiquities police – those I have dubbed the *merchant princes* – who now dominate the market. These dealers are a new breed. They are cosmopolitan. They may be Egyptian, or part-Egyptian, but they understand the world market. They flit between Cairo, Switzerland and the new market centre of Paris. Each of them works closely with his coterie of high-ranking officers, the Brigadiers and Generals who have the power in Egypt. They dine together.

JOURNAL: 12th June 1987, Cairo suburbs

Tutu's [Ali's brother's] wedding party. The family had simply commandeered a side-street, emptied some truck-loads of sand to cover the trash, put a stage at one end, and strung up the fairy-lights. The party was in full-swing, with the Cairo police band hammering away–courtesy of Ali's Uncle –when Ahmed's [Ali's elder brother] party arrived. They made a splendid procession, with generals of the antiquities police, and directors of Cairo Museum–past as well as present– and amongst them G...[a Swiss Dealer] and her sister. Ali murmured to me:

*–'G... works with my brother Ahmed. She buy many things. But she cannot come to Egypt, because the police arrest her. She has four passports, and always she use a different name. They know all this. They know all about her. But she is good for business, so they give her three days before they know she is here. Then they **must** arrest her.'*

The Cairo police band at Tutu's wedding, which was also attended by the international antiquities market, the dealers, the antiquities police, and the museum officials.

JOURNAL: 27th January 1992

Apparently, our friends the antiquities police–they're most definitely that now, and pledging eternal friendship–are 'having big problems' with G... They've been sending things via her nephew in Alexandria, and G.. has been bouncing them all back because 'published'–because they've been recorded in a book or article, and would be recognised as 'stolen' if they turned up in the outside world.[17] The stuff has all ended up in the their 'secret room in Zurich'–whatever that means–where the famous shawabti[18] is now.

Now the main hazard to these merchant princes is not from the authorities, for they work together, on a daily basis. No, the real danger is from each other. They are battling for dominance, for customers and sources. Add their internecine jealousies, their readiness to betray and denounce to further their own cause, and you can understand the feuding that runs through the market.

When these squabbles occur, the only real beneficiaries are the antiquities police. They can always benefit from the rending of flesh. They can revert to their official duties, and diligently enforce the law, or at least give that appearance. Money changes hands, everything is quietly forgotten, and after a decent interval it is business as usual. What you must never do is take things as they appear. Appearances are only for the gullible West. Consider the tale of P..., a Canadian, and a major 'source' of 'fresh' antiquities for the New York market. A while ago, he found himself in a spot of bother.

JOURNAL: Wednesday 10th June 1992
P... was arrested the day before yesterday. The whole thing was televised, and headline news, because the raid uncovered 'gold statues' estimated at '50 million American dollars'. In reality they're gilded wood, as the Colonel told Ali with an eloquent shrug, and worth no more than $100,000 (probably not even that, as I've severe doubts about their authenticity) but, after all, the authorities don't often get such an opportunity to strut their stuff. Apparently the raid followed a detailed denunciation by Ahmed [Ali's brother]. He directed them to P...'s stockpile, and gave them $10,000 to get a move on (otherwise they'd have taken the money from P..., and qui-

---

[17] If an antiquity has been published whilst it is still in Egypt, and after Law 117 of 1983 forbade the export of antiquities — and if it then turns up in the outside world — it follows that it has been 'smuggled', and is officially 'stolen from the Arab Republic of Egypt' — whoever actually owned and sold it — and is liable to a civil courts action by the Egyptian regime. What they do with it after they have it back is another matter entirely. See *Journal*, 4th December 1986, page 242.

[18] The Shawabti of Iurudef, see *Journal*, December 21st 1991, page 234.

etly forgotten about it). This splendid act of national devotion was Ahmed's retaliation for a very tiresome month in Switzerland, after somebody had denounced him for having a cabine in the freilager *[freeport]. The authorities knew **that**, of course–or at least some of them did, the ones who'd been providing his shipping documents–but it was anyway embarrassing. The irony is that Ahmed denounced the wrong man. It wasn't P... at all...*

JOURNAL: Wednesday 15th July 1992
Everything very jittery after P...'s arrest, with dealers trying to offload of their stock, because of the authorities' new strategy–publicly announced on the television–that any dealer arrested will have his assets confiscated, all of them, and not just the antiquities (which, incidentally, is way beyond the prescription of the law, of Article 117 of 1983).

JOURNAL: Sunday 6th September 1992
P's trial was yesterday. His photo's in all the magazines, with a shaven head, rather shocking. The judgment against him? Confiscation of all his Egyptian assets–house, flat, bank funds, stock etc.,–and an order to quit the country within ten days, and never return. This is actually rather lenient–he should have faced a minimum of ten-year's hard labour. Money has obviously changed hands.

All very convincing, of course, unless you knew the whole story — what went before, and what came after. And what was moving beneath the surface. For after such a public ceremony, with newspaper and television coverage, you would naturally conclude that P... could never return. No, never. He had been disgraced, and hounded from the scene. And yet, fifteen months later, he was back in Egypt, and once again he was trading. He had simply negotiated through his own coterie of officers, and paid a bribe of $180,000.[19]

And so it continues. Antiquity has become a resource, which can only be handled by dealers and by antiquities police working together. It's little more than a game.

---

[19] The journal entry, detailing the officers concerned, has been edited out to protect their identities.

JOURNAL: Friday 25th June 1994

Just as I was becoming exasperated about Ali's late arrival, Fat Hassan arrived to say that there's been a 'play' with Ahmed [Ali's half-brother]. We took the back alleys to the shop–Hassan explaining that the 'government people' had been closeted with Ahmed for half-an-hour, and when Ali had dropped in to see what Ahmed was up to, he'd triumphantly been shown photographs of Horemhab [a fake head by the Berlin Master] and 'George' [a genuine Old Kingdom statue], for which Ahmed had just paid $20,000 on deposit. What Ahmed didn't know was that the pieces were in England and New York respectively, that I'd taken the photos myself, during my restoration, and Ali had supplied them to the Colonel. Ali had great difficulty keeping a straight face. But, oh, the scallywags!! What can you do but laugh...

It would be rather fun if Ahmed paid a lot for Horemhab, because then he'd sell it to G... in Switzerland, at which stage it would bounce. Also, because it made Ali's position very strong. The secret police would be pushing him hard to take delivery of Horemhab, having already sold it to Ahmed. And Ali obviously hasn't mentioned that it's still in England...

Horemhab, as sculpted by the 'Berlin Master' (who also probably made the head of Meryet-Amun, see page 5.)

Sometimes, however, it can all get out of hand:

JOURNAL: 15th May 1992, Luxor

Interesting news from Qurna. F..., the patron of the Abul Kasim hotel of ill-repute, had had a fake statue manufactured in his alabaster factory, which he left with some farmers in Edfu. Then he took a merchant from Qena, and persuaded him to buy it for a princely £40,000 Egyptian. Unfortunately the merchant overheard that his purchase was counterfeit. He went back to F..., who washed his hands of it all, and sent him back to Edfu. At Edfu the farmers explained that the money was actually with F... (minus their commission, of course), and that the piece had been F...'s all along. This outraged the merchant, who despatched four armed men to the village, where they managed to shoot and seriously wound three others before kidnapping F...'s son. They then demanded a ransom of $100,000. As a result the police have thrown everybody in jail, in F...'s case for 'selling antiquities'. Ali's uncle, the state governor, is on the way to sort it all out, for a fee (in his case, a modest £5,000 Egyptian).

Summary

- There are many antiquities for sale in Egypt, and from various sources;
- from the peasantry, the bourgeoisie and apparatchiks, and increasingly from the authorities (those responsible for guarding the 'national heritage').
- These are not 'stolen' goods, or not in any conventional sense. The word is being used as propaganda.
- The market has been distorted, however. New finds are increasingly being made by builders,
- and the major dealers, of necessity, have formed a symbiosis with the antiquities police.

CHAPTER 17

The Egyptian Authorities
Are Involved

Shenanigans like this, however, are far from the norm. For the most part it all goes smoothly. It is strictly commercial, after all.

For one who has watched all this, moreover — and watched it very closely, I have to say — it is difficult to resist the conclusion that the authorities are taking control of the market. Yes, indeed they are, but largely for their *own benefit*.

As the supply of new finds begins to dwindle (as the Prohibition begins to bite) their own stockpile increases in importance. They already have a huge surplus of 'moveables', of antiquities that are held in the depots because, quite simply, there is no display space for them. However they've been acquired — whether confiscated from *fellaheen* or dealers, found by themselves, or received from foreign expeditions — they are now *surplus to requirements*.

The economic mechanism of all this is familiar to us in the West. OPEC used it against us in the 'eighties, when they had gained complete control of the world's oil-supplies, and thought to make themselves rich by hiking the prices.

Attitudes to the Egyptian Antiquities Service

There are two historical attitudes to the Egyptian Antiquities Service — and its successor the Egyptian Antiquities Organisation (the EAO). One regards the service and its officers with a degree of compassion — as honest men, undervalued and ill-paid, who are doing their best in difficult circumstances. The other regards them with contempt — as scoundrels, both venal and corrupt. Traditionally the English tend to the latter view, partly because the service was dominated by Frenchmen, but mainly because it's consistently turned out to be true — and Englishmen, at least in the past, were still able to tolerate the truth.

It is worth remembering that the Antiquities Service was not founded to 'conserve' Egyptian Antiquity. Oh no. Its task was to channel as many looted or excavated antiquities into government hands as possible. As the great Flinders Petrie observed:

> Mariette [the first Director of the Service] most rascally blasted to pieces all the fallen parts of the granite temple by a large gang of soldiers, to clear it out instead of lifting the stones and replacing them by means of tackle... Nothing seems to be done with any uniform and regular plan, work is begun and left unfinished; no regard is paid to future requirements of exploration, and no civilized or labour-saving devices are used. It is sickening to see the rate at which everything is being destroyed, and the little regard paid to preservation.[1]

From the beginning the service was corrupt and incompetent, the museum was in a shocking state, and the curators busily selling off the stock, even as new stuff was arriving. Petrie wryly observed that 'the museum had a peculiar way of doing business without cheques'.

It is interesting how little has changed over the last hundred years, despite the apparent change of intellectual fashion. A description of Sir Wallis Budge's antics in the 1880s could stand as well for now, and the same is true of the widespread corruption in the Antiquities Service. They are still, as ever, cheerfully selling what they are supposed to be guarding. These recent events in Egypt, for instance. Are they a noble attempt to suppress an illicit market, or are they just part of that market — factional struggles between antiquities police and their client-dealers to control the *resource of antiquity*?

I sympathize with the British Museum, anyway, who are required — by diplomacy and the Foreign Office, if not by good breeding — to regard the Egyptian Antiquities Service as worthy colleagues, when they must know better. They must. But I have to say it makes them look foolish — if they actually believe what the Egyptians serve up for their consumption — or else blatant toadies, who are afraid of having to give back some of their own collection.

---

[1]   *Ten Years Digging in Egypt 1881-1891*, London 1892.

But I am disappointed that archaeologists generally are so easily cowed into silence. There are many who know what is happening in Egypt — that antiquity is being treated as an economic resource, as a commodity, and treated appallingly — but none of them dare speak up, as the great Egyptologist Bernard von Bothmer did. Presumably they are afraid of having their precious licences revoked. But their contempt of the EAO is clear enough, if you have eyes to see.

In some cases, however, it can only be naivety (or neo-colonialism perhaps, treating the natives as *grown-up children* — charming enough, but hardly responsible for what they do). John Romer, for example, in his otherwise devastatingly good book *The Rape of Tutankhamun* — which everybody should read, incidentally — first tells the heartless truth about Western archaeology, but then eulogises the EAO in a most unconvincing way.

Firstly, he claims, that 'each year, the EAO spends colossal sums on maintenance and conservation'.[2] They don't. They spend even less than they earn from the sale of tickets to the sites and the museums, almost nothing of the $2.5 billion that tourism earns each year for Egypt — though most if not all of that is antiquity-driven — and less than 3% of their World Bank loans for tourism.[3]

Then he manages to suggest that a large proportion of the EAO's 15,000 employees are somehow involved in conservation. They aren't. No more than a few hundred have ever picked up a scalpel, according to Dr. Hussein. And he should know, if anyone does. The EAO, like the American army in Vietnam, has a very long tail, and very few infantry.

Lastly, and caressingly, he praises their abilities, that 'for the most part the Egyptians have to manage quite alone. It is fortunate for the world heritage that they are both skilful and resourceful'. They are not. They are *busy* enough, as I have already explained. But they are utterly incompetent. There are barely a handful that would be employed by any Western restorer, and I am not speaking of their technical ability — their specific knowledge of current techniques and materi-

[2]   *The Rape of Tutankhamun*, John and Elizabeth Romer, 1993

[3]   Nearly all of which is spent on 'infrastructure' — roads, airports, ferries and hotels — getting more and more people more efficiently into Kings' Valley without coming into contact with ordinary Egyptians. There is little or none for rectifying or preventing the damage the tourists do when they get there, see page 255.

als—but of how good they are with their hands. In fact, in Egypt, most of what they do is *pretend* work, which keeps them out of trouble, and safe from judgement and its consequences. Only a diplomat would claim otherwise.

But will the Egyptian authorities always be corrupt?

There are really two questions here, and the first is an easy one. Yes, in my opinion—and knowing what I know—I would say it was inevitable that each new generation of officers will end up with their hands in the till. There is no welfare system in Egypt, no safety net for the indigent. The Egyptian extended family is their only buffer against a harsh world—against calamity that passes for the will of God, and the inevitabilities of old age and sickness and officialdom's tyranny. The family must find the resource for all these, and a man of authority or wealth will be looked to by his numerous kin and dependents.

At a purely practical level it has been my experience that any officer over the rank of major in the antiquities police (or Inspector in the Antiquities Commission) is a dealer—in *posse* if not in *esse*. Either he has already sold government antiquities, or will as soon as he gets the chance. Or he has already helped with shipping them out of the country. This is my working assumption, after an extensive experience of the species:

> ### JOURNAL: Wednesday June 10th 1992, Cairo
> The Colonel's solved the problem of repaying Ali's loan. He instructed to Ali to hire a flat-bed truck, and wait until the [antiquities] depot was closing. Then the Colonel marched out a large crate, born on the shoulders of four squaddies, and simply told Ali to bring it back tomorrow. Ali drove it to Dokki, where the street market greeted him like a hero, and everybody carried it up to the flat. There must have been thirty men helping. The crate itself was about four ft. by four by three, and very heavy, maybe 300 lbs, maybe more. The lid was nailed down, and covered with government stamps. When this was removed, a vast quantity of yellowing newspaper was revealed. Everything was wrapped in the stuff: all sorts of antiquities, from amulets to lumps of stone, and from every period, all jumbled together. The only concession to good practice was that the heavy stone slabs—which would have crushed the delicate stuff—had been thrown into the

This government crate, measuring 5' by 4' by 3', contained over a hundred assorted antiquities, from a large stone relief in six pieces to tiny amulets. They were piled in anyhow, amongst a mass of rotting newspaper. Few had stock-numbers, there were no photographs, and no overall records. Most interesting of all, however, was that over half the contents were fake.

bottom.[4]

The Colonel had told Ali to take what he wanted, and replace them with copies bearing the same numbers. He'd been most particular about this. But very few things had numbers at all. And the really peculiar thing was that half the contents were fake. Did that mean they'd already been replaced–by Ali's predecessors, or some other general's customers, and this had been going on for years–or that poor farmers were being thrown in prison for selling tourist copies?

And the same logic applies to the military:

JOURNAL: Tuesday 5th July 1993, Cairo
Tutu [Ali's brother] arrived about 2am, just as I was getting to sleep, and full of braggadocio. He'd been to Beni Suef to

---

[4] Appositely, the only thing that reached the West from this (and a subsequent crate) was an Old Kingdom relief from Sakkara, which had been scattered unrecorded through the crates in seven pieces, and effectively lost. They were identified by myself as belonging together — itself no mean feat, given their condition — and then re-assembled and extensively conserved. I personally consider — knowing everything I do — that this relief has been saved for posterity, from such neglect as would have reduced it, given time, to unrecognisable stones in the bottom of a forgotten crate. And no, I didn't make any money from this. I lost by it.

*organize with the relevant general about an excavation of
the land his father owned twenty-five years ago. This is to
take place on Saturday (read: sometime this month). It
sounds like a minor temple cache, and previously yielded
various large bronzes–Sekhmets, Horuses, Osirises etc–to
his father. Apparently it was the original source of the family
wealth. His father had closed the area, having taken enough
to establish himself and his sons. The arrangement seems
to be that the general, for turning a blind eye, and arresting
any interlopers, as well as manning the perimeter and providing safe passage out of the area in a provided car, will
receive 75,000 Egyptian pounds (or more on a half-and-half
basis).*

It is clear, for example, that tombs under government protection cannot be robbed without the compliance of the
authorities. I do not believe, you see, that it is possible to rob
a tomb which is constantly guarded — as the Americans say,
twenty-four/seven, and by soldiers armed with assault
rifles — unless there is complicity. I simply do not believe it
possible. At the very least the soldiers must be distracted —
persuaded to *watch the wall, my darlings*. And if the soldiers,
then also their officers. And if the officers, then presumably
the Antiquities Inspectorate:

JOURNAL: Tuesday 24th June 1994, Minea, Upper Egypt
*Dr. Hussein was called out in the night to accompany some
militia. They drove to el......[a notable site], and found a tomb
with its roof cut open. Whilst they were inside some shooting
started outside. Hussein had to sleep inside.*

*Apparently the army had burgled the tomb, using heavy
cutting equipment brought from Alexandria, the whole site
being sealed off by the Chief Inspector of Antiquities, and
the site guards being paid (£E100 each to watch the wall).
The whole thing was funded by a politician in Alex–or maybe
a businessman, nobody seems sure–who was to get the
sarcophagus (a rather fine Schist one). It had only gone
wrong when an NCO refused to drive his lorry with the sarcophagus on board through the military check-point at Beni
Suef. Whilst they were trying to sort this out–the Inspector of
antiquities saying it was an army matter, and the Brigadier of
Engineers saying it was out of his area–the head of the site
guards panicked and told local police (not the antiquities
police) what was going on. The subaltern there rang the*

Interior Ministry in Cairo, secretly because he was heavily outranked. The Ministry assumed that everyone was involved–the local government, the military, the Antiquities Commission, the Antiquities Police–the whole damn lot of them. So they scrambled militia from the neighbouring governorate, who'd collected Dr. Hussein on the way (I assume because he'd only just got back from Germany, and was the only one they could trust).

JOURNAL: July 10th 1994

Ali's solved the problem of the fire-fight. He actually went to the village. Apparently the Chief Inspector had told the guards he was taking the sarcophagus to the museum, so when some trucks turned up in the middle of the night, the guards assumed they'd come to steal it, and took a pot-shot or two at the militia.

JOURNAL: June 14th 1994, Anglo-American Bookshop[5]

Ahmed and Tutu were in the shop with Dr. S...–the former director of Cairo Museum, the very same–the one who'd eventually got himself fired for losing over three hundred pieces from the Museum, some of them rather large (including a three metre sphinx), which he'd claimed he was re-arranging for display. Now they were discussing the recent tomb- robbery. S... said that 'nothing would happen about army thieves. Maybe the Inspector finish his work [retire, that is, on full pension], but nothing more. They all laughing about it.'

If we learn nothing else from history, it is indeed that nothing changes. Those famous trials of the XXIst Dynasty (circa 1200BC) arraigned the craftsmen from Deir el Medina, the royal workers' village — whose job it was to prepare the royal

---

[5]   At that time, the main entrepôt for 'fresh' antiquities in Cairo, and clearly recognised as such by the authorities. The antiquities police kept it under surveillance during the day but, as Ali had explained to me:

JOURNAL: 27th April 1993 [continued]
'they finish their work at ten o'clock, maybe eleven. Then they make report that 'nothing happening here', and go home. Then we open the shop for the farmers. Sometimes they stay longer. But they very kind, and they let us know. Sometime they make raid on the shop, but they always telephone before, so Tutu is ready. If they ask 'what's in the safe?', he say 'is private', and if they ask 'what's upstairs?', he say 'is only fakes'. Everybody is happy, they make report, and Tutu he give them whisky. They very fond of whisky, you know'

tombs in Kings Valley — for robbing those self-same tombs.
The trials ended in some confusion when it became evident
that they *couldn't have done it alone*. You can hear a brooch-pin
drop at night in the Kings' Valley — let alone a shovel-full of
earth, or a pick-axe — and it's inconceivable that the Kings'
Valley guardians — the ever-present *Medjet* — could have
been unaware of what was going on. And if they were aware,
then so were their bosses, and so was the high priesthood
over-the-water in Karnak. Indeed it would have been impossible without their assistance. To put it bluntly, they were the
ones with the map. How else could a tomb have been rifled in
Kings Valley, whilst the front door remained undisturbed?
Somebody had told the tomb-robbers where to dig.

No, the conclusion to be drawn from those trials — and
nothing has changed over the intervening centuries — is that
when a guarded tomb is repeatedly looted, it has effectively
been sold, in one form or another, deliberately or by deliberate inattention. The notorious tomb of Hetep-ka, for instance,
has been under armed guard since its discovery and publication in the early 'seventies. During that period — if the official
records are to be believed — it has been robbed and rifled no
less than seven times. Oscar Wilde springs to mind: once
may be a misfortune, my dear, and twice a carelessness — but
seven times? Oh no, that's something else entirely. And as I
have also said, the officer corps in Egypt is all-powerful.
Only the military and the police can get things done:

JOURNAL: Sunday 9th August 1992

*T…'s store-room has been burgled. Nothing so strange
about that, but his reaction was remarkable. He stomped
down to antiquities police headquarters, and demanded
they get the bloody things back. These were 'stolen' antiquities he'd lost, please note. And these the dedicated police
whose task it was to prevent them from being stolen. If
there'd been any justice, T… would've been arrested on the
spot. But he is a powerful politician, and they don't call him
'the Prince' for nothing. Anyway, the police set about it, with
all the diligence you'd expect from a conscientious constabulary. They arrested two of T…'s former employees, and
held them for two days. Ali collected them when they were
released.*

*— 'They use electric shock, you know, on feet, and lips,
and between the legs. But these are village men. They very*

strong. They know if they say the truth, they stay in prison for long time. But if they say nothing, the police must make chuck-out.'

And so it was. T... was outraged, and the police were apologetic. But without a confession, they said, what more could they do?

If a captain can effectively kidnap a citizen and hold him in detention, without any of the checks and balances that coddle us through in the West, it follows that this captain's superior, his general, is a very powerful man indeed. Egypt is run by an inner circle of such generals. They are effectively beyond the reach of the law:

JOURNAL: Sunday 25th April 1993, Cairo

Ali arrived with a new tale to tale. This illustrates something, but I'm not quite sure what. He'd arrived back last night to the following. The secret police, in the guise of one of their highest- ranking officers, had been pretending to buy antiquities from Ali's cousins... The official had only been offered fakes, but when he'd revealed himself one of the brothers had grabbed his identification, thrown it aside, and then actually attacked him! This was the real crime. Ali had interceded, and then Tutu and Ahmed. By six in the morning it was settled as follows: that the police should have two of the brothers, who'll come to court today, and be charged with draft-dodging (this old chestnut came to light, apparently) and with selling antiquities. The general confided to Ali, 'we know now that they were only fakes, but we've changed them with antique pieces—all part of the deal, you see—and then we can free the old man, and the third brother, who is just commencing a career in law'.

The sentence, as with V... [airline cabin-crew, caught with a suitcase of papyri] will commence with a custodial of, say, four days, followed by one of thirty days, followed by the possibility of a bribe to scotch the whole.

And just as these generals have fought to their present exalted position, so they intend to use it while they can:

JOURNAL: Saturday December 21st 1991

Ali just returned from antiquities police headquarters, where he'd been closeted with a full general. Rather intimidated by the experience. Two guards behind him with machine-pistols. He'd been offered, with magnificent condescension;

The Shawabti of
Iurudef. Where is it
now?

— 'a shawabti in black schist, Dynasty nineteen, and very important. The big man, he want $100,000'.

I asked whether he'd actually seen this marvel?

— 'No, is in Suisse. They say they have a room there, for keeping things. And they can transport. But he give me photograph.'

But what Ali had wasn't a photo. It was a photocopy of a fax half-tone, and it had the fax print-outs, just discernible, if you knew where to look. It had been sent on February 19th from Switzerland—from Galerie M… in Zurich, [G…'s gallery]. As for the photograph, I felt sure I'd seen it before. The American University book-shop had what we wanted: The Hidden Tombs of Memphis, *Professor Geoffrey Martin's book about the Anglo-Dutch expedition. And there it was, plate 94,[6] a full-page black-and-white photograph of the Shawabti of Iurudef,[7] the same as the General's fax half-tone. Clear evidence that the secret police—as Ali calls them—have inadvertently been selling excavated items, and having them returned because they're published.*

This, incidentally, was further proof of the symbiosis—of the necessity for symbiosis—of which I have spoken. The Egyptian antiquities police have the *custody* of antiquities excavated by foreign expeditions, after they have been handed over. Many of these are published in the West, in

[6] Which the author was refused permission to reprint by the Egypt Exploration Society. One wonders why? and what they're afraid of.

[7] This eleven inch 'masterpiece of the figurine-maker's art' was, according to our reports from the antiquities police secretariat, later disposed of as an embarrassment. As Ali reported: 'they make chuck-out, into the water'. This could be wrong, of course. It would only require the Egyptian authorities to produce the piece from storage. And whilst they were at it, they could also produce the Head of Horemhab's wife, plate 57 of the same book, which they'd previously sold to the same Swiss dealer—for $50,000—and also had returned. The book shows the statue intact. The police told Ali the head had been 'broken in transport'. 'Broken for transport' sounds more likely.

scholarly journals. For a long time the Egyptian authorities seemed unaware of this. They seemed to have no idea which antiquities had been published, and what this meant. In short, that they couldn't be sold without being immediately recognised — and returned. For this they needed Western expertise, and preferably before the items had been paid for.

A recent development, however, suggests they've become aware of this inconvenience, and learned how to get round it:

> **JOURNAL: 14th June 1995**
> *Long discussion with Fred [Schultz, President of the American Dealers Association], who told me that a valley temple has recently been discovered in Memphis–or, more correctly, the temple causeway that connects it with higher ground. When it was discovered, the causeway decoration was splendidly intact. But almost immediately–within two months–sections started appearing in the New York market, before there'd been any chance to record them, or even to photograph. The obvious conclusion–given that the site's been under armed guard–is that they've been deliberately removed before they could be fixed in time and place by publication. And that this constitutes a sale rather than a theft, and a decidedly cynical one.*

Is this really a *corruption*, or just the 'Egyptian way'?

The second question is the more interesting one: that of the *Egyptian way*. Is this really a *corruption* — a despicable form of betrayal, as seen from our Western perspective — or is it just the *Muslim way of life*, where family is put firmly before duty? The Koran tells the Muslim to serve his family, to care for them and provide. And it is a duty that overrides any other duty, whether to state or the tribe. And how is the good Muslim to manage this — except through the *perquisites of position*?

Egypt is a poor country where government salaries are held down, but consumption — and inflation — floats free. The national average income may remain below $500 a year — and a major's $90 dollars a month seem grand by comparison — but not in the city, where each middle-class person needs $80 a month to live appropriately.[8] The major will be badly squeezed to maintain the dignity — the *face* — which his

[8]   My figures refer to the early 'nineties. They may have climbed by now — one would expect them to, given an undeclared inflation of perhaps 15% — but the proportions will remain intractably the same.

rank and position demands. Luckily, position has its perquisites, and any man of rank is expected to use them. There is wide scope for bribery in return for favours or denunciation.

It is not that I sympathize with the antiquities police, merely that I've accepted the inevitability of what has been happening — and what will always happen, until the *Prohibition* is lifted, and a little common sense can return.

Putting it bluntly, corruption is a falling away from the norm — a rotting down, if you like. But this just *is* the norm. This is their way of life, and nothing will change it. We achieve little by being priggish about this, and nothing by taking them seriously when they denounce the practice and play the hypocrite for our benefit — when they say the things they think we would like to hear. With Egyptian affairs, it is wise to assume that *what lies on the surface is usually what has been placed there for somebody else's consumption.*

We are naive, therefore — and more than naive — if we accept things at face value. When the Egyptians brandish outrage about the threat to their heritage, I simply do not believe them. They protest too much, and the ones who protest the most have a nasty habit of being caught with their own hands in the till. Dr. Nuur el Deen, for example, who in those days was the supreme authority for Egyptian antiquities, and responsible only to the president and the arts minister, came to England in 1996, and viewed the antiquities that had been confiscated from myself. Whatever he might have said in England, he was forthright enough in Egypt. He declared that if dealers were involved in *depriving the Egyptian nation of their rightful heritage* etc., etc., then they should be hanged. You cannot be plainer than that. All the more amusing, therefore, when he was dismissed, allegedly for shipping container-loads of Egyptian government antiquities to one of the Gulf states.[9]

He was not sacked for this, of course, or not immediately. That would have been too embarrassing. But the antiquities police were delighted at the outcome — they had been fighting a form of civil war over who was to guard this lucrative resource, and had been threatened with demotion by none

---

[9] This information (and documents), was provided, from 1993 to 1996. by a general in the Antiquities Police Secretariat in Cairo, whose almost daily briefings were diligently recorded in my journals. If these differ from the official pronouncements, I leave it to you, dear reader, to decide which is the truth and which is spin.

other than Nuur el Deen. Yes, they were just delighted. It was another six months before another lapse enabled his dismissal — a minor burglary of Cairo Museum — and it seemed this had been fabricated for the purpose:

JOURNAL: August 14th 1995

Our general in the antiquities police secretariat tells us they've finally found a ruse to get rid of Nuur el Deen, a good six months after his arrest. They've arrested somebody going through the scanner at Cairo Museum–on the way out, that is–with his pockets crammed full of goodies. Apparently he'd been in the museum all night. The peculiar thing is that the scanner, as far as we know, has never been wired in, and is certainly never switched on. So how did it manage to pick up gold jewellery and a couple of shawabtis in the man's pockets? In fact, so the general told Ali, it was one of their own men who'd been tasked to get himself caught, and provide grounds for Nur el Deen's dismissal, on the grounds of a security lapse–even though El Deen's report about deficient security was already on the arts minister's desk.[10]

The West will remember Nuur el Deen as a man who spoke loud and clear about the iniquities of the market. The Egyptians — those in the know, that is to say — will remember him as just another official who fell from grace.

So, why don't the antiquities police just close down the market?

If you have followed the argument this far, you will understand that this is actually a rather silly question. It is clear enough, you see, that if they really wanted to close down the market, they could do so overnight:

---

[10]   The official version of events, for instance...

Saudi Gazette: 'Egypt Busts Robbery Plot to Deprive it of Antique Wealth', by Mervat Mohsen, Special to Saudi Gazette, Cairo, Sept. 16 1996
A storm in a teacup displaced a senior official in the tourist department
With disbelief and raised eyebrows Egyptians received the news that three attempts to upset the [sic] Egypt's ancient treasures were foiled within the week. In the first attempt 23 years [sic] old Amr Sabry almost managed to run away with the priceless dagger of King Tut Ankh Amun, the sculptured pieces of two cats, 18 rings, a gold bracelet and a necklace. The echo of such an attempt was so great that the renowned and learned director of the antiquities department Dr Abdul Halim Nour el Din was replaced...

...was quite different from what we were getting on the ground. I know which one I believed.

> **JOURNAL: Monday 20th July 1992**
>
> *Ali has been spending time with our general, who seems very confident. However it began, the general feels that the antiquities police are now 'controlling the situation'—whatever that means–and largely because of the 'quality of their intelligence'. He assures Ali that they know the names of all the remaining dealers, including [his half brothers] Ahmed and Mohamed. He also seems well informed about G…–that she has a fistful of passports, and that she only comes to Egypt for a couple of days at a time. He doesn't know the names of any farmers, however, although he's aware of them, and seems to be giving Ali his blessing to continue…*
>
> *By the end of the month, the General says, the majority of dealers will have been arrested–if only for embarrassment's sake–and by the time it's over, we'll be the only dealers left in the market (and, one presumes, Ahmed and Mohammed). The general intimated that all this was by design—or at least with his blessing–and that we carry his protection. At this point I found myself wondering whether another general–in the very next office, maybe—was saying exactly the same to our competitor, and with the same contented expectations of profit…*
>
> *– 'And the big man, he say if we have any problems–if other antiquities police make trouble for us–we must tell him very fast, and he fix the problem for us'.*

They *know* who all the dealers are — well, they should do, they provide their shipping paperwork — and they have the manpower. It would only require a gesture, a demonstration of intent. For example, they could introduce the death penalty for dealers, as Dr. Nuur el Deen suggested in 1996. They did that for heroin dealers, after all, and solved that problem quite efficiently.

But unless they do something like this, they can hardly be taken seriously. There is too much money involved, after all, and the flesh is weak…

But isn't the Egyptian government putting its house in order?

That is certainly what they would like us to think. And it is certainly what they *need* us to think, if they are to have any chance of bullying the British Museum. But I am not convinced. Far from it.

Consider the Egyptian Trial of 1996.[11] This was a show trial in the best Soviet tradition. As a serious attempt to discipline the Egyptian market it can be discounted. But as an illustration of freemasonry between the leading dealers and their government associates — and of propaganda for Western consumption — it speaks volumes. We are dealing with a symbiotic market, remember. A market in which the real danger to dealers is not from the authorities — for they are so close as to be inseparable — but from other dealers, from competitors. A market in which the main danger, perhaps the only danger, to the calm unruffled delicious flow of commerce and intrigue is denunciation.

For denunciation disrupts everything. When there's denunciation, there must be investigation and that, in Egypt, inevitably means bribery. Money changes hands to ensure that innocence is revealed. And when there has been one denunciation, there is likely to be another in retaliation for the first. Which in turn provokes another, and so on. A feud is in progress, and the only real beneficiaries are the police — unless one side runs out of patience (or money) and quits the field.

Just such a feud had started in the late 'eighties. I have already touched on this, and the parties involved: the Farags, a dynastic family of traders, and the most powerful Egyptian dealers of the 'eighties and 'nineties; a Canadian P...; and a politician T..., known as 'the Prince' because of his high connections within the regime. The charm of the affair was that, although T... frequently found it prudent to take his family on extended Moroccan holidays — to escape assassination, or so it was rumoured — he never seemed to be directly implicated. It seemed a straightforward slugging match between the elder Farags and P..., with the junior Farags and myself caught up in the mêlée. But that was misleading.

More misleading was the idea, widely believed in England — and fostered by the British police to their advantage — that the whole affair had started with the British arrests in 1994. In Egypt nobody believed this for a moment. They all knew the previous events.

They knew, for example, that P... had been denounced by Ahmed Farag in 1990, arrested, convicted and thrown out in 1992 but, after eighteen months of exile, had returned to

---

[11] Case Number 391 of 1995.

Egypt and the Egyptian market in 1994. They knew this had cost him bribes of $180,000 to the antiquities police. They knew that he had denounced Ahmed Farag in turn, starting the 'first case' against the Farags, which had ended in total failure.[12] They also expected that

> because of this [the failure], they will attempt to bring another charge against the Farag Family, which is unsupported by facts or the law, in that there is no evidence, and there are no confessions, or anyone caught in the act. It is based solely on inventions and false investigations.[13]

The real significance of 'foreign involvement' was that it injected some real meat into this feud. For the first time, the anti-Farag faction had something to go on.

> The investigation of the whole Farag Family in this case, because of the presence of some inspectors of the Antiquities Department in the indictment, who were public employees, and also a number of merchants and some archaeological workers and restorers, has resulted in the case being called in Egypt 'The Case of the Great Egyptian Antiquities Theft.[14]

That is why, although all the antiquities inspectors for Sakkara were 'arrested', all twenty-five of them, only fifteen were eventually indicted—the ones who had been working with the Farags. It was anyway a very large trial, with over thirty separate defendants. The first sixteen were all high-ranking officials in the Antiquities Commission. Then came the senior members of the Farag family. Then came the junior Farags and ourselves, who had nothing to do with the senior half-brothers and their high-ranking connections, but had been caught up in the scrum. And then came an assembly of

---

[12] This concerned illegal sales from the Anglo-American Bookshop collection, see *Journal*, 27th November 1992, page 208. The 'investigative committee' found numerous items were missing from the collection (as they were, having been sold), but the 'higher committee' immediately formed to check their results found that not only weren't there any pieces missing, but that there were several *additional* pieces in the collection [Case report No. 3116 dated 21/11/1994, and Resolution No. 3211 dated 30/11/94, from the Egyptian Higher Council for Antiquities]. Quite remarkable as a turnabout—money had obviously changed hands.

[13] Section 2, from an antiquities police secretariat internal memo, of 1995—concerned, please note, with the activities of their own investigative department (here referred to as 'they'), and evidently supportive of the Farags.

[14] *Ibid.*, section 3.

minor players, all of whom had been associated with the Farags in some way.

As I say, it was an impressive affair. Farouk Hosni, the Egyptian arts minister, referred to it as 'probably the most important trial of the century'. And the evidence against the Farags—provided by the British police—was absolutely damning. In any other national court it would have secured a conviction. But not in Egypt. None of the government officials were convicted. In fact, none ever made it to court, despite that initial splash of publicity. And the senior Farags were acquitted, at a cost of $240,000 in 'ancillary legal fees'.[15] The junior Farags, my partners, were convicted because temporarily impecunious. They were sentenced to fifteen, ten and five years' hard labour respectively, but they served *not a day*. They took a loan from their elder brother, lodged an immediate appeal, and have been acquitted.

The only conviction, in fact, was mine, and only because I had declined to attend, and was automatically found guilty in absentia under the Napoleonic Code. But that was sufficient. A 'foreign devil' had been found responsible, and I was declared the 'second greatest smuggler of the century' (the first, rather churlishly, was said to be Howard Carter and his infamous box camera).

Meanwhile, the feud had progressed to the next round, with another show trial in 2000, and this time with T... on the receiving end. *Plus ça change*, I'm afraid, given what had happened a decade before, just a year before he'd had the antiquities police running around for him, trying to recover his stolen 'stolen' antiquities:

> **JOURNAL: Christmas Day 1991**
> *Apparently T... has been arrested in Alexandria with a sizeable hoard. Ali had some unpleasant moments with the brigadier–who was clearly very windy about T...'s powerful friends, and what might happen, if he found himself on the wrong side–but was able to swear on the Koran that he'd had nothing to do with the denunciation.*

And so it goes on and on, and more fool us for taking any of it seriously:

---

[15] A phrase used by the Professor of Law at Ain Shams University, when speaking of the means to secure *acquittal* on appeal. She even specified the figure.

JOURNAL: 18th August 2005

The head of antiquities police in charge of checking regis-
tered collections—Abdel Karim Abu Shanab, one of Ali's 'se-
cret police'—has just been given life imprisonment for 'taking
bribes, for supplying smugglers with certificates that said
genuine antiquities were fakes, and for stealing records
from the Supreme Council of Antiquities'. His 'group' is said
to have 'stolen 57,000 artefacts from state warehouses and
smuggled thousands of them abroad. Police found coins,
statues and sarcophaguses in tunnels under the villas of
three relatives—businessmen who were convicted in an ear-
lier trial.' He vigorously protests his innocence—'This is injus-
tice. I have done nothing'—and says he'll appeal. Within a
few months he'll be out and about, as if nothing had hap-
pened. But it'll cost him several years earnings.

What gives it all away is that figure. How could they ever
know that fifty-seven thousand antiquities have been lost?
Of course they can't. Their records are abysmal. Mostly
they're just numbers, painted on the objects, and no descrip-
tions better than 'a stone relief' here, or a 'bronze Horus'
there. As the colonel told Ali 'They can't tell whether the
objects are fake or genuine. But they don't need to. It doesn't
matter. They just check the numbers'.

So are they claiming that 57,000 numbers are missing, or
that 57,000 numbered fakes have been found? And what
about all the objects—about a third, if the famous crates were
anything to go by—that have no numbers at all, and are just
crammed into boxes? No, it's just a figure they've plucked
out of the air. Sounds impressive, but the whole thing is just
a game. It's nothing but a game.

Even the grand and public ceremonies should be taken
with a pinch of salt:

JOURNAL: 4th December 1986, London

Delivered restoration to N..., and got to talking about the
Egyptian authorities. N... was scornful, and told me about
the B... Museum. They'd been embarrassed some time
before for circulating line drawing of a large wall-decoration—
from its publication, it seems. Parts of this they'd already
bought—they'd marked these on the drawing—and the other
parts they were now trying to locate.

So when they discovered, some time later, that they'd mis-
takenly bought a published object, they thought to regain

> *some brownie-points, and immediately returned it to Egypt, with all appropriate ceremony. But the thing re-appeared in Europe after three months. 'In the front door, and out the back', as N... wryly commented...*

Some conclusions

This should suffice for the antiquities market. You will have gathered, I hope, that the market continues in Egypt, but that it's been corrupted by the Prohibition—and is now being run, or so it seems, for the benefit of the very authorities who were tasked with its suppression. This is not a healthy state of affairs, if only because many sites and many antiquities are being lost that—in a saner world—would be brought into the light.

I have also tried to explain why this is so, and why the vital ingredient—the correct and laudable passion for antiquity—what I call the emotional response, and the trade calls object-mindedness—has never developed in Egypt. If it was there, in the hearts and minds of all Egyptians, then there would be little amiss. But it isn't there, and this is the most worrying thing of all.

And because it isn't there, this sentiment, there are many of us who have come to regard our task as quite simple—that of rescuing what we can before it is too late. This is the sentiment of the world market, make no doubt about it. As I said in an earlier chapter:

[6] **Antiquities should not (be expected to) remain in their country of origin, if they are likely to be destroyed or damaged there.**

Summary

- The Egyptian Antiquities Service has always been corrupt, and always will be, given their circumstance, their creed, and the wealth they have on hand.
- The ultimate proof is that they *could* suppress the antiquities market overnight—but they don't, and never will.
- Indeed, it achieves little to disparage the Egyptians as corrupt. It is just the norm we have to work with,
- and our task becomes the traditional one of *rescue*.

CHAPTER 18

The Real Threat to Egyptian Antiquity

I shall now consider the monuments of Egypt — the glorious temples and the tombs. These are marketed assiduously, as a lure for tourists. They spring to mind whenever Egypt is mentioned. They are the reason, direct or subliminal, why people go to Egypt. And they are in danger of disappearing.

The things that ought to be done — that desperately need to be done, before it's too late, if they are to survive intact for the future — are just not getting done. The Egyptians may respond to the grand and the glorious — or so they would have us believe — but apart from the rhetoric, there is little enough to show. Oh yes, there's plenty of intrigue, and denunciation, and jostling for position. But the proper work just seems to get overlooked. Again, there must be a reason...

The physical situation in Egypt

The situation in Egypt is serious. Make no mistake about that. The Aswan High Dam has changed things forever. The Nile used to flood every year, sweeping away the salt that leached from the bedrock. This annual cleansing has ended, and the salt and pollution now accumulates.

For thousands of years the annual flooding of the Nile cleansed the valley, sweeping away the salt

Worse, the intensive irrigation which followed the high dam has raised the water-level of the soil, and this chemical brew threatens many of the objects and sites that used to be safe and dry.[1] Worse still, the towns and villages have been released from their ancient boundaries — their raised areas above the annual floods — and sprawl out to accommodate the new flood, the flood of population.

A peasant's house in the nineteenth century

A similar house (foreground) being menaced by the city (along with any archaeology that lies beneath it)

[1] All this was accurately foreseen by the British, who refused to fund Nasser's grandiose project (as did the Americans in 1956). Nasser abruptly 'nationalized' the Suez Canal, so its tolls could pay for the dam. The result was the Suez war of 1956-57 and the USSR moving into Egypt on a grand scale. The Soviets built Nasser's dam — creating his eponymous lake — and the largest destruction of Egyptian (and Nubian) antiquity there has ever been.

How Egyptians build nowadays

Since the High Dam the population of Egypt has nearly trebled—three-quarters of Egyptians are children—and to accommodate this surging population, a vast programme of building is underway. Very few of these new buildings are the traditional mud-brick. Most are pillar-and-platform construction—that blight of the socialist East—and rely on reinforced concrete. These buildings need deep foundations, perhaps 15 feet or more. And these, in many places, are the first ever such excavations.

Many of these new buildings are sitting on antiquity. Literally so. Sites are being built over and lost from view before they can be excavated. And when they are discovered—when the contractors turn up something ancient—it is invariably destroyed. It is just too troublesome to do anything else.

The problem of salt

Ancient sites, in short, are everywhere under threat—from development and also from *chemistry*. Development is a political problem. It may seem intractable, but it can be solved. Common sense and political pressure should suffice, if they can be brought to bear.

The problem of salt is less tractable, however. Eighty million years ago the Nile was a vast estuary, the full width of the present valley. The present valley's escarpment was its bank. Egypt lay beneath salt water, and everything was impregnated. Taste Egyptian stone these days, and you will taste salt. The salt is everywhere. It is in the stone, in the desert sand, in the very dust.

The physical problems in Egypt all come down to this salt or, perhaps one should say, to salt plus water. Left in the baking sun, and the salt does no harm. It sleeps benign. But bring *water* to it, and the consequences can be disastrous.

Consider an Egyptian tomb. It may have been carved from the bedrock, tunneled into the escarpment, as were the West Bank tombs at Luxor. Or perhaps constructed from prepared blocks of stone, as with the tombs at Sakkara. But invariably there is an inner space, a closed-space—a room, in fact—which is surrounded by salt-infested stone.

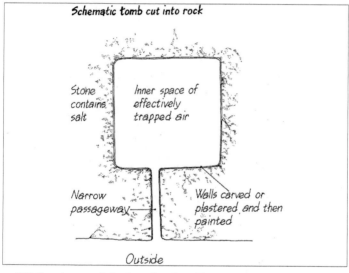

Whilst the tomb is dry, this hardly matters. But now introduce some tourists, on a hot summer's day. The tourists are northerners, and they are sweating. Egyptians may survive on the occasional small glass of sweetened tea, but northerners drink by the gallon, and then perspire it away. In this hot climate they are little better, biologically speaking, than *leaking bags of water*. Their lost water hangs in the air as humidity, and as the air cools in the evening it falls out as dew. It settles on the walls, which absorb the water like a sponge. Once absorbed by the stone, this water dissolves some of the salt. The next day, and the room and walls heat up again. The water returns to the surface and evaporates, leaving the salt behind, but now slightly closer to the surface.

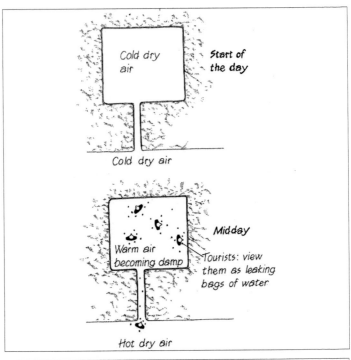

Cold dry air

Start of the day

Cold dry air

Warm air becoming damp

Midday

Tourists: view them as leaking bags of water

Hot dry air

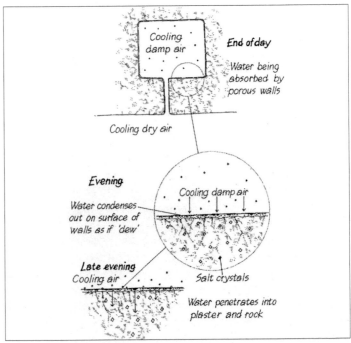

Cooling damp air

End of day

Water being absorbed by porous walls

Cooling dry air

Evening

Water condenses out on surface of walls as if 'dew'

Cooling damp air

Late evening
Cooling air

Salt crystals

Water penetrates into plaster and rock

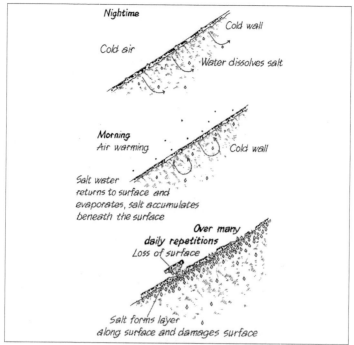

Each movement of the water — each daily cycle of absorption and evaporation — carries the salt ever closer to the surface. Like pebbles on a storm beach, the movement is always one-way. Day by day, week by week, season by season, the salt accumulates under the surface skin. Eventually it crystallizes out, long delicate webs and needles, as delicate as gossamer but strong enough to penetrate the surface and disrupt it, and to crumble the stone.

I have seen surfaces where the paint layer — a base wash of white, bound with acacia gum or animal glue, and on top of this the other colours — is literally floating upon a fairy-web of salt-crystal, and where a fingerprint leaves its mark like a harsh footfall in soft sand. And I have seen floors littered with flakes of paint and fragments of rotting stone, entire fragments, that have been forced away by the pressure behind, the inexhaustible, insidious pressure of expanding crystals.

During my years in Egypt, I have watched the entire process. I have seen the most vulnerable tombs, the smallest and the most fashionable, where the tourists are squeezed in like cattle, day after day after day. At first they were pristine and

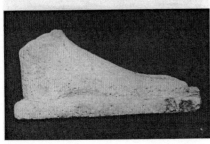

Such a growth of salt crystals as this can be removed by repeated immersion in pure water, but only if the object is 'free-standing'. Walls cannot be treated so.

flawless, as if painted only yesterday, almost unbearable in their beauty. And for some years there was nothing to observe. This is the insidious way of it—that until too late there is nothing to be seen. Only the daily cycle that repeats itself, the thousands of *leaking bags* that come and go, spending a few minutes in their busy schedule, and leaving their water behind.

There may be a trifle more dust, scuffed from the floor and caught by the granular paint. There may be the odd stain, trifling enough, where fingers have reached out and touched, again and again, and left behind their sweat and their dirt. For tourists must always touch if they can, if only to reassure themselves. But these are minor matters, after all, and the surfaces still seemed pristine.

Then at last the first signs. A slight glint, perhaps, as the light catches a crystal, tiny among the dull matte of the paint pigments, or the slender feather of the growth, like a brittle mould sprouting. And then another, and another, until the whole surface seems eaten and obscured, as if a fungus has infected it. This is when ordinary people begin to notice— that something is not quite right—but already it is too late, and the damage mostly done. Like many a cancer, it is only noticed when death is already closing in.

Detached pieces of the surface can be treated in our northern workshops. I have treated nearly seven hundred

The entire sequence – the horror of it – caught on one wall relief. 'A' shows an area where the carved surface is obviously 'floating' on a bed of salt crystals, some of which are already punching holes in that surface. With 'B' and 'C' these holes are getting larger until, with 'D', the entire surface falls off, leaving raw stone. Until this last stage, something can be done. After this, nothing.

myself, for collectors and dealers throughout the world. Many of them I have saved from complete dissolution. The north is incurably damp, remember, and every Egyptian stone fragment needs to have its salt removed, or at least to be stabilized. Without this, it will be in danger.

The principles are simple enough, as with the processes – some of which I have developed myself – but they are easier to describe than to manage, as these things usually are. The salt itself can easily be removed, by immersing the fragments in distilled water, and dissolving away the salt. If the stone surface is far gone – if it has already being disrupted by crystals – the decoration can be held in place with a *consolidant*. And if the fragment is heavily infested – so that removing the salt leaves a latticework of tiny spaces inside the stone where the crystals used to be, which weakens the stone, and even makes it crumbly – then it is an easy enough matter to impregnate it.[2] By such means the stone has its salt removed and is strengthened again. It looks unchanged, but is now immune.

But this is only possible in a workshop, and for pieces which are small and detached. Walls cannot be handled like

---

[2] By a charming technique, or so I think. The stone is immersed in a thin plastic solution, and the whole placed in a vacuum. As the suction begins to bite, thousands of miniscule bubbles are pulled free. These come from the empty spaces in the stone. When the pressure is returned, the solution is forced into these tiny spaces, the plastic is deposited, and the entire stone is provided with an unseen skeleton of tough plastic. It is now said to be *plasticized*.

this. They cannot be immersed in water to remove the salt, or put in a vacuum bath to impregnate with plastic. Like a cancer, the problem for tombs can only be contained, and only if it has been caught early enough. It can never be cured, or even reversed. Please remember this.[3]

Tombs are being worn out by display

The real problem for tombs, you see, follows from *the desire to display them*. A slight simplification, perhaps, but only slight. If tombs were left in peace—unvisited, un-watered, and hence undisturbed—they would sleep benign, with no further damage than the gentle damage of time. But display them to tourists, and especially to *leaking northerners*, and they are brought into danger.

It is possible, with experience, to predict the future of any tomb. Its prognosis, if you like. Given its structure, its starting condition, and its daily quotient of leaking bags—say five hundred or five thousand or whatever—it is possible to predict when that tomb will fail, and by what stages. When its first freshness will dull, when the first damage begins to show, and when it's been damaged beyond repair.

Or perhaps one should say *damaged beyond touristic attractiveness*, because the point—the vulgar point, I am afraid to say—is that these tombs are being used up as a resource. They really are. And it is tourism that is using them. That much is clear. Tourism might contribute funds to the Antiquities Commission, and funds that—in the best of all possible worlds, or at least a slightly less venal one—could be used to patch the tombs up again. But tourism *causes* the damage in the first place. And the Egyptians know this. They must know it. They cannot be so obtuse as not to know it.

But it seems they choose to ignore it. They continue to advertise, and to expand their tourist facilities. They entice more and more visitors to the tombs, and they fill their coffers. And it is easy enough for them to ignore the damage, because the damage never shows until it is all too late.

---

[3] There is one site, however—Kings' Valley, thankfully unique—where the predominant problem *is* water, and the problem of salt I'm describing is perhaps only the final straw. See *The sad plight of Kings' Valley* in the Appendix.

Nefertari and Tutankhamun

Consider Queen Nefertari — 'the beautiful one'. Her splendid tomb in Queens' Valley — arguably the finest surviving tomb in Egypt — is somehow symbolic of the whole shameful process. It was open to visitors before the war, those long leisurely halcyon years before mass tourism. The visitors were few, but quite enough to dilapidate the tomb. Eventually it was closed, and remained so until the Getty Conservation Institute arrived on the scene, and undertook to restore the wall paintings. But the Getty could only rectify the visible symptoms of decay. They did cosmetic restoration at enormous cost. But nothing was done — and nothing could be done — about the underlying cause, which is a massive concentration of salt, including a large number of large crystals, probably the result of ancient flash floods.

The walls have been cleaned, sure, and the visible salt-growth removed. And the damage to the paint layer has been made good.[4] The tomb could even be protected, in the future, against further flash floods — by isolating it from the surrounding rock, and installing a damp course.[5] But there will never be any way to remove the salt from the walls. The tomb of Nefertari, alas, will always be highly vulnerable to leaking bags of water. The salt will always be there, a sleeping cancer behind a blameless skin.

Given this terrible vulnerability, the Getty Institute recommended that Nefertari be left in peace. They asked the Egyptians to resist the temptations — those of publicity and revenue — and keep the tomb firmly closed. They made the dangers abundantly clear. Perhaps they had begun to realize what they were dealing with. They were honourable and unambiguous about this. At first their warnings were heeded, and the only visitors were visiting VIPs. But in 1996 the tomb was declared 'safe for display', and re-opened to the general

---

[4] Either 'correctly', by the *sgraffito* technique, whereby missing areas are re-painted, in the correct colours, but using a series of vertically separated strokes — so that the design is complete at a distance, but the newness is also revealed upon a closer inspection — or 'incorrectly', with 'invisible' touching-up. The Italian restorers used both methods, much to the disgust of Dr. Hussein, who regarded the latter as a form of cheating, of conservator's vanity, and complained about it to the arts minister, Farouk Hosni, see footnote, page 275.

[5] This was recommended by the Getty, but has yet to be attempted. And nor will it, now the Getty have been cold-shouldered from the scene.

public, by none other than the supreme authority for antiquities, Dr Nuur El Deen. Why? Quite simply, because the tomb would make money, and Egypt needed revenue after the fundamentalist outrages had scared tourists away. And, more importantly, because Nuur el Deen disliked the Getty, and would probably have reversed any recommendation of theirs.[6] Besides, when the damage becomes undeniable — when the 'beautiful one' is again dilapidated, and this time irredeemably — there will be nobody around to blame. And certainly not Nuur el Deen.

Now consider Tutankhamun. He was not an important pharaoh — his tomb is more iconic than glorious — but it attracts the faithful in droves. In high season, between October and April, up to 16,000 a day squeeze into this tiny space — little larger than your dining room — and jostle and perspire for an average of seven minutes, before departing — supposedly in a state of grace, but almost certainly damp. Their influx leaves three-and-a-half to four gallons of sweat each day, and raises the relative humidity from 15% in the morning to 97% by mid afternoon. By contrast a closed tomb would show no variation (and would, hopefully, be bone dry).

During the night much of this water was absorbed by the walls, only to be released again, as the tomb re-heated the next day. Because of the quantities involved — and these daily fluctuations are huge for a delicacy like Tutankhamun — by the early 'nineties the tomb had developed a fungal infection, and disfiguring blotches had appeared on the walls.

Dr Shawky Nakhlar, the head of conservation for Egypt, was under mounting pressure to do something about this — *anything* in fact — just so long as he was seen to be doing it. His wife was a biochemist, and she suggested a fungicide. He thought to combine this with the inevitable B72 — the all-purpose conservation cure-all — and paint the walls with the mixture. It was a diplomatic response, the reaction of a man in a tight spot. He had used the politically-correct materials — nobody could seriously object to B72, or denounce him because of it[7] — and he had done no apparent harm.

Western conservators might cavil that a water-based fungicide cannot be expected to work when wrapped in plas-

---

[6]   See *Journal*, 11 October, 1994, page 277.

[7]   Just as 'nobody ever got fired for buying IBM'.

tic—which is what the B72 was effectively doing—or that he had sown the whirlwind by inserting a plastic sock inside the tomb.[8] But I had a considerable sympathy for the man. His hands were tied, and there was almost nothing else he could do. The cause of the damage was tourism, but he could not rectify that. He couldn't close the tomb, for example. He could not even restrict the number of visitors. But at least he had gained a breathing space. He had treated the symptoms and put off the evil day.

The dangers of mass tourism

You can understand everything from a single visit to Kings' Valley during high season—if you have eyes to see, that is, and a mind that can scent humbug. If this is your first visit, and you approach these glories as a *sacrament*—and so you should, for they are without parallel in archaeology—you are in for a rude awakening. For there is nothing of the sacred here. There is only chaos, and commercial opportunism. It is a menagerie completely out of control.

The Egyptians create the *infrastructure*. There are copious funds for this, it appears. In 1979, for instance, the World Bank loaned them $20m to modernize tourist facilities in Luxor. An international airport was built, and new roads. Clean water and telephones were laid on. As a result it is now possible to fly directly to Luxor, and to reach Kings' Valley within the hour. More and more tourists can be more and more efficiently brought to the Valley, without coming into contact with ordinary Egyptians. But almost nothing is spent protecting against their onslaught. Of that World Bank Loan, only 3%—yes, a measly three—went on conservation.[9]

---

[8] What Dr. Nakhlar had done was to coat the walls with impermeable plastic, so that water could no longer settle on the surface skin, and be absorbed. Some might regard this as dangerous because it also trapped water *behind* the skin—and stopped the skin from 'breathing'—but I'm more worried about the idea of a temporary coating, which does the job now—and keeps tourist humidity at bay—but has to be removed at some point in the future before it cross bonds and turns nasty. I just can't imagine the Egyptians being able to remove it without a catastrophe—or getting round to it, for that matter—or even remembering that it has to be done before it's far too late. But then, I've seen the Reserve Head, see page 270 ff, and numerous other disasters, and no other Westerner has had these doubtful pleasures.

[9] And that was mostly for the Tomb of Nakht, see page 262 ff, an experiment which the Egyptians then rejected. There is another loan on the way to speed

The Kings Valley 'rest-house' (now demolished) was built smack in the middle of the Valley. Its 30,000 gallon septic tank became famous, because it never seemed to need emptying. The horrible truth eventually dawned, when Tomb KV5 was opened, and found to have been doing second duty as a reserve tank: the pipe going to the septic tank had cracked, and tens of thousands of gallons of tourist sewage had been pouring into the tomb, and thence into the Esna shale bed that underlies the valley's limestone. This shale expands dramatically when wet, hence the series of massive movements and tomb falls in the valley since the 1970s. See The sad plight of Kings Valley *in the Appendix.*

And when the tourists arrive at the sites, and are jostling each other to view the tombs? The Egyptians watch helplessly, as if nothing can be done. No attempt is made to control the number of people who enter a tomb. The size of parties is limited only by the size of their coaches. It is ironic that a process that began in Europe — about the economics of motorway travel — should now determine how many sweating tourists should squeeze themselves into an ancient tomb in Egypt. And when the sweating tourists are inside, there is no protection for the decorated walls, whether from casual touching, from bumping or even deliberate scratching. If the visitors carry heavy bags and are jostled, their bags will scratch the walls. There is nothing to prevent it.

> ### JOURNAL: 23rd March 1988, Kings' Valley
> *With Dr. Hussein and the Inspector to Seti's tomb, now almost permanently closed because of the subsidence after Sheikh Ali's excavation. But at about 3:00 they opened the main doors—for some reason they'd decided to open it to the public—and we could hear the stampede down the stairwell towards us. We were squashed against the wall. Within minutes there must have been five hundred people in there, all*

tourists to these sites but, again, nothing to protect these same sites once the tourist hordes arrive.

squeezing and shoving, with their [Egyptian] tour leaders trying to shout over each other. The din was tremendous, like a rush-hour in a railway station. And this was supposed to be a sacred place! Within five minutes I counted fifteen contacts—serious ones, I mean—between shoulder-bags and the painted walls. Not that it really matters, I suppose, because Shawky Nakhlar's [the head of conservation for all Egypt] men have slapped on such a thick coat of B72 [plastic] that the walls are like formica.

The only guards are villagers, untrained, poorly paid and mercenary. They are energetic enough about their *baksheesh*, but indolent about everything else. They allow brushing and leaning against the walls, jostling for position, drinking from water bottles inside the tomb, and the inevitable splashing. They preside contentedly over a bedlam. But one thing they will never allow—almost on pain of death, it seems—and that is flash photography. They have raised this prohibition to a sacred edict. It seems to justify their other failures.

The Antiquities Commission is convinced, you see, that camera flash produces ultra-violet light, which is, and I quote, 'dangerous to the tombs'. They have a point, arguably, but their own tomb-lighting is more at fault. Their hundreds of neon striplights should be sheathed to suppress the ultra-violet they emit. But they never are. The Commission delivers more ultra-violet, therefore—and more damage, if damage there be—then any number of flash guns. And they do it day-in, day-out, over the years.

Anyway it's common-sense that ultra-violet can only degrade pigments. In other words, it can only affect the painted tombs. It is childish and absurd to forbid it elsewhere, on the assumption that it could harm carved and unpainted stone.

Tourists, bloody tourists

As you may have gathered, I am no great fan of tourism. I don't blame the *leaking bags* for their damage, however. I blame those who stand back and let them do it. As John Romer has observed, the same tourists who behave impeccably when they visit a bird sanctuary—because they have been prepared, and understand the real value and fragility of what they are about to see—can behave like irate rush-hour commuters in Kings' Valley, scrambling to get inside the tombs, jamming the corridors, and then fighting each other for precedence, as they would on the Underground.

But then nobody has taken the trouble to prepare them. They are harangued about the drinking water, about 'gippy-tummy', and tipping the natives. They may even, nowadays, be exhorted not to flaunt female flesh, because this offends Islam. But nobody ever mentions the tombs, and how vulnerable they are.

We can hardly expect the Egyptians themselves to do this, because they are not object-minded, and only their senior officials are aware of the problem—have ever been told about it—and they are unlikely ever to visit a tomb.[10] But somebody has to set the *mise-en-scène*. Somebody has to make the tourists realize they are about to see something rare, glorious and ephemeral—and that they may well be the last generation to have that privilege. If they approached in this frame of mind, they would not lean against the walls, or touch them, or jostle each other. They would behave as they would in a *sacred* place.

Sophisticated crowd control is mostly social psychology. Very few people have visited an ancient tomb before, and they have no idea how to behave. They can only pick up hints as they go along. They observe, for instance, that the tombs are marketed like consumer goods. They notice that the guards are venal and ragged and cadging, that there is neither maintenance nor control, that the tickets are ridiculously cheap, and that there is no preparation before they are allowed—encouraged even, by their Egyptian tour-guides with a schedule to keep—to pile in and barge their way to the front. In other words, they will conclude, the people in charge are not bothering about the tombs. And they will draw the obvious conclusions. Either these tombs are unimportant, or they are bomb-proof.

Impose a *ritual of preparation* upon them, however, and they would approach with a suitable sense of reverence. Make them wear special clothing, for instance, gloves, masks, slippers and the like; restrict them to only one tomb per day; charge the correct world-class fee (about $10 is the norm everywhere else); and issue them with strict instructions as to fragility and rarity and privilege etc.

---

[10] Forgive this lurch into the cynical, and consider *Journal*, 22nd March 1988 Queens' Valley, page 274.

All this would create an ambience of *sanctity*. After all, Parkinson's Law tells us that response is proportional to the expectation that has been created—in other words, that the sex is much better when you have had to work for it. The behaviour of visitors to the boathouse at Sakkara, for instance, is already much better—they invariably talk in awed whispers—merely because they have to remove their footwear and put on slippers. These immediately create an aura of supplication (even though they are actually quite unnecessary, and only serve to keep the floors polished, and to give some dignity to the custodians, who hand out the slippers).[11]

I hate to say this, but the problem begins at home, in the way some of our own museums display their wares. The mummy room in the British Museum, for instance, as often as not resembles a railway station. School parties are running here and there, and adults are pushing and bumping their way along the walls—almost as if, as John Romer observed, they were 'getting into training' for a trip to Kings' Valley.

And then there is 'Ginger', the most widely viewed Egyptian exhibit in the world. Ginger is a naked pre-dynastic man, mummified by the desiccating sand, curled up and dis-

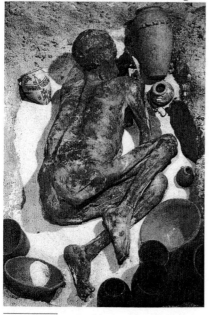

'Ginger', exposed to all the world's prurience, is best regarded as a nineteenth century 'cabinet curio', somehow stranded in a serious museum. Or kept there because of marketing. His retention – as part of the display – asks questions about the seriousness of the curators. See footnote on page 118).

---

[11] There's an interesting Islamic parallel here, as if the boathouse has been created like a secular mosque.

played like a household object, stripped of his dignity, and surrounded by giggling children, whose predominant concern seems to be his private parts.[12] Is this how we should be preparing visitors for Egypt? Is this the dignity and reverence we need to inspire?

Compare this with a modern museum of natural history, where arguments for conservation are subtly woven into the display. Modern children, as a result, are far more impressed by the dignity and power of elephants than by the monuments of their own ancestors.

Cultural heritage — or a 'bed of coal'?

Egypt's antiquity, be in no doubt, is the bait for tourism. And tourism keeps her economy afloat. That much is painfully clear. Cotton production is falling, oil production has peaked, and the $10 billion per year the tourism brings — mostly in hard currency[13] — just about keeps her in the black. Few foreigners would ever dream of visiting Egypt — the clear leader in the dysentery charts — were it not for her antiquity, even when that is absorbed at the vulgarest level, as a sort of background muzak, the 'Land of the Pharaohs'.

But this same tourism is destroying the architectural sites. It is a slow process, and one which the 'responsible parties' can ignore on their daily rounds. There are other factors, of course — the burgeoning population, the demand for space, the rising water level in the Nile Valley, and the lack of annual 'cleansing' by the river's flooding — but tourism is the central factor, the *only one that can be controlled*.

Unless tourism is strictly controlled, the major tombs — those that form the tourist staple — will be dilapidated within twenty years. And for most of them the damage will be irreversible. It is an irony of the process that the damage is done long before there is any appearance of it, and that when it finally shows — so as to convince those who would much rather not be convinced — it is too late to do anything about it.

But the Egyptians are well aware of what they are doing. They have encouraged a huge increase in tourism — the num-

---

[12] I attended a conference where his restoration and re-display was being described, and asked the BM's curators whether they had considered the 'ethical' problem of such a display. Their response was bemused. 'Oh, we've never thought of that', they said.

[13] The Egyptian pound is not an internationally listed currency.

The problem is not limited to the insides of tombs. The great temple complexes are also at risk. These splendid carvings—the lower walls of Luxor and Karnak temples, the two greatest Egyptian temple complexes, and the most visited – have been simply written off by Egyptologists. They blandly assume they will 'fall off within twenty-five years'. The temples have been largely re-constructed, and are now acting like giant wicks to the risen water level (courtesy the Aswan High Dam and permanent irrigation). The stones were already full of salt, and then long immersed in sabakh, *the dung-rich Egyptian topsoil. This chemical brew is now being dragged to the surface. The very fact of rebuilding – without the common-sense of a damp course – has doomed them.

ber has increased ten-fold in the last decade — and they hope to increase it even more, by further expanding the infrastructure. And they know the consequences of their policy. They have been many times informed, by the international community of archaeologists (and conservators) for whom they bear a certain — although reluctant — reverence. And they can already see the results, if they care to look. The condition of some of the major tombs, such as Tutankhamun and Seti, is already considered to be a national disgrace.[14] And yet they continue to allow untrammeled access.

It is hard to resist the conclusion — which I reached myself after several years of bitterness and frustration — that the Egyptian regime is treating its heritage as a short-term economic resource — consuming it like a bed of coal — to get them through difficult times. In other words, they don't value Antiquity for itself — except those close enough to sell it off bit by bit — but only as a means to some other end, the survival of an embattled secular regime.

---

[14] The Tomb of Seti illustrates just about everything that's gone wrong in Egypt since Napoleon arrived off Alexandria.

But surely the tombs can be protected?

In theory, yes. And with foreign expertise, easily so. Modern museum practice is expert at managing large numbers, without causing harm to the displays. As for the threatened tombs themselves, a little common sense would suggest that if tourist humidity could be neutralized—somehow prevented from getting into the tomb, or at least from remaining there long enough to be absorbed—the threat could be held at bay. The salt in the walls is benign, after all, as long as it is kept dry. Only when exposed to water does it become malignant. The problem, therefore, is relatively simple. It is one of housekeeping. The water must be prevented from reaching the salt.

There would appear to be three options:

[1]   Closing down the whole show—preventing any water from entering the tomb, by preventing any visitors.

[2]   Using a prophylactic—allowing visitors, but keeping them isolated inside a glass or plastic container.

[3]   Evacuating the water—allowing visitors inside the tomb proper, but getting rid of their moisture before it can reach the walls and be absorbed.

The first option, as I have suggested, is a political impossibility. Egypt's economy is kept in the black by tourism, and deprived of tourism the country would sink into fundamentalism and chaos. And tourists will only visit in sufficient numbers because of her antiquities—because of the famous sites themselves, or just the pervasive ambience of the past. No, closing the tombs is just not an option.

The second option has already been tried, in the Tomb of Nakht on the West Bank. As a gift—and also a suggestion for the future—a Swedish expedition equipped this small, exquisite eighteenth-dynasty tomb with an air-tight envelope of glass, an air-conditioned foyer, and a visitors' exhibition.

The glass envelope was mounted six inches away from the walls. It acts as an inner sock—a sort of giant condom—which isolates the *leaking bags* from the tomb proper. They can walk into the 'tomb space' freely enough, but in one sense they never enter the tomb at all, because the atmosphere inside the sock is kept separate from the atmosphere of the tomb. Behind the glass, therefore, the tomb's environment continues undisturbed. And if there is a need for the

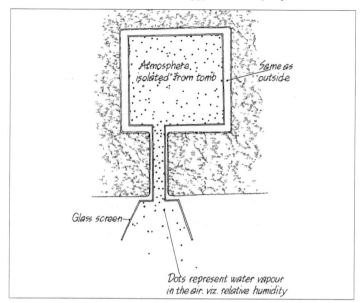

Atmosphere, isolated from tomb

Same as outside

Glass screen

Dots represent water vapour in the air. viz. relative humidity

walls to 'breathe' — for air to pass unhindered through the surface skin — there is still space enough.[15]

Inside the glass envelope the atmosphere is air conditioned, and inside the foyer — created by roofing the ancient Offering Court — there are coolly-lit displays, line drawings of the tomb paintings, commentary and historical background.

This had to be the future — at least for the small tombs — or so it seemed to me. The display created an ambience, everything, in fact, that the intelligent visitor now expects from a Western museum. It was unobtrusive, but it seemed to suggest that here was something special, something that could not just be captured with a photograph and then forgotten — just another glanced impression between a felucca-ride and the hotel swimming-pool — but something that required *effort and study* to master, and that really rewarded the effort. It created esteem where there had been none. It even hinted at the sacred.

---

[15] The chemistry of this 'breathing' is rather complicated, and I am not convinced that anybody understands it yet. Pending this, it obviously makes sense to allow free passage of gases through the surface skin. Shawky Nakhlar's temporary 'fix' in Tutankhamun — slapping an impermeable plastic coating over the painted-surface — would certainly prevent this, quite apart from the problem of having to get the stuff off again.

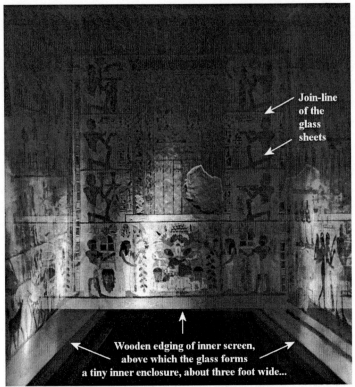

Join-line of the glass sheets

↑
Wooden edging of inner screen, above which the glass forms a tiny inner enclosure, about three foot wide...

Before the installation, this tiny space was crammed with a dozen tourists a time. Now it is completely protected. The only disadvantage is the glass reflections, which interfere with photography. Against that, however, the air-conditioning enables visitors to take their time, and the ambience encourages them actually to look.

By shielding the decorated surfaces from the viewer's touch and breath, moreover, it also emphasized their fragility, and hence their value. And maybe, just maybe, it would plant the idea that the other tombs—those as yet unprotected—were still at risk.

Apart from a certain gaucherie in the construction—this being a prototype—I thoroughly approved. But the Egyptians hated the whole idea. They were uniformly hostile—even Dr. Hussein, which surprised me—claiming that it separated the visitor from the art, and made the whole thing into a circus. So it did, of course, but a better regulated one, and that was surely the point. I think it was the Scandinavian efficiency that offended, however, and the suspicion that—for this small tomb, at least—the modern Egyptians were redundant, and only necessary to switch off the lights.

And surely tourism can be managed?

And the third option? Well, we tried that one ourselves, Dr. Hussein and myself. And we failed, but instructively so. Given that air conditioning a large tomb is prohibitively expensive, we opted for a pressurized air system (see diagram). The technology for this is simple and sturdy, and well-proven. It is also inexpensive. Our scheme was fashioned by English Heritage, and welcomed by the Egyptian arts minister and by his deputy. In fact, it became identified with this deputy, a trouble-shooting American-Egyptian. And this was its downfall. For when he threw in the towel and returned to the 'States—worn down by intrigue and obstruction and malice—our scheme went with him. At this level, we had discovered, it was all a matter of politics, and the games politicians play to keep their advantage.[16]

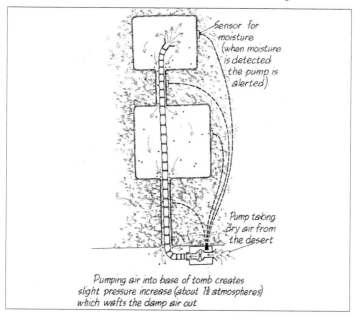

Sensor for moisture (when moisture is detected the pump is alerted)

Pump taking dry air from the desert

Pumping air into base of tomb creates slight pressure increase (about 1½ atmospheres) which wafts the damp air out

So, yes, tourism could be managed easily enough, if there was foreign expertise on hand, and domestic goodwill. Except that goodwill tends to founder on the Egyptian Way, the unfortunate obdurate fact that most Egyptians whose job it is to care for antiquity are—how shall I put it—propelled

---

[16] See *Conservation – how (not) to get things done in Egypt* in the Appendix.

by other ends. They should have the attitude for antiquity that doctors have for their patients. Of course they should. They should have an overwhelming care, something that puts everything else in the shade. But they don't. For these fine fellows, antiquity is invariably a means to some other end, and a decidedly grubbier one at that.

You might dismiss this as the *African problem*, that however much money is thrown around in Africa, it always ends up in the wrong pockets, and nothing will ever get done, or done properly. But I think the problem is rather different, and rather more tractable.

In the end, again, it all comes down to *value*

I am afraid it does. Antiquity will never be cherished — for its own sake, that is — unless it has a *real and proper value*, and for everybody concerned, not just for the few. And this, I have to say, can only be a *monetary* value. It cannot be a false sacrament, such as Egyptianization has tried to engender — a sort of nationalist pomp. It has to be a monetary value, all the way along.

If all Egyptians came to believe their antiquity was genuinely valuable, they would never harm it so. They would husband it. And the converse — until Egyptians care for their antiquity with a passion, they will never imagine that anyone else could do so.

Summary
- There are various physical threats to archaeological sites in Egypt;
- the pressures of development, of *modern irrigation*, and of *salt*,
- but the greatest hazard is *mass tourism*, which is wearing out tombs as if they were an expendable economic resource.
- It is possible to *manage* tourism, and the dilapidation it causes, but only with foreign expertise, investment (and attitudes).

CHAPTER 19

The Politics of Conservation

If they take away our past, they take away our future as well.
Zahi Hawass, Egypt's supreme authority for antiquity[1]

It is a platitude — at least for conservation in Egypt — that the natives desperately need our help. They don't have our technology. They don't have our materials. But their real problem, as I have been at pains to explain, is that they don't have our *attitude* — our passion for the art, our object-mindedness. Without that the materials and the technology are useless.

The strange ineptitude of Egyptian conservators

The ancient Egyptians were arguably the greatest craftsmen ever. Their only rivals were the Saxon metalworkers, who finessed upon Celtic techniques. But examine Egyptian Middle Kingdom gold work and you will conclude it was more than a match. The ancient Egyptians were *sans pareil*, but now they can barely change a car tyre.

There are many reasons for this. Much as I dislike the social sciences — with their fatuous assumption of man's innate nobility, and society's blame for any corruption — I have to agree with them in this case. The present Egyptians are predominantly the same race as their forbears. If they are now incompetent, therefore, it must be their present culture. But which part? The other-worldly disregard of Islam? Its latent iconophobia? Or the modern lassitude, seasoned by bilharzias or some other African parasitic disease?

Perhaps it doesn't much matter. Given the right *incentive*, you see, the true craftsman will always respond. He will apply himself, and discover his latent abilities. He will rediscover old skills, develop new ones. And if he doesn't respond, it is because the incentive is lacking.

---

[1] And the willing inheritor of Nuur el Deen's legacy — a tomb of Nefertari that has been re-opened to mass tourism — against all the expert advice — and thus effectively doomed, probably within Hawass's own lifetime.

Now incentives are of two kinds. There is money, and there is pride. Status and its symbols, *amour propre*, self-regard and rank — they all boil down to these.

In our own culture, conservators have a problem of pride, what the moderns call 'self-esteem'. They are busily trying to make themselves more important, to make themselves a proper profession, with all that goes with it — the conferences, the academic accoutrements, the esoteric rules of membership. The money is important, of course, the fact that they're not particularly well paid. But the resentment — the feeling of near servitude, when they enter a swish gallery, with its redolence of wealth, of a life that's beyond reach — this can be soothed by self-importance. Conservators may not be rich, but they are closer to heaven.

In Egypt it is much worse. Impecunity is worsened by disregard. They are two sides of the same coin. Egypt has a stultifying soviet-style bureaucracy, which provides a minimal level of security, but little reason to work. The rates of pay are secure, but they are also risible. And there is no prestige.

My colleague, Dr. Hussein, may have been head of conservation for Cairo, with troops of workers at his command, and billions of dollars of ancient real estate — from the Sphinx and Pyramids down to the humblest shawabti. But he was still paid less than the under desk-clerk at my three-star hotel.

Myself with Dr. Hussein (on my right) and the restoration crew at the Tomb of Mentuemhat. What Hussein and this entire crew earned in a month would have taken eighteen minutes in my studio. Therein lies the problem.

The crew foreman and his mate, although illiterate, have assembled this from the thousands of fragments lying around. There is a certain honest pride in this, but it is hardly conservation.

Small wonder that the best and brightest take their degrees in Egyptology, and promptly find work as tour guides. That is what their degree qualifies them for (and precious little else, if truth be told). And that is where the money is. Only the rump and the time-servers remain in the Antiquities Commission—and the occasional honest man like Hussein.

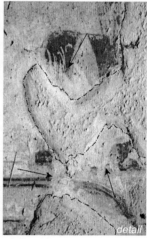

Typical – and typically shoddy – Egyptian restoration (in Tomb No.89 West Bank, Luxor). The painted surface is a very soft plaster, and the modern infill contains cement, which is considerably harder. All the more unfortunate, therefore, that the infill has been liberally smeared over the painted surface, and cannot now be removed without destroying that surface.[2] As an objective measure of worth, this painted wall would realize $200,000 plus in auction (and has had its value noticeably reduced, for less than $30's worth of Egyptian 'investment'.

---

[2]   Well, not by any Egyptian—there is simply nobody good enough, by which I mean good enough with their hands—and not by any foreigner without a considerable expense (and Egyptian permission). Hence not by anybody.

And small wonder that those who remain do little or nothing, and do it as slowly as possible. The government pretends to pay them — as the old soviet maxim had it — and they pretend to work. As long as they make no mistakes, their minimal security will continue. Avoidance of error becomes more important than achievement. And doing nothing at all is the safest way to avoid mistakes. Parkinson's Law applies.

The results are drearily familiar. I could cite a score of disasters, for Hussein was conscientious, and consulted me in his distress. But one example should suffice, not only to show that something is seriously wrong, but also a fair idea of what it is. It's the underlying attitude I'd have you ponder.

JOURNAL: 8th January 1988, Cairo Museum

Back-stage to the 'scientific section', yet again, with a surprisingly cagey Hussein. He wouldn't say why, only that 'the restorers would be very happy for my advice' and then, as an afterthought, that I was 'very lucky to see their problems'. If I'd worked for a foreign institution, he intimated, a museum or an academy, I'd never get to see these things. But I was an independent—no laurels to tend, I suppose—and therefore they'd take me into confidence. 'Something to do with B72' was all he'd say. He'd venture nothing more.

I was intrigued, I have to admit. Egyptians have something of a love affair with Paraloid B72. This conservation plastic is something of an ideal for them. It represents modernity and technology, Western expertise and flair. And if action became unavoidable — if someone had to be *seen to be doing something* — then the safe option was to slosh on the stuff. This was undoubtedly an *act of proper conservation*, and nobody could make trouble by claiming the wrong materials were being used.

JOURNAL [continued]

We wandered through the dreary rooms, deserted as usual, and almost without equipment, and eventually found a tiny room with a table in its centre, and half-a-dozen restorers around it drinking tea. But I hardly noticed them, once I'd seen what was on the table. They'd got a reserve head![3] I'd seen them in the Boston Museum, which has the largest

---

[3] The rarest and most beautiful of Egyptian antiquities: life-sized heads in pure white limestone or gypsum, whose function was to sit in the owner's tomb — an Old Kingdom Tomb, that would be — and provide a haven for his wandering soul, his *Ka*. Something that the *Ka* could recognise, if it got itself lost.

collection–Fred told me there were only about fifteen in the world–but there were none on display in Egypt, and I didn't even know they had one. And this one was just stunning, with a necklace of brilliant blue faience embedded around its neck. As far as I knew, this was the only reserve head anywhere with such a decoration. There hasn't been one on the market for a long time–certainly not while I've been restoring, these last twenty years–but you'd have to assume a price tag of $3 million or more.

Now the extraordinary thing was this. Here we all were, in a small, bare, and slightly grubby room, and in front of us the finest of Egyptian antiquities. But none of the Egyptians were paying it any attention. They looked around it at each other, and appeared to be discussing it, but they delicately ignored it, as we do with cripples or the incontinent. And now they were asking my advice about B72. What on earth was going on here? I began to state the obvious:

– 'But Hussein, it doesn't need anything. It looks fine to me. It certainly doesn't need a sacrificial layer.[4] Why not just...'

But then I saw the real problem, and burst out laughing.

It must have happened like this. Someone had decided to paint this reserve head with B72. God knows why, but he had. Or perhaps the order had simply got muddled. Anyway, someone had fetched a bucket, poured in the transparent beads of B72, and enough acetone to dissolve them. But as he hadn't bothered to clean the bucket – it had sand and gravel and muck in its bottom – all this got mixed with the B72, and the result resembled vomit.

And then, somehow, he had managed to empty the bucket and its horrible contents over the reserve head. Yes, right over it. Perhaps he had been passing by, quite the innocent, and simply managed to trip. Perhaps it was deliberate, and more sinister. Perhaps someone's enemy had infiltrated after hours, and done the dreadful deed.

Anyway, here it was, in a back-room of Cairo museum, the world's greatest collection of Egyptian antiquity. A reserve head, probably their only example, and probably the best anywhere, with a large pile of gravel and sand and half-

[4] A *sacrificial layer* is a surface that is put onto an antiquity, or an antique for that matter, with just that purpose in mind – the sacrifice of itself, so as to protect what lies beneath.

dissolved B72 beads, nearly an inch thick on the top, and stuck down with what was now a rock-hard orange plastic, and dribbling gracefully over the face like a custard pie in a Chaplin movie.

I looked carefully, but couldn't see any obvious damage—no bucket-shaped indents in the soft plaster of the head, no embedded shreds. One had to be grateful for that much. It could have been much worse. The bucket could have been stuck on like a helmet from the Keystone Kops.

Of course it could all be removed, without trace of lasting damage. And it was this that made it so funny, rather than tragic. All that was necessary was a large clean tank and a lot of pure, clean acetone. The head could be immersed, and left untouched until the B72 and its custard-pie junk had dissolved away, as if it had never happened.

JOURNAL [continued]

But as it was so easy, why hadn't they done it? This was where Hussein got embarrassed. Because, he said, they didn't have a big enough container, and they hadn't enough acetone. They only had Tupperware-type containers, or more dirty buckets. To get something suitable–a stainless-steel vat or a sink–they'd have to go to the chemistry department. And then they'd have to explain what they'd done. And even if they could get a suitable container themselves, they'd still have to indent with the chemists for the acetone, and explain why they needed so much. Either way they'd find themselves denounced. And even if they managed to find a commercial source of acetone, and were able to sneak it in undetected–all fifteen gallons of it–they couldn't raise the money between them. Or, more importantly, they wouldn't.

Besides, as Hussein told me, some of them still thought that acetone would damage the head, like primitive tribesmen and the internal combustion engine.

Let me reassure you. That reserve head could have been left in acetone until kingdom come, and no harm done. In short, these fine fellows were stymied, and were now considering mechanical means—that is, chipping the stuff off with chisels! This drew me up short. Until now I had found it funny, but now the horror caught me. A prime rule of conservation, you see—and again it is little more than common sense writ large—is never to remove harder materials from the softer. This B72 vomit was much harder than the plaster of the head, and the result could only be butchery. It was at this point — myself protesting, and half disbelieving — that Hussein hustled me out.

I never saw the reserve head again, so I have no idea what they did (and Hussein was too embarrassed to enlighten me). But I still see the room in my nightmares. I see six men, earning perhaps $150 a month between them, plotting to escape detection, and trying to avoid an expense of $40 along the way — the cost, in Cairo, of fifteen gallons of industrially pure acetone — but risking the destruction of an irreplaceable work of art valued at over $3,000,000. Putting their ambitions — and their tiny wallets — before the welfare of such a magnificent object. And the real *tragedy*, of course — in the correct Greek sense of the word — was that there was nothing else they could do, given the system.

Do not assume these were isolated incidents, and that I am taking journalistic advantage. Don't do me that injustice. We travelled the length of Egypt, Hussein and myself, and everywhere we saw the same incompetence and disregard. The barbecue-fuel boat at Heliopolis, wax-stripped sarcophagi, or the scrubbed tombs at Minea. Any of these would have our own press screaming the odds. But in Egypt they are all suppressed. Nothing ever gets reported by the government-controlled media. Manipulated for propaganda, yes. But reported, never.

The Getty Affair

If simple common-sense would obviate these 'problems' — and it would, I am sure — then why are the Egyptians so concerned to keep them hidden? Why do they no longer turn to us? For left to themselves, the Egyptians will fail. That much is clear. Their officials will follow each other, like mosquitoes in the Egyptian night, each determined to have his fill. To put it with more dignity — and these gentlemen enjoy their dignity — each is determined to preserve what he has. Each is skilled at prevarication. Each is ready to denounce his competitors And the modern accusation is that the *wrong materials have been used.*[5]

---

[5] From which it follows, strictly speaking, that the safest conservator is the one who *uses no materials at all.*

This partly explains their wariness. They fear exposure. But there is more than this. They are suspicious. They rarely accept us for what we are—or what we jolly well ought to be—as a powerful *force for the good*. On the contrary, they doubt our motives. They are convinced that whatever we do is largely for our own benefit—for publicity, for aggrandizement. And for that they'd expect us to pay.

But why so suspicious? Partly, I suspect., because of the *Getty Affair*. The Getty Conservation Institute, based in California and splendidly endowed, was hoping to establish itself as the world leader in the field. There was nothing wrong with that. It struck many of us as an excellent idea. They had persuaded the Egyptian government to let them restore the magnificent Queens' Valley tomb of Nefertari, First Queen of Ramesses the Great. There was nothing wrong with that either.

But what followed was perhaps less dignified than it might have been. Looking back, one just marvels at the publicity. It was so relentless. There were glossy reports. There were talks and lectures. There were television programmes showing the young foreign restorers, robed in white and sweeping off the ferry like young gods, bringing salvation to Egypt. And, finally, there was some neat but unadventurous conservation—largely cosmetic, and conducted at inordinate expense.

And almost overlooked in all this self-serving publicity, there were also some Egyptians involved. Hussein and his friend Maglad—as the country's leading restorers—were selected to work alongside the Italian students. The idea was to improve the standard of Egyptian conservation, by establishing a native store of excellence. A laudable idea, but undermined from the very beginning. The two Egyptians, you see, were expected to work alongside the Italians—performing the exact same tasks—but on their Egyptian government salaries, whereas the Italians were paid by Getty:

JOURNAL: 22nd March 1988, Queens' Valley, Luxor
To Nefertari Tomb with Hussein, to examine his restoration. Hussein seemed unusually animated–almost resentful. He explained how Maglad and himself had had to maintain their families in Cairo, travel by train to Luxor, and feed themselves there, all on their salaries of $27.50 per month. They'd had free lodging, but so had the Italians–and whereas

Adequate restoration, but only treating the symptoms, and at huge expense.

they'd been billeted in the government hostel–not the most salubrious, as I'd just discovered–the Italians had been in the Sheraton, at $130 a night. And the Italians had had free air-fares home–at $900 a round-trip–any weekend they wished.

*And–this was the really big and, according to Hussein– the Italians were paid $250 a day tax-free, (rising to $300 in the second year). Over the two-month season, therefore, they could accumulate $8,000 tax-free ($9,600 in the second year), whilst the two Egyptians, some years their senior and both family men, only had their $54 of salary. Putting it another way, the six Italians were doing exactly the same work as Hussein and Maglad, but **got paid in half an hour what the Egyptians took a month to earn**. This didn't bode well...*[6]

---

[6]   And there were other iniquities:

> **JOURNAL [continued]**
> *It's true–as Farouk Hosni [the Arts Minister] had disparaged, when he'd inspected the work-in-progress–that the Italians' sections seem fresher, brighter. Their background positively gleams, compared to the Egyptians'. But, as Hussein indignantly explained to his old friend, the Italians had been 'touching up' their entire background with titanium dioxide [white]—which in this context counts as serious cheating. Oh dear, foreign gods with feet of clay.*

> *Eventually Hussein complained to the Mexican supervisor of the project and, once the Getty had grasped the problem, they very decently despatched a stipend from California–another $100,000–to 'make it all good', as Hussein quoted the supervisor. Personally, I'd have thought it more correct to reduce the Italians' salaries, or expected them–if they'd taken on board the ethos of their craft, when they'd learned its tools–to work in such a glorious tomb for nothing more than living expenses, and the immense honour of it. They were only students, after all.*

If the Getty were at fault—and I do not suggest they were—it was perhaps their naïvety. They expected too much good will, or at least disinterest. They certainly didn't understand the Italians, who were quite evidently milking the project. And they so little understood the Egyptian character, that they thought the problem could be solved by throwing money at it.[7] But desert sand is thirsty for water:

JOURNAL [continued]

Well, the money eventually arrived. But then a crowd of Egyptians officials emerged, fifty-four of them to be exact–and from the woodwork, I'd be inclined to say–all of them, according to Hussein, claiming to be essential for the project's success. Now some of them, he graciously admitted, had actually visited the tomb. And some might have needed placating–because they really were capable of harming the project. But the Getty didn't consider this. They simply handed the money over. And after the gulls had been gorged, Hussein and Maglad–the only Egyptians actually doing any of the work, remember–were left with $450 apiece.

---

[7] As my host in Egypt carefully explained—when he was urging me to engage an Egyptian agent for marketing my aircraft in the Middle East—'as soon as your project is proposed a crowd of officials will appear, all of them claiming influence. They are not offering to help. They are threatening to close you down unless they're mollified. This is when you'll need an Egyptian to tell you which ones can really harm you—they'll the ones you'll have to pay—and which are only bluffing.'

As a demonstration he had me observe the annual inspection of his hotel by the Ministry of Tourism, who promptly threatened—'as they always do' to revoke his licence unless they were 'satisfied'. As these were officials who could fulfil their threat—however ignorant—they had to be paid.

The souring of the conservation market

In the long term the Nefertari Project was to leave a sour taste in the mouth. The Egyptians, you see, came to regard Getty as buying recognition on the world stage — and buying it very cheaply at that. They became resentful. They envied Getty's wealth, but they despised its presumption. The Egyptians may have been naïve at first — or so they considered themselves — but the next time they were ready. A second grand project was proposed, this time to restore the tomb of Tutankhamun:

> **JOURNAL: October 11th 1994**
>
> *Hussein tells me that Dr. Nuur el Deen–that 'half-honest man', as Hussein calls him–when he heard of the Getty's munificence in sending his predecessor [Dr. Muhammed Bakr] for a $25,000 check-up in California[8]–which had secured permission for the Getty's next project, to 'restore' Tutankhamun–promptly cancelled that permission. He told Hussein privately that The Getty 'were only doing it for their own glory.'*

Another long-term effect of l'*Affaire Nefertari*, of course, has been to inflate the market. I doubt that any foreign institution could now suggest such a project. No, the Egyptians would expect too much. They would expect a fulsome budget, and above all they'd expect bribes.

In another sense, however, they would expect too little. They no longer believe in the altruism of foreigners — in the altruism of professional archaeology, that is to say. They now assume that such schemes are just a *vainglory* — a means to purchase world publicity at Egypt's expense, to strut the world's stage wearing Egypt's borrowed clothes.

In other words, they assume that *Egypt is being used*, yet again, and for the benefit of others. Ridiculous of course. Or is it? We have spawned a minor industry, telling the Egyptians that they have been exploited. There was always the danger that they would take this seriously, and turn the sword on those who forged it. The Getty intended well in Egypt, and they behaved correctly. But they seem to have seeded the ground with salt.

---

[8] Which perhaps counted as the 'fraud and malpractice', for which Bakr was sacked the previous year.

The Sphinx and the puzzled crab

The Sphinx Affair is perhaps another corruption. You could take it for hopeless bumbling of course, but there is more it can teach us.

The Sphinx herself is a *cause célèbre,* and a minefield for Egyptian conservators. I pass over our dismay, when we first confront her. We have arrived, remember, with a feeling of easy familiarity. We know the lady from a thousand care-fully-angled photographs — photographs that create the impression of something that sits seraphic, isolated in the deep desert — which makes us all the more astonished to find her sitting in the middle of a raucous bazaar.

In the 'sixties the city was still a mile away and more, a dis-tant haze down the Giza road. But it was coming closer, seep-ing along the road like an infection, and now the tide laps around her paws. If you want that same long-shot photo nowadays, you must press your shoulders against the slum. For many new visitors — those who come in search of inscru-table antiquity, and find only the *shock of the squalid new* — the contrast is already too much to bear.

Now the whole world knows the Sphinx is in poor health. Her woes are rehearsed. There are television programmes. There are magazine articles. There are talks and conferences. But her problem is actually rather simple. The Lady has been performing as a *gigantic wick* for five thousand years.[9] Water is constantly being sucked up, evaporating from her head and shoulders, and depositing its salt beneath the surface layer. And this has not been helped by the burgeoning slum, whose water table has risen dramatically. The wick is now drawing directly from sewage water. The Sphinx's stone is literally rotten. The pragmatic thing — at least until some-thing can be agreed upon — would be to bury her again in the sand, and prevent the flow.

But the technology to restore the Sphinx *is* available.[10] It is less a matter of restoration, in fact, than of civil engineering. In scale it would match Abu Simbel. The problem, therefore,

---

[9] I pass over the recent *pyramidiocy* of the Sphinx's age; that she is older than archaeologists assert, was made by an older race than the Egyptians, and a better race, as the insinuation is. I just note that this is an argument of patination, of surface decay, which can easily be induced by intensifying conditions, which is precisely what a wick does.

[10] In one sense I have no right to an opinion about this. I restore objects. I'm not a monuments man. But the principles are the same, and so is the science. The

is a *political* one. With so much at stake, who will carry the responsibility? And who will reap the glamour and the publicity — and the risks — of what would become the greatest art theatre the world has ever seen, and the greatest advertisement?

There is a phenomenon of biology that is pertinent, a sort of *pressure-valve for indecision*. Approach a shore crab just so, on the exposed sand, and you will confuse him. His rather limited circuits cannot decide whether you are a threat, or possibly a meal. Whether to attack you, that's to say, or just run like hell. As the tension mounts in him — you can almost feel it, as you move in closer — you will observe that he starts to do something else entirely — something apparently irrelevant. He will pretend to feed himself, and almost in a frenzy.

We call this *displacement activity*, and in the peremptory world of the sea shore, it has obvious survival value. It may well him alive. It keeps him occupied, it keeps him quiet and still and — in case you yourself are hungry, and haven't yet noticed this small and succulent meal — it will keep him from the larger decisions, the ones which might deposit him in your cooking pot.

Crabs pretend to feed, and ducks pretend to preen, but what of Egyptian officials? They call conferences, and they keep themselves busy, making their pretend decisions. These serve little purpose — or perhaps none at all — but they do no harm, and most importantly they don't rebound. The real aim is to *keep busy, and be seen to be so*.

----

research literature is on hand. And so is the common sense. I am aware, for example, that the Germans have developed the machinery to impregnate large pieces of stone with silane. They operate this *in situ* for their civic statues. They immerse the troubled statues in mobile tanks, apply a vacuum, and impregnate the stone with silanes. This stabilizes the stone, and allows the next stage, the removal of salt through a series of water-baths. This technology is well-established, and does not endanger the stone, once it has been strengthened.

I am also aware that we managed successfully to slice up Abu Simbel, and to reassemble it without mishap. Nothing revolutionary there. And I am aware of such things as damp courses. What I would suggest, therefore, is that the Sphinx is sliced into manageable pieces, the pieces carefully numbered, and then treated with silane before having their lethal salt removed. They can then be re-assembled. The cosmetic work — the making good of surface damage — this is child's play, once the stone is free of salt, and made strong again.

This resolute engineer's approach would solve the problem, once and for ever, and save what is surely part of mankind's 'heritage', if that care-worn word means anything at all.

Thus Hussein was despatched, whilst he was still head of conservation for Cairo, and laboured conscientiously on the Sphinx's lower face and beard. It was a cosmetic work, cementing back fragile sections, and of course, being Dr. Hussein, it was painstakingly done. And it hardly mattered that the fragments soon fell off again—forced off by the relentless pressure of the salt. In an anthropological sense, his work had served quite a different function. It was *seen to be doing something*, and it kept the critics at bay. It managed to put off the evil day.

The late 'sixties produced the classic of the genre. A certain architect had gained political favour, despite his archaeological ignorance—or perhaps because of it—and he decided that the higgledy-piggledy restoration of the Sphinx's lower haunches and paws should be 'rationalised'. All the previous efforts were to be removed, and replaced by larger, purpose-cut sandstone blocks of a uniform size. A new outer skin was to be rebuilt over the rotting sandstone of the original.

The result was pleasing enough, in a cavalier 'sixties shopping-mall sort of way, but unfortunately the higgledy-piggledy had *itself* been ancient. It ranged from the famous restoration by Tuthmosis III, circa 1500BC, right up to the late Roman work. It had become an integral part of the Sphinx—an acquired patina if you like—and very important indeed. Oh dear.

JOURNAL: Tuesday 24th April 1994, Cairo

Out to the Sphinx with Dr. Hussein, where we inspected the restoration in progress, and learned more of the politics of restoration. To the left of the Sphinx is a smart wooden hut, and in this hut is the wall chart–a doctoral thesis by an American–that saved them all from disaster. It recorded and dated every individual stone used in the lower-part, all of the successive ancient restorations. This chart was reassuring. It gave the impression that everything was under control– until, that is, you realized the entire lower concourse had recently been rebuilt. All these small blocks had been removed between 1983 and 1987, and replaced with purpose-made 15 inch by 12 inch edged blocks which, because they were only sitting on the surface of the new cement layer–which had been made using unwashed desert-sand, chock-full of salt–buckled off almost immediately. The entire restoration work of the 1990 to 1993 seasons, therefore, has painstakingly replaced **what the previous restoration had just ripped off**.

 Thus the Egyptians can show themselves vigilant and workmanlike, whilst conveniently ignoring the condition of the neck and haunches, which really are the problem...

The Sphinx's bright new paws in 1989, courtesy of an archeologically illiterate architect

Meanwhile, pieces were still falling off the face and mouth with monotonous regularity. And after each one there'd be outrage in the press, and a demand that *something should be done*. Just as well, perhaps, that everybody could show that *they'd all of them been so very busy*. And meanwhile, the politics raged on...

I personally doubt that anything will ever get done about the Sphinx. Consider our friend the crab, caught in the open and paralysed by huge choices, frozen but feeding himself in frenzy, and feeding himself nothing.

This is what we should expect from the Egyptians, because they are well aware of the power of the Sphinx. They know that whoever handles the restoration can *strut the stage*. They will refuse the gift to anyone else, therefore, but are paralysed at having it themselves; at having to decide what to do – and being scorned by the whole world if it goes wrong. And so they stage endless consultations and conferences,

*...and as they had been, a repository of archaeological knowledge,
back in 1982*

hoping against hope that the world's conservators might manage to agree perfectly — shout their solution in synchrony, and spare the Egyptians any responsibility for the wrong decision.

But the West has yet to grasp the psychology, the importance to the Egyptians of *saving face*, and their preparedness to slam the door on outsiders, rather than expose themselves. The world's conservators, that is to say, have yet to understood what is really required.

B72 and the cargo cult of new materials

And yet, and yet. If the approach were made in good faith, and without ambition to cloud it, there is no reason why the Egyptians should refuse. No reason in principle, that is. For the Egyptians themselves have a sort of love affair with foreign expertise. On the one hand they disdain it — as corrupt, as somehow taking advantage. But on the other hand, they display an almost abject reliance upon the latest Western conservation materials, the latest cure-all.

The problem, however, is that every synthetic material has a life span, after which it changes — and almost invariably turns nasty — and has to be removed again. Even in the West there have been some notable cock-ups because — in the first enthusiasm for the latest 'wonder material' — this simple fact was overlooked.[11]

Paraloid B72 is no exception. It may be the world's first purpose-designed conservation plastic — but it is a synthetic, and as such it is inherently unstable. It is presumed to age excellently — without turning yellow, becoming insoluble or inflexible — but no one really knows, because none has been exposed to air and light and heat for long enough. The experiment — as to its ageing properties — is being conducted in the field, as it were. And on antiquities.

Bu we'd be wise to assume that, after exposure to sufficient ultra-violet light, it *will* change into something else. The molecules lying side-by-side will form cross-bonds — like parallel reeds binding themselves together — and a new material will have formed, with different properties from the original.

Western conservators bear this in mind, and are suitably cautious. This is our nightmare; the small-print, if you like, at the bottom of our contract with industrial chemistry. The wise restorer assumes, therefore, that whatever he puts onto an antiquity will have to be taken off again — with some difficulty, if he leaves it too late — within twenty-five years.

As a working restorer, indeed, most of my time has been spent doing just this — rectifying the damage caused by past restorers. Not so much the work they have done, but the materials they've used. I can even date a restoration by the materials I am having to remove. And as my career has pro-

---

[11] Soluble nylon, for instance, the wonder consolidant of its day, close to perfect — or so everybody thought — until it stopped being soluble at all, and seriously damaged the objects it had been used to protect.

ceeded, so the disasters have gradually changed. When I first started it was shellac, the cow-hoof derivative beloved of Victorian restorers. Then it was wax, as popularised by Howard Carter and Flinders Petrie. And now I am removing epoxy compounds, and the early synthetics.

What surprises me is that the profession—for it likes to think of itself as a profession, it preens itself—has forgotten this salient fact. Time and again we working restorers have had to clear up the mess. Even the British Museum has skeletons in the closet (soluble nylon, for instance).

No, the small print is always there with synthetics, sitting ticking at the bottom of the contract, and only the arrogance of conservators ignores it. Let us be quite clear about this. Conservators are not scientists. They are just not bright enough. And what counts for research in conservation is little more than picking up the scraps that are thrown out by dental technology—for that's where the money really is. Most of the cock-ups could have been avoided if conservators had been more humble, and remembered that the quality of their work—how they use their hands, that is—is a damn sight more important than the materials they use.

But if this is the danger in the West, imagine how much worse it is in Egypt, where there's a veritable *cargo cult* about materials. In Egypt, B72 is used without any thought for the future, simply because the future is unimaginable. Twenty-five years is a vast time for an Egyptian. In twenty-five years the humblest tea boy will have risen to be departmental head, and then retired—and with him evaporates all responsibility for his work.

Hence I had actively come to dread the misuse of B72. Hussein took me into Seti's Tomb, for example, and we inspected the wall-paintings.

JOURNAL: 23rd March 1988 (continued)

The stuff has been daubed on so thick—over an eighth of an inch, and running down with obscene dribbles like wallpaper paste, some of them a quarter of an inch thick—that it's become a ticking death-knell for the wall-paintings. Now they'll only live as long as the B72. When the stuff cross-bonds, it will rip the surface off completely. As for removing it, I can't see that happening, and neither can Hussein. We just can't see them taking it on—all that acetone, patiently applied in swabs, and no rubbing, no trying to speed it up, no resorting to the scrubbing-brush. And without industrial-quality breathing-equipment it'd be bloody dangerous.[12] No, it won't happen. The stuff can never be removed.

Whether they can be saved or not, these wall paintings, the Egyptians have created a monumental task — a multi-million dollar task — of taking the B72 off again without destroying the paintings, when they had no sensible reason to put it on in the first place. Another disaster in the pipeline.

Summary

- Egyptian conservators need foreign expertise and investment,
- but recent episodes have soured the field, and convinced Egypt that Westerners are still taking advantage, only offering help for their own ends.
- In other words, there is a serious *credibility gap*.

----

[12] B72 should be removed by dissolving it in acetone, applied on successive swabs, and without rubbing, most definitely without rubbing. In any confined space the sheer amount of acetone required would be near lethal to any unprotected worker. Heavy-duty extraction equipment would be necessary. The Egyptian government lacks this. Nor would they allow any foreigners to undertake the work.

So, in such a case as Seti — and there are many others — the B72 will remain where it is, as a thick coating, unless some faster method is attempted, like rubbing off with abrasives. But this would simply destroy the painted layer.

CHAPTER 20

But Archaeology is a Safe Pair of Hands. Isn't it?

If I had an antiquity in one hand, and a publication about it in the other, and a gun to my head, I'd throw away the antiquity. The knowledge is the more important.

Curator of a US west coast museum, recently[1]

As we have seen, there is a credibility problem. The Egyptians are deeply distrustful of foreigners. They feel they have been deceived, time and again. Indeed they have. And they are only half convinced that the West has antiquity's interests at heart, even now — her clear and unequivocal best interests, that is to say. I would certainly be more at ease, if I believed it myself. But I don't.

Ruthlessness reconsidered

The mythology of the age has it that dealers are ruthless — ruthless in their pursuit of profit, that is — whereas academics are benign and caring, untrammelled by ambition or self-interest. The idea certainly has a pedigree. Auguste Mariette, the founder of the Egyptian Antiquities Service, set the hare running in the 1860s:

It is more correct to say that the desecration of Egyptian tombs...is the work of dealers in antiquities, or even the tourists themselves

when he couldn't bring himself to admit that most of the desecration was by the academics themselves — yes, the seekers after knowledge — those hungry for Champollion's 'un-hoped for enlightenment'. And that Champollion — the great scholar who translated Egyptian hieroglyphs, and opened the mysteries of the Egyptian language — had himself started

---

[1]   Source: Craig Duff, producer, New York Times TV.

the trend, by hacking the first head out of Seti's great tomb, simply because he could now put a name to the portrait.

A practical example

A modern example to confuse your pieties, if you have read so far and are still a believer. It concerns Tutankhamun's magnificent arcade, which he donated to Luxor Temple – as the price of re-instatement, you might say – after the disgrace of his Uncle Akhenaten's heresy.[2] The work is exquisite, a swathe of delicate relief, an elaborate documentary crammed with movement, all of it jaunty and expressive, in the lingering *Amarna* style of his unfortunate uncle.

The limestone blocks of this wall had recently been unearthed, and the wall rebuilt. But nothing had been done to rectify the salt damage, and over large areas there was an almost cancerous infection, as if a pathogen was frothing from the interior, forcing the surface lines and the curves away from the healthy core, twisting them and distorting. This was the effect of the salt, crystallizing just below the surface and creating a hollow space. These cancerous areas were very fragile. A blow or compression could crush them to powder.

I had been pondering the matter. I couldn't bear to see this, and not to rescue it, if only in my imagination. I had considered what the technology offered, and I had considered my own techniques. I had even given thought to the politics –

[2]   The Pharaoh Akhenaten has been lauded as the first monotheist. He certainly imposed sun worship on his unwilling populace, a single-god religion that discounted all need for a priesthood – save for himself (and wife) as direct intercessors between God and people – but his reasons were as much political as theological.

Egypt's Middle Kingdom had ended in chaos when the feudal aristocracy became so powerful as to overwhelm the centre. The New Kingdom pharaohs sought to avoid a repetition of this by keeping the spoils of empire away from the aristocracy, entrusting them instead to the priesthood. This worked, but only in part. It certainly kept the nobility in their place, but it created a new power-base in the priesthood – especially those of the God Amun – who themselves became a threat. Amenhotep the IIIrd (see page 202) began to rein them in, but it fell to his nephew Akhenaten to complete the task. Eventually he nullified the priesthood altogether – by the simple expedient of abolishing their gods. This may have worked, were it not for his strategic mistake of quitting the capital, and isolating himself from the offices of empire. The result was confusion and loss, and his successors – in particular the boy-king Tutankhamun – were forced to re-instate the *ancien régime*, and make an expensive peace with the clergy. The imbalance remained and yes, eventually, the clergy took the throne.

really the most important part, this being Egypt. I had mentally assembled what I would need, and how long it would take, and who would be there to aid me, and how much it would cost. In my imagination I had completed the task. It would be painstaking and arduous — and certain parts could only be managed by myself — it seems arrogant, in cold print, for me to say this, but I suspect it is true.[3] But anyway, it was possible. The arcade could be saved. And for the expense of some few thousand dollars — I was assuming that we foreigners would be working *gratis*, merely for the honour of lending a hand — a monument of many millions would be saved.

Imagine my frustration, therefore, when I chanced upon a young epigraphist from Chicago House — The Chicago University Centre at Luxor:

> **JOURNAL: 26th February 1987, Luxor Temple**
> *There she was, in the spring sunshine, perched contentedly on a ladder, and correcting her photographic proofs. But the top- bar of the ladder was leaning against one of the swollen areas, although some modern cement infill was immediately below. This was more than carelessness. It was outrageous. I went up and asked her–with commendable restraint, or so I thought, and not mentioning that I was a restorer of exactly what she was about to destroy, and how much it would be worth if it ever came onto to the market (about $100,000, I'd imagine, just for that tiny section), and what the f... she thought she was doing?–whether she was aware that her ladder was resting directly on a fragile part of the design, and was likely to crush it?*
>
> *She went all embarrassed–like a naughty child caught out –and told me 'the wall was doomed', that it'd be 'completely gone in twenty years'–that 'under ordinary circumstances, of course'–but the only important thing now was to publish...*

[3] The rotten areas of stone could some of them be saved, by injection or immersion-under-vacuum, and then by teasing and re-aligning. I had developed this technique in my own studio, and saved many such fragments. The only difference here was one of scale, and of course the constraints of working in situ. For some areas, however, there was simply nothing to be done, and here I inclined to boldness. I would insert pieces of healthy stone — saving the originals for posterity — and then recut the design, much as we do without qualm for our own weathered cathedrals. As I say, it was a thought exercise, but it reassured me that the arcade could be saved — that it was *only a matter of politics and resources*, and that there *was* time enough to spare. Not much time, but surely enough.

*This may not be the precise spot, but it does make the point. The bottom part is healthy hard stone, the middle is modern cement infill, and the top is diseased and fragile. But **that** is where she lent her ladder.*

She was young, she was pretty, and I dare say she believed this nonsense. But who had told her the wall was doomed? And why was she so complacent? Was it only my impression, or did she really believe that **publishing** the wall was actually more important than **making sure it was still around?** That by publishing an object she somehow took it under her wing, and made it safe?

Just imagine the public outcry if the RSPCA were to content themselves with merely photographing and filing the animal they'd been sent to rescue...

The ambition of archaeologists

But academics actually *believe* this. The University of Chicago writes that 'time has never seemed so pressing in our struggle to save the monuments of Pharaonic Egypt.' But when they use the word 'save', they don't mean conservation as we know it — the business of repairing sites, and saving them for the future — but only drawing them in extraordinary detail, and publishing them in scholarly journals!

But this is the traditional response of Egyptologists when faced with decaying monuments. Professor James Henry Breasted called it 'saving the past', when he visited Howard Carter in Tutankhamun's tomb. Luckily, Carter took a different, and more pragmatic, view and was willing to spend an entire decade conserving the contents before he would let the Egyptians ship them up to Cairo.

Dr. Vivien Davies, Keeper of Egyptian Antiquities in the British Museum, recently observed that 'there is more than one way of conserving a site. In my view the best way is to document it properly, record it and publish it'. And he added with splendid aplomb that those who protest about merely documenting monuments as they crumble — rather than marshalling the forces to save them, that is — are being 'oversensitive'.

Would anyone dare claim that there were 'various ways to save the tiger, and the best was photography'? And those who complained about their impending extinction were being 'over-sensitive'? I suspect not. Because the corollary — however anodyne it is made to appear — is that the poachers might as well take over, and exterminate the remainder, because the professionals have learned everything there is to learn about tigers, and nobody is interested anymore. Interested enough to publish, that's to say.

As I say, I find this outrageous, simply outrageous. Instead of saving Egyptian antiquity — or at least making the attempt — Egyptologists are happily converting it into a library, and claiming this as an act of conservation! Dusty publications on dusty shelves, that can only ever be read by Egyptologists.

No. The sentiment is unworthy of the profession. As are those who mouth it. And when they rail with righteous wrath at those of a more practical bent, who have decided to do something practical, they add hypocrisy to the charge sheet.

Modern archaeology has its own credo

I began this chapter by quoting a modern curator. I was astonished — horrified, in fact — when I first heard of this. But at least the curator was being honest (well, reasonably so, because he omitted the caveat that if the article was written by his academic rival, he'd probably have thrown that away first — substitute his own article — and only *then* discard the antiquity).

I am sure that many academics *do* actually care about antiquities, but their scholarly life ill-equips them for the hard realities of countries like Egypt. And I am sure that many know what is really going on. I don't see how they cannot, if they have been to Egypt with eyes to see, and ears to listen. But moral courage is a rare commodity, as rare in academe as in politics. And speaking openly will have immediate consequences. They will have their licenses revoked by the Supreme Council for Antiquities.[4] And if they cannot excavate in Egypt, they cannot publish. And if they can't publish, they can't make professor. Or am I being unkind?

I daresay that many Egyptologists — like my epigraphist on her ladder — have simply written off the great monuments of Egypt as unsavable and best abandoned. It has been said of Kings' Valley, for instance, that 'if the mountain is moving, we'd best get what we can, whilst we can', without admitting *why* the mountain is moving — which is arguably because of the archaeologists themselves.[5]

---

[4]   Neatly demonstrated by the German expedition of the early 'nineties, whose crawler robot had been exploring one of the sloping passages in the Great Pyramid at Giza. When it reached a wall, and proved by soundings that the passage continued on the other side, an argument erupted. The state-controlled press accused the Germans of 'treasure hunting', and 'stealing Egypt's heritage'. The leader of the expedition, Herr Gantenbrink, was injudicious enough to express a few home truths about the respective levels of knowledge and self-interest in his Egyptian 'minders' — and his licence was immediately cancelled, and the work curtailed. But, as always in Egypt, there was more to it than this...

[5]   See *The sad plight of Kings Valley* in the Appendix.

The real problem, that Egyptology itself is not 'object-minded'

The real problem, unfortunately, is that Egyptology has always been more interested in the ancient Egyptian language, and what it teaches us, than the artefacts that bear it. There is a reason for this. Traditional scholars hold that erudition — the study of texts — is the central part of wisdom, and Egyptology is nothing if not traditional. Scholars have always taken *texts* to be the key. Monuments might be interesting — for what they can teach us, that is. But they are less important than the texts, and mere antiquities — those 'defaced remnants of history that have escaped the ship-wreck of time' — are altogether lesser things:

> **JOURNAL: 13th December 1992, Luxor Museum, evening**
> *In the museum's new extension, built for the Luxor Temple Cache.[6] Amazing things. Several life-size Horemhabs, and an astonishing standing Amenhotep III in a purple-speckled crystalline. I'd been there forty minutes, trying to cope with this, when some Americans from Chicago House [the American expedition] arrived. I could hear them coming—they were deep in office politics. When they arrived they broke off, made a few comments– 'Oh, he's on a sled. That means he's a statue of a statue'– and then turned on their heels, and were back to politics before they'd reached the door. They'd never seen the statue before, that much was clear. But they never really looked at it–probably the most important and beautiful in the world–never expressed any appreciation or pleasure–let alone awe–and rated it less than two minutes of their time. These people...*

It was not until quite recently, for example, that museums were regarded as anything more than rather vulgar if amusing cabinets of imperial curios. Probably the idea of art and of beauty only arrived on the scene with the Americans and their great museums, particularly the Metropolitan in New York. But some Americans, it seems, have yet to embrace the idea:

> There are big private collections and museum collections of art — not archaeological objects — with very little information

---

[6] A group of statuary, found by accident in the Great Court, when some drainage engineers sunk a trial shaft.

about them at all. The only thing you can do about them is to talk about their beauty and style — their 'art' [sic].[7]

Because of this obsession — this getting of knowledge — Champollion's 'un-hoped for enlightenment' has always been Egyptology's over-riding aim and justification. You could call it their Creed. There is a deep ambiguity here, of course, which some might call hypocrisy. Scholars wish to stop others from damaging antiquities or taking them away, for example, and they denounce dealers with contempt. But Champollion's creed has, until very recently, justified archaeologists themselves in buying 'stolen' antiquities from Egypt — if they could learn something from them, gain un-hoped for enlightenment, that is — and even to argue (if only in private) that many monuments would be 'best-preserved away from Egypt' (Bernard von Bothmer). Champollion himself complained to the Pasha of depredations to the monuments, but still demanded the right of archaeologists like himself to continue their own very destructive excavations…

This is a very different position from my own, please note, although the effects sometimes coincide. Mine is the simpler position. I am *object-minded* like collectors, and curators (I would hope) and most dealers. I value the objects for themselves, and only want to get as many as possible through to the future. I don't much care where they are — or who has them at the moment — as long as they are somewhere that is *safe*. I leave the future to argue the rights and wrongs of it — as long as the objects are still there for them to argue about. That is my concern:

[2a] Antiquity (as much of it as possible) should get through to the future.

Egyptologists are *text-minded*, however, and value the objects for some other reason. Their working principle is:

[2b] Knowledge of antiquity (as much as possible) should get through to the future.

which is not quite the same thing. They are quite prepared to allow objects out of Egypt if they can learn from them, but are also content to discard them — or the monuments supporting them — once these have given birth to a text. The examples I have given may be striking, but they're hardly unusual.

---

[7] Ricardo Elia, vice president for 'professional responsibilities', American Institute of Archaeology.

It has always disturbed me, what happens to an archaeological site after the academics have excavated and published it. Knowledge-driven archaeology is a destructive art, after all. It digs down through time, and destroys the upper time levels as it moves to the earlier. It discards what it cannot use, and after the work has been 'finished' — after the site has been drained of its 'knowledge' — archaeology just discards it, as if it were now an empty husk, leaving it to the developers' bulldozers, or to the elements. I have said this before, but it bears repeating.

The British expedition's excavations at Memphis were excellently done, a model of good practice. But what of the sites now? They have been discarded, left to decay, like wrapping paper denuded of its chocolate.

Archaeologists will always claim that knowledge is more important than a hill of sand. And that sacrament will protect antiquity from the peasantry. But where is their own sense of reverence? Where is their sense of the sacred — that the sites of our ancestors are holy ground, and should be treated as such? Their only *sacrament* seems to be the quarterly academic journal. I find this profoundly worrying. In fact, I think it stinks.

I would mind it less if they accepted some responsibility for the huge destruction of Egypt — rather than just blaming it all on the dealers and the rapacious natives. But they do not. They still claim — yes they do, especially those who have never been there[8] — to be the natural guardians of ancient Egypt. As if they morally owned it, just because they have spent their lives studying it, and mostly from other texts.

It seems that publication — the business of writing articles, and getting your name on them — has now assumed a life of its own. It is the way to advance your academic career, and with it your sense of your own importance. *Toujours l'égoisme*, or am I being cynical? Surely it is only in Italy where academic progress is measured by the weight of publication — where it is a commonplace that 'to make professor, you need to have published two-and-a-half kilos'?[9]

---

[8]　And there are quite a few of these. Several prominent Egyptologists refuse to go to Egypt, and regularly despatch their graduate students to do their footwork.

[9]　Dr. Laura Vazzoler, Faculty of Letters, Rome University, as early as 1982. Having said that, the RAE (Research Evaluation Exercise) would appear to be

Collectionism re-considered

The *collector's impulse*, I suspect, is more pervasive than academics like to think. It is a profound biological urge, and it assumes many forms. Some are admirable, and others less so. Professor Renfrew may pour contumely on collectors as a class, because he holds them responsible for the *rape of heritage*, but that — as I hope you have now come to realize — is a child's tale only fit for children.

Because this very same urge that drives collectors — the *urge for neatness*, for arranging things in patterns, and the feeling that they are thereby brought under control — this same urge drives much of academe, especially in the *taxonomic sciences*. It is probably something that has been hardwired into the brain, our joint and shared Palaeolithic brain. And it can get out of hand, this urge, and threaten to displace the first task of archaeology, which should surely be to *save* things, and get them through to that uncertain future.

We must rid ourselves, I fear, of the idea that *archaeologists are the natural guardians of the past* — of what our ancestors have bequeathed us. They are not.

For one thing is painfully clear. The exposed monuments of Egypt are really falling apart. A combination of exposure after long immersion in a chemical-rich *sabakh* (dung soil), salt problems, raised water-tables after the Aswan High Dam — and now a tourist flood — is bringing it all to the boil. Many of the finest wall sculptures of Egypt — such as Tutankhamun's arcade — are simply falling off their walls. And this despite the fact that the technology is available in the West, and the money.

But what do archaeologists do? Do they delicately negotiate with the Egyptians, using their undoubted goodwill as foreign 'experts', to bring in the funds and the expertise that the Egyptians need so desperately, but are so suspicious of? Do they hell. They bury their heads in the sand, part cowardice and part indolence — and another part shrewd ambition — and they get on with what they call the real business of Egyptology. That is, 'saving' the sites and the monuments by recording them meticulously in line and photographs, and

---

moving the UK in the same direction. It is no coincidence that the number of new books published has *doubled* in the last five years, and that the average journal citation rate is *zero* (sic) and that includes authors citing their own papers.

then publishing their work in scholarly volumes. As you can see, I am not impressed.

And I am even less impressed by the gathering ambience of *realpolitik*. Archaeologists are quite prepared, it seems, to pay lip-service to the Cultural Heritage Crusade, to its gathering sanctimony. They are quite content to urge in their museum journals that curators should now be 'aware of cultural pieties', even to the extent of denying access to some classes of religious artefact.[10] But not enough, it seems, to return these artefacts to those they now implicitly regard as their 'rightful' owners. And certainly not enough to consider the much larger matter of their bulging Egyptian collections, which were unashamedly stolen in the past.

On the contrary, in what strikes me as a suspicious new development, they seem intent on returning the occasional bauble to the natives, to preempt them from asking for anything more substantial. This seems to be politically acute. It certainly is political.

I dare say there will be a chorus of outrage from the academics at what I have been suggesting, and further attempts to discredit me. I would ask them, however, to see it from the point of view of the natives themselves, the suspicious and corrupt and demoralised Egyptians.

Summary

- We tend to assume that Egyptologists have a duty to safeguard antiquity, much as doctors have for the lives of their patients.
- But their idea of safeguarding is often merely that of publishing (as if a patient's notes were more important — to his doctor — than the patient's health)
- In fact, modern archaeology has a political (or politically correct) credo — 'in the beginning was the *word*...'
- It follows, therefore, that a little scepticism is in order — that Egyptologists should relinquish their claim to speak for antiquity. In other words, develop some humility.

---

[10] For example the recent case of Red Indian religious art being held incommunicado, and only available to accredited Red Indian scholars — but not to the general public — and the shameful *Alice through the Looking Glass* logic that is used to enforce this dictum (whilst still retaining the objects).

CHAPTER 21

Uncomfortable Conclusions

JOURNAL: Wednesday 28th May 1992, Princeton
*My passion for antiquity was still intact, a concrete and pro-
saic passion for the objects themselves–for the beautiful
things that would remain long after we are all dust–and the
compunction to pull them back into the light. It was this, after
all, that had driven me on: the growing conviction that modern Egypt was not a safe place for antiquity, that it was one
of the enclaves where the new common sense–that of the
market and free trade and openness–was being ignored.
Academic complacency and nationalism were doing their
damage, and there was still a need for people like me–
literally enough–to pick up the pieces. In one sense, it was
just part of the conservator's faith. And it was indeed a faith.*

Time to pause and reconsider. Time to draw the strands
together. For this book, as you will hopefully have gathered,
compares two positions that derive from opposing world
views. The difference between them is radical.

One is liberal and optimistic, naive perhaps about human-
kind, but almost proud to be so, always forgiving of some –
the politically favoured, in this case the new nations, their
governments and those who produce the platitudes on
demand; and unforgiving of others – our recent selves, the
free-enterprise market that makes us strong, and the collectors who drive that market. It is revanchist and liberal. Call it
the *UNESCO School*.

The other is suspicious of government, wary of its recent
excesses, a trifle cynical perhaps, but optimistic in a different
way – the way of the proven world. Call this the *Libertarian
School*.[1]

---

[1]   Our recent ancestors would be astonished that the adjectival and substantive
       forms of a single Latin root – *liber* (free) and *libertas* (freedom) – now define
       diametrically opposed political camps. Ho hum…

The UNESCO credo

• **Cultural heritage requires** *state ownership*, even when the claimant states have neither racial nor cultural continuity with the former inhabitants of their territory, whose property they are claiming, or with the manufacturers of those objects, when they were traded in antiquity.

• **That educating people to 'accept their cultural heritage' is akin to** *recovering memories* (rather than just propaganda for cultural nationalism).

• **That** *private ownership* **is somehow a turpitude**; that collectors are responsible for damage to ancient sites, as are the ignorant peasantry of the poor countries.

• **Whereas** *archaeologists* **are not responsible for any damage**, and neither are the modern politics of the West, hence archaeologists can gain access to foreign sites without compromising themselves or their science.

• **That antiquity should never be regarded as a** *resource* (and isn't, by archaeology or the nations that archaeology favours).

• **The way to preserve antiquity is to deprive it of** *monetary* **value** and substitute a *sacramental* value, even in Islamic countries, where this is offensive to the prevailing doctrine, and where antiquity could actually compete with economic and demographic pressures.

I believe that *every one of these propositions is demonstrably false*, either logically (doesn't make sense), or contingently (as a matter of observable fact, the world doesn't work that way). The only possible exception is what Hassan Fahty called the *problem of peasantry*, the hidden assumption that is never openly acknowledged, at least in the liberal West (because it is politically incorrect) but which is actually the key to the problem, and for which there *is* a simple answer.

In short, archaeology has saddled itself with a political agenda. It is politically adept. That much has to be admitted. But it has compromised itself, so as to retain access to the sites (without which its career professionals cannot publish).

The LIBERTARIAN credo

begins with some articles that many UNESCO liberals would accept (albeit with coy restrictions):

• **Antiquities can be legitimately collected and retained where they exist in profusion**. No one would suggest, not even Zahi Hawass, that all the mummy cases in the world be shipped back to Egypt.

• **Or the people who created them no longer survive** (in any real sense).

• **Or their descendants are incapable of looking after them** (or demonstrably unwilling).

What will be anathema to UNESCO liberals, however, are the following:

• **That antiquities will only survive if they have a value**. The diaspora proves as much, and the present destruction in Egypt. It is clear that antiquities have come down to us — in brute terms, they have survived — only because they were *valued*. A simple empirical point, which ought to be self evident — blindingly so — but seems difficult for some to accept.

• **This value can be of various types:** Sanctity, prestige, or vulgar lucre. Some antiquities have been treasured because they gave sanctity to a place or an era, or thrilled their custodians with the past. Some were representative of tradition, of heritage. Some were simply saleable. But unless they have been valued — considered important, or holy, or sacrosanct, or currency — they would never have made it through. And the same harsh logic still applies. They'll either be valued, or cast aside. Moreover

• **The whole population must share this value**; all those that come into contact with antiquity. In one sense this is a political aside, or a caveat. But the *elephant argument* gives it force. It's of little use having a salaried elite which idealistically believes in something (or opportunistically, as in Egypt) whilst the impoverished remainder looks on with cynical disbelief. That will only breed poachers.

• **If they don't, they'll never become 'object-minded'**. Object-mindedness is a propensity — to care and respond — that has always protected antiquity. I am arguing, you may remember, that our response to art is nothing less than a *biological inheritance*, something that is hardwired into the brain. Not that we are born with it fully-fledged — this true collector's passion — with its objects already specified, be they Egyptian antiquities, teddy bears or vintage cars. Or that it always develops, in every one of us. Or that it develops about the right things.

Only that we are born with a *propensity* — to collect things, to cherish them, and eventually to respond with laudable emotion. As I say, this isn't something that comes fully-developed. We have the capacity to respond, all right — but first we must specify the field. We need to fix our gaze, as it were. And this can only be where we have discerned some value, some importance. Then we need the expertise. And only then will the emotional response — the true collector's passion — begin to show.

The market calls this 'object mindedness', a rather dull name for something so glorious — that links with our profoundest feelings, with the sacred — and that preserves so much for the future. When all the parties are object-minded in this sense — when they all share the passion — then no harm can come to its objects. Without it, however, bad things can happen. And Egypt proves the point.

Professor Renfrew might argue, perhaps, that if this is part of our biological inheritance, then it's an aspect that's well past its sell-by date, and had much better be suppressed. And I'd reply that this is academic silliness. Or worse.

• **But the same type of value won't do for all countries**. It must suit their particular circumstance. Unless the currency is *pertinent*, it simply will not work. This is the heart of the argument, the real bone of contention between Professor Renfrew and myself. The Cultural Heritage Crusade claims that the world has changed — a sweet new dawn entices — and the only type of value needed to save antiquity is the Value of Heritage, of the sacrosanct past. But I am not convinced. I can only repeat, that *unless the currency is pertinent, it will not work*, and the antiquities themselves will be cast aside in the struggle to survive in a harsh world.

• **In the industrialized West, this value can't be commercial**. Apart from anything else, antiquity just cannot compete with property prices. Archaeology for us is usually a last-ditch attempt at rescue, before it's too late.[2] We scrabble to extract *knowledge* — and a few commercially worthless artefacts — before the bulldozers move in, and replace the site with a fac-

---

[2] The 'Time Team', with all its irritating showmanship, its Blue Peter presenters and specious 'deadlines', is symptomatic of the light-hearted afterthought that is Western archaeology.

tory, or a lay-by, or a swarm of bungalows. This is the world that Eliot decried and which, for better or worse, we now inhabit. It's a world where ancient sites and the ancient objects cannot compete with human greed.

In the West, therefore, the value that attaches to archaeology has to stand apart from the currency. We can only try and make archaeology a sort of extended graveyard, a nostalgic sanctity that cannot be touched by commerce, that's forever out of the modern play. There is really no other choice, given commercial pressures — given a world where the most expensive and glorious antiquity is valued less, in hard currency, than a look-alike semi in a London suburb.

• **But in poor countries-of-origin it cannot be anything else**. In some countries, however, antiquity can *compete commercially* with the pressures of a modernizing world. Egypt is one of those countries. Its archaeology needs no protection against the ruthlessness of modern commerce and development. In Egypt a free market would actually — and at last — begin to serve antiquity's best interest. In developed countries land is just too valuable, and would never be spared because it happens to shelter ancient remains. Mere archaeology will be pushed aside. But in Egypt the converse applies — antiquity *enriches* the land, and can make its own way.

• **Antiquity will only survive if it benefits everybody**. And that, inevitably, means money, Marx's 'universal equivalent'. The ordinary Egyptians, for instance, are struggling hard to survive. The forces of rectitude are straining equally hard, trying to push antiquity out of the frame — their frame — by making it more and more hazardous to sell. But what cannot be sold is valueless. And what is valueless to a hungry man is scorned. And what has value only to the ruling caste is doubly scorned.

Sites are now being discovered by people who cannot benefit from them, at least without considerable risk. They are being destroyed before the authorities become aware of them. It follows that our *bien pensants* have been stoking the wrong fire. What works for the liberal West — if it does work, which is arguable — can never work for the poor countries.

• **Nor is nationalization the answer**. The Cultural Heritage Crusade assumes that confiscation by the state — in *loco parentis* for the populace — will serve the best interests of antiquity, although nationalization has proved generally disastrous in the West. All the more ironic, therefore, that Egypt has been nationalizing her antiquity — and attempting to remove the commercial value that is antiquity's saving grace — whilst the West, these last twenty years, has been going in *quite* the other direction, and busily privatizing everything.

In Egypt, moreover, this policy has ignored Islamic doctrine — its anathema for polytheism — and caused antiquity to be strictly identified with the secular regime. And this is sowing the whirlwind.

Egyptianization has been a disaster, in fact, because the mass of the Egyptian people have seen it as a virtual theft of something that was previously theirs — a *Gift from God* — and that should be theirs again (if it's to survive). It has become, quite simply, an argument about a resource. And the result has been a Prohibition in the classic American 1920s sense — with the same consequences of venality and neglect.

The Egyptian antiquities authorities have always been corrupt, of course. Given the importance of 'face' in Egyptian society, the paucity of the salaries, and the apparent wealth of antiquities on hand, it is difficult to see how it could be any other way. But the present regime has done nothing to rectify this. If anything, it has intensified, by bringing so much more of the market into government hands.

• **In the countries of origin antiquity has become a political plaything**. In some cases it has become a mythic resource, little more than propaganda for cultural nationalism — a prop for unsuitable regimes, and political manipulation at it most blatant.

In other cases it's become essential for tourism. This *may* be a good thing, in the platonic sense. But it reduces antiquity to an economic resource, a means to hard currency. The Egyptians, for example, have been bailing themselves out, in the short-term, but using up their sites in the process.

In fact, the regime treats antiquity like a bed of coal. Western archaeologists are also aware of this. They *must* be aware, unless they are impossibly innocent. But they prefer not to speak out, for fear of losing their licences, and hence their access to sites. So much for Western archaeologists.

In other cases — Egypt springs to mind again, as does Iraq — antiquity has become a personal resource of the ruling regime, a rain cheque against political reverse.

The Egyptian government might object that if the peasantry were allowed to own antiquities, they would sell them to foreigners, and this would result in a massive flow of objects abroad. But so what? The argument may have had some force in the socialist 'fifties, but now it is laughable. A massive flow of objects out of the country would mean a massive flow of wealth in.

Besides, these pieces are surplus to the requirements of display and tourism. The authorities could easily retain the best pieces for themselves — which is all they actually need — and as for little things, Egypt already has a superfluity of them. What Egypt needs — as does archaeology — are the important sites, and the important pieces. And she would have first refusal.

• **Only a commercial market can serve the best interests of antiquity**. Our aim — at a purely practical level — should be to get as many sites and objects as possible through to the future. That should be everybody's aim. And the best way to do that is by placing them where they will be cherished and protected.

And there is only one way to manage this — as Bernard von Bothmer understood. Bothmer argued for the re-establishment of an open but controlled market in Egypt. He saw the market as the only means of breaking the cycle of neglect and venality. The market needs regulating, of course. It needs to avoid the excesses of the past. But properly managed, it will save the day. It is only zealots who cannot grasp this fact, and probably won't until it is too late.

If a man is starving, the sensible way to stop him stealing other people's food is to make some of his own available to him. If a properly regulated market such as our own were re-instated, a vast new wealth would enter the system and, quite simply, there would be no further need for ordinary Egyptians to steal from government-guarded tombs — and no further need for the authorities to collude in that theft.

If antiquities could again be owned and traded, it would restore their value for the populace at large — for *fellaheen* and farmers and shopkeepers, and not just the harried black marketeers, and the antiquities police sitting on their stockpile.

And from this, everything else would follow. This is my central contention.

Ordinary people would no longer despise antiquities as the perquisites of the ruling-caste. Instead, they would learn about them, so as to understand what they were now able to possess. And from this knowledge they would develop pride in their heritage. In other words, they would at last become object minded.

Once the Egyptians become 'object minded' — and actually learn to love the objects in themselves, then the battle has been won. The eventual idea, you see, is to produce a nation of devoted collectors

• **Regardless of how much private property is distrusted.** You still think me inconsistent? That I am advocating something — free enterprise — that in the past was cheerfully dismembering the tombs? Ah, but that *was* the past, when the West was actively encouraging the destruction. Bring in the modern Western market, with its sophisticated idea of property — which embraces intellectual property, and the duty of care — its discipline and expertise. Bring in the auction houses and the proper Western prices, and the corruption that goes hand-in-hand with Prohibition will wither away.

There would be an immediate and immeasurable benefit — the new sites that would otherwise be lost or deliberately destroyed. They could now be openly declared without fear of loss. Where appropriate the government could insist upon controlled excavation, to be funded from the finds themselves, so that the knowledge is conserved as well as the artefacts.

When modern nations claim antiquity as 'their inheritance' it follows that certain questions have to be asked[3]

• **Have they any grounds?** As a *body* (rather than as individuals).

• **Who is actually doing the claiming?** It is vital to distinguish between the *people* and their *rulers*, because of the extreme rarity of democracy.

• **Is it, for example, the people?** Who act with a synchrony which suggests a *truly common culture* and a purpose to match,

---

[3]   These follow from Chapter 9 (in the 'support' section).

- **Or their rulers?** Be they tyrants, cadres, party or regime — who are manipulating them, having them chant in unison, and then claiming to represent 'their' interests.

- **If there is no legitimate claim**, is it merely *realpolitik* and manipulation? And if so,

- **What is being proposed for antiquity?** Its use as a *mythic resource*, as a *touristic resource*, or simply as a means of denial?

- **Is that in antiquity's best interest?** It is vital, that is to say, to distinguish the interests of antiquity from the interests of government policy. And,

- **Is archaeology being compromised, as a profession?**

- **Archaeological knowledge is also a 'commodity'.** The way to protect the sites from premature destruction[4] — what archaeologists call 'illicit' excavation — is to recognise that *the value of a site resides in more than its artefacts*. Correctly excavating those artefacts yields knowledge — which is an intellectual property, and which also has to be preserved. And the only way to do that is to honestly acknowledge its value. This is how to solve the *problem of peasants* — by broadening their concept of property — of what an ancient site really contains.[5]

- **But archaeologists must also pay for this.** Until now, they have visited distant places, extracting Champollion's 'unhoped for knowledge' from the sites — as if it was a mineral deposit that only they could refine — and merchandizing it. But knowledge is no longer free. It probably never was. If archaeologists want to retain access to these sites, therefore, they will have to admit the fact, and pay recompense. Otherwise the countries of origin will confiscate that knowledge — just as they are busily confiscating the artefacts — by preventing Western access.

Putting it bluntly, archaeologists have doomed themselves. They have been agitating to prevent anybody else earning money from the sites — so they can have sole access to the resource and the earnings — and they have been irritatingly sanctimonious about it. But the countries of origin don't see it like that. Hobbit Man is only the beginning.[6]

---

[4] Assuming that archaeology is most efficient at destroying them.

[5] See page 142 ff (support section).

[6] See page 146 ff (support section).

• **It follows that academics should stop striking poses**. We all of us have the well-being of antiquity at heart — the archaeologists, the conservators, the dealers and collectors, even the tourists. Academics do not own compassion. Virtue is not their sole prerogative (and nor is common sense, apparently). We all want to get antiquity through to an uncertain future. We all want the same thing.

The difference between us is how much we know about what is actually happening. And whether we are prepared to admit it. Most coffee-table books, for example, now include a summary of the current pieties:

> The great majority of museums and public collections are extremely careful today when purchasing 'new' objects... Only a documented provenance ensures that they have not come from recent illegal excavations. In the last few years illegal trading in Ancient Egyptian artefacts has been made a lot more difficult thanks to pressure from *international experts* and a new offensive, both at home and abroad, by the Egyptian antiquities authority...which must have made it clear to all that *traditional greed for profit and collecting Egyptian antiquities must become a thing of the past.*[7] [my italics]

This is the Cultural Heritage Crusade in triumphalist mode. Notice the easy moral assumption of the last sentence, that 'greed' and 'collecting' must — the self-assured moral *must* — become things of the past. But put that alongside another assertion, again the received wisdom, that:

> The requirements of today's inhabitants of the Nile Valley are far more important than any of the needs of archaeology and ancient history. The rapidly increasing need for space for living and for business activity in contemporary Egypt will inevitably lead to more and rapid building over ancient towns that will thereby be lost to archaeology, or will at least become inaccessible. *In today's Egypt, archaeology is no more than a question of salvage. Ibid.*, page 505, my italics.

And you may be forgiven for scratching your head, and asking yourself why any sensible man — or body of supposedly sensible men — could be so obtuse. The pieces of the puzzle are all there, but they refuse to put them together, and admit what needs to be done. That is, to give back value to

---

[7] Professor Daniel Polz, from the German Expedition in Cairo, in Könemann's *Egypt, The World of the Pharaohs*, pages 506-7. These extracts are entirely typical, only made more poignant by the fact that the good professor is based in Cairo, and has to mind his 'p's and 'q's.

the sites and to what they yield — both their intellectual value and the value of their artefacts. Do this, and they could remove the dread word 'salvage', and put 'mutual benefit' in its place. The same author, and this is also par for the course, states that:

> *Today the question of long-term or even short-term preservation of monuments is perhaps more urgent than ever before...* Some Kings Valley tombs are visited in High Season by up to 2000 visitors a day, yet scarcely a single tomb has proper climate control...the very real and constant deterioration could in fact now *only be prevented by the immediate and complete closure of the tombs. Ibid.,* my italics.

Has he not noticed a connection between the 'requirements of today's inhabitants of the Nile Valley', those same 'collectors', and that 'mass of tourists'? Again, the pieces of the puzzle are all there. He only needs to look.

* * *

My last word on the subject: It is a universal desire of people to handle beautiful things. This desire has preserved the past for us, those thousands of objects that have come down to us. Otherwise they would have been lost. We owe our present richesse to this desire, and to its practice — what we choose to call 'the market'. Beneath the sophisticated veneer of our Western culture this same brute fact remains. And without the market, the properly disciplined organized market, with its expertise, its candour and its resourcefulness, there can only be loss and despair.

Summary

- There are two diametrically opposed positions about antiquity, each of which derives from a particular world view, a *weltanschauung*.
- One is the *UNESCO stance*, held by the Cultural Heritage Crusade, by modern archaeology, and generally by 'liberal' academics.
- The other is the *libertarian stance*, held by collectors, the market, and various countries of origin (*de facto* if not *de jure* — by their behaviour rather than their public pronouncements).
- Each has an explicit credo.
- This book has disproved the *UNESCO credo* and confirmed the *Libertarian credo*, point by sensible point.

CHAPTER 22

Postscript, and Political Malice

Is it too late for common-sense? Apparently it is.

As we have seen, we are faced with two rival world-views; the *UNESCO* and the *Libertarian*. In practice, the choice is between a mix-and-match approach, taking each country on its merits — whatever its political claims — and locating the best mechanism for getting its antiquity through — and a one-size-fits-all approach, which treats all these countries the same, whether they happen to be G8 property-rich industrial, or third-world cheap-land agricultural.

On one hand, a free trade in antiquities would ensure that they end up in the hands of those who most want them, and who are most likely to look after them, and that archaeological knowledge has a sporting chance of being gathered. However, such antiquities will not be 'public property'. The interested public will still have access — collectors love to 'share' their pieces with the cognoscenti — but they will largely be denied to the gawpers and the vulgar.[1] And nor

---

[1] An interesting question this; whether articles made for the exclusive use of an exclusive group — a group that alone had the trained sensibility to appreciate them — should now be openly displayed to those who are neither exclusive, nor capable of the refinement necessary (to make head or tail of them, let alone appreciate them in the more subtle sense). Whether this counts as a *deliberate defilement* of the objects themselves.

Egalitarians will get hot under the collar about this, and mutter the present pieties. But that in itself proves the next point — that we can only display these objects, and display them without qualm, because we actually have nothing to do with the ancient peoples whose intimate property they were. And what is more intimate than a tomb, and its private tomb-goods? We can only expose them and their intimate selves to those who are clearly not their 'family' — international package-tourists, for example — because we, also, are not their family — they are not our ancestors — and we feel no guilt about blatantly flaunting their pieties and their most evident wishes. You would not do this to your granny's grave, any of it. You would be inhibited by a sense of sanctity. You would think it a sacrilege. Ponder this. It was President Sadat's

will they — except the important pieces — be kept at the sites of origin.

On the other hand, keeping antiquities at the sites of origin, as far as the Islamic countries go — and that covers all of the ancient Middle Eastern cultures, remember — is almost sure to end in their destruction. When the Moslem Brotherhood takes over Egypt the museums will be looted and the major sites defaced (whether or not the minor 'moveables' are sold for ammunition, as happened in Afghanistan).

This is the stark choice before us. And whilst this book was being written, the choice has apparently been made. At least it has in Britain. And made behind closed doors, by a government in thrall to political correctness, and without bothering to ask the British people.

In Britain — and to a lesser extent America — the Crusade seems triumphant. There have been, in quick succession, a series of high-profile trials, a ratification of the UNESCO convention, and some knee-jerk legislation in response to Iraq. It is hard to resist the conclusion that the Crusade — and in particular its zealots — have been manipulating the media, and feeding them false information. In short, that the British government has been 'bounced'. It is also hard to resist the feeling that it were content to let this happen.

Rather than congratulating the British antiquities market on its probity — the fact that the world's second-largest art market has less than one thousandth of the world's misbehaviour about antiquity[2] — it has effectively destroyed that market, just to 'send out a powerful message'. Who the message has been sent to, and what they will make of it, seems less important. The temptation to strike a pose was just too tempting. And the Crusaders, as I have already hinted, were never interested in 'reforming' the market. They wanted to *destroy* it on political and class grounds, irrespective of the consequences. But unfortunately there *will* be consequences.

What does international law have to say?

A large number of things, I am afraid, and most of them muddled. Firstly there is no such thing as 'international law'.

---

opinion, when he decided that the Egyptian Royal Mummies should never be placed on open display. A decision that was later overruled, on grounds of publicity and revenue. And, yes, of cultural propaganda.

[2]   The government and UNESCO's own figures, as we shall see.

There is maritime law, but apart from that there is nothing that legally obligates nations, in the way that nations obligate their citizens — nothing to punish them if they fail, or coerce them if they waver. The United Nations is merely an association, and its edicts have little more than moral suasion. Not even that, given its blatant corruption. The International Court in the Hague is only effective when it is recognised. Both can be flagrantly disregarded, and for every Milosevitch that is brought to book there is many a Burma or Rwanda that passes unchecked. *Realpolitik* is the only 'law' of international affairs, and that means power, and power inevitably means ourselves. 'International law', for better or worse, is the present plaything of the Western conscience.

As regards antiquities, there is no worldwide agreement, nor any apparent convergence. Antiquities laws vary hugely from state to state. In some places it is a simple matter of Finder's-Keepers. In other countries, such as Egypt, there is a blanket nationalisation, and everything under the ground, in collection or in territorial waters has been claimed by the state. Between these two extremes are countries such as our own — which I previously regarded as paradigm — where there is a free trade in antiquities, but with mechanisms in place to identify pieces of archaeological importance, and ensure they can be retained for the nation.

The irony is that nobody seems aware of the differences. UNESCO passed its convention thirty-five years ago, and it has a hundred signatories. But they have only just thought to list the various laws, and put them on the same page.[3]

The law is one thing, however, but political correctness is another. Western countries may have had sensible enough laws — until recently, that is — but they have also harboured the *market-haters*. And these are the ones who have been up to mischief.

The Crusade and agitprop

What has been interesting — perhaps more interesting than the events themselves — has been their coverage by Western

---

[3] Only in 2004 did they get around to allocating funds to create a 'database' of the various laws of the signatory states. If they had done this a little earlier they might have discovered that much of what they choose to regard as 'illicit' — against the law of the particular states — is no such thing. It may show moral turpitude — as in 'nineties Iraq — but it is perfectly 'lawful'. See page 322.

media, and what this reveals about their agenda. Or, perhaps, the interested parties who have been briefing the media. The press coverage of recent trials was extensive, for example. For those who knew the actual events, however, it bordered on the hilarious.

Firstly, the Egyptian people and the Egyptian authorities were deliberately conflated. As we have seen, Law 117 of 1983 distinguishes sharply between the two. The Egyptian people are forbidden any contact whatsoever with 'their' heritage, from which it follows that the real owner is Mubarak's regime. But Dr. Anthony Leahy, honorary secretary of the Egypt Exploration Society, has blandly asserted: 'These treasures don't belong to private collectors, they belong to the Egyptian People'. Tell that to the farmers, Dr. Leahy, who have been thrown off their land merely because a handful of antiquities have been found there.

Secondly, the foreign involvement in smuggling has been vastly exaggerated. I should know, because I was the smuggler concerned in these cases, and had been quietly pursuing my amateur pastime for several years, carrying objects in my own suitcase, and shunning the semi-industrial market, which ships containers to the Swiss free-ports using Egyptian government documentation.

But the British press, never noted for its restraint, spoke of 'lorry-loads of priceless stolen artefacts', of 'plundered tonnes of silverware [sic!],[4] jewellery and ceramics', of 'thousands of pieces recovered', which were not only 'priceless', but had 'incalculable value'. And this was just the broadsheets, the so-called 'quality' papers. The tabloids hardly bear quoting.

As for Scotland Yard, they had 'smashed a multi-million pound operation', and 'foiled an international ring of racketeers'. Much of this was the Arts Squad blowing its own trumpet, of course. This was a tiny two man and a tea-boy department, who had never managed a conviction, and as my solicitor explained to the Egyptian government, were 'more than eager to cultivate national publicity...to save themselves from being closed down.'

---

[4]   As a matter of fact, silver was rarer and more valuable in ancient Egypt than gold. Almost no silver of any description has been found. I have only ever possessed one tiny silver amulet.

Thirdly, the antiquities were invariably 'looted from guarded vaults', the 'sealed stores where treasures are stored', by 'hired gangs of labourers and thieves'. That is to say the archaeological site of Sakkara — that vast area of shifting sand, an ancient necropolis brimming with monuments and tombs — was being deliberately confused with the fortified storage depots where surplus antiquities are stored under armed guard.

Now getting into an isolated tomb is one thing, a matter for adventurous villagers, even if they do occasionally hire the front-door key. But helping yourself from a heavily guarded depot is quite another, and can only be accomplished by the antiquities police themselves. The two methods should be clearly distinguished. And if they haven't been, there must be a reason.

The reason, it seems — and now we're getting into my 'fourthly' — has been to play down Egyptian involvement, and heap all the blame on 'international art-traffickers'. Oh yes, Dr. Nuur al-Deen admitted 'there were Egyptians involved in the illegal trade in antiquities, as well as foreigners'. He even went so far as to 'believe that some corrupt guards and inspectors are giving inside help'. This, of course, before he himself was arrested.

His excuse, however, was that there were 'only 15 Inspectors and 120 guards for this vast site', and 'these ignorant guards are paid only £20E ($6) a month, so of course they are going to be easy to bribe'. The implication being that the flesh is weak, and it was nobody's fault if the stuff gets stolen.

Not so, however. These figures only refer to 'village watchmen' employed by the inspectorate. There were also antiquities police on hand, and land police, and the conscripted military. The correct figure was closer to five battalions, all of them heavily armed.

JOURNAL: Thursday 4th March 1993

Ali just rang with a splendid tale. Apparently, President Mubarak visited the Boat House at Sakkara, and for his delectation a dozen Middle Kingdom statuettes were put on display. After he'd gone there were only eleven. The word was that one of his retinue had pocketed it–they're only six-inches, after all–but the antiquities police took advantage, and decided on a house search of Sakkara. They brought in a couple of army battalions, sealed the entire vil-

lage, and went through it with a toothcomb. Various rogues have been netted, and a great deal of money changed hands, according to Ali (and his source in the secretariat).

Besides, Sakkara will always be the premier site on the tourist round. How many visit Egypt without the Pyramids, the Sphinx and the tombs of Sakkara lurking in their consciousness? As such it generates, directly and indirectly, an income of perhaps $8 billion a year. One might have thought that such a resource merited an adequate guard — and one that was adequately paid — and not just for the parts the tourists might see.

Anyway, the Egyptian government's internal papers, unseen by the Western media, make it clear that the blame lay fair and square with the Egyptian authorities. In the late 'eighties the entire inspectorate in Sakkara was quietly sacked — for facilitating tomb-access to those same 'gangs of hired labourers' etc., etc. In other words, for selling the tombs. In 1996 they were all sacked again, and this time also 'arrested'...

The only reason the antiquities police themselves were overlooked — though widely known in the trade to be selling antiquities from the depots — was because there had been a prolonged power struggle between the various factions, which they themselves had finally won.

JOURNAL: 14th August 1995 [continued]
General rejoicing in antiquities police headquarters [over Nuur el Deen's disgrace]. They'd been going through a rough time, with almost daily denunciations and resignations, and a gathering feeling of panic, that they'd lose their powers [of inspection and storage]. And then, out of the blue, Nuur el Deen himself was arrested–and his second in command–whilst he was away at a conference in Germany. And that meant–as the general from the secretariat told Ali–they could 'fix all their problems very fast.'

The British authorities, incidentally, were aware of this political infighting, if not its details. They widely spoke of the 'total confusion, and cross-purposes' of the Egyptians, and in 1995 the Crown Prosecution Service[5] referred to a

---

[5]   The public prosecutors, equivalent to the district attorneys in the US.

'civil-war over antiquity', in which 'your client' (myself, that is to say) 'had found himself embroiled'.[6]

But the CPS lawyers, through the Arts Squad, were urging the Egyptians to proceed against their own suspects, because 'if it is said that [these] smuggling operations were undertaken with the connivance of senior members of the Egyptian Antiquities department and police, but prosecution [of these suspects] was discontinued, it would undermine any sympathy which a British jury would have for [an English case].'[7]

Hence the British authorities knew of Egyptian corruption, but chose to deny it in public. Putting it bluntly, they condoned it, so as to attack the London antiquities market.

But the British had other concerns – other than mere muddled virtue. Their Egyptologists were 'terrified' that 'the scale of the racket might jeopardise the granting of excavation licences.' And British television companies reported the British Museum was 'paranoid that any appearance on television would jeopardise their licences to dig'.[8]

They had a very careful path to tread, it seems. Am I alone in finding this unseemly?

And that weasel word 'stolen'

The Crusade, as I have already mentioned, has deliberately misrepresented Egyptian law. Every report in the Western media talks about 'stolen' antiquities, and all involved, from dealers to smugglers, are accused of 'stealing' antiquities. But when does this barbaric act take place? I say barbaric, because the *insinnuendo* is that these same people have actually desecrated tombs, ransacked them, viciously hacked and sawn antiquities from their rightful resting place – rather than buying them, in any of a hundred ways, from Egyptians who considered them their rightful property, and who had probably bought them from other such Egyptians, stage after stage, until we reach the humble farmers – or workmen – who originally found them. That is how the vast majority of pieces are 'stolen'. That is the humdrum reality, however disappointing it may be to the tabloid mentality.

---

[6] Personal conversation, August 1995, between the Arts Squad and my Israeli Attorney.

[7] Internal memo from CPS to Arts Squad (disclosed to the crown court).

[8] Internal correspondence from a television company sub-contracting to the BBC, which entered the public domain (by subpoena) during a high court case, see *Grounds for a grudge*, in the Appendix.

The nineteenth-century romance of discovery: noble savages digging up what they quite evidently feel has nothing to do with them (and hence has no lingering trace of the sacred for them).

The modern romance: hidden tombs and native dress, subtle lights and smuggling (except that, in this case, we are looking at the gaffer and his mate in Mentuemhat's tomb).

And the prosaic reality: workmen digging a sewer in a remote village. A month before this photo, these same men discovered a large fragment – of Coptic Christian carved-limestone tracery, which had somehow got itself incorporated as a foundation in the village mosque (and still remains there, unless the Islamic puritans have discovered it and smashed it to pieces).

The Anglo-American trials

I link these trials, and not just because they involved the same evidence, and the same personalities. They shared something else, a peculiar modern obsession of the English-speaking world — the urge to feel morally superior, which we call 'political correctness' (PC).

The modern English will travel to the countryside — to admire its 'unspoiled' beauty — and they will throw out their trash whilst they indulge the sentiment, so as to keep their 'personal space' unsullied. PC does much the same. It claims the 'high-ground' — and it does this expansively — but it is actually content with a very small compass. It looks inwards. It is only concerned with the inner self, and 'feeling good' about it, and hardly at all with consequences and other uncomfortable realities.[9] It prefers to keep the beloved vehicle (of the self) spotless and uncluttered, whatever the cost to its surroundings. This is more than narcissistic, although it is. It is also dishonest, because it relies upon others — the

[9]   Thus Tony Blair's justification of the Iraq war focused on the purity of his intentions, contrasted with the 'evil' of Saddam's regime. The government could have made a better case for the war on long-term strategic grounds.

unseen 'untouchables', the fixers and movers – to actually clear up the mess. And because it cannot resist the temptation to strike a pose, even though it's partly ironic.[10]

The British legal situation in the 'nineties was quite clear, however. It was stated by the House of Lords in 1996, and re-iterated in 1997:[11]

> It is not an offence for a British Citizen to bring antiquities into the UK from a Country of Origin, knowing them to have been illicitly excavated and illicitly exported from that country.[12]

There was an obvious reason for this. Offences against British law have to be committed on British soil (with the sole exception of treason). Britain does not indict 'offences' supposedly committed in other countries, and according to their laws. If we did, we would find ourselves bolstering some very unsavoury regimes.

Lord Renfrew found it 'scandalous', that Britain did not forbid the import of 'stolen' antiquities. For those of a politically-correct persuasion, I dare say it was. But the solution, as the market had repeatedly and patiently pointed out, was for parliament to consider a new law, after suitable advocacy and debate. That eventually happened, in 2003, when 'loopholes' in the existing legislation were cited[13] as grounds for another law. It hardly matters, now, whether these really were 'loopholes', or merely common sense. What matters is that a sovereign people – through their parliament – should have had the opportunity to consider the claims of these countries of origin when they were busily demanding antiq-

---

[10] Well, some of us do. There is more to 'PC' than this, of course. It is also a retreat, a resignation, an admission of defeat against an uncompromising world, an acceptance that there is very little that can be done, and hence the only thing is to cultivate one's own garden, one's own inner self. This is Epicurean, and it is hardly what made the Stoic English the envy of the world.

[11] The House of Lords is the highest British adjudication, equivalent to the US Supreme Court.

[12] Baroness Trumpington in 1996, as reiterated in debate by Lord Inglewood, on February 17th 1997.

[13] 'The Theft Act 1968 does not apply...to items...illegally excavated or removed in circumstances not amounting to theft...for example with the consent of the landowner, or owner of the building, or where there is no legal owner of the item...or where *the person receives a stolen item for his own benefit, rather than for the benefit of another person*' [my italics]. Department of Culture, Media and Sport, PP639, January 2004. The first part refers obliquely to 'unsavoury regimes', but the latter is a straight quote from the Theft Act itself – see footnote on page 318 – and effectively admits that my indictment and conviction in 1997 was bogus.

uities as their rightful property, and hence 'stolen'. Specifically, whether the Egyptian *people* were doing the claiming, or their *regime* — and whether that regime could be trusted.

It is not for politicians to decide the issue in private, and then manipulate the judiciary, and through them the law, and for nothing more than political correctness. But back in 1997 that is precisely what happened. The CPS had already dropped charges against several antiquities dealers because they were 'out of jurisdiction' — because, that is to say, if they had committed a crime, it was outside Britain, and not a matter for British courts. And the CPS had explained this to the Egyptian government — explained, that is to say, why they could never bring such a case.[14]

The remarkable thing about the English trials of 1997, therefore, was that they ever happened — either the first one or the second. Because there were in fact two. The first failed immediately, and for the same reasons of jurisdiction. The second succeeded, but only by indicting the same owner — myself — in respect of the same pieces, as if I was no longer their owner, but merely the owner's servant, and assisting that owner from Britain. Which entailed that I would be committing a (lesser) offence in Britain jurisdiction.

The problem was, however, that I actually *was* the owner, and always would be, wherever I happened to be. I couldn't literally be in two places at the same time, or two legal persons in the same place. And therefore, by the existing law, I still couldn't be indicted.[15]

But to achieve the desired result, I was.

---

[14] Letter from Arts Squad to Egyptian Antiquities Commission, 1996.

[15] The Theft Act (1968) distinguishes *primary* handlers — people who knowingly buy stolen things, trade them, store them etc., and who are 'acting for their own benefit' — from *secondary* handlers, who are the servants of primary handlers, and assist them by driving their cars, running their errands etc, even though they may not come into contact with the stolen goods. These secondary handlers are said to be 'acting for the benefit of another'. Now the Theft Act was badly drafted, and much scorned by academics, but this bit is very clear. You are either a primary handler, or a secondary. These are two separate legal persons. You cannot be both of them. You either 'own' the stolen goods, or you help the person who does. You just can't do both. So if the primary handler is abroad when he takes the goods into his possession — the point at which he 'commits the crime' — then he is quite simply 'out of jurisdiction'. Only the secondary handler can be indicted, if he is helping the primary handler from inside Britain. But he can't be the same person...QED

This was clearly a legal nonsense.[16] But the goal here, the politically-correct end, was to create a precedent, however unsustainable. Something that would frighten the market and, presumably, that would appease the Egyptians. The government could not risk an attempt against Sotheby's — who had been recently undergone an exposé on Channel 4 — presumably because they had not broken UK law and they could afford the lawyers to laugh it all out of court.[17] What the government needed, therefore, was a scapegoat. Somebody they could throw to the wolves.

I daresay the 'liberals' would justify this by citing utilitarianism — that an individual had been punished *pour encourager les autres*. They would probably suggest that 'he'd really deserved it'. But these are not good arguments. Liberals are generally tetchy about 'civil rights infringements'. They are quick to quash them with human rights. But it seems they are selective with their indignation.[18]

It's an ill wind, however. As London's market shrank under the onslaught, so New York's grew. In fact, the US was fast becoming the world centre for antiquities, just as her art market was the largest. And the American attitude was correspondingly confident. They had none of our historical baggage. They had no guilt about empire. They believed passionately in the market, and the saving value it gives. And they also believed — as our forefathers had believed — that many antiquities were at risk throughout the world, and would be much safer under their capacious wing. They accepted that many countries could not be trusted to protect their 'heritage', either on doctrinal grounds, like the Taliban — and Islam generally — or because they just couldn't be bothered. And that the market's job was to rectify this.

The Frederick Schultz trial in New York, therefore, came as something of a shock. In one sense the attempt was cleaner and fairer than the British, if only because there was legisla-

[16] A *reductio ad absurdum*, in fact. see *Trials, The English* in the Appendix.

[17] What Sotheby's actually did was to shift their antiquities sales to Paris.

[18] Paul Johnson (Spectator, 20th August 2005) has blamed the present corruption of the body politic on the centre-left and centre-right politicians — my beloved 'Liberals' — who felt (and feel) so earnestly about their legislation that they consider it permissible to lie, blatantly and pervasively, in order to get it enacted. Pity they had not read Bertrand Russell's *Government by Propaganda*.

tion on hand — the recently enacted 'wire-fraud legislation'.[19] But the decision to use it was a political one. The US authorities were persuaded of a 'need to discipline the market'.[20] And it could only be claimed that Schultz had 'electronically transferred moneys overseas to purchase antiquities he knew to have been stolen', if these antiquities were first accepted as 'stolen'. And that was something the US had never done.

Because of this, feelings were running high in the art market, especially as Schultz was a former president of an American dealers association,[21] and a prominent trade spokesman.

What Schultz should perhaps have done — and what many expected him to do, the FBI and myself amongst them — was to have stood up, boldly and clearly, and admitted that, yes, he had been buying antiquities which he knew came from Egypt, as many others did,[22] but this was the correct thing, given the disgraceful state of affairs over there. That buying antiquities from Egypt was — as it had often had been — an *act of conservation*.

This would have earned him a fine — a mere slap on the wrist — but he would have been centre-stage, a hero, and the trade would have rallied around such refreshing candour and good sense. And so would the American academics, who are bolder and more straightforward than the British.[23] Besides, we reasoned, no American jury after 9/11 would convict a US citizen, if they thought they would be doing the dirty work of a corrupt third-world Arab regime that actively exported fundamentalism.[24]

But the Schultz Trial was hugely important, especially his appeal, which argued that the US had never recognized the

---

[19] Originally passed to combat drug commerce, it made the electronic transfer of moneys abroad an offence, if the transfer was for nefarious purposes.

[20] Personal conversation, 2001, with FBI Special Agent Pat Gildea.

[21] The National Association of Dealers in Ancient, Oriental and Primitive Art (NADAOPA).

[22] Schultz argued privately that all those — the dealers and collectors, the auction houses, and no doubt the museum buyers — who visited the *freilagers* in Switzerland to buy Egyptian antiquities assumed that what they bought had been 'legitimated' by the Egyptian government, without whose active assistance they could never have got there.

[23] Schultz had several times said that the [American] academics 'knew what [I, the author] was doing, and envied me for having all the fun.'

[24] What he actually did, once the lawyers got involved, was altogether less courageous.

'repressive' antiquities laws of other countries. The Appeal Court rejected this, and agreed that the US would henceforth recognise foreign laws in these matters[25] — the countries of origins' effective nationalizations — 'as long as these laws were rigorously enforced in their own countries.'[26]

And this signals that the national vanities of third-world regimes (however (un)elected, and however appalling their behaviour) are more important than the preservation of their antiquities. A strange concession from the country that has just invaded Iraq. It was Iraq, ironically, that proved the real gift for the Crusade.

UNESCO triumphant

The UNESCO Convention of 1970 — 'On the Means of Prohibiting and Preventing the Illicit Import, Export and Transfer of Ownership of Cultural Property' — enables signatory states to recover illicit antiquities from fellow signatories. This sounds fairly harmless, sensible even, until you realize how the convention defines 'illicit'. It simply means 'against the wishes of the incumbent government'. If any regime chooses to nationalize its antiquity, and claim it as an asset, denying its people any rights of ownership or access — as they have in Egypt — then that's fine by the Convention. And any antiquity which is not treated as such becomes illicit.

But the convention was very much a product of its times; a world chock-full of liberated colonies, of newly-hatched democracies. It trusted Big Government, and professional

---

[25] That the US National Stolen Property Act applies to objects 'stolen in violation of foreign patrimony laws', what has been called the *McClain Doctrine*.

[26] From which it follows that widespread and demonstrable corruption would nullify any requirement to prosecute US citizens. From which it follows that Schultz's attorneys missed another trick. This book — the evidence it presents, from the same source (my journals), that convicted Schultz — constitutes grounds for an appeal, and this seems to be the opinion of a leading US authority on art law.

You may be wondering why I decided to testify against Schultz. For several reasons: Firstly, I knew there was going to be a case, whether I participated or not, and that it would be based on my papers. Therefore, that I would be 'trashed in my absence, by the defence' (to quote the assistant defence attorney) unless I was there to see them off. And I'd had quite enough of being lied about. Secondly, I was told (incorrectly, it emerged) that, as a 'white-collar criminal', Schultz was only facing a fine. And thirdly the FBI offered me 'the world's greatest forum' to explain what was *really* going on in Egypt. Overall, this was probably a mistake. Courts are not for explaining these things, they're for convicting people. I should simply have written this book.

politicians, and their benign intentions. It distrusted peasants and private property. And it blamed colonialism for practically everything. These were the implicit assumptions.

As such, it has dated rather badly. For these beautiful ducklings have grown into ugly ducks. Nowadays there is only one recognisable democracy in the whole of Africa and the Middle East.[27] Nearly all are dictatorships, one-party states, or military regimes. Few are interested in 'cultural property' — at least as the UNESCO mindset would have them be — and many are hostile to polytheistic antiquity.[28]

The convention allows these governments free rein with 'their' antiquity. Uday Hussein, Saddam's charming son, was abiding by the convention when, as the 'competent authority of a legal government' — he had *de facto* (and probably *de jure*) ministerial rank — he not only helped himself from the national museum over the best part of a decade, but systematically pillaged thousands of sites across the country, and exported the proceeds, as a source of government revenue. None of this was 'illicit'. It was done with government consent, and was therefore allowed within the convention.[29]

The same applied to the Taliban, who destroyed their Buddhas under the outraged gaze of UNESCO's cultural watchdogs. They also acted within the convention.[30]

This was belatedly grasped by UNESCO, who issued a supplementary 'declaration' — Concerning the Intentional

---

[27] I am obviously using 'democracy' in an empirical sense — where a people can not only select their masters, but also bend them to their collective will.

[28] Hostility which UNESCO blatantly ignores. The Director of Kabul Museum, Dr. Omar Khan Masoodi, pleaded for help to evacuate his museum's contents, before the Taliban got round to destroying them. UNESCO repeatedly refused, piously intoning that it was 'not UNESCO's policy to export works of art from their Country of Origin', until it was too late — bloody idiots — and most of the collections had been destroyed. And this is not the only example.

[29] You may find this hard to stomach. In that case I would suggest you study the convention itself. You will find it solely concerned with 'illicit import, export and transfer of ownership of cultural property', and never considers the possibility that governments might be actively hostile or indifferent to the stuff (to the very idea of another culture's property). Iraq accepted the convention in 1973, but the only aspect Uday Hussein could possibly have breached was Article 6, which enjoins signatories to 'introduce an appropriate certificate...[of] export' without which an export could be judged 'illicit'. But few signatories have ever done this, and UNESCO itself has no idea which ones have.

[30] Unlike Iraq, Afghanistan was not then a signatory. They did not join until recently. But even if they had, it would have been within its remit.

Cocking a snook in the grand style, and the wages of UNESCO's meddling

Destruction of Cultural Heritage.[31] This began resoundingly enough: 'Recalling the tragic destruction of the Buddhas of Bamiyan that affected the international Community as a whole', and 'Expressing serious concern about the growing number of acts of intentional destruction of cultural heritage', and 'Mindful that...this... may have adverse consequences on human dignity and human rights'.

All well and good and uplifting. But it ended quite lamely with 'A State that intentionally destroys...[its] cultural heritage...bears the responsibility for such destruction, to the extent provided by international law'.[32] If this is anything more than circular — if p does q then q is because of p — it has a blithe fatuity about it. As we have seen, 'international law' is a club that has to be joined. It can also be blithely ignored. And nobody, surely, expected the Taliban to turn up at The Hague, and meekly submit to judgement by the infidels.

The UNESCO Convention, therefore, is little more than a moral exhortation.[33] It has no teeth. But it is having an effect. It is condoning antiquity as a resource, a merchandise for

---

[31] Paris, 2003, at UNESCO's 32nd Session.

[32] Article VI: State Responsibility.

[33] And from a discredited source, to judge by recent revelations from Baghdad about the infamous Oil-for-Food Scheme, and the UN's involvement. A source that is morally bankrupt, and hopelessly corrupt.

government's unrestricted use. That use can be corrupt and brutal, and there is nothing UNESCO can do about it. The irony is that archaeologists—as a largely Western profession—assumed that UNESCO would keep the sites intact until they got around to excavating them. In fact, it has made them a hostage to political fortune. And Islamic fortune is turning against antiquity. 'Hobbit-man' will soon be par for the course.[34]

In October 2002, with much fanfare and some very dodgy statistics,[35] the British government did what it had stoutly and sensibly refused to do for thirty years. It signed this ridiculous residue of Bandung, and claimed to be 'sending [a] strong warning to those who do so much damage to the world's cultural heritage...that the UK is serious about stamping out the illicit trade in cultural objects'.[36] Not quite, I'm afraid. It sent another message altogether.

The looting of Baghdad Museum

As wars go, the second Gulf war was a very good war. At least it was for the Cultural Heritage Crusade. It provided a horrifying event, and horrifying images of the same. And these provided superb propaganda. I refer, of course, to the looting of Baghdad Museum, which seemed to confirm everything the Crusade had been preaching, and converted many to the faith. But view it from a distance, and there is more than a hint of manipulation.

The fertile crescent between the Euphrates and Tigris was one of the original 'irrigation states', the other being Egypt. As a 'cradle of civilization', it is exceptionally rich in archaeology, having nursed a succession of empires. Compared with Egypt, however, there has been almost no systematic excavation. Iraq is an unexplored storehouse of archaeology.[37]

After the first Gulf war, there was widespread looting of provincial museums, those temporarily 'liberated' from Ba'ath Party control. The significance of this was overlooked.

---

[34] See page 148.

[35] See page 331 ff.

[36] Baroness Blackstone, announcing ratification by the UK government, 1st August 2002.

[37] The reason for this, of course, is that Mesopotamian archaeology has never been sexy enough—compared to Egyptian—and has been consequently ignored. There are no fat fees in it for coffee-table books, and none for television punditry.

In the next decade, and for the first time, there was widespread and systematic *excavation*. Although Babylon and Ur were untouched, most of the other sites were 'got at', in one way or another. Again, the significance was overlooked, that this would not have been possible — even less so than Egypt, in fact — without the cognisance and approval of Saddam's regime — and almost certainly their direct participation. It seems, that is to say, that the oil-for-food programme was not their only source of revenue. Any other conclusion is naive.

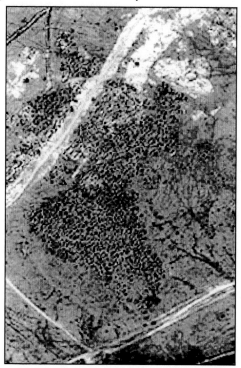

This satellite picture shows hundreds of rows of neatly-spaced excavation holes. Notice their regularity, their uniformity—their sheer 'in yer face' blatancy. They are not 'proof of organized professional gangs.' Or only to an armchair archaeologist. Such excavation may well be, from the publishing viewpoint, 'worse than what happened with Baghdad Museum'. But it is very organized, and very systematic. And consequently impossible without Ba'athist government consent and, probably, direct Ba'athist control. Orderly lines mean surveyors and site foremen. As the Kurdish leader in Faladjah[38] has said: 'Saddam was in charge of everything. If a bird was killed, Saddam knew about it'.

---

[38] Where the Kurds were notoriously massacred with Saddam's chemical weapons.

With the fall of Baghdad, however, there was an outbreak of general looting. This should perhaps have been foreseen. There were cultural advisors attached to the coalition, who suggested as much,[39] and agents from US Customs, some of whom were deliberately embedded with the combat troops. And there were resignations after the event.[40]

An outburst of spontaneous joy — at the fall of Saddam — had been widely expected. But the pent-up resentment — its sheer pervasiveness — seemed to catch everybody by surprise. Practically all government buildings, and all Ba'ath party offices, were savagely attacked. Anything and everything associated with the regime was taken or smashed. Even hospital beds were removed. And Baghdad Museum was no exception.[41] The immediate impression was that the entire museum was either smashed or carted off in wheelbarrows.

The 'international community' — which in this instance meant the UNESCO faction — swung into action with commendable speed, if not clarity of thought. The director of the British Museum personally took a team down to Baghdad[42] under UNESCO auspices. This was closely followed by a UNESCO conference in Paris, an 'intervention' by Interpol, a British Museum conference, an Interpol conference, a UNESCO plan, a UN resolution, and promises of rapid legislation. And all this within a month.

---

[39] Dr. Peter Stone for example, CEO of the World Archaeological Congress, who advised the MoD for two months before the invasion, had suggested that 'both opportunist looting and stealing of treasure to order would be likely after the liberation'. The standard party line, in other words.

[40] 'It didn't have to happen. In a pre-emptive war, that's the kind of thing you should plan for.' Martin Sullivan, resigning from the Presidential Advisory Committee on Cultural Property, 18th April 2003.

[41] It is difficult to know — it will probably never be known — if it fared better or worse than other targets. The contents were probably seen as valuable, and marketable. But they were also *taswir*, and anathema, not to mention the personal treasure of a secular and hated regime. Nor shall we ever know whether the important pieces were 'stolen to order' by collectors, or 'saved to order' from the mob. Only time will tell. If the refined middle classes were responsible, for instance, they would be unlikely to return these items until assured that the next regime was sympathetic to them. As for myself, I am confident they will re-appear in time. I also suspect they are still in Iraq. They certainly have not been 'destroyed', which is the important thing. Remarkably little has.

[42] On the stated grounds that the British museum 'traditionally' hosts the world's second collection of Mesopotamian art, 'gathered' during the nineteenth century.

The assumption, widely canvassed by the Crusade, was that the looting was the work of 'organized gangs' of 'international art traffickers':

> It looks as if the looting was a deliberate planned action... They were able to take keys for the vaults and take out important Mesopotamian materials put in safes. Probably it was done by *the same sort of gangs* that have been paying for the destruction of sites in Iraq over the last twelve years, and smuggling the objects onto the international market'.[43] [my italics]

> It would not surprise me at all if international dealers had a hand in the plundering...I would be very surprised if it were not the case that some of it had been stolen to order — although I've no cast-iron evidence of that...initial reports... suggest... that replicas have been left in their cases.'[44]

There was much more of the same, and it rapidly became the orthodoxy. Unfortunately, it has proven *completely wrong*. Little short of opportunist nonsense, in fact. The Baghdad Museum looting was nothing to do with the 'international antiquities market'. Nothing at all.

Firstly, it emerged that the museum staff had hidden most of the exhibits in three bank vaults before the war, and taken others into their private care. But they had been reluctant to reveal this until they were certain that Saddam was safely off the scene. This meant that, within a few months, the 'crime of the century', with at least 170,000 'priceless' antiquities stolen, had shrunk to several dozen un-recovered items, and a couple of thousand small beads and amulets (and an unknown number of cuneiform tablets, unknown because nobody knows — or nobody is telling — how many were still there when war broke out). Given the surrounding events, this was already remarkable.

Secondly, it emerged that the museum records were in an appalling state. Nobody has much idea of what the museum

---

[43] Professor McGuire Gibson, Chicago University, although how he could assume from the evident chaos — or the use of conveniently available keys — that there had been advance planning, or that 'gangs' had been paying for hundreds of sites to be destroyed under the eagle eyes of Saddam, quite beggars belief.

[44] Dr. Peter Stone, Director of the International Centre for Cultural and Heritage Studies, University of Newcastle, as if thieves were necessarily illiterate, and couldn't read display labels, which specified that they were copies.

originally contained,[45] except the staff. And since the museum had been effectively closed since the first Gulf war, with Uday Hussein using it as a personal resource,[46] it is unlikely they will be forthcoming.

Thirdly, and perhaps most interesting, was the ease with which most of the looted material was recovered, either by amnesty, by negotiation, or by tip-offs from ordinary Iraqis which lead to seizure (from other ordinary Iraqis). Almost none of the pieces left the country, although there has been slanted reporting — some of Uday's previous exports have been seized, and confused or deliberately conflated with museum lootings — which seemed to suggest as much.[47]

As for 'international smugglers', it did occur to some, fairly early, that there just weren't any foreigners in the country, except for accredited journalists. They were briefly accused, it's true, but Interpol eventually admitted that smuggling was effectively impossible, because non-accredited outsiders had no access to the coalition-controlled country.[48]

There were other puzzling aspects, which nobody seems to have noticed. Dr. Donny George, Director of Baghdad

---

[45] 'We don't yet have a complete record of all the stolen objects, and we don't have any means to verify that a certain object is indeed coming from that collection.' Giovanni Boccardi, UNESCO World Heritage Centre, Paris.

'Records were so poor it could take years to work out what was in the museum in the first place, let alone what was stolen by looters'. Colonel Matthew Bogdanos USMC, in charge of museum security.

For example, nobody seems to know whether the 4,500 'very important' cylinder seals that are no longer in the vault — but had definitely been there once — were recorded as one item in the *journal d'entrée*, or 4,500. If this was Egypt, I would be rather suspicious.

[46] 'Many of the missing artefacts...were probably stolen several years ago by senior figures in the Ba'ath regime: Saddam's eldest son, Uday, is known to have made huge profits from the international trade in antiquities.' Parliamentary select committee 'Cultural Objects: Developments since 2000', 2004.

[47] 'Three London antiquities dealers have been arrested in a secret police operation for allegedly dealing in artefacts looted from Iraq. Police recovered an Assyrian stone relief looted in 1991 after the Gulf War' *ibid*. But there has been no subsequent admission — or no publicity for that admission, more like — that these objects were lawful by existing British law, or that the other such 'seizures' in France and Kuwait were similarly *Uday's exports*, and nothing to do with the Baghdad Museum looting. This is the way publicity is being manipulated.

[48] 'Quite limited traffic of stolen art at the moment...these are items which would be very hard to get out and which are very well known to major dealers and experts internationally [because published], so practically impossible to sell' Jean-Pierre Jouanny, Interpol, 2nd October 2003.

Museum, pronounced 'the theft of the entire museum' as the 'crime of the century', when he must have known that most of it was safely in storage. If he knew this, and systematically deceived the West, what was he up to? Watching his back, in case Saddam came out of hiding? But if he'd been unaware of the storage, then what were his staff up to? One suspects the shadow of Saddam lay heavily on them all. But either way, the Western 'experts' were badly deceived, and believed everything they were told. Or wanted to believe it, because they were so full of hatred against 'the market'.

The response to the looting

If the usual suspects were not responsible — the unscrupulous collectors stealing-to-order, the professional smugglers, the 'international art-traffickers' and the 'same sort of gangs' — then who was?

The simple truth is that ordinary Iraqis took their revenge. The Iraqis are Muslim, and these antiquities were the *taswir* of previous polytheists. They had long been the property of a thoroughly secular dictator, who had waged war on Islamic puritanism. As *jahiliyyah*, therefore, they were an obvious target for retaliation.

The fact that ordinary Iraqis were content to destroy these wonderful things — the smashing had always been more significant than the looting — showed that, as far as these modern Iraqis were concerned, the Sumerians, the Akkadians, the Babylonians and Assyrians and all their goods might as well have been from Mars. If this really had been the Iraqi's 'family silver', they would not have dreamt of destroying it. But nobody seems to have noticed this.

As a result of the furore, however, the UN Security Council passed a resolution[49] which vetoed all trade in Mesopotamian art. This was a radical departure. It effectively assigned Mesopotamian antiquity, in toto, to the care of just one nation, Iraq, which was in the painful process of re-inventing itself, and which might well become a Sharia-based theocracy similar to Iran, or split into three separate states, with or without a bloody Lebanese-style civil war and enormous bloodshed. Several of these outcomes, if not all, would be hostile to antiquity. Rather like entrusting Save the Children to slave traders, in fact.

---

[49] Number 1484.

And this was not even taswir, *but a fairly recent ruler*

If other Western states follow Britain, who dutifully passed the Iraq (UN Sanctions) Order 2003 — which outlaws any Mesopotamian antiquity 'thought to have been exported illegally after 1990', and allows up to seven years imprisonment for it — their own markets will follow Britain's, whose 'trade in Mesopotamian antiquities has collapsed to virtually nothing in the aftermath of the Iraq war.'[50]

Dr. Stone may opine that:

> the looting continues unabated...somewhere there must be warehouses bulging at the seams, because the stuff isn't showing up on the [Western] market...the people who are storing it are perhaps long-term family firms of antiquity dealers. They may be assuming that if it's not this generation then it's...the next generation that's going to reap the profits.

But this, again, is naive.[51] Even if it was possible to tell whether sites had been looted before the war under Uday's tender ministry, or afterwards, in the general mayhem — which it evidently isn't[52] — it is clear that almost none of 'the stuff' has been reaching the Anglo-American market. Since

---

[50] *'Cultural Objects: Developments since 2000'* §64.

[51] Actually, it is worse. Academics who know nothing of a given human sphere, because they regard it as *untermenschen*, should refrain from pontificating about it. The twentieth century provides example enough.

[52] Because nobody had access to the satellite imagery until recently, and certainly no-one with this unfashionable distinction in mind.

the early 'nineties, in fact, there have been very few Iraqi pieces passing through London, and almost none that was 'fresh' from Uday's excavations. I should know, for I restored for all the Middle Eastern dealers, and saw all their stock.[53] The interesting question, therefore, is where has it all been going? Dr. Donny George gets closer to the mark:

> There's a definite connection between these looters and the collectors outside the country. We know there are people sitting in Saudi Arabia and Jordan asking for specific material from specific sites.

You might raise an eyebrow about a man who didn't even know his museum had been put into safe-storage before a major war, but he does have a point. These antiquities are not bound for the Anglo-American market. Not at all.

And the recent British legislation

In 2000 the British Government set up a committee,[54] whose remit was:

[1]   To 'examine the world trade in illicit antiquities', and

[2]   how much Britain was involved in it, and

[3]   how Britain could (help) rectify it.

By their own figures, the British art market is the world's second largest, after the US. It has a turnover of $9,000 millions. That is rather impressive. The British antiquities market, however, has shrunk considerably since the early 'nineties, because of the various attacks upon it—including the EEC regulations of 1992, the show trials of 1997, the 'Sotheby's Affair' and subsequent removal to Paris.[55] It now has a turnover of only $26 million. The government may claim this is a 'considerable part' of our art market,[56] but it is actually 0.3%.

---

[53]   see *Stolen Antiquities – how many are there (in circulation)?* in the Appendix. My figures are probably the only accurate ones since—as a restorer of international reputation— I was the only person with complete access to the market, to dealers' stock, and collections. No academic had such access— they'd have refused it with disdain—and neither did any government agency.

[54]   ITAP, The Illicit Trade (in cultural objects) Advisory panel, set up in May 2000 under Professor Norman Palmer, a barrister.

[55]   Removal of their antiquities department, that is to say.

[56]   'Britain has the second largest art market in the world, *with antiquities making up a considerable part of it* [my italics]...the British art market was worth

Only a politician could claim this as anything but miniscule, negligible.

We have no idea of the size of the world antiquities market. And nor does anybody know how much of it is 'illicit', that is, supposedly against the wishes of the countries of origin.[57] There are various claims, figures plucked from the ether. UNESCO claims that $500 millions is illicit. The Crusade claims over $4,000 millions.[58] But if, as our government admits, only a small part of the British antiquities market is dodgy[59] — say a tenth, or $2½ millions a year — this means that Britain carries less than a thousandth part of the world's sin, even though she is a world leader for art trading. That strikes me as commendable.

So, the common-sense answer to [2] is 'hardly at all'. And, it follows, the common-sense answer to [3] would be 'nothing, because it's nothing to do with us any more (even if it had been in the first place).' Passing legislation would be superfluous. And claiming that this 'sends a powerful message to those who do such damage'[60] would be fatuous.

Let us be clear about this. The Crusade and its zealots have taken every opportunity — especially their self-appointed spokesmen[61] — to accuse the trade. But their claims are patently false. And they have been disproved by the government's own findings:

£4,500m in 1999, of which antiquities contributed £15m'. Baroness Blackstone, for the UK government,

[57] It is doubtful, for instance, whether antiquities exported from Egypt with government authorization — by government agencies, or with documentation supplied by them — should seriously be claimed as 'illicit', and hence claimed back. These countries cannot have their cake *and* eat it. They really can't.

[58] Professor Renfrew's famous 'worth billions' of his New York Times article, and various others. Some newspaper articles claim even more, $5,000m plus. But these are drifting into fantasy, and could only ever be justified by strictly identifying 'un-provenanced antiquities' (those lacking a complete and written history) with 'illicit'. But as I have already shown, this would mean putting any antiquity that has 'gone through the rooms' — been sold in auction — into the sin bin. And that is simply disingenuous.

[59] 'The market generally operates in an honourable way, but we did find evidence of illicit activity.' Professor Palmer, quoted by Baroness Blackstone.

[60] 'Part of a package of measures to combat the international illicit trade in antiquities,' Baroness Blackstone. Herod would have been impressed.

[61] Richard Ellis, formerly of the Arts and Antiques Squad — 'the nearest thing to a national unit on these matters' *Cultural Objects: Developments since 2000* §18, — who is always popping up to 'link' antiquities dealers to the fashionable horrors. But there is never any evidence, never any proof. Only his 'opinion' please note.

Neither HM Customs nor the National Crime Intelligence Service have any specific intelligence of links between cultural goods and money-laundering, drugs or arms-trafficking.[62]

There is no 'problem of illicit antiquities' in England, and there is no proven connection with drugs, or terrorism, or the white-slave traffic, or paedophile rings, or anything else that is fashionably nasty. And sooner or later history will have to admit it.

The ITAP committee, not unsurprisingly, reached another conclusion.[63] It recommended the UNESCO convention and also 'the criminalisation of dealing in tainted cultural objects'.[64]

Now this *tainted* concept is actually very interesting. A 'tainted' antiquity is defined as 'illicitly acquired after December 3rd 2003'. That is, 'acquired *against the laws of its presumed country of origin* after 3rd December 2003'. This has a bureaucratic neatness about it which is very satisfying, at least for bureaucrats. And it captures the moral nuance, that of contagion, of something that has been sullied by unclean hands.

Unfortunately it is impossible to apply, unless applied unfairly. How can we ever know a given object is tainted? Is there anything about a tainted antiquity that identifies it? Of course not. There is only its lack of continuous history — what we call a provenance. But as we have already seen, almost nothing in ordinary life has a provenance. How many pictures or antiques or collectables in your house have a 'continuous history'? You may vaguely remember how they came to be there, but can you prove it? Can you provide the list of their successive owners, the dates, the places?[65] Of course

---

[62] *Ibid.*, §23.

[63] I say not unsurprisingly, given their choice of witnesses, only one or two of whom — for example James Ede, the president of the World Antiquities Dealers Association — *actually knew anything about the market and its praxis*. The rest were allowed free rein to accuse without foundation. And many had undeclared interests. The Salem witch trials had as much chance of a balanced verdict.

[64] *Cultural Objects: Developments since 2000*, §19.

[65] David Gill, an archaeologist from the University of Swansea, surveyed seven 'major collections' of antiquities in 2000. He discovered that '75% of the 1,396 antiquities were of 'unknown origin', and that many had 'surfaced' for the first time well after the passage of national antiquities regulations. His insinuation — following the Crusade's agenda — was that they were therefore 'dodgy'. The common-sense conclusion, however, would be that they had

not. And why should you? So why should antiquities be any different? The only objects which can be proved to be tainted are published pieces, those that have been excavated and published, and then reappear where they shouldn't. But 'illicitly excavated' sites, by definition, are unpublished. If they had been 'properly' excavated, they would have been published.[66] QED.

And the problem with published pieces is that nobody seems to know which ones they are. The countries of origin certainly don't. If they did, the Egyptian antiquities police for one wouldn't keep selling them by mistake. There is no comprehensive list to which anybody can refer. UNESCO certainly doesn't have one. Thirty-five years after their convention, they have not even got a list of their signatories' various and contradictory laws, according to which certain antiquities (by definition) become 'illicit'.

So the British government committee also recommended a 'database' — admitting that any law about tainted antiquities would be impossible to apply unless there was actually a list of tainted antiquities.[67] But this sparked a major argument, because somebody had to pay for the database, estimated at twelve million pounds.[68] The trade did not want to pay, not surprisingly, because their entire turnover was now only

passed through several hands — especially auction houses, which are by definition anonymous as to seller — and their 'attached' memories had been lost, as with any other antique or craftwork. Did Dr. Gill think to ask what percentage of these 'major collections' had been bought at auction (with vendor unknown)? Of course not. Why is common sense in such short supply with academics?

Jerome Eisenberg, a prominent New York and London dealer, estimates that only 10% of the 3,000 scarabs he sold in the 'sixties have retained their provenance — that is, are now remembered, by their present owners, as having been bought from his galleries.

I can confirm Eisenberg's figures. I have restored, bought, cosseted, and sold literally thousands of Egyptian amulets, and kept accurate photographic records of them all. Despite that, I have several times actually bought amulets that I had already restored, without realizing that I had already owned them, or already restored them. If *I* cannot remember, with my records, then who can? And who can be expected to, or be required to?

[66] Unless, of course, they happen to be recently excavated sites in Egypt, which might have been kept unpublished for a reason, see page 235.

[67] 'The database is an essential...cog in the prosecution wheel... How are people going to show they had no reason to believe [it] was stolen if they cannot say 'I checked the register, and it wasn't there?' Professor Palmer, *Cultural Objects: Developments since 2000*, §21.

[68] 'The problem we have...is the profound disagreement between the police...and the art market and industry. Both want a database, but they want

£15m. And the British government did not want to pay, because they tacitly admitted — at least when it came to opening their wallet — that they did not think there was a (criminal) problem for the database to solve, and they were not even certain it was worth spending the money to find out.[69] And the main people who had been urging the pace for the Crusade — and for the database — were now revealed as those with most to gain from it.[70]

The Dealing in Tainted Antiquities (Offence) Act of 2003, therefore, was preceded and followed by years of confusion. As such, it has been a masterpiece of British muddle, or of British guile. I suspect a bit of both. The Act supposedly 'confirmed the UNESCO Convention, and closed a few loopholes.' But it has proven impossible to apply, and I don't think the British government ever meant it to be. They have actually admitted as much.[71] But by dangling a Sword of Damocles over the British trade — what remains of it — they are actually completing the task that the Crusade and its zealots originally set themselves, that of destroying the British antiquities market.[72]

As such, the Act compares well with the British government's 2004 hunting ban. It is virtually unenforceable, but that was never the point. It is in practice oblivious to the fate of antiquities — whether they are destroyed in the ground through lack of buyers, or drift into another diaspora — just

it for different purposes, and neither wants to pay for it.' Secretary of State, *Cultural Objects: Developments since 2000*, §33.

[69] 'The link between *investment* in such a database, and *dealing* with money-laundering, drug-trafficking and other criminal activities...remains to be proven by the Home office' Secretary of State, *ibid.*, § 22.

[70] Richard Ellis, for example, now director of *Trace,* one of two private organizations that were in the running for the lucrative database contract (until somebody noticed that, under EU law, tenders would have to be invited Europe-wide).

[71] 'We don't intend to put anybody in jail, merely to change the culture of the marketplace — encourage due diligence and enforce 'good practice.' Dr. David Gaimster, Senior Policy Advisor, Ministry of Culture Media and Sport, *Cultural Objects: Developments since 2000*, §43.

[72] Richard Ellis, formerly of Scotland Yard's Art Squad, was generally regarded in the trade as a 'zealot', a tireless advocate of Renfrew's position, who strictly identified 'un-provenanced' antiquities with 'illicit', and repeatedly declared his intention of 'closing down' the trade. During his time there were many investigations launched into un-provenanced antiquities. Since his sudden retirement 'the level of police activity has considerably diminished,' Philip Barden, solicitor for the Antiquities Dealers Association.

as the hunting ban is oblivious to the fate of foxes — whether they are poisoned or snared or shot in their thousands, whether they survive or die in agony.[73] That was never the point. The point, it appears, of both Acts was class warfare: as Roy Jenkins famously observed in the House of Lords debate 'are my Lords aware that the antiquities trade is a 'posh trade'?[74]

No, I'm afraid this was 'feel-good' legislation, driven by political malice, with common sense trailing a poor second. 'The British government wishes to send out a warning.' Well, it has. And the warning is that it wants nothing to do with what it regards as an unseemly mess — even though it has the best pedigree in the world for getting in there and sorting it out. Or am I just being cynical again? Perhaps I have just seen too much of reality. It's always easier being ignorant.

The future of the great museums

A few parting words about our museums. As we have seen, the *argument for restitution* is merely an extension — a militancy, if you like — from the *argument for retention*. Cede the one, and you'll find yourself morally bound to the other. To expect otherwise is illogical, even for a director of the British Museum:

> [it is] very disturbing, anti-world, worryingly anachronistic, that countries want to reclaim what they've made.[75]

It is no surprise, however, that Western museums are getting rather windy, despite their much brandished piety. They are beginning to look distinctly embarrassed. Scarcely a month passes without some former dependency or colony demanding the return of its 'cultural heritage'.

Some few of these claims have merit, but they are swamped by the noise and the clamour. So far returns have been decided on grounds of political correctness. That's to say, fascist confiscations are returned — such as Mussolini's obelisk from Ethiopia — and the rest are being ignored or obfuscated. But how long can this go on, before the countries of origin simply turn the screw — close their frontiers to

---

[73] It is now officially confirmed that many more foxes have been killed since the Act became law than was the norm before.

[74] *Hansard*, February 17th 1997.

[75] Statement to BBC News, referring to Greek claims for the Elgin Marbles.

Western archaeologists, and revoke their licences to dig?
Zahi Hawass has already started, by forbidding any new foreign expeditions in Egypt. Soon he will be threatening the
existing expeditions.

The fear of the museums is clear enough. They're worried
about being emptied:

> Museums are concerned that, if they acquiesce to one request,
> everyone with a claim will do the same, and they will lose the
> incentive to be the museums they are. As a result, many shy
> away from [such claims] completely in order to protect their
> entire collections. (Rochelle Roca-Hachem, UNESCO)

Their belated response was the *Universal Museums Declaration*, signed in 2002 by many of the world's great museums.[76]
This confirms that there will be no return of (their) antiquities, because 'Universal Museums are good for the world'.
And they are good, it explains, because:

> [they] have provided access to artistic and ethnic objects [and
> created] universal admiration for ancient civilizations...

That is, they have been useful in the past, because they have
educated the public. And they are still better than the alternative – returning things like the Elgin Marbles to 'non-
universal' museums – because 'only here [in the British
Museum] can their *worldwide significance be fully grasped*' [my
italics]. In this case, 'their distinctly Greek aesthetic...appears
all the more strongly as the result of their being seen and
studied in direct proximity to products of other great civilizations.'

I find these arguments puzzling. They roll sonorously off
the tongue. But I am not at all sure what they mean – other
than something very obvious – and I am not sure these
museums do either. Are they arguments for *keeping things
where they are best cared for*? But that has been my point all
along.

---

[76] The Art Institute of Chicago   The Bavarian State Museum
The State Museums, Berlin   The Cleveland Museum of Art
The J. Paul Getty Museum, LA   The Louvre, Paris
The Los Angeles Museum of Art   The Metropolitan Museum of Art
The Museum of Fine arts, Boston   The Thyssen-Bornemisza, Madrid
The Museum of Modern Art, NY   The Prado, Madrid
The Whitney Museum, New York   The Hermitage, St.Petersburg
L'Opificio delle Pietra Dure, Florence   The Guggenheim, New York
The Rijksmuseum, Amsterdam   The Philadelphia Museum of Art
The British Museum didn't sign, but 'fully endorsed'.

Or is it just a way of saying that the past should be forgotten, simply because it *is* past,[77] and *benefit* is all that matters nowadays? But that would be little more than vulgar utilitarianism—whatever the deedy talk about humanity, and showing the world to itself, and grasping significances, and so forth. It would boil down to the claim that more happiness—in whatever the currency—follows from the pieces being here, than if they were back there in their countries of origin. And that is debatable. Those who live by votes can also perish by them, as I've repeatedly mentioned.

All the more disturbing, therefore, that the British Museum now suggests that its own constitution—which neatly enough prevents any artefacts from being returned to anybody—can be overridden when 'sacred items' or 'human remains' are involved.[78] Given the otherworldliness of curators, I would hate to think of them handling the flood of claims that, for example, the Benin Bronzes from Nigeria are 'sacred' and should immediately be returned.[79]

Better by far if these museums started arguing about *property*, its rights and its duties. The simple point, for example, that saving the Elgin Marbles gave the British Museum property rights over them.

The new diaspora of antiquities

As I have said, the antiquities from Iraq, and increasingly from Egypt, are not heading our way. Since the seventeenth century's first fascination with antiquities, the West has been their main consumer. We have gathered them in—by fair means and foul—and we have studied them. Antiquarianism and archaeology are Western pastimes, which followed from the Western world view. If the West now imposes a prohibition upon itself—that archaeological sites can only be excavated with due process, with Western-trained archaeologists on hand, and the contents of these sites can only be the property of non-Western governments—then the result will be

---

[77] It seems so, judging by the following: 'the objects and monumental works that were installed decades and even centuries ago in museums throughout Europe and America were acquired under conditions that are not comparable with current ones' Neil McGregor, Director, British Museum.

[78] Because it is a British charity, and therefore subject to the Charities Act.

[79] So they are, of course, and that was precisely why they were confiscated—to symbolically emasculate the king, their holder, and thus prevent 'the genocide, barbarism and human-sacrifice' they enabled.

another *Prohibition*. And, I would predict, the largest and most brutal diaspora the world has ever seen.

The reason for this? That the bulk of antiquity is outside the West, and effectively outside Western control. The Middle East is the most concentrated source of archaeology in the world (outside China). The Middle East saw the birth of Indo-European culture, the two great 'irrigation states', the succession of empires and the birth of monotheism. And the Middle East is *Islamic*. It heartily despises the West.

The world is moving on. There are new sources of wealth. The Pacific Rim, South East Asia, China and India. All these have abandoned collectivism — that failed and murderous Western export — and adopted Adam Smith and free market economics. What they will *not* do, however, is embrace the market-hating Western 'liberals'. They will ignore UNESCO — except when it is clearly to their advantage — and they will ignore the Cultural Heritage Crusade's prohibition.

If Dr. Stone is looking for a warehouse that's bulging at the seams with Uday Hussain's exports, he should look to Saudi Arabia, and the Gulf states, and secular Arab wealth wherever it is to be found.[80] He should look to the French and Arabic-speaking markets.

The signs were always there, if anyone had cared to look. There was a marked change in the London market — and not for the better — after the Middle Eastern dealers arrived in the 'seventies, the diaspora of Persian Jews after the Shah's demise, and the Lebanese after Beirut. These dealers were cavalier. When I worked for them — and I tried them all, at least once — they might have been selling potatoes, for all the care they had. We wondered how they survived, with their ignorance and cupidity. But they did. They sold to their own clients, the oil-rich Arabs, and for prices we natives could never aspire to.

It is these dealers and their clients, all of them Arabs, and most of them secularised Moslems, who form the new market. It is a market that Britain — which had been the world centre for antiquities until the 1970s, and which had the world's leading expertise and probity — and I am not refer-

---

[80] It only needs the Chinese demand for aphrodisiacs to see the African rhino exterminated, whatever our Western anguish. What if China became interested in Egyptian antiquity? Do you seriously think — having read this book — that the present regime in Egypt will feel in the least embarrassed about selling them their surplus?

ring to the museums — could have educated. If we had done this, we could have saved the day.

I am now afraid, very afraid, that antiquity will be caught in the middle of a cultural war. As for Western archaeology — its squeamishness and its politicizing — it will go the way of the Munich generation. I could be wrong. I hope I am. But these are matters that need *thought* — hard and sensible thought. Fairy tales and fancies are no use anymore. The Crusade has sown the whirlwind, and now it must reap.

Summary

- Common sense and proof may have come too late, however.
- The various Egyptian 'show-trials', 'arrests' and 'prosecutions' might best be regarded as mere propaganda (for western consumption),
- but the Anglo-American Trials of 1997 and 2002 were more serious, and constrained our markets,
- especially the US Appeal Court decision to acknowledge restrictive foreign antiquities laws, 'as long a they were rigorously enforced',
- and Britain's recognition of the UNESCO convention, and hence of 'illicit' antiquities (as specified by those same laws).
- The museums' response to pressure for restitution, the Universal Museums Declaration, is an argument from simple utilitarianism, and vulnerable to votes, as all utilitarian arguments are.
- The looting of Baghdad Museum in April 2003 was cleverly manipulated for publicity purposes, and the Cultural Heritage Crusade now appears triumphant.
- But it may be a hollow victory. It can only restrain the Western markets, and Western archaeology will find itself cold-shouldered.
- The new markets — the Arabs and the Far East — will be unaffected, and far less scrupulous. The result will probably be the largest diaspora of Middle-Eastern antiquities the world has ever seen. The next twenty years will be critical for antiquity.

Appendix

Conservation — how (not) to get things done in Egypt

In the early 'nineties Dr. Hussein and myself wanted to equip a demonstration tomb — preferably on the West Bank — with a system to protect it by evacuating tourist-generated humidity as soon as it was produced. The chief mechanical engineer at English Heritage drew up the plan. Air-conditioning would have been expensive and bulky — a small house full of equipment would have been necessary beside the tomb — but there was another method, widely used by ourselves — the pressurized air system.

It was a simple and effective scheme, and one that used a proven technology, and removed water vapour as it was being produced. In addition, a proper visitor management regime would have imposed some order on the carnival, and generated enough resource — by charging suitably for the experience — to equip another tomb, and so on. We estimated a capital expenditure for the first large tomb of £250,000, recoverable within four years (at the slowest-rate calculation). With proper management — without corruption, that is — we could equip a string of tombs, and without the Egyptians needing to go cap in hand to anybody.

The humidity control was simplicity itself. A pump housed outside the tomb would suck in dry air from the valley, and pump it through a duct laid on the floor. Microchip sensors placed throughout the tomb would detect moisture as it leaked from the visitors. These sensors would activate the pump, which would deliver dry valley air to the innermost part of the tomb, creating a slight pressure there — about 1½ atmospheres — and hence a gentle breeze outwards, sweeping the moisture before it. As more moisture appeared, so the pump would accelerate. As the humidity fell, so the pump would slow. As a consequence the humidity would never rise above a certain level, and there would be no damage to the tomb. A simple idea, and one already employed at numerous European sites.

The visitor management scheme was also simple. A pigeon-hole rack outside the tomb, such as hotels use for room keys, would hold a set of numbered plastic paddles. As each visitor arrived, his baggage would be exchanged for a numbered paddle and a pair of cotton gloves. When all the paddles were in use the tomb was deemed to be full, and no further visitors could enter until a paddle had been returned.

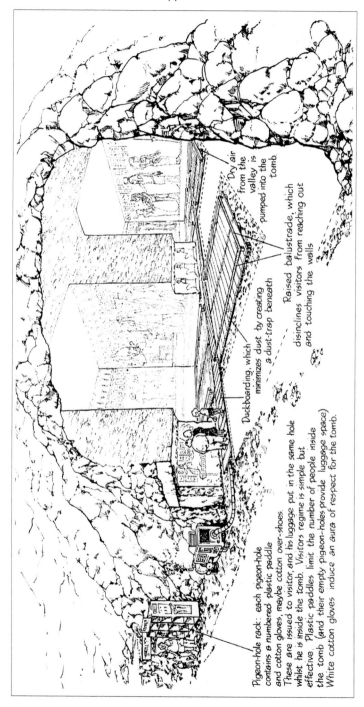

Dry air from the valley is pumped into the tomb

Raised balustrade, which disinclines visitors from reaching out and touching the walls

Duckboarding, which minimizes dust by creating a dust-trap beneath

Pigeon-hole rack: each pigeon-hole contains a numbered plastic paddle and cotton gloves, maybe cotton over-shoes.
These are issued to visitor, and his luggage put in the same hole whilst he is inside the tomb. Visitors regime is simple but effective. Plastic paddles limit the number of people inside the tomb (and their empty pigeon-holes provide luggage space) White cotton gloves induce an aura of respect for the tomb.

No paddle, no entrance. Hence a ceiling was imposed on the tomb's capacity, and a ceiling that couldn't be subverted without everybody else noticing.

The gloves — and possibly the face-masks — were there as theatre — a very useful theatre — to create a sense of caution in the visitor, an ambience of fragility. Similarly the low balustrades, that threatened the would-be toucher — and you always get some — with the risk of overbalancing, and making a complete idiot of himself, if he leaned too far. Lighting would be UV shielded. Oh yes, and the ragged meretricious guards — little better than beggars — would be replaced by trained graduates, who could be well paid from the tomb's own revenue, and who could afford to be genuinely proud of themselves and their tomb.

Things moved very quickly. Hussein took the project to Farouk Hosni, the arts minister — they knew each other from Rome — and he immediately passed us to Dr Fekhri Hassan, his newly appointed supremo. Within a few days we found ourselves in the arts ministry, a small bustling office full of sunlight. Hassan was an archaeologist but had the American's zest and pragmatism. His plan was simple. He would draw up a list of projects and international expertise, draw up another of funding, and then match the two. After everything I had seen, and my developing sense of hopelessness — that muddle, incompetence and massive venality would swamp every urge toward the light — this was just glorious. This man was honest. He felt clean, and we were well-placed, and could do great things. I felt like Icarus, taking his first flight.

Perhaps it is this *legerdemain* that so confuses the novice at Egyptian bureaucracy. After all the delays and the obfuscation — the sense of a dense and cloying mist, which dulls and resists every attempt — the vista suddenly seems to clear, and close at hand you can see the finishing post. But then it changes again, leaving you helpless, with the ground sliding away remorselessly. When we returned with a detailed and costed version of our proposal, we found that Fekhri Hassan was gone. His bright fresh office was empty. As he'd explained to Farouk Hosni, he'd found nothing since his arrival that he could rely upon — except unthinking resistance to any proposal he made, simply because it was his proposal. And of course the treachery of his colleagues. He was far too busy a man to waste his life among such political wolves. And so he'd departed in disgust.

But with Dr Hassan went our project. This is the Egyptian way. The virtue of a project hardly matters — only its adherents. Our project bore the imprimatur of Fekhri Hassan, and now it was doomed, and presumably any other attempt.

The consequences of this were profound. I had thought myself in a position to help. I had glimpsed a better world, where common sense and application might be allowed to put things right. Nothing had seemed impossible. But that departed as abruptly as it had come, with the dynamism of Fekhri Hassan. And we were back in a world of expediency, where anybody striving to put things right will be opposed by the legion of those who would much rather do nothing.

Soon after this the roof collapsed in Seti's Tomb, and Dr. Mohammed Ibrahim Bakr, Chairman of the Egyptian Antiquities Organisation, made an emotional appeal at Turin[1] for foreign help with conservation. Make of this what you will, but bear in mind that Dr. Bakr was prominent in the demise of Fekhri Hassan.

If I had been a lover — and in a sense I was only and ever that, a lover of Egyptian antiquity — this was the point where it broke my heart, when all hopes of a future were quietly put aside, and my eyes were lowered in despair to the ground, to see what could be saved from the wreckage.

Corruption — does it matter?

The ad hominem argument would suggest that it does — that by dealing with corrupt men, a man is himself corrupted, and his arguments can be dismissed. The liberals would certainly argue as much against me. But, again, the world is a trifle more complicated than may appear from an academic's armchair. There is wisdom to be gained, and for that one has to observe the things that happen, and to compare them with their descriptions.[2]

When I first went to Egypt, it was with curiosity, both about the market — whether it still existed, and the form it held — and about conservation. This curiosity gradually deepened into dismay, as I saw the incompetence and disdain of the Egyptians, and their insouciance.

---

[1] The Sixth International Congress of Egyptology, 1991.

[2] This was F.R. Leavis's requirement, after all.

JOURNAL 10th October 1990 Amsterdam
The Dutchman, having inspected the restoration, asked me why I 'spent so much time helping the Egyptians with their conservation...and then smuggled things out of their country?' Wasn't there a contradiction? But then he burst out laughing, and answered the question himself. 'Don't worry' he said 'I've lived in Egypt myself. I know what it's like. It' s just the academics who are fooled by it. But then they want to be. Saves them having to do any thinking for themselves.'

At a certain point my thinking hardened, perhaps after the failure of our project.[3] I began to work out the ideas in this book. By a certain stage I had decided that our forebears had been right after all—that our first duty was to get as much through to the future, and it didn't much matter where it was. Correct ownership was a problem one could safely leave to the future, and a problem they would be grateful to us for bequeathing them. Unless they had the things in safe keeping, no-one could complain about their ownership.

From then it became an anthropological problem for me. I wanted to know exactly what was going on. I wanted to know the centre.

JOURNAL Monday December 23rd 1991
Was all this knowledge too dangerous for us? These were powerful men, dangerous perhaps, and I wasn't at all sure I'd ever invite them to dinner. But Ali seemed unruffled. He assured me his family is very strong: not only his uncle the general, but armed factions in the mountains. And what was it LBJ had said, after all? Better have them on the inside of the tent pissing out, than outside pissing in?

What worried me was more vague, a sense of unease, a shadowy sense that it wasn't quite clean, and that these people were selling things that didn't belong to them. Whereas, with the *fellaheen*, I'd always felt—whatever the Egyptian law might have to say about it—that they had every right to own and sell what they'd found. And the traditional collectors in Egypt—the natural people to buy from the *fellaheen*—were the middle classes and the professionals.

But what finally decided it for me, I think, was simple curiosity. This was Alice's *Through the Looking Glass* world, after all, and having started I wanted to see more. I wanted to get

---

[3]   See the previous section in this appendix.

to the bottom of it. I was intrigued, and how many other westerners would ever have such a chance?

But having seen and understood — seen everything that was going on, and understood why it was — my conviction was clear. We should only work with the rightful owners — those who had found the objects, and those who correctly felt themselves the owners, by Islamic tradition, if not by the dictates of a bullying and secular regime. This was a moral conclusion.

The wickedness of dealers

It is a charming myth, at least amongst the English, that dealers are naturally unscrupulous. I have to disabuse you, I'm afraid. They may be richer, some of them, but they are the self-same clay as yourselves, and if they behave worse on occasion — or at least differently — it is only because they are being tested in ways that you've probably escaped. Depressing though it may be, it's rare to find someone behaving decently in trying circumstances. Most men sink soundly to the occasion,[4] and dealers are no exception.

Well, that was the view of old Sartre. He was speaking about politics of course, but the same may apply to the art trade — or at least to antiquities, which have problems and temptations peculiarly their own. It may be impossible to do such work without getting your hands dirty. It may be impossible to deal and also remain honourable, or even honest. That seems to be the view of the museum curators, at least in England (where they have no money to buy, hence every reason to denigrate what they cannot enjoy). If so, we would just have to hope — as we despairingly do with politics — that in the end it's worthwhile because of the good that comes of it. The means may accuse, but the ends will excuse.

As I say, this may be the case, but I think there is a better way of looking at it. It has to be admitted, you see, that dealers are naturally playful. Dealers like to outwit each other, and score points off each other. They like to prove that they know more than the next man, that they're faster, quicker, smarter than he is. In short, that they are better players. And of course they play to the audience. 'For why are we here' as

---

[4] Witness the Germans during the 1930s and the French during wartime occupation.

Jane Austen's Mr. Bennett would have said, 'but to make fun of our neighbours, and be laughed at in our turn?'

Nobody has yet attempted a sociology of art dealers. Nobody has looked at art dealing, as Wittgenstein might, as a form of life.[5] Which is rather a pity, because many of the actions of dealers can only correctly be understood under another description.

If you came from the planet Zog, for example, and happened upon a game of cricket — or even baseball, God forbid — you would reach quite the wrong conclusion about what was going on. You would see a group of men throwing stone-like objects at another man, who was defending himself with a stick, and then trying to run for it, but being chased by his attackers. You would assume it a punishment, perhaps, or a ritualised hunt. Or a trial by duress, in the medieval manner. But once the rules had been explained, and you had interpreted what you were seeing according to those rules — no mean feat with cricket — you would view it all differently, as a form of play.

You would have grasped the idea that an action can be quite different, when it's done with rules in mind. The man hitting the stone-substitute, for example, is not defending himself from attack and trying to escape (although, in special sense, a rule-interpreted sense, he may be described — commentated — as doing just that). No, he is executing a high cut — a definite chance for the wicket-keeper — which he follows up with a brisk single. And more than that, he is farming the bowling by changing ends at the end of the over, keeping the score line ticking over, and protecting the tail-ender. That is how he sees it, how he interprets it according to the rules and the communal lore of cricket. And that is how all the other players see it.

This is an extreme example — games are extreme after all — and you can't take the actions of a dealer as an attempt to play the game, pure and simple. There is a lot more going on than this. He has to make a living, after all. But neither can you take his actions out of context, and hold them up in a court of law, as was recently done in New York.[6] For then

---

[5] The notion of a *form of play*, and of rule-guided *forms-of-life*, are from the *Philosophical Investigations*.

[6] *US–v–Frederick Schultz Jnr.*, New York, January 2002, in which I was the principal witness.

they will appear horrific, as if dealers were all of them engaged in fraud and deceit of a particularly shameless sort — doing things that really ought to land them in jail.

The difference, of course, is their intention — what they themselves would claim they are trying to achieve. If one dealer has an antiquity restored, for instance, so that it looks better and becomes more valuable — and then sells it to another dealer, without mentioning the restoration — is that a fraud, something to be indicted and convicted? Or is it really meant to be something else? The dealer who's been duped — who buys the restored piece, and then discovers his mistake — would be as horrified as anyone were his antagonist to be indicted, his actions taken out of context, and everything held up to the harsh unforgiving light of the courts. For him, and for everybody in the trade, such a response would be quite wrong, quite out of proportion. Much better would be a slap on the wrist, and the biter bit.

If the good sociologist is the one who describes things in a way that the participants could accept, then he would conclude that antiquities dealers are more playful than wicked, with a playfulness that is not the preserve of any particular race or creed, although the rules may differ slightly, place to place, and with them the penalties and rewards.

Drug money laundering — is the antiquities market involved?

Professor Renfrew claims that 'the trade in looted antiquities is one of the most valuable criminal trades in the world, second only to drugs. It is now a multi-billion-dollar-a-year business'.[7] But Renfrew goes further. He argues that the 'illicit trade in antiquities is intimately involved with drug-money-laundering.'[8] In fact, it has become part of what one might call The Crusaders' Agenda to establish a link between antiquities and drugs. If they can do this, you see, they efficiently besmirch the antiquities market, and everyone who works in it, whether dealer or collector. Except, of course, the saintly curators and academics, with their recently acquired 'ethical buying policies'.

After the looting of Baghdad Museum, it was claimed that:

---

[7] New York Times, 23rd February 2004.

[8] *Ibid.*

This is becoming the second traffic — after drugs-traffic — in the world. Cash-strapped farmers are digging up 'find-sites' to acquire the objects because they know they'll find a willing buyer.[9]

Given UNESCO's own figures, this is arrant nonsense. It verges on the meretricious. US sources suggest the world drugs-market is now running at several hundred billion dollars a year, although nobody really knows. But the 'illicit' antiquities market, UNESCO admits, absorbs no more than $500m a year, of which perhaps $50m is in the Middle East. This, by comparison, is 0.25% of the drugs-market, yes, a quarter of one percent! Hardly in the same league.

The British government, although it would perhaps prefer on political grounds that there was a link:

We are aware...that there are links between the purchase of these [cultural objects] with a view to laundering money, and we also have some evidence to suggest that they are being used by terrorists...[10]

also admits there isn't one:

Neither HM Customs nor the National Crime Intelligence Service have any specific intelligence of links between cultural goods and money-laundering, drugs or arms-trafficking. [*ibid.*]

But mere facts rarely deter. A recent article confidently claims that in antiquities smuggling:

Pieces move along the same routes, and often through the same people's hands, as do drugs. Four years ago, for instance, a huge collection of Greco-Roman antiquities worth more than $1.5m, snatched from a museum in Corinth, Greece, was discovered hidden in fish-crates in Miami. It had been packed in precisely the same manner as a shipment of Mafia-controlled cocaine worth £15million. There's a clear upside to pursuing a career in art crime rather than drugs: getting caught with a Sumerian tablet, the legal owner of which died 2500 years ago, is not going to earn you the lengthy stretch you'd expect for smuggling heroin.[11]

Apart from being bloody nonsense, there's a great deal of interest in this. The way it creates the impression that 'they're all in it together'. The way that 'looted' antiquities — in this

---

[9]   Mounir Bouchenaki, UNESCO's Assistant Director General for Culture.

[10] Evidence given to parliamentary sub-committee 2004 by Caroline Flint MP, Home Office minister responsible for international crime and anti-drugs co-ordination.

[11] The Art of Crime, Sunday Telegraph Magazine, 21st September 2003.

case stolen from a museum by obvious criminals — are conflated with 'fresh' antiquities generally. And the suggestion that all items smuggled in a certain way must be smuggled by the same people.

Cleverly written of course. But you might as well suggest that all European car-makers steal each others' designs, because all their car bodies look the same — whereas, in fact, each company has independently reached the same solution to the same set of technical problems. Boring of course, but honest. Similarly, hosts of things are smuggled in Samsonite suitcases — everything indeed from duty-free fags to heroin, with antiquities somewhere in the middle. But is this an argument against the people who use Samsonites, that they are equally evil? I think not. I think it says something about the reliability of Samsonites.

Yes, I'd agree that antiquities are used as a 'reserve currency'. And I'd certainly agree that the international antiquities trade is involved in the smuggling of antiquities — in the sense that most dealers and collectors knowingly and contentedly buy 'fresh' pieces. But the trade as a whole would run a mile from the sort of people who have anything to do with drugs, and use the occasional antiquity to launder drug-money. If they knew what goes on — as I discovered purely by chance — they would be horrified. In truth, they are blissfully unaware.

For the two worlds are completely separate. There is the antiquities market, the network of galleries and dealers and catalogues and collectors and, yes, of academics. And then there is another shady world, a criminal world, where drugs are bought and sold, and drug money is laundered — but nothing at all to do with the antiquities market I've been describing in these pages, and by very different and very nasty people.

One huge difference is in the prices. I remember my astonishment when I heard the figures involved in money laundering. An antiquity, you see, has a definite price, which varies only slightly between countries. An object may be a third dearer in Switzerland than in London, say, but no more than this. Some dealers with 'captive' clients, Persian Jews selling to Arabs for example, can sell for higher prices than Anglo-Saxon dealers selling to thrifty Anglo-Saxons. But again it's only a matter of percentage points.

But money-launderers are selling for ten times the real value of the piece. A Cycladic figurine, for example, which was worth perhaps £250,000 on the 'kosher' market — if it had been genuine, that is — was apparently sold for £6 million as a drug-money laundering exercise. Such figures are astounding. But they occur in a criminal vacuum, without contact with the real market.

You could almost take money-laundering as a back-handed compliment to the antiquities themselves — because they hold their value against the vicissitudes of the economy, and are small and portable (like gems and postage stamps, the other main candidates for laundering) But, anyway, very little harm is done — for the simple reason that most of the pieces employed are fake. The joke is on the launderers.

Grounds for a grudge

The Arts Squad had no reason to appreciate me. A fortnight after I was arrested 'on suspicion', they committed (or so we thought) an illegal and very unpleasant act. They 'smuggled' a BBC film crew into my mother's house, pretending they were policemen, and therefore covered by the search warrant. This constituted an illegal use of a search warrant. The effect of this upon my mother, who was elderly (eighty-one), and in poor health, was dramatic, and required years of treatment to rectify. This constituted trespass and damages. The eventual television documentary — *The Art of Crime* — made use of this illegally obtained footage.

Eventually the senior officer involved was taken to the High Court by my mother. And with him, the Commissioner of the Metropolitan Police, the Chief Constable of the Devon and Cornwall Constabulary, the BBC, their subcontracting film company, and the other officers.

Their defence was that the senior officer had been invited into my mother's house, had carefully explained his intentions, and obtained full consent from my mother for the proposed filming. Only when that consent was given, did he re-enter with the film-crew.

When the defence finally examined our evidence, however — we had sub-poenaed the unused footage, and re-assembled it in real-time, thus demonstrating that there had been no such interview, no such pause in the proceedings of 'up to half an hour', but that he'd knocked on the door and immediately inserted the film-crew with no attempt at consent, and no revelation as to their real status and, hence, that his statement was untrue, as were all the corroborating statements[12] — when all this was revealed, the defendants immediately offered to settle out of court.

The Home Office was required to foot the bill, a substantial one (mostly legal fees, of course), and insisted on 'confidentiality'[13] — what the press delights to call a 'cover-up'. Our counsel, Lord Lester QC, who had only undertaken the case in an attempt — his second attempt, after Princess Diana's 'gym-photos' case — to establish a law of privacy by precedent, appealed personally to the Home Secretary, but was informed by Jack Straw that 'he was not prepared to have the Met humiliated at this time'.

However this affected the officer's career — Philip Barden, my mother's solicitor, wrote to James Ede, the president of the World Antiquities Dealers' Association, explaining that the officer's 'credibility was shot', and he suddenly retired, soon afterwards and whilst being investigated for corruption in respect of my case — it left him outwardly unblemished. No-one had any idea of what had happened. Nearly all of the subsequent falsehoods to be found in the press, I believe, can be traced to him. And he is very vocal.

The sad plight of Kings' Valley

Kings' Valley is unique. Everyone knows that, even without the relentless marketing that packs in two million tourists a year. Few foreigners would dream of visiting Egypt were it not for Egyptian antiquity, and Kings Valley is invariably top of their list. It is, therefore, an essential staple of Egyptian tourism — together with the Sphinx and the Great Pyramids — and hence of the $3 billion from tourism that keeps the Egyptian economy afloat.

But Kings' Valley has unique problems, and unless there is serious change, the Valley and its glories will soon enough be little more than folk memories — and of course, the beloved publications of Egyptologists. Whether such publications really 'save' or 'conserve' Kings' Valley depends, the

[12] With one noble exception, DS Steve Toms from the Devon and Cornwall Constabulary, who not only told the truth, but later apologized.

[13] Except for myself, who was the only party not required to sign any such Agreement of Confidentiality. An unfortunate oversight perhaps.

cynic might suggest, on whether you get your dinners and your reputation from them (see page 294). For myself, I'd prefer to keep the Valley itself intact. But to achieve that would require a multi-national effort, and some very blunt talking.

The problems of the valley are four-fold:

[1] Flash-floods, which act upon
[2] the Esna Shale Bed,
[3] and have been exacerbated by archaeology,
[4] and tourist grubbification.

The last of these, the familiar salt-meets-tourism problem that I describe in Chapter 18, is the least of the valley's problems. It is, if you like, the devil's gloss on a job well done.

If you fly down the western edge of Egypt, you will observe a fascinating pattern along the desert's edge, a sort of ramifying lacework of gullies. These are caused by the rain storms that occasionally rage over the desert. These streams and gullies combine and combine again, growing in volume, until they sweep as a flash flood into the Nile Valley—thousands of gallons of water pushing debris and boulders before it. King's Valley is one of main conduits, and every couple of hundred years, a cataract of water roars through the valley. The ancients were well aware of the problem, and tried in various ways to minimize the damage. They used breakwaters and dams to speed the water past the tombs before it could enter. They sealed the tombs, and they built in water traps—sumps, if you like—to catch the water that may have entered. On the whole they were successful, and when Kings' Valley was re-discovered, at the end of the Eighteenth Century, some fifteen tombs were almost untouched by the water, including many of the major decorated Royal Tombs.

The ancients also knew about the system of fault lines in the limestone that runs through the central group of tombs in the valley's floor—the group that includes the show-stoppers: Tutankhamun, Ramesses VI and Ramesses IX. They may not have realized the mechanism involved,[14] but

---

[14] If small amounts of rainwater enter such a crack in the limestone, the 'absorption causes the limestone to swell, developing enormous pressures parallel to the ground surface. The limestone expands vertically, also, but there is no resistance in this direction, and it can move upward freely. Laterally, however, it cannot move, so it deforms slightly or "creeps" down-slope. When the water dries out again, the limestone contracts, leaving

they managed to stop water entering, by simply plugging the cracks.

But the ancients had no idea of the Esna shale that lies directly beneath Kings Valley, in places only thirty feet below the surface. At least they had no idea of its menace, for they actually exposed it at floor level in several of the tombs. When water comes into contact with this shale — a type of soft mudstone with a clay content — there is a chemical reaction as the shale hydrates. It expands dramatically, and exerts an incredible pressure, literally heaving the limestone hillside above it, and shattering the internal architecture of the tombs. This can take decades. Then as it dries — again a matter of decades — the tomb is left suspended, and starts to collapse internally. This was all demonstrated in the Tomb of Ramesses III, whose

> burial chamber filled with water between 1883 and 1910. Immediately the shale in the floors of the tomb's lower-sections thrust up with massive force, pushing the limestone walls and columns against the mass of rock above, causing massive fracturing and collapse.[15]

Kings' Valley, in geological terms, is like a broken tile draped across a sponge.

What is appalling, however, is that Egyptologists seemed to have had no idea of this menace either — until John Romer, an Englishman of empirical bent and vast common sense, thought of the obvious expedient, and called in some geologists. Because of this ignorance the trade of archaeology — supposedly the natural guardians of the treasure — has done immense damage to the Valley — more in the last 150 years than in the previous three millennia.

Excavations have exposed the tombs to flash floods, as with Seti I, which was discovered by Belzoni intact and pris-

---

a joint that is now opened slightly. The next rain can now penetrate into the joint still further, and the joint can hold more water. The process continues with every rain, gradually opening the joint further and further and deeper and deeper. The time necessary to develop large openings in these joints must be tens of thousands of years...the importance of this mechanism for Royal Tombs is that many joints occur directly above the tombs [especially in the central group] and are undoubtedly permitting water to penetrate deeply enough to dampen the wall-surfaces of the tombs, with consequent displacement of large blocks of limestone and spalling of the walls themselves.' Professor G.H. Curtis, Earth Sciences, UC Berkeley.

[15] 'History and Experience in The Valley of the Kings', presented by John Romer at the The Sixth International Congress of Egyptology, Turin, 1991.

tine, but immediately flooded because he filled in the sump just inside the tomb, and enabled the next flash flood to roar straight in. The real damage there, however, was done by Sheik Ali's excavation in the late 1950s, when he emptied one hundred and fifty yards of debris-packed tunnel at the furthermost point of the tomb. This tunnel had probably been acting as a secondary sump for the original flood of 1817 — it was anyway soaking wet, when Sheikh Ali's workmen emptied it — and by exposing the shale bed again he enabled a rapid desiccation of the soaked and expanded shale. The tomb has been collapsing slowly ever since.

The major disaster, however, was courtesy of Colonel Nasser's enthusiastic government, who built a lavish Rest House, complete with toilets, smack in the middle of the Valley, which used KV5 as its personal septic tank.[16]

As if this Egyptian disaster wasn't bad enough, the present rash of Western excavations will be emptying central area tombs of their flash-flood debris — which they will find to be wet, of course — with the result that the shale bed will begin to desiccate rapidly, and shrink. The archaeological community, it's clear, has been pursuing its own scholarly course with bland disregard for what they are purportedly 'saving' for the future. There ought to be a moratorium on Egyptologists.

The market and 'illicit' antiquities:
How much does 'the trade' really know?

Given that smuggling brings illicit objects into the 'legitimate' world-pool of antiquities — we can now ask the sixty-thousand dollar question. Does the trade know what's really going on? And how is an innocent collector to know, when he sees an Egyptian antiquity on display — in the auction rooms say, or one of those discrete and elegant galleries in Zurich, Paris or New York — whether it left Egypt two hundred years ago, or only the previous month? Whether in the open market before 1983 — and hence entirely above board — or after that date, and hence against Egyptian law? Whether 'fresh' from the ground, or blameless?

Any collector will tell you that he relies upon his gallery or auction house, upon their experience and probity that is, and above all their tact. But how are these poor fellows to know?

---

[16] See above, page 256.

In one sense their problem is the same as any antique dealer's anywhere. Or anybody who goes out to buy a second-hand car, for that matter. They must separate the rogue from the respectable. It's just the definition of 'rogue' that's different. For just as the majority of antiquities, or antiques — or second-hand cars, for that matter — are legitimate, with very few stolen, so the majority of antiquities in London or New York have long been out of Egypt, and are irreproachable. But there definitely are 'fresh' items, because people like me have been supplying them.

Given, however, that very few antiquities ever have a provenience — a fully documented history of where they've been over the years, and who has owned them — and given that this is unavoidable — and given that pieces are still being smuggled out of 'countries-of-origin' like Egypt, how can dealers avoid buying these 'stolen' objects?

Quite easily, in my experience — if they really wanted to, that is. It's not so much the ability to discriminate that is in question. Rather, it's the desire to. For what it is worth, I would say that a dealer in London or New York has a fairly easy time of it. A simple examination will normally suffice. If I can immediately tell, from the mere feel of a piece — from the degree of dirt, the extent of damage, the evidence of past cleaning and restoration, and the form of the wrapping — or even the presence of gold-specks on the surface[17] — then so can the dealers. Or they can hire me, or someone like me, to tell them.

In many cases the vendor himself gives the game away. He may not be as forthright and open as myself, but if he were an Arab gentleman, say, with a suitcase full of objects wrapped in Arabic newspaper, it wouldn't require an investigative genius to conclude that these were 'fresh' items from a 'source country' — and that the fellow himself was a 'runner'. And if he were Italian, and obviously a countryman, and again with a suitcase-full of Etruscan or Roman antiquities? As I say, it is relatively easy to distinguish 'fresh' things from

---

[17] It was a standing joke amongst the London dealers that if an Egyptian antiquity had minute specks of gold on its surface — caught in its pores, so to speak — then it was 'one of Tokeley's', and had just been smuggled out of Egypt. My technique, you see, was to camouflage my objects, by shrouding them in gold leaf, making them look like a tourist copies, the sort of thing you would expect to buy in a bazaar. And my cleaning process, once they were in England, sometimes left minute flecks of gold behind (see above, page 10.)

things which have long been in the flow, as they say — bought
and sold, restored and handled, and bought and sold again.

With objects in auction however, it is slightly more difficult. The auction system conceals the vendor's identity. He is
rarely named, except when famous or landed — when his
prestige might be expected to 'push up' the bidding. It has
always been easy to put 'fresh' items through the rooms, sa
they say, and the mere mention of Switzerland — the glamour
and the rectitude of that splendid country — has usually been
enough to establish the *bona fides* of an object.

For the dealer who trawls his way through the hundreds of
items in an antiquities auction, therefore — and whether on
his own behalf, or because he has been commissioned by an
institution or a wealthy collector — his only real clue is the
condition of the objects, that is to say their patination. The
presence of crusted earth, of calcium-crust, of raw breaks
and damage and dirt — all the things, indeed, that would
have been seen to by the very first Western owner — these are
clues for the experienced 'eye', and tell him that this particular object has never been in anybody's collection, but is
'fresh' out of the ground.

Whatever their public piety, therefore, I would say the
dealers' position was — and perhaps still is — very close to
mine. They were perfectly content to buy objects coming out
of Egypt — because they know what's going on in that
benighted country — but they are slightly wary of making a
mistake, that is, of buying something that has only just been
cut from its site, or has already been published.

And how many dealers were buying 'fresh' antiquities
(fresh out of their country-of-origin, that is to say)? Until the
late 'nineties — before political correctness, that is, and the
antiquities trade became the new fur trade — the answer
would have been simple. All of them. I sold to nearly all the
London dealers, after all, and many foreigners.

And I never deceived them, or even tried. There was no
need. The dealers I sold my things to were perfectly aware —
and well before they'd agreed to meet me — of the provenance of my pieces. They knew I'd just brought them out of
Egypt. As did the dealers they sold them onto, I dare say.

The trade's attitude could be summarized in the words of
one reputable Bond Street dealer, although it could as easily
have been Madison Avenue, or the Bahnhofstrasse in Zurich:

We don't mind, of course we don't, as long as we know.

But if this is the case – and I'm in an excellent position to confirm it, after all, because they were most of 'em buying from me, and with full knowledge – then they'd do much better to stand up and be counted. Boldly to admit the practise, that is, and explain how widespread it is across the world, and that the blame – if blame there be – lies elsewhere.

Professor Ricardo Elia of Boston University is almost correct, therefore, when he says 'People are wrong to think there's an illicit market and an illegitimate market. In fact, it is just the same.' But only in a strictly technical sense. He should consider the *motivation* of the dealers. Obviously, some are motivated by greed and blatant disregard – which is what Elia and the Crusade would have us believe. Many, however, have made a clear moral decision.

Because, in the end, if a dealer cares about antiquity – as he certainly should – and yet continues to buy 'stolen' pieces, it can only be because he feels he is doing the right thing. Oh yes, of course there is profit involved. But more importantly, and at a deeper level, there is the conviction that there's no harm to these beautiful things, and probably only benefit. This is at the heart of the matter. Not whether a dealer is breaking somebody else's rules, but whether he's doing the right thing by the objects.

How does the trade cope with being caught out?

The next question, naturally enough, is what happens when it all goes wrong – when a dealer or collector or museum curator is caught out, when he buys something that he really shouldn't have bought. For example, when he buys a published piece.

Published pieces, so-called, are those that have appeared in the academic press, and usually with photographs on hand. A side effect of publication is that they are shown to be in a certain place at a certain time – in Egypt say, after Law 117 of 1983 has claimed them for the 'Egyptian people', and forbidden their export. It follows that, if you inadvertently buy such a piece outside Egypt, you have an unwelcome dilemma on your hands. Your piece should officially be in Egypt, and under Egyptian government care and protection. The fact of its publication confirms this. It follows either that it was taken out of the government's protection without it knowing, or that it was voluntarily relinquished. In other words, it was either 'stolen' from them, or it was 'sold' by them. Which you plump for—and what you decide to do about it—rather depends upon how much you really know about what's been going on. And to that particular can of worms we'll be returning.

In theory, of course, there is no real problem. The piece can simply be put back. If it had been in government storage, it can be returned to its correct depot and its correct container. And if taken from a tomb or temple, the Egyptian conservators could simply replace it—make up the missing edges—with no apparent harm done. They have the publication, after all, which tells them exactly where the thing should be. And if uncertain of their own competence, they would find many foreign institutions eager for the task.

But the problem is that this never happens—and I'm really not sure why. I'm not sure there's any reason for it, that is, other than laziness. But I do know, from direct experience, that any relief—any decorated stone fragment—that has been returned to the Egyptian authorities will simply go into storage—find itself wrapped in newspaper, and crammed into one of those dusty crates—never to be seen again.

Unless, of course, it's sold, or sold again. Witness the Boston Museum, who bought a relief in the late 'eighties, discovered it published and hence 'stolen', and promptly returned it to an apparently grateful Egyptian government —only to see it re-emerge in Europe some four months later. In the front door, one would have to say, and out the back.

Hence the dilemma of any foreign dealer who finds himself with a 'published piece'. He can return it to the Egyptian government, knowing that it will never be re-instated in its tomb, but consigned to obscure storage—and half suspecting that it will find its way back into the market. And if he is cynical he may speculate on the Egyptian government's part in its original removal. He may wonder, for instance, how it is possible for a tomb which is under armed guard to be robbed, and often enough robbed again and again and again...

Or he can 'place' the offending piece with a collector until enough time has passed for the dust to settle[18]—that is, until

---

[18] Twenty years or more, it would seem. The Dutchman, JB, told me that in the early 'eighties he'd been strolling down the Luxor Corniche with a purchase under his arm—when he came across a postcard of the very same piece! His

title deed has clearly lapsed, and the piece can be brought into the open and acknowledged for what it really is.

Either way, this is a nightmare for Anglo-Saxon dealers, although less so for French and Belgians (and, of course, for the Swiss). Their collectors have fewer scruples than we English and Americans — or perhaps they've less hypocrisy. In Europe, indeed, a common practice with a published piece is to alter the hieroglyphs — the signature, if you like — so that it can no longer be identified from its publication. In some cases, indeed, a published piece may actually be worth more — carry a premium, you might say — simply because it's published, and has a proven provenance.

What our dealer chooses to do depends, in the end, on how much he knows — and the clarity of his thinking. Whether he clearly acknowledges, that is, that his only real duty is to the object itself, and getting it safely through to the future. Nothing else really counts. At least, amongst those who really care for antiquity, nothing else should count — neither the fashions of the day, nor political correctness.

The problem of reliefs

The market in Egypt is less healthy than it might be, but it certainly exists. There is a steady flow of objects, and from a variety of sources. The huge majority are what we in the West call 'free-standing' antiquities, and what the Egyptians call 'moveables'. These are separate objects — small statuary, utensils, devotional objects and suchlike — the contents of a room, one could say, rather than the room itself. They can give an archaeologist information about that room, but are in no real sense attached to it.

But there are also architectural items — what the Egyptians call 'immovables' — things which strictly speaking belonged to a site, because they were physically part of a building or the bedrock from which the building was hewn. These are the reliefs, or friezes, and you are no doubt familiar with them. They are the typical Egyptian slabs of stone, adorned with hieroglyphs and the outline figures of gods and men.

These reliefs occupy a peculiar position. Once detached from their original wall, you see, they can be mounted and

---

decision then was to 'place' it with a Belgian collector, with strict instructions to keep it discretely out of sight for twenty years. A move was recently made to sell the piece, but it proved too early.

displayed as if they were separate art-objects. Because of this, over the years, the market — and the museums — have come to regard them as 'free-standing'.

And since the first Napoleonic enthusiasm for Egyptian art they have been detached from their sites — thousand upon thousand of them — and scattered around the globe. Like it or not, every relief in every museum across the globe has been treated in just this way. They have all been removed from their architectural home — ripped or savaged, as the zealots would prefer, or more demurely sliced — trimmed to make them manageable, and then mounted for display. And the man who started the fashion was none other than Champollion, the man — the legend — who first translated hieroglyphics, and first gave significance to the inscriptions that abound on reliefs. He it was who sliced the first chunk off the walls of Seti I's tomb in Kings' Valley.

There are still thousands of these reliefs in the flow of the market — in the auction rooms, in the galleries and the mail-order catalogues. Fashions have changed, however, and the present museum fashion now sneers at the practice, conveniently overlooking the fact that — until it had completed its own collection, at least — it obviously rather favoured it.

As I say, it is the fate of these reliefs that rouses the ire of the market haters. If the zealots have their way, and all antiquities are commandeered, locked away in dusty boxes — unless exceptional enough to be displayed — it will be because of reliefs, and the mob's fury they arouse.

It only takes a few shots of fluffy benign foxes being dismembered to turn city-dwellers against the hunt. And it only takes some footage of denuded tombs to do the same for the antiquities market. When the market haters want to attack the antiquities market, therefore, they know where to go for copy. Here be beastly looters, or so it seems.

It is also an unfortunate fact that most 'published' Egyptian pieces are reliefs. This is because Egyptology is most interested in inscriptions (for reasons that were outlined in Chapter 20). They are the most easily traced, therefore, if they go missing. Reliefs have become, you might say, the Achilles' heel of the market, where it will be attacked — where it is on the defensive — where it can be discredited by the *bien pensants*.

And the barbarism of cutting them from tombs

Reliefs, therefore, are a sore point for all concerned. And as I say, there are plenty of reliefs about in Egypt. I used to see them wherever I went. But it did not follow — and I never believed it for a minute — that tombs were being butchered to feed a ravenous demand. In many cases it was clear from their patina that these reliefs had been removed from their sites a long time ago — that the harm was long done. And in some areas the buildings themselves had disintegrated because of salt — for instance Mentuemhat's Tomb on the West Bank — and when discovered were nothing more than monumental piles of small fragments.

Of course there were some that had just been removed, and some of these — however it came about — from tombs guarded by the Antiquities Police, and inspected by the Antiquities Inspectorate. There were not many, thank God. I would estimate, overall, that one in fifty had been recently removed, and the rest had been long in the flow. The only thing, it seemed to me at the time, was to tread very warily, and when the evidence was clear — that a given example had just been cut from its site — to shun it like the plague.

As I say, there were rogue pieces about in Egypt. But this was no reason to shun the market. We do not abandon a currency because of the occasional rogue coin. No, it was only another reason to despair of the present situation.

I agree, of course I do, that cutting reliefs from their original sites is a barbarism — unless it is an act of conservation, that is, the only way to save them, and pass them safely to the future. But the practice has only recently come to be regarded as a barbarism, and the museums, now so scornful, were quite content about it in the past — whilst they were still buying, that is. And I would suggest that if they feel so very strongly about the practice now, then they really should hand back the fruits of it — at least those whose original sites are known.

I suppose these same museums would argue that the damage was done by an age that knew no better — and that their present duty is only to preserve the reliefs in their care, and pass them safely on to the future. But this, interestingly enough, is precisely my own sentiment. It is the very reason I had no qualms about buying a relief that was in the flow in Egypt — if I could be assured that it really was in the flow, and had come from a collection, and not just fresh from a tomb – any more than I would about buying a relief that was in the market outside Egypt. I see no moral difference between the two cases.

Professor Renfrew would argue for a moratorium, however. He would say that anybody who bought an Egyptian relief in Egypt – or even outside Egypt, so the wider argument goes – was actively encouraging tomb robbers to go out and dismember another tomb. That only by everybody shunning such things could we persuade the pillage to stop.

I agree that if it were possible to persuade everybody to stop buying, it might well work – but it isn't possible, anymore than it has proved possible for elephant ivory or rhino horn. Liberal pie-in-the-sky, in fact. It only takes one country to disagree, or one consumer group, and the sanction becomes useless.

Besides, it's not even a good argument. The correct logic, unfortunately, was the *fellah*'s, when he explained to Lady Duff-Gordon that if he hadn't taken the piece, somebody else would.[19] It might not be a Frenchman, but there always would be someone who would buy. By refusing what was offered, we would only make it cheaper for that other person, and leave the *fellah* still hungry.

'Stolen' antiquities – how many are there (in circulation)?

Before I answer this – give a professional estimate, that is – some verbal accuracy might be in order. The Crusade, you see, uses various terms synonymously, more for emotion than accuracy. Sometimes it says 'stolen', sometimes 'looted' or 'pillaged'. And there's an occasional 'ravage' or 'rape'. The antiquities market is more sedate. It uses the word 'fresh', which at least has an accurate meaning. It refers to objects that have just left their countries-of-origin, and are therefore, quite literally, 'fresh' in the larger world market.

Now these 'fresh' pieces come from many different sources. Some come from chance new discoveries, and others from old established collections, from native traders or government officials. Some few, one presumes, have actually been stolen – in the usual sense of being 'nicked' from their

[19] See above, page 28.

rightful owners. And some — more sinister this — come from looted museums in time of civil unrest,[20] or from looted tombs. But only some of them are 'stolen' in the sense of being illegally exported from countries whose governments have decided to nationalize their antiquity, and claim everything for themselves — and only some of these have been 'looted' in the correct sense.

It is quite clear, therefore, that the number of 'stolen' items will be smaller than the number of 'fresh', and the number of 'looted' smaller than either. It is only the Crusade that would have us confuse them all. I would be inclined to suggest, in passing, that if a cause is so noble it should have no need of such a deliberate confusion. But that's by the bye.

Now for the really interesting question. Just how many items in the antiquities market — in that swish gallery in Madison avenue, or that Sotheby's auction, or that stall in the Portobello market — are actually 'fresh'"? And how many 'stolen'? And how can we distinguish the 'looted' from the merely 'stolen'? (And how — I suppose I ought to add — can I even maintain such a distinction, when the Crusade so deliberately conflates them?)

Of course the Crusade would claim a substantial fraction. It is in their interest to do so after all. A recent article suggests a multi-billion dollar a year trade in 'stolen' antiquities. Absolute tosh, I'm afraid. The entire antiquities world market can barely muster five hundred millions of turnover. So how a few percentage points of that can become a matter of 'billions' I'm at a loss to understand. Make of it what you will, but I've concluded that the Crusaders are living in a fairy world — or else they are being fed false information by unscrupulous people who can sense their agenda, and seek to profit by it. I'm giving you the down-to-earth figures, and I would have you simply imagine a broad stream of antiquities moving legitimately around the world, ever changing hands — and into this river there is a trickle of 'fresh' pieces.

In my experience, an experience probably unmatched in the trade over twenty-five years — in which I have inspected almost every item in every auction, and many many thousands in private and dealer's hands — and had access as a

---

[20] As in the recent case of Sarajevo but not of Baghdad, where most of the pieces were restored, to the great disappointment of the Crusaders. See above, pages 326-333.

restorer that's denied to any academic or dealer—I would say that no more than three in a thousand are 'fresh', and only two of those are 'stolen'. I dare say that this figure is accurate to within, say, twenty percent, and that no-one else is in a position to make any better estimate.

My assumptions are these.

Firstly, that as a restorer I have had far greater access to antiquities in the market than any mere dealer, or academic, or investigative journalist.

In the auction rooms, of course, I have only had the same access as dealers. I could inspect every item minutely, as they could. But I had the advantage in that—having restored perhaps ten thousand antiquities in my career, and of all types—I could distinguish when something had just been restored, and the type of restoration—and in particular the type of restoration that is habitually made to 'fresh' items which had just been unearthed. Putting it bluntly, I could smell the rats.

As regards collectors, I had access that would be denied to dealers. And as regards dealers in the London market, I worked for most of them, and saw the entirety of their stock. This is an important point. Another dealer who visits them will only be allowed to see certain items. But I would be given access to the entire stock, so as to recommend which items needed conservation, and which could be improved by restoration. The major dealer, in terms of the size of his stock, for example, habitually had me work in his country storage rooms, where his entire stock was on hand for me to inspect.

Secondly, that almost every 'fresh' antiquity requires some work—basic conservation, mounting or restoration. The only exceptions to this are Roman glass and gold jewellery and coinage. All other classes deteriorate, and need treatment when they have been unearthed, or at least inspection.

Stoneware, for example, is invariably dirty, and encrusted, and damaged by the chemicals of the soil and, if from Egypt, full of salt which needs to be removed before the stone comes into contact with humidity. Bronzes are encrusted with corrosion products, and this has to be stabilized and then 'cut down' to reveal the true and desirable patina that forms a part o the beauty and the value of the piece. Wooden pieces are friable, and often fragile, and need consolidating and perhaps internal strengthening. And so it goes on.

Thirdly, that 'legitimate' pieces in the market are only restored, if at all, every thirty-five years. This is because the materials used by restorers and conservators are constantly improving (as dentistry improves the technology upon which conservators largely depend), and because modern synthetics have a clear life span of about twenty-five years. We have to assume, that is to say, that any synthetic that is used in restoration will be degraded by ultra-violet light within twenty-five years and need replacing. This is the small print, if you like, on the contract with modern plastics chemistry. My own records show that the average time since items were last restored was in fact slightly longer, about thirty-five years.

Notice this difference. The huge majority of 'fresh' items need immediate work, whereas 'legitimate' pieces are only restored every thirty-five years. My records show that, between 1980 and 1994, when I was solely a restorer working for the London market, 1½–2½% of the objects I restored were 'fresh'. And of these, judging by where they came from, only 1½% were 'stolen' — mostly from Egypt and Syria. I think it's fair to assume, therefore, that about one in four hundred objects in the London market was 'stolen'. That's probably quite close to the number of cars in London that are stolen, or ordinary antiques, or mobile phones.

Fourthly, that the combined stock of all the London dealers was about 60,000 objects, and that the auction rooms, brought another 10,000 items into London from country collections, and from abroad.

It follows that, at any given time, about 175 objects out of 70,000 were 'stolen'. This estimate, I say, is accurate to about twenty percent either way, and no-one else could give a better estimate, because no-one else was in my position.

Fifthly, that about the same proportions would apply in the French, Belgian, German and New York markets — at least for Middle-Eastern antiquities. The Swiss proportion — if one included the *freilagers* — would be slightly higher.

The English Trials of 1997

The first indictment, of January 1997, averred that the defendant (the present author) was 'acting for his own benefit' in bringing antiquities into England. That is, as their primary handler. This indictment was quashed, because the judge—quite rightly, and in accord with the CPS's own explanation to the Egyptian government, and in accord with the House of Lords, who debated the matter immediately afterwards, in February 1997—judged him to be 'out of jurisdiction'.[21] This effectively 'legalized' the 3,000 antiquities, mostly amulets, that the defendant had imported.

The second indictment averred—in respect of the same three antiquities, the only apparent exception to the first ruling— that the defendant was actually 'acting for the benefit of another', his courier, by buying him air-fares to go and collect the defendant's own property from Egypt. That supposedly made the courier the primary handler—the main-man, the boss—and the defendant the servant. Which was patent nonsense.[22] The defendant was the primary handler, since he'd been to Egypt and found and bought the objects, and left them in storage for the courier to collect. Also, the courier didn't know an antiquity from a hot dog.

The trial became a ludicrous haggle about who had actually 'carried' these pieces. If the defendant had carried them himself, he was legal. If his courier had carried them, he was legal. But if the defendant had bought the courier's air-fares in England, he'd apparently committed a crime, aiding and abetting a man who wasn't himself about to commit a crime.

The legal precedent that the second trial established, however, was that a British citizen could now be both a primary and a secondary handler at the same time—as long as they were in different countries.

But there is a clear *reductio ad absurdum* here. It follows that, because a man could now be both primary and secondary handler—as if he had become two legal personalities instead of one, a sort of legal schizophrenic—he could commit a crime by going into a travel agent in England, and buying himself an airfare, when he only intended to use that airfare for not committing a crime (viz, bringing things out of Egypt). And only his *intention* mattered. If he later decided not to do anything after all that was not committing a crime

---

[21] See page 317, footnote.

[22] The judge brushed aside the legal argument (made with the jury absent) that, as the defendant had just been tried as their primary handler—which he obviously was, being their purchaser and owner—he couldn't now be tried as their secondary handler. That would make him both at the same time, which the law proscribed. The judge simply observed that the prosecution could use 'whichever part of the law they thought appropriate'. This ignored the point.

(viz. bringing things out of Egypt) — because, say, there wasn't anything to bring out when he got there — he would *still* have been committing a crime when he'd bought the air-fare, because he'd had the intention at the time (of not committing a crime etc).

In fact, a double *reductio*, because no law punishes mere intentions. The law is only interested in actions. Otherwise we would all be indicted. That's why the precedent was never used again. And that's why Sotheby's were never taken to court, because Sotheby's would have had the money to buy good lawyers, who would have rubbished it.

It may puzzle the reader how this nonsense could have been got past the jury. That much is simple. The jury were prevented from knowing anything about it — about the first trial, and about the law, and specifically the difference between primary and secondary handling. They may have been puzzled about the small and technical nature of the charge, since the prosecution were making great play with other objects that were not on the indictment, and that had been declared 'lawful' by the first trial. But when the defendant's barrister began to explain this, he was immediately stopped by the judge, who sent out the jury, and ordered him not to say anything 'that might give the jury the impression that this was the prosecution's last chance to get their man.' Hence the trial proceeded with the jury in complete ignorance. They effectively completed the work of the first trial, and convicted the defendant as a 'primary handler' — even more broadly, as a smuggler (not an offence in British law).

For those of you who still believe the British judiciary to be independent — stoutly immune to political tampering, and a bastion against government infringement etc., etc. — this may come as a shock. Take consolation that it couldn't happen in the US, where trial lawyers do not aspire to become judges, and are unconcerned about offending those who will be selecting them. US attorneys want to earn a reputation, and then go into lucrative private practice. For this simple reason, they will stand up to judges. They have nothing to lose by standing up and being counted.

Bibliography

Anderson, Benedict (1991) *Imagined Communities: Reflections on the Origin and Spread of Nationalism* (Verso).

de Bernières, Louis (2004) *Birds without Wings* (Secker and Warburg).

Von Bothmer, Bernard (1968) in *Sauvetage des Antiquitées en Egypte* (Paris).

Budge, Sir Wallis (1920) *By Nile and Tigris* (London).

Colley, Linda (1994), Britons: Forging the Nation 1707-1837 (Yale).

Fathy, Hassan (1969) *Gourna: A Tale of Two Villages* (Prism Publications).

Goffmann, Erving (1984) *The Presentation of Self in Everyday Life* (Penguin).

Grabar, Oleg (2004) *Islamic Art and Architecture* (Könemann).

Graham, Gordon (2005) *The Institution of Intellectual Values* (Imprint Academic).

Keegan, John (1976) *The Face of Battle* (Pimlico).

King, Dorothy (2006) *The Elgin Marbles: The Story of Archaeology's greatest Controversy* (Hutchinson).

Hobsbawm, Eric (1992) *Nations and Nationalism since 1789* (CUP).

Hrdy, Sarah Blaffer (1999) *Mother Nature* (Chatto and Windus).

Johnson, Paul (1983) *A History of the Modern World* (London).

Laslett, Peter (1956) 'The Face to face Society' in eds., Laslett and Runcimann *Philosophy, Politics and Society I* (Blackwell).

Moran, Lord (1945) *The Anatomy of Courage* (Constable).

Mount, Ferdinand (1982) *The Subversive Family* (Jonathan Cape).

Plenderleith and Werner (1971) *The Conservation of Antiquities and works of Art* (OUP).

Ridgway, Brunilde Sismondo (1970) *The Severe Style in Greek Sculpture* (Princeton).

Romer, John and Elizabeth (1993) *The Rape of Tutankhamun* (Michael O'Mara).

Russel, Sir Bertrand (1924) *Government by Propaganda* (London).

Ryan, Alan (1987) *Property* (University of Minnesota).

Scruton, Roger (1998) *An Intelligent Person's Guide to Culture* (Duckworth).

Scruton , Roger (1994) *Modern Philosophy* (Sinclair Stevenson).

Smith, Adam (1776) *The Wealth of Nations* (Penguin, 1970).

Smith, Anthony (1988) *The Ethnic origins of Nations* (Blackwell).

Trivers, R.L 'The evolution of reciprocal Altruism' in *Quarterly Review of Biology* 46 (1971) pp 35-57.

Tylor, E.B (1871) *Primitive Culture* (John Murray).

Weldon T.D (1956) 'Political Principles', in ed., Laslett and Runcimann *Philosophy, Politics and Society I* (Blackwell).

Index